Gary Snyder:
DIMENSIONS OF A LIFE

Gary Snyder:

DIMENSIONS OF A LIFE

EDITED BY JON HALPER

SIERRA CLUB BOOKS

SAN FRANCISCO

The Sierra Club, founded in 1892 by John Muir, has devoted itself to the study and protection of the earth's scenic and ecological resources— mountains, wetlands, woodlands, wild shores and rivers, deserts and plains. The publishing program of the Sierra Club offers books to the public as a nonprofit educational service in the hope that they may enlarge the public's understanding of the Club's basic concerns. The point of view expressed in each book, however, does not necessarily represent that of the Club. The Sierra Club has some sixty chapters coast to coast, in Canada, Hawaii, and Alaska. For information about how you may participate in its programs to preserve wilderness and the quality of life, please address inquiries to Sierra Club, 730 Polk Street, San Francisco, CA 94109.

Grateful appreciation is extended to the Four Seasons Foundation, New Directions Publishing Corporation, and North Point Press for permission to print excerpts from Gary Snyder's poems.

Library of Congress Cataloging-in-Publication Data

Gary Snyder : dimensions of a life / by Jon Halper, editor.
    p.   cm.
    ISBN 0-87156-636-2. — ISBN 0-87156-616-8 (pbk.)
    1. Snyder, Gary.   2. Poets, American—20th century—
    Biography.
    I. Halper, Jon.
    PS3569.N88Z66   1991
    811'.54—dc20   90-35363
    [B]   CIP

Cover Illustration: *Rock Scallop* by Robert Davidson
Cover/Jacket design by Clifford Burke
Book design by Clifford Burke
Composition by Wilsted & Taylor
Production by Susan Ristow
Printed in the United States of America on recycled paper
10 9 8 7 6 5 4 3 2 1

Contents

Jon Halper   EDITOR'S INTRODUCTION   ix

1930–1952: The Rainy Northwest

Jerry Crandall   MOUNTAINEERS ARE ALWAYS FREE   3
J. Michael Mahar   SCENES FROM THE SIDELINES   8
David H. French   GARY SNYDER AND REED COLLEGE   16
Carol Baker   1414 SE LAMBERT STREET   24
Jeremy Anderson   MY FIRST ENCOUNTER WITH A
   REAL POET   30

1952–1956: Cascades to Sierra: Night Highway Ninety-Nine

Jim Snyder   RIPRAP AND THE OLD WAYS:
   GARY SNYDER IN YOSEMITE, 1955   35
Will Baker   POETS ON THE BUM   43

1956–1959: Japan: First Time Around

Burton Watson   KYOTO IN THE FIFTIES   53
Philip Yampolsky   KYOTO, ZEN, SNYDER   60
Hisao Kanaseki   AN EASY RIDER AT YASE   70
Will Petersen   SEPTEMBER RIDGE   76

1959–1969: The Wide Pacific

Katsunori Yamazato   SNYDER, SAKAKI, AND THE TRIBE   93
Nanao Sakaki   DUST FROM MY OLD BACKPACK   107

1969–The Present: Shasta Nation/Turtle Island

Doc Dachtler TRUE ENLIGHTENMENT 113

Bruce Boyd AN ENCOUNTER AT KITKITDIZZE:
SUMMER OF 1970 115

Steve Sanfield AS IT IS 117

Will Staple THE ONE AROUND THE CAMPFIRE 120

Gary Lawless MY APPRENTICESHIP AT KITKITDIZZE:
SUMMER OF 1973 122

Scott McLean "THIRTY MILES OF DUST:
THERE IS NO OTHER LIFE." 127

Kai Snyder HAVING A POET AS A DAD IS KIND OF LIKE
HAVING A FIREMAN AS A DAD 139

Gen Snyder WHAT I HAVE LEARNED 142

Jim Dodge TEN SNYDER STORIES 143

Peter Coyote GARY SNYDER AND THE REAL WORK 157

Gary Snyder HARRIET CALLICOTTE'S STONE IN KANSAS 169

Photographs

174

Poetics

Ursula K. Le Guin NAMING GARY 201

Allen Ginsberg MY MYTHIC THUMBNAIL BIOGRAPHY OF
GARY SNYDER 203

Michael McClure "PASTURES NEW" 204

Philip Whalen LIBERAL SHEPHERDS 207

Anne Waldman VOYANT 209

Alan Williamson SOME TENSES OF SNYDER 216

Gioia Timpanelli JUMPING OVER BEAR DROPPINGS 221

Clayton Eshleman IMAGINATION'S BODY AND
COMRADELY DISPLAY 231

Jerome Rothenberg THE POET WAS ALWAYS FOREMOST 243

James Laughlin NOTES ON GARY SNYDER 246

Robert Sund YES, IT'S REALLY WORK! 248

Wendell Berry   A TRAIL MAKER   252
Tim McNulty   THE WILDERNESS POETIC
   OF GARY SNYDER   254
Paul Hansen   FOR COLD MOUNTAIN'S STREAM   259
Robert M. Torrance   GARY SNYDER AND THE WESTERN
   POETIC TRADITION   263
Jack Hicks   THE POET IN THE UNIVERSITY   275
James Koller   "WE SHOULD GO BACK"   285
Drummond Hadley   GARY SNYDER   287
Frank Jones   EXCELSISSIMUS   288

Dharma

Robert Aitken   THE TOKU OF GARY SNYDER   291
Ryo Imamura   FOUR DECADES WITH GARY SNYDER   299
David Padwa   WHAT'S THE SANSKRIT WORD
   FOR COYOTE?   302
Dale Pendell   A RAVEN IN THE DOJO:
   GARY SNYDER AND THE DHARMA   312
Carole Koda   FIRST WINTER   321
Gary Snyder   OFF THE TRAIL   326

Culture and Politics

Dan Ellsberg   THE FIRST TWO TIMES WE MET   331
Paul Winter   IT WAS THE WHALES THAT BROUGHT ME
   TO GARY SNYDER   340
Richard Nelson   AN ELDER OF THE TRIBE   344
Lee Swenson   SWIMMING IN A SEA OF FRIENDS   352
Charlene Spretnak   DINNERTIME   359
Dave Foreman   GARY SNYDER: TRIBAL FOUNDER   362
George Sessions   GARY SNYDER: POST-MODERN MAN   365
R. Edward Grumbine   A WILD FOX BARKING   371
Peter Berg   BEATING THE DRUM WITH GARY   376
Dell Hymes   A COYOTE WHO CAN SING   392
Stanley Diamond   PRIMITIVE AFTERWORD   405
Thomas Buckley   FIXING THE WORLD   411

Ron Scollon   SNYDER'S CULTURE   416
Suzie Scollon   GENUINE CULTURE   421
Wes Jackson   EVERLASTING LIFE   426

Illustrations

Bob Giorgio   FROM "TRUE NIGHT"   I
Tom Killion   LAKE TENAYA, YOSEMITE   33
Tom Killion   MT. TAMALPAIS FROM CORTE MADERA
  GRADE   51
Tom Pohrt   UNTITLED   91
Michael Corr   "RAIN, RAIN . . ."   III
Will Petersen   FROM *MYTHS & TEXTS* SERIES, 1958
  (PREVIOUSLY UNPUBLISHED)   199
Mayumi Oda   MANJUSRI ON TIGER   289
Jacquie Bellon   WITH JOYFUL INTERPENETRATION
  FOR ALL   320
Arthur Okamura   TURTLE ISLAND   329

Notes on the Contributors   429

Index   441

Colophon

Clifford Burke   WE'RE STILL MAKING BOOKS   452

Jon Halper:
EDITOR'S INTRODUCTION

We were poking around Haida Gwaii, South Moresby, Lyell Island, in the Queen Charlottes, following the curve of islands, and had come to Skedans, a long-deserted Haida village. Skedans was, once, a place where longhouses and totem poles expressed *home* for human beings surrounded by the wealth of many other Beings. The wealth remains, but the people are gone (although there is a strong native and reinhabitory culture in the region). We were visitors, come there to imagine and explore lightly. Gary and I were alone then, and at one point we kneeled in the wet beach grass, looking at a fallen cedar, Bear and Eagle discernable still, if one looked carefully, but their once bright edges blurred, slowly returning to soil and wind. There wasn't anything to say and we didn't. I realized how special this moment was for him, the *now* of a life lived strongly, following dreams and imaginings, journeys begun in a childhood far south of here in Puget Sound and pursued in studies of this actual place and its people when he attended Reed College. Looking at him, I noted in silent acknowledgement how integral his perception and thinking were to who I had become, how inspired my life felt because of his, and knew that I was not alone in this inspiration.

No one lives forever. It seems too often we fail to communicate many of the things that matter most to those for whom they are felt. And we don't have forever. It was some time later when I thought that it would be meaningful to assemble an appreciation for Gary from his many friends and colleagues. I wrote him, including specific suggestions from my vantage of his life. He responded that he would be delighted if I wanted to do such a project, adding parenthetically, "unworthy as I am." I was interested and we explored the idea further.

From the outset it was clear he was not comfortable with something that focused solely on him, envisioning ". . . not just a book for me, [but for] the whole circle and period of time." Gary has a strong sense that he is a part (and not a leader) of a larger social and cultural movement that represents a continuum with the best of human relationship and what it truly means to be human, a subculture in line with the "Big Flow." He thought that a gathering of the sort I proposed might celebrate "something we've done for fun, for ourselves and each other—including those we've never yet had occasion to meet. Not just for [me], but for everyone who's been involved, as an affirmation of some of the hard work and play and crazy stuff we've been doing for the past twenty and more years. An affirmation of the direction and the energy we've all put into it."

Gary observes that his role "is to be catalytic, for the moment." He was plainly uninterested in anything that had an adulatory bent. But he liked the idea of a book about friendship—with room for stories. And we agreed that it might be useful to try to explore relations, ties, and interactions between him and his friends, since it was obvious that other minds had come at the same problems and broadened both their own minds and his. It was also obvious that he had affected people's lives in a very personal way and that this carried to community and culture, both everyday life and worldview.

Two hundred people were considered for inclusion. After extensive consideration, I chose to invite about seventy-five contributors, largely restricted by book size. This compilation, therefore, isn't a fully inclusive one; many more individuals might have been included.

The first half of the book is composed of sections entitled *The Rainy Northwest, Cascades to Sierra: Night Highway Ninety-Nine, Japan: First Time Around, The Wide Pacific,* and *Shasta Nation / Turtle Island.* These sections were envisioned and solicited as pieces from, and pertaining to, specific People, Places, and Times. Some contributors were assigned the recounting of one single day to illustrate some aspect of their own life or their relationship with Gary Snyder. Other pieces are tangential and serve primarily to present the milieu in which Gary moved, but in which he doesn't figure directly.

The second half draws from friends and fellow workers from the various fields of Gary Snyder's interests. These sections include *Poetics, Dharma,* reflecting both individual practice and community, and *Culture and Politics,* including anthropology and the environmental movement.

Some of these essays are highly personal and impressionistic and represent, for example, poet-to-poet thoughts. Others are more objective and critical.

As a whole, the collection begins to form the picture of a post–World War II period, largely West Coast/North Pacific Rim–centered, that amounts to a kind of cultural history, more than just memoirs about Gary Snyder. In a letter, Gary suggested "It seems as though there is a West Coast literary and cultural history that underlies some of the more widespread American social phenomena of the last thirty years that is virtually unknown."

In the twenty years since I first met Gary, I have been a part of a tremendous community, whose commitment and generosity continue to create the world we inhabit and envision. Compiling this book was further evidence of the community, as it expresses the influence of a most remarkable and important person as he continues to move through our midst.

• • •

I wish to express my appreciation for the great kindnesses shared by friends and correspondents alike in the compilation of this book.

My particular gratitude goes to Gary Snyder, Carole Koda, Clifford Burke, Yvonne Marquis, and my mother, Lee Halper.

JON HALPER   xi

The Rainy Northwest
1930–1952

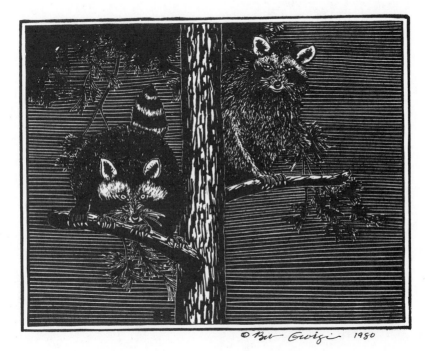

Jerry Crandall:
MOUNTAINEERS ARE ALWAYS FREE

There is something special about growing up surrounded by the natural beauty of the Pacific Northwest. A synthesis of invigorating clean air, crystalline water, and the ubiquitous greenery of forest, field, and lawn stamps an indelible impression on the evolving spirit and shapes character that is sensitive, strong, and independent. Surrounded by rugged mountain ranges dense with towering fir and cedar and hemlock, over which stand guard the snowcapped peaks like sentinel towers above a medieval fortress—Mount Hood, Mount Adams, Mount St. Helens, Mount Rainier—the young are nurtured on the joys of nature: the music of stream, waterfall, and lake, the delicate beauty of birds and flowers, the challenge of the trail. This was the environment of the young Gary Snyder.

Gary and I go way back, to before our teen years even. I think that we first met at the downtown Portland YMCA in the early 1940s when we were together in gym and swim classes (Y-style, barebutt naked, of course). We learned to play basketball (the Y game) and to swim like minnows, trout, and sharks—or so the classes named us. Working parents often parked their kids after school at the Y where they knew the boys would be well supervised, taught athletic skills, and led to participate in constructive activities bereft of economic, ethnic, or social distinctions. Regardless of our backgrounds, as Y kids, both in the city and at camp, we became familiar with the Triad of concern for Body, Soul, and Spirit (symbolized by the Y triangle); this was usually translated into the credo of "I am third!" (God is first, others second, and I third.) Thus, all our play and club participation was encouraged in an atmosphere of cooperation, fair play, and unselfishness—certainly a positive approach. I'm sure we all made use of this orientation in different ways; yet for many of us, it was a significant beginning toward developing our philosophies of life.

Gary and I became close pals when we started spending our summers at the Portland YMCA camp for boys, Camp Meehan, on the shores of Spirit Lake at the foot of Mount St. Helens in southwest-ern Washington. Mount St. Helens, like Mount Hood, was one of the impressive snowcapped peaks that we could see on the horizon from downtown Portland. If there was ever a place designed to inspire the soul, Mount St. Helens/Spirit Lake was it. We thought of the mountain as the Queen of the Cascade Peaks (actually she was a princess in native Indian lore). Sometimes called the Fujiyama of America, she stood regally amid a robe of green with a mirror of deep blue at her feet.

Most of the campers here, like me, were city kids who loved to spend the summers hiking the trails in the Gifford Pinchot National Forest between Mount St. Helens and Mount Adams and learning the lore of the great outdoors. A big help to us were campers like Gary, who had been raised on rural farmsteads and were already comfortable away from concrete and streetcars. Although some kids preferred to stay in camp—swimming, boating, playing softball— there was always a group who wanted to be out of camp on the trail, who couldn't wait to be backpacking again. Gary was one of these. We also learned the thrill of climbing such majestic peaks as St. Helens and Adams. By age thirteen we had become totally addicted to "mountaineering," which included backpacking, mountain climbing, and skiing. One day, we just knew, we would hike the Himalayas and climb Mount Everest. Or so we dreamed. For Gary, many of those dreams would be fulfilled.

I have many vivid memories of Gary from our Spirit Lake days. Some of these occasions may have foreshadowed the man to be. For example, on one of our many three- or four-day hikes, I remember that our trip leader—the camp's inspiring founder, white-haired J. C. Meehan himself—while taking a break on the summit of Mount Margaret, looked out over the panorama of the Cascade Range and asked, "What do you see, boys? What do you see?" Slowly, there were scattered replies, like, "I see a vast forest," or "I see sky and lakes and trees," or even, "I see the raw material for a thousand houses." Finally, after some moments of silence, I heard Gary say quietly, "It's God, it's all God." (Although Gary had been raised an avowed atheist to this point in his life, Nature as God was an easy and popular viewpoint—especially in these surroundings—for many of us who had not been nurtured with a formal religious doctrine. At the time, I imagined this is what he meant, although Gary could have been putting everyone on, knowing that such a response was probably what the Y leader was trying to elicit. Unfortunately, I didn't read his mind; I just heard his comment.)

On another occasion, when we were working our way at camp as kitchen helpers (Super KPs, they called us), Gary and I were sitting on a log eating our lunch and talking. Our sandwiches and peach halves in Sierra cups attracted several noisy camp robbers, Canada Jays, that swooped down into the closest tree boughs to mock us for food. They can be irritating birds and have been known to take the food literally right out of your hand. Without thinking, I picked up a piece of pummy stone (pumice) and threw it in the direction of the closest, noisiest visitor. As bad luck would have it, the stone glanced off the jay's back and knocked the bird to the ground. Gary was upset. He yelled at me for some minutes, telling me how insensitive I was and how cruel and how stupid to assault one of nature's fellow creatures, who had certainly meant us no harm. Of course, he was right; I've felt like the Ancient Mariner ever since. When I recall such experiences, it seems that Gary had grasped instinctively the fullest implications of nature, of ecology, of the interrelatedness of man and of earth much earlier and better than most of us.

There are other moments too: a bashful Gary, hands in his pockets, head down, embarrassed in front of his teasing friends, sheepishly greeting his girlfriend on visitors' Sunday as she eagerly runs to meet him. "Hi, Marty," he sighs, backing away slowly as we all laugh. For weeks afterward, "Hi, Marty" is a camp greeting. And an earnest Gary, presenting "Message to Garcia" with appropriate intonations and gestures "suiting the action to the word, the word to the action" during a morning campfire assembly. And a whimsical Gary, dressed as the farmer's wife in one of our campfire skits, chasing her old man with a broom. And, ultimately, a triumphant Gary, posing atop the wreckage of the old lookout on the summit of Mount St. Helens, staring across the peaks at Mount Rainier in the distance. Whatever the situation, Gary was involved and wholly himself.

Although we had gone to different grammar schools, Gary and I both attended Lincoln High School in downtown Portland, Oregon. Lincoln was an urban high school with rich, poor, and in-between students equally represented. There were lots of clubs and cliques, but Gary's school interests centered around the journalism club and the drama group. On weekends in the winter and spring we would ski the slopes at Mount Hood (11,226 feet), an hour's drive from the city, and party at the Mazama Lodge at Government Camp. Gary loved the camaraderie of the slopes, and he missed very few weekends.

We had both joined the Mazamas, a major mountaineering club in the Northwest, in 1946 after climbing Mount Hood. (One of the requirements for membership was to climb "a snowpeak on which there is at least one living glacier, and the top of which cannot be reached by any other means than on foot.") Previously, we had climbed other mountains, especially Mount St. Helens (9,677 feet), and had become climbing enthusiasts. (Alas! The wonderful Mount St. Helens is no longer as we knew her.) In the spring and summer, besides skiing (we could ski all year long on Mount Hood), we would go on club outings and climbs throughout the Northwest.

Often during the week, after school, Gary could be found at the Mazama clubhouse, which was appropriately located on top of the Power and Light Building in downtown Portland. Here, the library was filled with books, maps, and pictures of the great climbs and climbers, and the walls were adorned with inspiring photographs by Ray Atkinson, Ansel Adams, and other fine artists. I think Gary had read everything in the library, and we'd remember the stories and fantasize about our climbing the great peaks around the world— Mont Blanc, Mount McKinley, Mount Everest.

The Mazamas had a yearly magazine, the *Mazama,* and Gary, an avid "youngsteiger," a name he coined for the younger Mazama members, had his first article published in the December 1946 issue. The item is an amusing satire on a beginner's first snow climb. It ends predictably, with the author's desire to be "climbing [the mountain] again next week." The next year Gary was an associate editor of the magazine and again had an article in the December issue. This time he reviewed the climbing activities of the youngsteigers, who were swelling the membership ranks of the club. In this article he also clearly reveals his infatuation with the mountains that have inspired him. He wrote: "Few could forget the beauty of the Cascades and Olympics, or lose the appreciation and love for the mountains they first came to know."

During his high school years Gary was also involved in writing for the school paper, *The Cardinal,* and trying his hand at dramatics. In the senior class play, *You Can't Take It With You,* he played the fireworks maker in the basement, receiving the praise of all. However, he almost missed the performance. The afternoon before the play, the cast had a champagne party at which Gary, a novice drinker at this time, had a few too many. I had to administer two glasses of hot salt water and six turns around the school in the cold air before he was able to perform that night.

As I recall, Gary also worked part-time as graveyard shift copyboy for the *Oregonian,* Portland's major newspaper. Since his mother was a journalist, perhaps the propensity to write came naturally. At any rate, I believe he wrote regularly during his high school years.

Most everyone liked Gary, especially those who skied and climbed and the older members of the Mazamas who shared his love for the mountains. There were those at school who thought the ski bums were nonconformists, outsiders, but if that bothered Gary, I never noticed it. He had a ready smile for everyone, a sharp sense of humor, and a generous, open manner. But what I admired most was that he had the courage of his convictions. He was always an individualist. I never knew him to follow a high school fad in clothing or behavior. His style was always his own. Who else would wear lederhosen, Indian moccasins, and a Robin Hood hat to school in the 1940s? I admired him then, and I admire him now. We like to say up in the Oregon country: "You can take the boy out of the mountains, but you can't take the mountains out of the boy." Those who know Gary know this is true.

J. Michael Mahar:

SCENES FROM THE SIDELINES

Gary's mother, Lois, was the first harridan I ever met. She provided me with this brand new word for my "mean" list by scuttling a weekend camping trip that Gary and I had planned in the Linton Hills. Her reason: Gary had failed to get an A on his Latin quiz and had to stay home and do his homework. Since nobody in my circle did homework at all, this was a weird decree amounting to cruel and inhuman punishment for twelve-year-olds in the St. John's district of Portland, Oregon.

But then, Gary really wasn't a member of our peer group—children of the resident elite from the gas works, the woolen mill, and the foundry of Portland's blue-collar north side. Our parents didn't hassle us kids about homework and grades. We were headed for the kinds of jobs where formal education did not weigh nearly as heavily as one's abilities on the football field.

It was only with the years and from a ripened perspective that Lois Snyder's vital role in the development of Gary Snyder, poet and citizen, could be acknowledged. She differed from other mothers in that she was the first single parent I had ever met, other than the Norwegian widow Johansson, whose sea-captain husband had gone down with his ship. Lois was a newspaperwoman at a time when many other women did not even drive cars, let alone work outside the home. Her independence was accompanied by a sharp tongue, a sharp intellect, and a declared resolve to become a reporter, even though when first we met she was working in the circulation department of the *Oregonian*.

All the other mothers in our neighborhood were simply mothers—but here was this whirlwind breezing in from Seattle with Gary and his younger sister Anthea. Lois had come to Portland with her two children at the height of a wartime boom to reside in a housing project cheaply built for shipyard workers in the open fields of northwest Portland.

Unlike the rest of us, Gary didn't go to Roosevelt High, distinguished for its athletes—sons of boilermakers and other wage-earning families. His mother insisted that he commute downtown to Lincoln High, generally known as the most intellectually demanding in the Portland system. In retrospect, it seems clear that she was helping Gary lay the foundation of scholarly excellence that would enable him to attend the college of her choice. They didn't have the money to pay for higher education, but she was setting him up for scholarships that, combined with frugality, would buy him four years at a first-rate college.

Anthea, Gary's younger sister, was, from the perspective of a twelve-year-old, just another kid sister with freckles. I don't recall much about her, and in later years I never saw her again.

Gary's father never entered our conversations and scarcely figured in the rounds of our friendship. To this day I don't know if he was tall or short, fat or thin. At that time, I knew only that he worked for the government as a housing administrator in San Francisco. Years later, around 1951, when we were attending Reed College, Gary told me his father had been questioned by the FBI about his son's politics. The agent cited a report on the people and places that Gary visited, and its remarkable accuracy caused us to ponder the identity of an informer in our midst. About then, the Velde Committee (on un-American activities) came to Portland; it was McCarthy time. The visit led to the dismissal of Stanley Moore, a Reed professor of philosophy whose houseboat was a favorite place for parties and stimulating conversation. As far as political action was concerned, however, the most militant bit that anyone ventured was circulation of petitions to put William O. Douglas on the Oregon primary ballot for the presidency.

While I don't recall the first time Gary and I met, I suspect it may have been due to his mother's abortive effort to enroll him in the neighborhood Boy Scout troop in which I was active. Gary never became one of us, but he and I ended up going bird-watching in the Columbia Slough from time to time. He owned a pair of binoculars and I a copy of Roger Tory Peterson's *Guide to Western Birds*. We sloshed around in the midst of a lot of dead carp and willows, occasionally seeing a redwing blackbird. We also paddled about in a flatbottom boat made of spare lumber from my father's oar factory.

Long after those days, Gary and I met again, in the spring of 1949. At age seventeen, I had joined the Army and gone off to Korea for two years. I signed up under the GI Bill to go to the University of

Oregon and, noting how the collegiate crowd dressed, I bought a brick red shirt. Gary was going to a little college called Reed that I had never heard of, somewhere in the southeast part of town. He invited me to a student party that changed my life. It was the first time I had ever met a group of people who really liked to talk. Words that I had only read in books were used with ease and vigor, ranging over subjects from Leadbelly to broad jumping in Lithuania. I was enchanted and rushed down to campus the next day to apply for admission.

The first semester, I took the bus from home to school. Gary was a junior at the time but graciously led his freshman friend through such intricacies of college life as how to find the coffee shop, where he often held court between classes. This was also the arena for periodic battles with the manager over Gary's practice of brewing his tea with his own cup and tea bags brought from home. This was but one measure of the frugality prompted by his having to live on fifty dollars a month. At one point, denied use of the coffee shop's hot-water spout, Gary set up his Sterno stove and boiled his own water.

In the spring of 1950, Gary invited me to move in at 1414 SE Lambert Street—by far the most socially and intellectually stimulating environment I had ever encountered. The rambling old two-story house had been divided into a rabbit warren of seven apartments by the owner, a fundamentalist preacher from Vancouver. Gary acted as sometimes-manager in return for the privilege of living in the basement between the furnace and the laundry tub: an area about eight by ten feet. A casement window provided a view of the heavens and a steady stream of water whenever it rained. Typically, Gary defined the leak as a waterfall and running brook, which he channeled across the basement floor to serve a miniature Japanese garden. This "Zen retreat," with Gary as its centerpiece, attracted a constant stream of beautiful young ladies, especially children of the rich and famous. With a simple bed—a mattress on the floor—a Japanese print or two, and a draped cloth here and there, Gary somehow evoked the aura of a sheik of Araby.

Women of all persuasions found him attractive. Gary managed this with what struck me as a lot of bravura and not much sentiment. Robin was the exception. She was the essence of myth and legend— lean of leg, sensitive, intelligent, and delicate in matters of the heart. She came very close to Gary but then she withdrew, and it was a very long time before Gary could accept what had happened. Perhaps she sensed his underlying fear of emotional involvement with women, a feeling he never expressed in words but which was somehow implicit in the fleeting nature of his other relationships and his celebration of sex for its own sake—a posture that ran contrary to my own Lochinvar mentality. Although Gary married Allison in his senior year, I never understood their mutual attraction other than a common interest in nature and hiking and camping. I suspect they met at one of those times when couples are in the mood to marry. They eventually split and went their separate ways.

Of the many interesting women visiting the predominantly male occupants of Lambert Street, several were attuned to social changes that became manifest in the feminist movement a decade or two later. Not only were they college educated, in contrast to their mothers— they were career oriented and very much in charge of their own bodies.

Before Gary occupied his tiny basement seraglio, he lived in a real room on the second floor, one of four units sharing a common bathroom and occupied by various luminaries at various times. There was Roy Stilwell, a violinist in the Portland Symphony. There was Carol Baker, night operator on the police station switchboard, with her army of cats, and her husband, Bobby Baker, a former high school football star.

There was Ed Harper, a lanky, redheaded ex-Marine who was studying gypsies in the Pacific Northwest. There was me, and there was Philip Whalen. A portly fellow, Phil tended to sit back and dispense wisdom like a grandfather. As a counselor and commentator on life, he maintained a steady calm that somehow seemed to balance Gary's intensity.

More spacious apartments in the house on Lambert Street were occupied on the ground floor by the likes of Paul Chambers, who had spent two years on a destroyer in the South Pacific but couldn't swim; Martin Murie, who looked like a mountain man and whose father was president of the Wilderness Society; and Eddie Durham, who had the only car and tried to teach Gary how to drive. (It was to no avail. Gary never got to the hands-on part of the Oregon drivers' test because he always failed the written exam.)

Apart from me, the callow freshman, these occupants of Lambert Street were older students, several of them combat veterans from

World War II, with a serious interest in their studies and an awesome grasp of skills ranging from mountain climbing to Chinese calligraphy. Their spirit of sharing contributed as much to my education as the formal coursework in which I dabbled. Much of the talk was about literature since Gary and Philip were poets, and their friends, such as Lew Welch and Bobo Allen, were deeply immersed in the subject. Bobo and Gary were kindred spirits in many other ways, incidentally, sharing code names (Hoodlatch and Leitchswitch) and a penchant for deviltry. On one occasion, they fashioned a stippler for biology lab illustrations by lashing a pencil to the clapper of an electric doorbell: a timesaver not appreciated by the instructor.

My naiveté inspired the companions to such "experiments" as thrusting upon me copies of *Ulysses* (which I liked) and *Finnegans Wake* (which I didn't finish). My responses to the music of Bartók and the poetry of Blake were also probed, almost dissectingly, by such queries as "How do you like it?" Philip Whalen, a gentler teacher, initiated me into sipping tea with discretion while consuming the works of Marcel Proust, T. S. Eliot, and other authors who before had been only names to me. Gary introduced me to the wonders of the Salvation Army resale store, where I acquired my one and only Harris tweed jacket, while he built up his basic set of camping equipment. His approach to camping was rigorous concerning carefully planned meals of dehydrated food and other measures to minimize the weight of backpacks. But on the trail and on the mountaintop Gary's disciplined style gave way to a frolicsome air. Characteristically, in his climbing days he always peed from the highest point on the mountain. Nature was vitally important to Gary as it was to me at that time. Martin Murie introduced us to the Wilderness Society, and I subscribed to their journal, a strong precursor of the ecological concerns of today.

Cosmopolites though we were, there were situations and commodities about which Gary and I both lacked knowledge. At the outset of our trip up the Dosewallips on the Olympic Peninsula, we bought a bag of freshly boiled shrimp. But neither of us knew how to go about eating them, and since they were small shrimp, we just ate them, shells and all.

Gary as a student was as diligent as any mother could desire and his interests clearly foreshadowed his later life as well as the temper of times to come. One was American Indians. His B.A. thesis treated myths of the Haida Indians, a subject spanning his interest in English and anthropology. I began as a biology major, but when I learned through Gary of the Thursday evening soirees at Dave and Kay French's house, I trotted down to the registrar and changed my major to anthropology. Dave French, in his ineffable way, steered me into ethnobotany, which linked my interests and tied in with the attention of Gary and his friends to the peyote cult. I recall, after Gary's first encounter with the hallucinogenic effects of the peyote ritual, his turning to me and saying, "Mike, I think it has a great future." This and other experiences we had in the early 1950s lightly sketched what was to become a dominant social and cultural theme of the 1960s.

Another personal interest of Gary's was folk songs. He knew a large repertoire of labor and Wobbly songs, which he sang with great vigor while whacking away at his guitar. I especially enjoyed his rendering of songs learned from Leadbelly recordings long before that name had entered the mainstream of American pop music.

After graduation Gary and Philip Whalen moved to San Francisco along with Lew Welch. They quickly arrived at a novel conclusion: Two or three can easily live off the earnings of one if you scale down your standard of living. Scaling down in this case meant living in a little cabin in the hills behind Sausalito where Locke McCorkle maintained his family, home, and business as a carpenter before he shifted to Arizona as a house builder and finally, after liquidating all his worldly goods, to Majorca.

The cabin, reached uphill from the main house along a grove of eucalyptus trees, was simply shelter. A few sleeping bags provided bedding—with perhaps a tatami as the base—and a Coleman stove was the kitchen. Free food was in abundance at the Safeway loading docks where slightly wilted vegetables and tomatoes past their prime could be picked up every day and tossed in a wok with sesame oil and a little imagination to make nutritious and tasty meals.

Savouring San Francisco from the perspective of poverty and poets led us to some delightful settings, including the Japanese Tea Garden in Golden Gate Park, where Philip liked to drink tea, eat cakes, and visit his favorite orchid in the adjacent botanical garden greenhouse. Philip also introduced me to a beach of marvels—a strand outside the Golden Gate adorned by multicolored pebbles, the likes of which I had never seen; one could imagine them as lost settings from a costume jewelry factory. In fact, they were the sea- and sand-burnished fragments of broken bottles, deposited by the city's garbage scows.

Phil, as I recall, got a job as night watchman on a construction site. His serene detachment seemed to enable him to be the one most often able to keep a job, providing the little cash needed for a gallon of California red wine and a loaf or two of bread. My occasional brief visits to Gary and Phil left me with the impression that here were people reading, writing, talking, and thinking more about Asia and the arts than in any graduate school I had ever encountered. Never had I seen such energy, interest, and enthusiasm addressed to one's studies: certainly not in the groves of academe where I later pitched my tent. While their peers were breaching the walls of middle-class prosperity at the beginning of professional careers, Gary and Phil spent minimal hours in nontaxing jobs so that they could afford to practice Chinese calligraphy, read up on Asia, and hone their poetry.

I did not attend the celebrated poetry readings in the North Beach bars. I did visit the City Lights Bookstore and the neighboring bar with the inscription over the door, "We are itching to get away from Portland, Oregon," "we" presumably referring to the contingent from Reed. My strongest memories of the neighborhood are of the pleasant, quiet hours of early morning with the odor of fresh-baked Italian bread in the air along with the plaintive sounds of a piccolo played by a wandering, mad minstrel who wore a headdress to match the season. On one occasion it was a plastic helmet liner with a small Christmas tree sprouting from the top.

Kerouac and the other East Coast people had yet to arrive on the scene. When they did come, Phil was several years into Zen dharma and what went with it. As for Gary, his emerging primary interest during our last years at Reed College had been Asia, Japan in par- ticular. This was inspired in part by Charles Leong, a Chinese gentle- man scholar in his forties who was an occasional student. It was Charlie who introduced Gary and Phil, among others, to Chinese calligraphy. Ezra Pound and Lafcadio Hearn, encountered in an En- glish course, were stepping stones also to interest in the art and aes- thetics of Asia, although their particular works were soon left behind.

Gary's first stay in Japan was arranged by Ruth Sasaki and the First

Zen Institute of America in Kyoto, who invited him to come and work as a translator and researcher and also to practice Zen. I have always assumed that the austerities of the monastic routine placed physical and mental demands on Gary that were modest, compared to those made by his mother and the poverty of his college years.

David H. French:

GARY SNYDER AND REED COLLEGE

Gary Snyder's years at Reed College were from 1947 until 1951; I will focus on those years but will sometimes stray from them. Gary's major came to be an interdisciplinary one in literature and anthropology. I really got to know him when—as a sophomore—he studied introductory anthropology (in a course then combined with sociology). He later said that it was my junior anthropology course on the Far East that first attracted him to that area of the world. My courses were the only anthropology games in town, and he took various others as well, participating in each on its own terms.

The link between anthropology and literature (especially poetry) was particularly strong at Reed in the late 1940s and early 1950s. Among those who were involved were Gary himself, Dell Hymes, the late Lewis (Lew) Welch, and Philip (Phil) Whalen. They were party-sharers, friends, and intellectual colleagues; there were others associated with them, and the critical mass resulted in aesthetic and scholarly activity extending spontaneously beyond classrooms. Hymes was also an excellent anthropology-literature major; Welch was a superior student in anthropology courses, and Whalen absorbed anthropology outside of classes.

In standard literature courses Gary was a good student, but his actual grades in that field averaged a bit lower than those in anthropology. Why should this be? A critical look at the courses and faculty might be revealing. As at most colleges, Reed's curriculum was then based on the assumption that literature is one of the Fine Arts and that it was produced mainly by white males in Europe and the United States. These significant but then rarely articulated views are "culture-bound," a term referring to the nearly universal belief that one's own culture, including its morality, religion, and arts, are the world's best by universal standards.[1] (There were aspects of fashion in the course emphases: Certain modern, culture-bound writers, such as Hemingway, wrote literature, but Dickens and Mark Twain had not done so.) Gary's favorite faculty member in the arts was the late Lloyd Reynolds—best known nationally for fostering calligraphy. Reynolds taught creative writing and (earlier) the history of modern art; he was a printmaker and came to be an enthusiastic amateur Orientalist. He was later forced to disclose a Communist past. He was not culture-bound, and neither were Gary Snyder and his student friends. It is an easy inference that standard literature courses, though worthwhile, lacked the world perspective sought by Gary and his colleagues. For Gary, at least, the information and viewpoints of anthropology served him better than, say, academic history. For Gary, and especially for his friend Dell Hymes, many aspects of linguistics also proved to be compatible with the perspective sketched above.[2]

Mythology in general, and American Indian myths especially, were a significant focus for Gary. His senior (B.A.) thesis (a thesis is required of all Reed students before graduation) was entitled *The Dimensions of a Haida Myth* and had a Haida narrative as the starting point. Lloyd Reynolds and I were co-advisors, but Gary needed little advice by the time he was a senior. The Haidas are a coastal British Columbian Indian group, and the thesis included discussions of a particular myth in terms of its Haida cultural context, its distribution elsewhere, and presented a range of approaches to its interpretation. In due course, the existence of the thesis became known, largely to young people, in California and elsewhere. Xeroxed copies of it circulated and were recopied. There came to be pale and messy Xeroxes of Xeroxes of Xeroxes; I was told once that it was the most copied Reed thesis of all time. Eventually, in 1979, it was published with an expanded title, a new foreword by Gary, and a preface by Nathaniel Tarn.[3]

Let me employ a phrase that is almost self-explanatory: "to engage in an activity in a professional manner." Its use is indeed relatable to familiar occupations, called professions, such as medicine and law. My focus here, however, is not on vocations and on certification to engage in them, but instead on the quality of an activity. Doing an act in a professional manner is doing it well, usually in the way that specialists do it (that is, by following standards) or sometimes building on a tradition by means of an appropriate innovation. Gary was approaching the writing of poetry in a near-professional manner when he entered Reed, and he said later that evidence of this helped him to secure admission. At Reed, he soon undertook his education (and other activities) in a professional manner. Being intelligent was no handicap, but Gary was also motivated to learn; except in two courses as a freshman, his grades were all above average. Required courses in fields outside one's major areas of interest can defeat some students.

In college, parties sometimes happen even though the participants have assignments to read for the next day's classes or have term papers to finish. It was said that Gary could immerse himself in a party for a goodly part of an evening, then slip away after midnight and do the academic work needed for the next day. Those who stayed at the party are likely to include people whose names one can no longer recall. (It was not that Gary was work-obsessed; at Reed—and later—he certainly stayed at other parties.)

Gary was an efficient scholar. The senior thesis at Reed, mentioned earlier, is not a trivial undertaking (it is like an M.A. thesis at many schools). During Gary's period, there were students who did not finish their theses in the normal nine months and who lingered in Portland for two or more years, still writing or revising their theses. (Later, the requirements included a deadline system that did not permit such extended periods.) In 1951, most students barely met the spring deadline. Gary, however, submitted his 159-page thesis at a date that was earlier than any I heard about during my forty-one years on the faculty. Yet it was one of few theses that have been subsequently published.

There is evidence that Gary took seriously the suggestions of those involved in academic approaches to poetry. Since his graduation from Reed, he has returned a number of times, by invitation, to read his poetry, to meet with students, and (once) to lecture on ecology, especially that of China. Allen Ginsberg accompanied him during two or more of these visits. Immediately after one of their readings, in 1956, Snyder and Ginsberg approached Kenneth Hanson, a rather new faculty member and poet, to solicit his evaluation of their work.

As a student, Gary was alert, articulate, diligent, friendly, and amusing. Those who know the college know that Reed has always lacked some features prominent elsewhere: sororities and fraternities, exclusive clubs, and an emphasis on intercollegiate athletics. Big Men (and Women) on Campus (BMOCs) have always existed;

some are leaders in student-body affairs. Two kinds of high-prestige people, or "heroes," are more common than in most colleges: brilliant students and those with talent and experience who excel in the arts. Gary was a BMOC, or hero, as were a few of his friends.[4]

Intellectual play had its role in Gary's life, when he was a student and later. During one visit to Reed by Ginsberg and Snyder during the 1950s (perhaps it was late in the visit mentioned above), I invited them to my house to meet with students in the evening. No topic or format was specified in advance; an informal debate quickly emerged in response to the question, "Are poetry and science (broadly defined) incompatible?" Allen consistently held to one position, Gary to the opposite; students interspersed questions and comments. Occasionally, during subsequent years, I have asked people who know the poets (by reading, rumor, or otherwise) who took which position. Almost always, their guesses are wrong; Allen in fact said science and poetry are compatible, which I have believed was, and is, his true position. Gary's opposition was well argued, but I have suspected it was taken to create the happening. In a sense, the argument was a skillful, unplanned performance.

Being sociable, and because dormitory space was temporarily inadequate, Gary was an early participant in a trend that was probably also occurring elsewhere in colleges. What were sometimes called "Reed houses" were being established. Someone would rent or lease an older residence, typically within walking or bicycling distance of the college. Only men occupied them at first, but women also began to live in them. The houses usually acquired nicknames, such as "the Zoo." Disharmony could appear regarding such matters as eating and cleaning arrangements, telephone bills, and the rent. Nevertheless, such houses also fostered the intellectual and aesthetic stimulation suggested elsewhere. Of great importance in some houses was the family-like community that developed in them.[5] Such houses are still flourishing at Reed.

Beyond conversation, Gary and his friends sought new, firsthand experiences. Gary himself had come from a broken family, and he led a rather independent life before coming to Reed. The following account from his pre-Reed days reached me somehow: Gary had a small group of friends who cherished vivid events and who created them for each other. They were mountain climbers; an example of a special experience was to be pushed unexpectedly from a high place. My understanding is that the result was fear producing but not life threatening.

A good party can be a special experience; it is no surprise that some Reed students did some drinking, mostly wine and beer. There was no evidence of a true drug culture at Reed, but Gary's friends did experiment in this area. For example, they tried peyote, a cactus that can sometimes cause hallucinations and is associated with an American Indian religious complex.

Openness to experience is reflected in Jack Kerouac's novel *The Dharma Bums*, in which Gary is represented by the major character, Japhy Ryder. (In chapter 23, page 161 of my 1958 edition and printing, Kerouac and his editors slipped and called him Gary, not Japhy; this was corrected in a later printing.) I have not reread the book recently, though I would enjoy doing so. Kerouac, however, was probably not fully a member of the intellectual/poetic/truth-seeking group to which Gary belonged, and the novel surely does not give a balanced picture of the lives of Gary and others. After all, it is a novel, not history or biography, and it has its own rationale. The book does refer to Japhy's college days, but it is mainly concerned with a somewhat later period.

Prior to World War II, when I was a Reed student, religion had very little visibility on the Reed campus. Students were Christian, Jewish, agnostic, and atheist; a few individuals followed belief systems popularly called Eastern religions. Some Christians and Jews quietly left the campus for services on the Sabbath and special religious days. There were no courses in religion and very little discussion of it at the school. After the war, religious activity became increasingly overt, and the environment was appropriate for more students to explore ideas from South Asia and East Asia. I don't know when Gary decided that he was a Buddhist. He was certainly interested in Buddhism while he was at Reed, but perhaps a personal adherence to it came later.

Reed students have long been politically active, with regard to both college-internal issues and those of much wider scope. Prior to World War II, the two largest groups were Democrats and Socialists. Poll-like evidence indicated that Communists and Republicans were roughly tied at a lower level. An unknown percentage of students were basically indifferent to such politics, but many people in the general Portland community had an exaggerated idea as to how many "Reds" there were at Reed.

After World War II, changes in political activity occurred among younger people on the West Coast. In the Bay Area—for example, in Berkeley and San Francisco—Marxists noticed with dismay that anarchists were replacing them. At Reed, Marxists were fewer in number and less vocal, at least less so than they had been in the 1930s. Spokespersons for extreme conservatism appeared in the student body. Gary defined himself as a radical, but it was difficult to label or stereotype him. He associated with two of the conservatives; when queried about this, he said they were simply talented friends of his. When students argued about how to assess Ezra Pound, who had supported Mussolini, Gary expressed appreciation for Pound because of the quality of his poetry; in later years, Gary seemed less interested in him and implied that he was culture-bound (using other terminology). (Arguments about Pound still occur at Reed and elsewhere.) Meanwhile, at least one of Gary's good friends was and may still be a Socialist. Some of politics, as usually defined, was probably not in the forefront of Gary's concerns. He has cared very much about natural environments, about human understanding, and about many other matters that could be labeled utopian. He has said that Kropotkin is one of his heroes, but this has hardly indicated clearly which candidate or party he would support in a current election. Were there a German-like Green Party available to him, he would perhaps have supported it at times. In the real world, he became an appointed member of the California state arts council and a personal friend of a Democratic governor.

Before beginning to write these pages, I was asked what Gary's contributions to anthropology have been. Because he chose not to obtain an advanced degree in any field, he could scarcely be expected to have published in standard anthropological journals. Yet he has made contributions. He has plugged our weirdly diversified discipline as one of the superior ways to gain perspective on mankind.[6] In the early 1950s, he spent time working at logging-related projects on the Warm Springs Indian Reservation. He came to know Indians there, and he collected oral literature. Such experience, as well as his formal and informal education, is reflected in some of his poetry, and in other written and spoken modalities. It is as if he has been a teacher of anthropology to audiences who did not always know that it was anthropology they were learning. Often, he told them it was.

Edward Sapir and Ruth Benedict were anthropologists who also were poets. Dell Hymes and Stanley Diamond are among those who have more recently functioned in the two roles, while at times merging them. Gary, as a friend of both, has joined them and others in participating in an activity sometimes called "ethnopoetics." He was a contributing editor of the journal *Alcheringa,* and was a participant in an "Anthropology and Poetry" session at the 1982 annual meeting of the American Anthropological Association. The subtitle of the session was "Another Way of Looking at Reality." In sum, Gary could scarcely have done more to link the two activities.

An interesting question concerns the extent to which certain Reed students independently invented the Beat Generation approach to life in the late 1940s in Portland. At Reed they weren't unusually "countercultural." I have indeed suggested that they were not culture-bound. They did, however, experiment with alternatives to the usual American ways. In the 1950s, various Reed graduates and dropouts moved to the Bay Area. Dell Hymes chose to learn more anthropology and to earn a Ph.D. in linguistics at Indiana University, but Gary and his other friends joined with Californians and some who had moved from easterly areas, such as a city called New York, to make a substantial contribution to well-known Bay Area developments. Just what contribution did the Reed contingent make to the changes that occurred in the 1950s, 1960s, and later? It's clear that there was a contribution, but I don't feel that I know the size of it.

Admittedly, this has been written with personal biases, all of them decades old: I remain enthusiastic about anthropology, linguistics, mythology, Reed College, democracy, the arts (including poetry), and Gary Snyder.[7]

NOTES

1. David H. French, "The Concept of Culture-bondage," *Transactions of the New York Academy of Sciences* Ser. II, Vol. 17, No. 4 (1955).

2. Nathaniel Tarn, "From Anthropologist to Informant: A Field Record of Gary Snyder," *Alcheringa* 4 (1972), 106.

3. Gary Snyder, *He Who Hunted Birds in His Father's Village: The Dimensions of a Haida Myth* (Bolinas, California: Grey Fox Press, 1979).

4. Gary himself has summarized his Reed education in *The Real Work: Interviews & Talks 1964–1979* (New York: New Directions Publishing Corp., 1980, p. 64): "I went to Reed College in Oregon, I had some marvelous teachers, I learned how to use a library, I was in an atmosphere that challenged me and pushed me to the utmost, which was just what I needed. They wouldn't tolerate bullshit, made me clean up my prose style, exposed me to all varieties of intellectual positions and gave me a territory in which I could speak out my radical politics and get arguments and augmentations on it. It was an intensive, useful experience."

5. Gary Snyder, *Earth House Hold: Technical Notes & Queries to Fellow Dharma Revolutionaries* (New York: New Directions Publishing Corp., 1969, III).

6. An example of his support for the field is this statement from an interview in *The Real Work*, p. 58: "If I were recommending anybody to study anything in the university over anything else, I would either recommend biology or anthropology. Anthropology is probably the most intellectually exciting field in the universities. The most *intellectually* exciting, the one where something's happening in *humanistic terms*. If you want to get exciting science, you go into biochemistry or something like that. But if you want to get interesting ideas you go into anthropology."

7. I would like to offer thanks for valuable assistance from Kathrine French, Edwin Gerow, Jon Halper, Dell Hymes, and Christopher Roth.

Carol Baker:

1414 SE LAMBERT STREET

Memory is very strange. I can't remember who told me back in 1949 that a room (with kitchen) was for rent at 1414 SE Lambert Street not far from Reed College, but I do remember moving in. I can't really remember about what shape the room was in, although I do know that one of the first things I did was to rent a steamer and steam the old wallpaper off. After the walls dried, I painted them a pretty color, a warm light brown. These were "furnished" rooms, but the only piece of furniture was a bed. I took the bed off the frame and put the mattress on the floor. It made the room seem much bigger.

The Lambert Street house was big, cut up into apartments. The rooms, only a mile or so from Reed College and usually rented by students, were small and cheap. I was one of two females who lived in that rambling place, and the only one who was single. Rosemary Thompson lived on the main floor with her husband, Les, and their son, Gregory, but they moved out soon after I moved in. I was also the only tenant who had a telephone and the only one upstairs who had a refrigerator. My room became a popular place.

Martin Murie and Ed Harper lived on the top floor, and at the back with their own private entrance lived Don Berry and Erich Wheeler. We all shared a bathroom down the hall. In the middle of the house, on the same floor as the Thompsons, Paul Chambers and his brother Carrol shared a place, and Eddie Durham lived in the rear portion of the house. Down in the basement were Philip Whalen and Gary Snyder.

Thinking back on those days, when I close my eyes the Gary that I see is always laughing. He had a great big grin, a friendly way about him, and a love for telling jokes. Some were fairly raw but all were funny. Gary was a rather small man, with a slight build. He'd suffered from rickets as a child due to his poor diet.

At the Lambert Street house, Gary had struck a deal with our landlord, the Reverend Cranston (whom we called the Shadow). The basement had once been a coal cellar, and Gary promised to clean the cellar and make it into another apartment in lieu of rent. Gary, being a man of his word even then, did the cleaning, and Gary and Philip set up housekeeping, but I believe the Reverend balked at the reduced rent.

As I recall, we gave our landlord a case of the hives. He didn't know what to make of us. He probably was aware of the "Reed Reputation," and we certainly did our best to live up to it!

Money was always a problem; none of us were rich. I was working my way through Reed by manning the switchboard for the Police Department. Gary was a scholarship student, and the other fellows were mainly GIs. We were serious students, however, and these were serious times. We had just won a righteous war; we felt it was up to the survivors to realize a righteous future. Peace, prosperity, and progress were the watchwords. Being full of almost too much energy, vitality, and brains for our own good, we were all flaming radicals—left of center, you bet, but by God, we were going to do it right! I don't know for sure which of us belonged to the leftist groups of the day, but we *all* believed in the power of intelligence as addressed to the problems of mankind. Long before Martin Luther King Jr., made the phrase popular, we knew *we could overcome.*

Although we lived almost as one big family unit, most of us had outside romantic attachments. Gary was in love with Robin Collins, and I was Lew Welch's friend. Later I met Bill Baker, a friend of a friend. Bill was beautiful, and before I knew it, I'd fallen in love.

But as a group, we spent a lot of our time together talking, arguing, and playing canasta or mah-jongg. I can't be sure, but I think we may even have studied occasionally. Gary, Philip, Bill Baker, Ed Durham, and I would argue, discuss, rant, and rave into the night. Social injustice was a big item on our agenda. Under Gary's aegis I began to pay attention to the underclasses—the Native Americans, the Japanese-Americans, the blacks. He talked to me about growing up as a Depression boy, and he showed me his rickety ribs, caused by not enough good food—his family was poor. He told me the story of the Wobblies, the local name for The Industrial Workers of the World, a radical union formed early in the century by loggers and others who worked in the forests. They'd formed their union to work for equitable rights in a time when exploitation of workers by the rich was the name of the game. Gary explained that right up the road in Centralia was the site of one famous conflict between the Wobblies and the wealthy lumber kings.

Gary had a saying: "I want to create wilderness out of empire." Funny? He meant it. A love of the natural world was deep in his bones, and he intended to make his point. I think I can say without challenge that he has. Both his books and his poetry show not only his gentleness for nature but his fierceness about what is happening to our world.

As I think back on those good times, I get many disjointed memories, such as those of funny incidents involving me, the lone female, sharing one bathroom with more than half a dozen young men—all of whom needed to shave when I wanted to take a leisurely bath. Finally I put my foot down and said that I intended to relax in the tub, drink my glass of wine, read my paper. If they wanted to come in and use the facilities, fine. They just shouldn't expect me to hop out of the tub. Years later one of the guys said that the high point of his day had been shaving while I bathed. But at the time it was no big thing to me—I think I simply felt like one of the guys.

I particularly remember Gary's pot of split pea soup—a huge pot that seemed to last forever. Even though Gary never seemed to have much, he was good with money; he knew how to make it last, how to stretch it out. He was a resourceful young man. He could always find a job. He worked as a firewatcher in the forests, as a logger, and as a choker setter on the Warm Springs Indian Reservation; one summer he even got a job at Fort Vancouver working on a dig for Indian relics. Nor will I ever forget the day Gary took me to the Goodwill. In those days the Goodwill warehouse was one huge room with everything piled in the middle. There were boxes and boxes of stuff to go through, and I was amazed at what I could find and buy for next to nothing. It was like a gigantic rummage sale. We got all of our clothes, kitchen goods, and furniture there. Cheap!

Something about that year (1949–1950) and that group of people is still very special in my memory. We had a great time—everything was either fun or funny. Gary had a gift for language and an ear for the ridiculous. He absorbed idiom and cadence. He could tell wonderful stories about the loggers or about the Indian girls that the men took to parties.

I believe that the teachers at Reed at that time were all men. Interesting and stimulating though they were, the one who most impressed us was Lloyd Reynolds, who became famous for his teaching of calligraphy. Reynolds was the mentor for several in our group, and

I'm sure he encouraged the poets in our midst. His impact on us was immense, explainable only because of inexplainable factors—good old serendipity.

About this time the witch-hunts began; intellectuals everywhere were hounded, and we were not to be excepted. Sure enough, the Velde Committee came to investigate us Reedies. Several professors were interrogated—one was let go—and everyone was worried. One day the FBI came to the door of 1414 SE Lambert. From my window I could see the two men coming, wearing suits that were out of place in that they were too tidy, too expensive, and too severe for the area. We thought we could tell the FBI by their shoes. These two slick big-city types had on black shoes. I met them at the door. They wanted information about Gary, and smart-ass that I was, I pretended not to know him. Apparently, he had applied for a passport, and his application was denied. Gary's politics were too questionable. After the FBI came to our house, we were sure my telephone was tapped—there were funny sounds on the line. But rather than be secretive, we delighted in being mischievous, saying rude things about the FBI and the Velde Committee, and pointedly injecting loaded and satirical comments into many of our phone conversations.

We all had nicknames. We called Bob Allen Bobo and Gary Gaygo; I was Caddie. (A few years later, after Gary had made friends with Allen Ginsberg and the sixties had arrived, I acquired the auspicious nickname Queen of the Hippies.) Two of the guys became Big Schiveik and Little Schiveik, based on characters in the novel *Good Soldier Schiveik*. In addition, Bob Allen sometimes called himself Hood-latch and Gary would playfully use the alias Leitchswitch. Both were writing poetry in those days. They even had a muse called Adelaide Crapsey, which none of us took very seriously.

As I think of it, we were a literary bunch. Lew was also doing some writing then, along with Philip and Don Berry, who later became a novelist. The Chambers brothers were interested in witchcraft and eventually wrote several books about witches. (I believe they also started a communal farm in southern Oregon.) I don't know if Les Thompson wrote much at the time, but he did later own a bookstore in Los Angeles. Today, Martin is a professor and Erich Wheeler teaches at the Metropolitan Learning Center in Portland.

One of our favorite topics of discussion in those days was religion—especially world religions. We explored, studied, and argued over such disparate faiths as that of the Rosicrucians, Scientology, Zen, and Buddhism. Gary eventually went to Kyoto, Japan, to study Zen Buddhism, and today Philip is a Zen priest living in San Francisco.

Back then, we were mostly young, trying everything we could. Gary introduced us to his mother, Lois, who was a stringer for the *Oregonian*. We called her Mummy Lo. She liked to come to our establishment, but she caused quite a ruckus one Thanksgiving. We had pooled our money, and I'd cooked a Thanksgiving dinner for us all. Mummy Lo thought the dinner was a scoop and wrote about it for the daily paper. In the Thursday, November 24, 1949, *Oregonian,* the William Moyes column read, "Sixteen bachelor gals and guys from Reed College who live at 1414 SE Lambert are going to cook their own Thanksgiving dinner." For some reason, the dean of women, Ann Shepard, hit the roof. She called me into her office and read me the riot act. She kept asking me what my mother would think if she knew. Funny stuff—I was twenty-three at the time, out on my own, and long gone from home. As I look back, it completely mystifies me that she could have pulled anything from that innocuous sentence that would upset her so. My, how times have changed.

As I think back, it is hard to evaluate Gary's influence on us all. He was a critic and a friend. He stimulated us. He was our leader. But it wasn't all seriousness. On the weekends, we would play. If anyone had money, we would buy wine and have a hoot. When Leadbelly died, we had a wake. I suppose we were a sort of commune: We had to share and it worked out pretty well for everyone. In some ways we were breaking new ground; we were probably the original hippies.

Those days ended abruptly. All of a sudden, Gary got married to Allison Gass, and almost as suddenly they separated. Then Bill Baker and I got married. (It took us sixteen years to separate.) Gary was one of our witnesses. It was January 27, 1950, and it was snowing. We put on our boots and heavy clothes, got on the bus to downtown Portland, and got married in the judge's chambers. That night I dutifully went to work. Someone had to pay the bills. At the end of the term, I quit school. A married woman, my job was to put Bill through school. This was common in those days. Maybe it still is.

After that, things changed. Bill and I left Lambert Street. Gary and Phil Whalen graduated. Gary left for San Francisco, where he did graduate work in Oriental studies at Berkeley. We lost touch a bit, but whenever Gary came back to Portland, he would stay with us. I especially remember one summer in '65 when Gary brought Allen Ginsberg with him. They were on their way north to climb mountains. It was Allen's first mountain experience. Allen and Gary laid out the ropes, ice axes, and other mountain gear in our front yard. Our neighbors must have been puzzled when Allen sang the "Sunflower Sutra" to my garden sunflower while accompanying himself with finger cymbals.

I was raising kids and the rest of our group was working on careers. And all this time, Gary was getting famous. Fancy that.

I always knew he would.

Jeremy Anderson:

MY FIRST ENCOUNTER WITH
A REAL POET

In July or August of 1952 our Scout troop took its annual nine-day summer hike in the North Cascades. That year we drove east of the mountains, up the Methow Valley to Harts Pass. From there we backpacked down Canyon and Ruby creeks to Ross Lake. The second or third night out we camped at Granite Creek and the next morning my friend Howard and I got permission to hike up to the lookout station on top of Crater Mountain. We didn't know if it was manned or not, but preferred climbing to fishing since we both had personalities that repelled trout.

Our camp was at about a 2,000-foot elevation, and we lunched at a small lake below the summit; we reached the lookout on the 8,100-foot summit about 2:30 in the afternoon. We were surprised to find a small cable tram leading up to the summit, as well as fixed ropes on the steep, rocky trail up the final few hundred feet. But even more surprising were the many pieces of cloth with strange writing on them flapping from the guy wires that steadied the lookout cabin on its summit perch, and from several poles stuck into surrounding rock cairns. Most surprising of all was the lookout ranger himself, barefooted and in shorts, stretched out on his cot, sipping tea from a handleless ceramic cup and studying conversational Chinese.

The ranger was equally surprised to see us. His first reaction was to scold us for not stopping at the guard station to see if there was any mail for him. Then he made us some green tea and we learned something about him and his home in the sky. He was a poet studying Chinese in order to translate the work of some ancient Chinese poets whose work he admired. He worked as a lookout during the summer in order to make a grubstake to allow him to spend the winter in San Francisco writing and translating. He explained that the flapping cloths were Tibetan prayer flags with the Buddhist prayer *Om mani padme hum* being repeated with every flap in the wind.

He also told us that this lookout was one of the highest in the Cascades, so high and isolated that he was the only ranger in the district who didn't have to repair trails on his days off. His water came from a snowbank a few hundred feet down the northeast slope, and his food was packed in on horseback at the beginning of the season, lifted up the last stretch by the aerial tram we'd seen. We admired his view, took a few pictures, and headed back down the mountain, reaching camp at sunset. We knew we'd met an unusual ranger, but not until I discovered and read *Earth House Hold* twenty years later did I realize I'd met the poet Gary Snyder on top of Crater Mountain in the summer of 1952.

Cascades to Sierra:
Night Highway Ninety-Nine
1952–1956

Jim Snyder:

RIPRAP AND THE OLD WAYS: GARY SNYDER IN YOSEMITE, 1955

The literary chronology is straightforward. Gary Snyder wrote "Riprap" while working on a backcountry trail crew in Yosemite in 1955. "Riprap" was first published in *Riprap* in 1959. Collected with *Cold Mountain Poems* in 1965 and 1969, "Riprap" was soon widely read by people working in the backcountry of the Sierra, as were the poems in *The Back Country* (1968). Gary's season on trail crew took him north of Matterhorn Peak, which he climbed with Jack Kerouac in 1957, an expedition chronicled in Kerouac's *The Dharma Bums* (1958). "The great rucksack revolution" Kerouac envisioned led a number of people to trail crews and other mountain work in the sixties and seventies. Many copies of *Riprap* and *The Dharma Bums* have become dog-eared by the campfire or under a gas lantern after a long day on the trail. The experiences described in them, too, have been relived many times, and a lot of folks have examined their experiences in the broader light of Gary's original perceptions.

With the chronology outlined, we can turn back to "Riprap" and its context, which invariably reminds me of a story. Some years ago I had a trail crew near Muir Gorge in Yosemite laying a lot of riprap to repair the Tuolumne River Trail where it had been blown out of the rock after World War I. One day we participated in an exhausting rescue followed by a bit of a party to relax ourselves. Feeling pretty rocky the next morning, we got up to start breakfast, but the Coleman stove flared up, caught the fly over the woodstove afire, and damn near burned the cook tent down. Our montane chef, wearing a red beret above his silver Ho Chi Minh moustache, shook his head, threw up his hands, and cried, "Burn, baby, burn!" Starting all over, and feeling even worse, we were in the midst of breakfast when a group from San Francisco marched in to see a trail crew camp and to learn about trail work. The camp looked odd, to say the least, with its charred ridgepole still dripping with shreds of plastic-coated canvas and with sand and water all over everything—hardly typical. We quickly ducked out to the trail to show what we were doing. There on the trail, things got back to normal when I did what I always do with trail crews to explain the work—that is, I read Gary Snyder's "Riprap" over a stretch of riprap in progress.

Riprap is a kind of rock pavement that can be laid in just about any rough or eroding trail. The technique came to Yosemite from Scotland and England with people for whom working with stone was as much second nature as is working with wood in the Northwest. A man who manages trails in England's Lake District has been studying the riprap laid by monks for burro trails to their mines a thousand years ago; he calls it by its older name, "pitching," rather than "riprap." The tradition among those monks went back further, to the Roman roads. The laying of riprap, then, is based on a long oral tradition carried erratically by the migration of people who knew it and preserved it by doing rather than by writing. Riprap has become the single most important erosion-control trail technique in the Sierra, and it is carried still by an oral tradition. The only thing written about it has been Gary Snyder's poem.

Riprap is a "cobble of stone," Gary wrote, "laid on steep slick rock to make a trail" in the mountains. Rocks are laid tightly, joints broken, spaces chinked, so that the work is, in John Muir's words, "hitched to everything else in the universe": "riprap of things: cobble of milky way," as Gary put it. One cannot throw just anything into riprap, though some have tried. To lay riprap one must try to understand the nature of the rock and its linkages. That is why this poem is worth a thousand photographs and why it has been shared with so many trail people laying riprap. The poem helps people make the leap from their work to the trail and the land around their work. Riprap is one of "the old ways," a key to knowing the "where" of who we are. The technique and its tradition stand in opposition to the heavy blasting that originally cut the trail through Muir Gorge, because with riprap you must accommodate yourself to what you have without the luxury of cut-and-fill blasting through any obstacle.

Gary learned riprap from Roy Marchbank on a trail crew in Yosemite where Gary worked in July and August 1955 as a laborer for $1.73 an hour. The crew worked through Pate Valley and through Pleasant Valley, finally camping at Bear Valley (where they were the last crew to do so), when Gary left to head for Japan. During that time, Gary and the crew laid quite a bit of riprap and did many small blasts to smooth the trail or to remove rocks. They drilled holes in the granite by hand. "With dynamite on mules like frankincense,"

Murphy packed that and nearly everything else for the small, mobile trail camp out of which the crew worked. They heated water on an open fire, often called a jungle fire after the hobo tradition of the thirties, cooked on a small woodstove moved from camp to camp as a mule's top load held with a diamond hitch, made rude furniture for each camp with materials at hand, kept their food without refrigeration, and had cold running water in the creek nearby. Little had changed in trail work or trail camps for close to a hundred years.

Many of the people who worked trails then probably belonged in a different century and certainly worked and lived with a different experience of world and place than most of us do now. Gary's growing up in the Northwest woods and working in the mountains and logging camps made him an inheritor of some of those traditions, but he also had the ability to stand outside of them, writing about them during the same period of time when he was reading Milton by firelight. Stacking hay in the barn built by the cavalry before there was a National Park Service, Gary worked with hay-truck driver Clarence Harris, who remembered thinking when he was seventeen,

> "I sure would hate to do this all my life.
> And dammit, that's just what
> I've gone and done."

Many people who came to trail work after the war had ridden the rails in the thirties or had worked in the mines. Others lived on seasonal work around the poor mountain county of Mariposa, where their families lived and died. Roy Marchbank, the foreman of Gary's trail crew, was one of those, as were Jimmy Jones, who cooked that season for Marchbank's crew, and Packer Murphy. Their hands reflected their lives and work.

Roy Marchbank, born in 1900, had family in Mariposa and had worked near there much of his life. He worked in the Blue Glory Mine near the Merced River's South Fork. The Depression made working the mines an even more precarious living, so Roy began working seasonally in Yosemite in 1934 as a laborer doing carpentry and other odd jobs, returning to the mine for the winter. After World War II, Roy came back to Yosemite and began working trails, using his long experience with mining explosives. Promoted to foreman, he took his first crew in the spring of 1953, continuing each season after that through 1967. Roy and his trail cook in later years,

Marty Pleasant, married sisters in the mid-sixties. "Wouldn't you know it," Roy noted with a grin, "Marty married the rich one." Roy and his wife moved to the South, where they lived on a boat until he died about fifteen years ago.

Marchbank was the foreman everyone liked—personable, easygoing, knowledgeable. Gary remembered, in "Milton by Firelight,"

> Working with an old
> Singlejack miner, who can sense
> The vein and cleavage
> In the very guts of rock, can
> Blast granite, build
> Switchbacks that last for years

Roy knew the country by feel, inside and out, and conveyed that sense to many on his crews. He also loved to drink and fish and did both generously. He got angry with his boss once because the powder he had ordered had not been sent up by mule when it was needed. So Roy called quite late at night from one of the rickety bare-wire backcountry telephones. "What the hell do you want, Mudbank?" growled his boss, Doug Thomas, when he finally answered the phone. "Well," replied Roy, "you can start with candles and five gallons of table wine." Thomas came looking for Marchbank and another fellow in Yosemite Valley one day when they had not shown up for work. As it happened, both were sleeping off a night of carousing in a cabin near the trail office. Thomas caught them and ordered both out on the trail with a crew. Roy told the story later, concluding, "And you know, the son-of-a-bitch didn't even bother to knock!" Roy looked forward to unemployment—he called it "rockin' chair"—after a season's work, living winters in the Mariposa Hotel on unemployment and credit until work began again in the spring, when he would take his fishing pole and full brim hard-hat and head back into the mountains once more.

Forrest Murphy, or Spud, as he was also known, often packed for Marchbank, bringing in the groceries each Monday with his mules and then packing dirt on the trail. They were friends, and Marchbank knew how to work with this wonderfully cantankerous soul. Born in 1910, Murphy was also a local who had had little schooling and had lived by doing a lot of different jobs around Mariposa—working with cattle, powder, packing, anything he could find in his modern-day version of subsistence living. A friend with a large ranch provided Murphy a bunk in return for odd jobs during most of Murphy's career. His first job in Yosemite in 1941 lasted only a week. Not long after that he found himself in the army. Perhaps that is where the nickname Spud came from. In 1950 he came back to Yosemite as a laborer, running a jackhammer, using explosives, or just working around until he began packing out of the barn in 1954. He packed mules in Yosemite part of each year after that through 1967, when he "retired" with Social Security to a small cabin in Hornitos, where he continued as a local institution until his death on June 8, 1989. Some years ago I asked him if he remembered Gary. He tugged at his chin, thought, and announced, "Oh yeah, that writer fella."

Spud was one of those people on the social and economic fringe. He worked out his own means of adjusting to the economics of the world, and he handled his physical requirements as best he could. His rancher friend, his boss in the park, and another friend in Hornitos helped him manage his paychecks and Social Security to keep him in clothes and meals. Like many other people, Spud did not have good teeth—he pulled several out himself with a pair of fence pliers—and that affected his ability to eat. Of small frame, often unshaven, in Levis and a weathered cowboy hat, Spud often found it easier to drink than to eat, and he did that. He was one of the few packers who could pack up, leave the barn sober as a judge with his string of mules, and be so drunk he could hardly sit on his horse by the time he was a mile away after tapping the bottles he had hidden in the talus along the trail.

Generous to a fault, Spud would periodically buy a whole new fishing outfit only to give it away a week or two later. He bought new clothes (Levis) once or twice a year, and wore them year-round. At least one trail crew threw him in the river to give him a bath. He complained about his mules, often trying to get another packer or trail crew man to bring them in for him. But he was proud of his calling. I remember his well-known cry when I first met him: "Outa the way! Got Damn! Gov'ment Packer comin' through!" He played the tough old packer and went through the same ritual with his favorite mules many times. He'd saddle up in the morning when the mules were cold and did not want to go: "Maude, you whore! I'm gonna knock a fart out of you that'll whistle like a wire nail!" He'd try to kick old Maude, or Clarabelle, but his legs were too short, always too short. The mule would sidestep him and then snort, and the show would start again.

Marchbank and Murphy were among a group of people who worked best when far back in the mountains, away from frontcountry temptations. Doug Thomas would ship them north or south of Yosemite Valley, never to Tuolumne Meadows if he could help it, because there was a store and booze there. Nevertheless, Murphy had a mule with an endearing quirk, or talent: Should he get away, which could be easily arranged, Whitey would make a beeline for Tuolumne, and Spud would have to go after him. Naturally, Murphy would return to camp with Whitey loaded with the goods for another party. Only in the far northern part of the park where Gary worked was the distance too great to use Whitey's homing-pigeon sense to benefit self and crew.

Trail crews were usually small in those days, six to eight people including foreman, packer, cook, and laborers. *Riprap* was dedicated to Marchbank and Murphy, among others. The cook on that 1955 trail crew was Jimmy Jones, whom Gary remembered in "Look Back," published in *Axe Handles*. Coming back to Yosemite after a winter in school, I'd see Jimmy on the trail. "Back in school again?" he'd ask. "Yeah, another year. What'd you do?" "Oh," Jimmy would say with a big smile, "I spent the winter drinking that sweet wine." Like Roy and others, Jimmy used his first paycheck to pay off his winter bar tab, but his comment belies the experience of the man and what he knew and felt about mountains.

Jimmy Jones was a Chukchansi Indian man, a small, short leprechaun, I thought, wearing a little canvas hat. His weathered face and warm smile had the suggestion of an amalgam the Gold Rush had brought into his family. In Gary's poem, he recalls a time when he was studying Chinese at the campfire when Jimmy asked,

> "Those letters Chinese?"
> "Yes," I said. He said, "Hmmmmm.
> My grandpa they say was Chinese."

Born in 1887, Jimmy spent his life around Yosemite working in many jobs, then filling out the season as he could in the lower country. He did not drive but walked nearly everywhere from his small cabin on the edge of Mariposa. To the end of his life he was well-known as a guide for deer-hunting parties, a skill he used often to put food on his family's table. My first day on the trail in Yosemite, we put a hundred tons of hay into the old cavalry barn, as Gary had, and then worked up the Pohono Trail out of the Valley—"That's to get you young boys in shape," said Doug Thomas with a laugh. I didn't know what I was doing or supposed to do with the shovel and rake, but I made a lot of motion with them. Finally the young college kid caught up to Jimmy Jones, foreman, and asked, "What should I be doing?" Jimmy smiled at me and said, "Oh, just do what I do," and turned back to his work. Used to reading things in books or manuals to learn explanations in college, I was here introduced in short order to a different way of learning, by experience and an oral tradition. When we got up the trail a mile or so and crossed the old Wawona Road, built into Yosemite Valley in 1875, Jimmy called a break. He'd light a cigarette and lie down in the prenatal position, head on his arms, hat over his eyes. When the cigarette burned down to his fingers, break was over. But before he closed his eyes, he looked around at all of us with our peach-fuzz cheeks, new Levis, and callous-free hands; then he looked down the old road and said, "In 1910 I worked on this road; now it's a trail."

Jimmy worked in Yosemite in the late twenties as a woodcutter in the days before modern utilities, when the Park Service regularly supplied its employees with winter wood. He held a number of jobs in the thirties, usually woods jobs using an axe or saw. The war brought severe cutbacks in park hiring, and Jimmy did not come back to work until 1953. His wife died shortly thereafter, but he continued to support his family and grandchildren as best he could with seasonal work on trails. Some years in the fifties he was a cook and some years a foreman, an alternation shared by a number of people during that time. Rain, snow, sun: It did not matter to Jimmy on the job. He would sit out a hard afternoon thunderstorm under the broad protection of a fir or hemlock, going back to work when it was over. Once, however, when lightning hit a tree not far from his, he jumped up, eyes wide open and a little pale, shouted "Home!" to his crew, and took off toward camp.

Because of Jimmy's age, the Park Service was eventually reluctant to hire him back, and 1963 was his last season. After that he was cut loose without so much as a fare-thee-well. Jimmy worked at what he could around Mariposa, passing away about 1970. Age indeed! The man knew mountains like the back of his hand. And he could walk, as if that were such a simple thing. "I used to run the ridges all day long—just like a coyote," he told Gary. He spent his life with the place and could move along the old Indian trails; he knew how to pace himself because he and the country were attuned.

These were among the people Gary worked with in 1955 who influenced his writing and for whom "home" meant "mountains." Knowing the country, hardship and hard work, time and distance, laughter and booze, mules and madness, was all part of daily life. Except for Gary's poems, these people were anonymous inhabitants who saw, as Gary wrote in *The Old Ways*, "the world they know crumbling and evaporating before them in the face of a different logic that declares 'everything you know, and do, and the way you do it, means nothing to us.'" They knew the "where" of who they were. They were natives of a place.

That is what riprap—the skill and the poem—is about. And not only "Riprap," but the other poems Gary wrote during those early mountain years. Gary was an ethnographer of trails, much as Kroeber was of California Indians, at a time when much of mountain oral tradition was being swept away by monoculture, and mountains were being replaced by offices with paintings and photographs of mountains hanging on their walls. That the skill of riprap continues, without technical manuals or week-long government training courses, suggests a viability to some of the old ways of the mountains that flow along, perhaps almost subversively, separate from the lives of managing organizations. Gary said later that he did not think much of the poem at the time he wrote it. But the poem has become a part of the persistence of the oral tradition and the old ways it portrayed.

—*Yosemite National Park*
January–June, 1989

NOTE

My thanks to Jim Murphy and Bob Barrett for sharing many tales and experiences of backcountry people and work around the campfire.

Will Baker:
POETS ON THE BUM

The English Department at the University of Washington was, in 1956, housed in Parrington Hall, a Victorian monster of damp stone and warped wainscotting. To me the inhabitants looked like cadavers, gnomes, and phthisic damsels haunted by some early tragedy. It must be kept in mind that I had come there, rather directly, from a boyhood spent in the logging and cattle towns of northern Idaho, and that Modernism was in full, evil flower: snobbery at best and fastidious Fascism at worst, challenged only by Existentialism's bleak intellectual ardors.

My own mind was understandably something of a mess. I was parking cars at the Outrigger Club at night, one of a bawdy, cretinous crew of jockeys from the nation's most corrupt chapter of Teamsters, while by day I slipped into my sportcoat and loafers to try and convince my profs that a natively acute sensibility made up for a deep ignorance of the classics. On weekends I drank home brew with my roommates, practiced my trumpet, or rode a bus many hours in order to neck all night with a girlfriend in Spokane.

Fatigued and disoriented by this schedule, I somehow allowed a good-hearted fussbudget professor to cajole me into attending a meeting of something called the Undergraduate English Club. Only a half-dozen students showed up. Most of them knew and voted against each other, which brought about my fluke election to the office of president.

The fussbudget announced then that for years the UEC had been largely symbolic, and she thought it was high time for us to seize a more active role for ourselves. We could, for example, sponsor a series of informal lectures on Careers for English Majors, inviting various teachers and other professionals to talk to us about the lives we might ultimately lead. She had already ascertained that we might use the department's faculty lounge, a big room on the top floor with rugs, chandeliers, and soft chairs. It would be a lively and educational experience, she just knew.

Dutifully I accepted someone's motion to launch this project, though I doubt whether the maker of the motion or the second or I had even the faintest hope that anyone would be interested. We all assumed that ultimately we would have to teach. What else did English majors do? In the meantime we had avoided the Korean War and indulged an addiction to reading. A few, like me, nursed a secret hope that the poems we hid in a notebook would someday be discovered by an influential critic and lead to fame and wealth and many beautiful people falling tragically in love with us. But only one young man—a friend of mine who is still at it, by the way—openly confessed this preposterous and shocking ambition, and he dropped out after a semester.

In the first three programs, as I recall, a Shakespeare professor elaborated forebodingly on the rigors of graduate study, a technical writer from Boeing proved to us that making a living with one's typewriter was possible, and a book salesman confessed that his best advice was to get a second degree in business administration.

For the fourth program nobody had any ideas. We appeared to have exhausted the possibilities for our future. In desperation I asked my favorite prof, Frank Jones, who was, among other things, a translator, if he would talk to us. No, he said, but a former student of his and another young friend were passing this way. They were poets and might give us a reading. But, I replied, our series is on *careers* for English majors. Well, he said, poetry *is* a career for these two. They are on the road just now, hitchhiking and hopping freights, reading everywhere they can, sometimes in nightclubs.

The idea was so radical it took me a couple of days to come to terms with it. I thought you wrote poetry and then died, after which your career really developed. Or at best you wrote for many decades and were luckily discovered in time to have a career as an almost-dead writer. The hottest, hippest poet to blow through so far that year had been W. H. Auden, who was not technically dead, but was at least English, a mitigating circumstance.

But a *young* poet? *Two* young poets? Reading in *nightclubs*? Ultimately, of course, the prospect of presenting so outlandish a program (especially after the book salesman) was irresistible. We did more than the usual publicity and bruited about that an evening out of the ordinary would finish our series. We had learned from Jones that these itinerant bards had recently been in San Francisco, where there was already, according to rumor, strange business afoot—jazz and tea smoking and men impersonating women and so forth. Someone in some office also had the fatal idea of sending notices to the local alumni, of which more anon.

On the day of the program I came to Jones's office to welcome the new arrivals and discuss the format for the evening. I believe I shined my shoes. Certainly I wore a tie. So it was a shock to encounter this pair. One of them, a Mister Ginsberg, looked like an undernourished deckhand. Pale, wearing spectacles thick as bottle-glass, he hunched into a peajacket even indoors. The other, a Mister Snyder, I recognized instantly from his boots, his mackinaw, and a beard several weeks along. This was surely an unemployed logger. Each of them needed a bath, and I was stunned to realize that the allusion to freight hopping had not been a joke. These poets bore a striking resemblance to young bums, despite their free-and-easy manner with Professor Jones and the ragged notebooks they carried.

Still, I assumed there was plenty of time for them to wash and borrow decent garb before the reading. Jones agreed to introduce them, so I looked forward to a diverting evening with only nominal responsibility. I was already confident that attendance for this event would set the record for the Undergraduate English Club and redeem my term of office.

Indeed the department lounge was packed and buzzing with anticipation. A mixed crowd, too. Many faculty and their wives, dressed in the rumpled sweaters and flaring skirts of that period. Strong representation, too, from the cadavers, gnomes, and phthisic damsels. Then a whole row of vigorous elderly ladies, alumnae thrilled to be especially invited to an evening of inspiring poetry. These were matrons of some substance, wearing hats and giving off potent perfumes.

I had premonitions of the ensuing *éclat* when the two poeticals came into our well-appointed room, still in their dungarees and boots. My voice skidded around announcing that Professor Jones would introduce his young friends; my hand shook pouring a glass of water at the lectern. These intimations of immorality were entirely trustworthy. Mister Ginsberg, after very little ado, launched into a long poem entitled, fittingly as it turned out, *Howl*. He spoke with a ferocity I had never heard before, dragging this roomful of perfectly nice people down Negro streets toward unspeakable acts. Or he sang, rather. A nasal tenor that honked like a saxophone and blatted like a trumpet through a wa-wa mute. Images that blazed out of heaven into the mire, and vice versa.

We must recall here that this was all before the sexual revolution. Before you could obtain *Lady Chatterley's Lover* without going through a disapproving librarian and a locked case. Before you could see guitarists below the waist on teevee. Before Lenny Bruce was hounded to his grave for using the commonest words in American argot.

So here in dark, dank Parrington Hall the unthinkable was happening right before the eyes and ears of the nice people. The first graphic sketch of the pastimes of lonely sailors went by most of the alumnae ladies, but soon even the most dumbfounded among them grasped that they were, in fact, hearing the very words they at first could not believe they were hearing. One by one they reeled to their feet, some with kerchiefs clutched to their lips, others supporting themselves on gallant volunteer cadavers.

The rest of us, however, had been effectively nailed into our chairs. There were gasps, of course, and inadvertent moans, but absolutely none of the usual symptoms of a poetry reading—coughs and shuffles, vacant eyes, and the empty, knowing smile. I don't know if anyone present sensed a historical dimension in the scene, a creaking hinge or tide-shift, but I remember thinking to myself: *This is tremendous. They can say anything they want to. This is like jazz, it really is.*

I also remember thinking, as Mister Snyder took over the lectern, that he had a hard act to follow. It was impossible to imagine any further extremity of outrage, perversity, or hallucination. There were deep sighs, the rapid blinking of those waking from dreams, a redistribution of weight on chair bottoms. What could be next?

This stubby man with copper whiskers and eyes squinty from too much sun exuded high spirits, something approaching hilarity just under control. He brought us out of the urban maelstrom with the solid jerk a hungover wrangler gives to a string of balky mules going over a pass. He was taking us, he said, to the mountains and rivers. And he did.

Like a big, fresh, cold wind, he carried us out of poetry, out of school, out of all the particular madnesses of our time and deep into pine trees, ice-scoured granite, and the elusive brains of birds, frogs, deer, coyotes. And also into the laconic, lewd brain of working man.

I was startled, exhilarated, to hear my own home language, heretofore unacknowledged in these chambers where Prufrock prevailed. The language of the woods—chokers and cruisers and sawbuck saddles—was now sung proudly forth.

For he was a singer too, this unemployed lumberjack. Deeper, resonant notes, with now and then a western twang. A guitar of a voice, meant to calm and thrill alternately. Again and again he gave us poems as pure, direct, and bracing as a sip of glacier-melt. No complex ambiguities. No trace of Greece or Judea. Only glancing allusions to Bashō or Buddha, the Anasazi or Salish.

At some moment, in the midst of my intoxication and delight, I was stricken by a disturbing thought. *Maybe this isn't poetry at all. This is too easy. Too clear. Too much fun. John Crowe Ransom wouldn't like it.* But a moment after that, I knew it was all right. This guy didn't care what we called it. He knew and we knew we liked it. We were there—clapping madly, sighing out loud, behaving in fact more like a crowd at a nightclub than an audience for a poetry reading—because we wanted this to go on and on. We had never heard of Mister Snyder or Mister Ginsberg, and this was surely not poetry as we had been taught to appreciate it, but who cared? We were excited and alive, becoming aware finally that the world would not be quite the same after tonight.

The cadavers had fire in their cheeks; the gnomes sat straighter and took on stature; the pale young ladies exhibited a hectic flush that looked suspiciously like desire. When the pair did their final riff, long after the scheduled terminal hour, a party seemed the natural way to continue this lively and educational experience; so almost the whole audience (minus the alumnae ladies) stampeded for Professor Jones's place.

There we sat on the floor, listened to more poems, and consumed a deal of cheap wine. Rapt, we heard Mister Ginsberg and Mister Snyder confirm our wildest, inmost fancies. Poetry was possible for everyone. All you needed was some experience—sitting in a lookout tower on a mountain, standing watch as an ordinary seaman, getting high in a flat in North Beach. And then of course the hard work, the craft, and so on. But at our age we tended to hurry past this less glamorous aspect of a career in poetry, which was by now the career we all wanted to pursue, the winner over professoring or tech writing or bookselling by a huge margin of enthusiasm.

Not least of the advantages of this new trade, for a group of us young men, was its apparent power to blow the hatches off the libido. What yesterday were dirty words we now perceived as allusions to exquisite, tender sensations that no healthy man or woman should resist. We understood from an offhand comment or two that even college chicks (pardon the unconscious chauvinism of that era) dug these heretofore unnatural acts. We were electrified.

We observed our insouciant hobo troubadours closely, and indeed they said things we could hardly believe to a surrounding bevy of admirers. A faculty wife broke down and cried over Mister Ginsberg's aloof, Byronic manner; a longhaired blonde sat so close to Mister Snyder that he was in danger of inhaling her. Flushed with drink, ties askew, some of our professors seemed to have forgotten the dead poets and sat deferentially at the feet of these young interlopers, just as we did.

Certain japes and anecdotes from still later in the evening do come back to me, but in the twilight of my middle years I have learned a measure of tact. Mister Ginsberg and Mister Snyder are distinguished men of letters now, approaching that antechamber of immortal fame, the almost-dead poets. Collected works are out, occasional professorships undertaken, honorary titles and royalty checks in the daily mail. No need, then, to recall the unruly and irrelevant; that is the material of second and third biographies.

I must note, however, our farewell in Professor Jones's driveway at three in the morning. Young, drunk, and maudlin, I got one foot into the last car leaving and then said that I wished—oh how I *wished*—that I could just drop out of school and go on the road too. Come ahead, Mister Ginsberg promptly replied. Travel with us. Mister Snyder shrugged. Up to me.

One foot out, one foot in, I hesitated. Memory plays a trick here, and my impression that this moment went on immeasurably—and is still going on, still presenting me with some terrific challenge—is surely inaccurate. I must have mumbled my reasons—only a semester away from graduation, no money except from the Outrigger Club— and fallen into the back seat in a matter of seconds. But I have never been sure that I fell the right way, and that uncertainty has been useful, over the ensuing thirty-odd years, in driving me to take other chances, risk other kinds of foolishness, consider the mad alternative as really possible.

What I did learn for sure that night was simply this: The purpose of poetry is to take over a life and make it generate incandescent language, which moves then to awaken a glow in other lives, to rouse in them feelings so deep and daring that no return to ignorant sleep is possible. This night, in the faculty lounge in Parrington Hall in 1956, I witnessed for the first time this chanting of flesh into fire. I have learned since that it is just as these two young hoboes claimed: Anyone can do it, even the dead.

Japan: First Time Around

1956–1959

Burton Watson:

KYOTO IN THE FIFTIES

I arrived in Kyoto in 1951, five years ahead of Gary. But the city didn't change very rapidly then—almost no building was going on—so it was not much different in 1956, except that the Occupation had come to an end.

Kyoto had not been bombed and was presumably much as it had been at the time the war started: sprinkled with large Western-style office buildings and theaters along the main streets, but essentially a city of small Japanese-style houses and shops, two or three stories in height, with here and there a temple roof rising above them.

Also it was essentially a city of the pre-auto era. There were a few taxis on the streets but almost no private cars. Bikes and trolleys were the main modes of transportation, with some electric train lines and bouncy buses running out into the countryside. Side streets in the city were unpaved, and once you got outside the city it was almost all dirt roads. The mountains and farmlands around Kyoto were still very beautiful, unmarred by the superhighways, scenic drives, motels, and drive-in restaurants that crowd them now. Cable cars ran up both sides of Mount Hiei, but the top of the mountain, which now bustles with cars and sight-seeing buses, was an area of quiet paths threading among the trees. Farming methods were those of previous centuries: oxen pulling plows and wagons, planting and harvesting done by hand, and crops fertilized with night soil carted out from the city.

Charcoal hibachis, or braziers, were the main heating devices, kerosene and electric stoves coming a little later, though whatever device you used, Kyoto winters were damp and chilly. In summer one slept under a mosquito net and kept cool through vigorous fanning. Housing was usually a problem for Westerners staying in the city. Few places rented to foreigners, and it was hard to find accommodations with the sort of privacy and freedom of access Westerners were likely to take for granted. Clashes of life-style, misunderstandings over what was and what was not permitted, occurred frequently. Some houses had bathing facilities, but the public baths, costing the equivalent of five cents and providing unlimited hot water, were more pleasant, especially in winter. Flush toilets were rare; most houses had the kind that were emptied at intervals by men who came around with buckets. In old-fashioned Kyoto dwellings, where the toilet is located at the back of the house and the bucketbearers have to pass back and forth through the kitchen, this could be a harrowing procedure to witness.

Rice was rationed and there was little variety in foods, but food prices were cheap, a meal in a student cafeteria running around 60 or 80 yen (the exchange rate was 358 yen to the dollar). A cup of coffee was relatively expensive, but coffee shops were well heated and you could dawdle for hours over one cup, reading, writing, listening to classical music or jazz, or simply basking in the warmth. Japanese cigarettes averaged 30 yen for a pack of ten; haircuts (now costing the equivalent of about 23 dollars) were 150 yen, or 40 cents. As TV had not yet become widespread, movies were the most common form of entertainment and the Japanese film industry was in its most flourishing and creative era. Other forms of entertainment included traditional Japanese drama, vaudeville, and strip shows.

Drinking was a highly popular recreation among the Japanese and foreigners I knew in Kyoto, and there were a variety of places to choose from. Western-style bars were usually small, with assorted young ladies to pour your drink or light your cigarette, but no prices were posted and they could be alarmingly expensive. Beer halls and highball stands were cheaper and livelier, though not much fun if you were drinking alone. People like Gary and I usually patronized *aka-chōchin*, or "red lantern" stands (so called because of the lantern that hung by the door), small places seating ten or fifteen customers and commonly run by an older woman, often with another woman to help. They served bottled beer, sake, and sometimes an illegally manufactured, unrefined sake called *doburoku* (that was very cheap but could give you a nasty hangover), as well as such simple foods as the stewed vegetables known as *oden* or bean curd dishes. In the course of drinking, I also learned a lot of Japanese in such places from the women behind the counter, who didn't mind talking slowly for my benefit and explaining things.

Kyoto in the fifties, especially if you had a dollar income, was a pleasant place to live: few cars on the streets, no smog in the sky, the countryside as yet unspoiled. Litter hadn't become a problem because there just wasn't that much in the way of packaging, empty cans, or outworn articles to throw away. People were generally quite friendly, and though there was a certain amount of anti-American feeling in the air, particularly among left-wing students, I seldom felt it was directed at me personally.

Kyotoites tell you that the economy of the city rests on three pillars: tourism, educational institutions, and Buddhism. Tourist spots—the temples, palaces, shrines, and festivals of the city—were always among the prime attractions for me, and in the course of twelve years of residence I thought I had seen all there was to see. I was wrong, though, as almost every year some temple or garden previously closed to the public is opened up.

The schools were my reason for being in Kyoto in the first place. I was enrolled as a graduate student in the Department of Chinese at Kyoto University, and initially earned most of my living by teaching English at Doshisha University. Kyoto University, along with its Research Institute for Humanistic Studies, was famous as a center for Chinese studies, and since it was impossible to go to Peking to study at the time, Kyoto seemed the next best place to be. Many European and American sinologists felt the same. During my years in Kyoto, nearly every leading figure in the field of Western sinology turned up at one point or another, including Gary's teacher of Chinese at Berkeley, Ch'en Shih-hsiang, who twice spent a sabbatical year in the city.

The third pillar, Buddhism, was Gary's main reason for coming to Kyoto; in that respect his case differed from mine. I was at that time specializing in the history and literature of pre-Buddhist China and was little involved in Buddhist studies.

I met Ruth Fuller Sasaki, the American who arranged Gary's first trip to Kyoto, through Hisao Kanaseki, a professor of English at Doshisha who assisted Mrs. Sasaki as an interpreter. She took an interest in the few American students who were in Kyoto at the time, including Al Craig, Walter Nowick, and me, and on occasion invited us to sumptuous meals featuring such imported foods as whole hams or Boston baked beans that were nearly impossible to get in Kyoto then.

Around 1954 I began to do odd jobs for Mrs. Sasaki in connection with her work on Zen Buddhist texts, and later, when she established the First Zen Institute of America in Japan, I worked there regularly one or two days a week. That was where I first met Gary.

By that time—the late fifties—the cost of living in Japan was rising rapidly, and I was glad to have the extra income from the work I did for Mrs. Sasaki. But I never got involved in Zen practice. I was busy with my own work on Chinese literature and sure I had no leisure to take up Zen, particularly as it seemed to be something one had to devote full time to. Moreover, there were things about Mrs. Sasaki, and about her descriptions of the Kyoto Zen world, that gave me a distinctly negative impression of the religion.

I don't think I knew much at the time about Gary's involvement with Zen. Japanese, to convey the highest approbation of someone pursuing Zen practice, will often say, "I've never heard him/her so much as mention the 'Z' of Zen!" (in contrast to a superficial person who chatters constantly about Zen practice). In that sense, Gary came close to the ideal. To explain why he would be absent on some occasion, he might remark that he was going into the temple (Daitoku-ji) for a week of *sesshin*, but otherwise I hardly recall him alluding to the subject, though this may be because I took little interest in it myself. When Gary and I talked, it was usually about places to eat or drink, or good trails for hiking in the nearby mountains.

Another subject I don't remember Gary discussing at any length is poetry. I knew he was a poet, particularly as Mrs. Sasaki was fond of making jocular references to the fact, though I don't think I had read anything he had written. On several occasions, though, he was of great assistance to me in matters pertaining to poetry.

In 1958, when I finished the first draft of my translations of the Chinese poet Han-shan's *Cold Mountain,* I asked Gary to look it over. Sometime later, he told me he had arranged for the poet Cid Corman, who was living in Kyoto at the time, to go over the translations with me. Perhaps he felt it would be easier for me to take criticisms from Cid, who was my age, than from someone like himself, who was five years my junior. Cid and I were accordingly invited to dinner by Will Petersen, an American artist living in Kyoto and a friend of Gary's—Gary couldn't be present for some reason—and after dinner, while Will smiled at me in a manner clearly intended to be friendly and reassuring, Cid proceeded to tear my translations apart on the grounds of bad or sloppy English. It was an unsettling experience, but one that proved to be extremely valuable. Though Cid went over only the first two or three poems, I could see the kind of things he objected to, and on that basis go through and revise the whole manuscript.

The translations still leave much to be desired, and I've always regretted I didn't have more practice in translating poetry before I tackled Han-shan. Perhaps I wasn't quite ready for him, but then most of us translate texts not when we are "ready" for them, however that is to be judged, but when they first attract our interest. Ideally, I suppose, one should translate the text once in order to acquire the proper readiness, and then, when one comes to the end, go back and translate it all over again.

Gary gave me copies of his own books as they came out, and also lent or gave me other books of or on poetry that were of great use. Memorable among these was the Donald Allen anthology, *The New American Poetry: 1945–1960,* that came out from Grove Press in 1960. At that time I had read little contemporary American poetry and had the impression it was rather dull and academic in tone. The Allen anthology was a revelation, and thereafter I read as much modern American poetry as I could get hold of, a fact that I hope is reflected in my translations.

I had long ago quit the teaching job at Doshisha, but in the meantime had been asked to teach a course in English composition at Kyoto University. Students in the English department were required to write a graduation thesis in English and needed practice in English composition. I decided to use some of the poems from the Allen anthology for class discussion and to have the students write papers on the ones they liked. I accordingly typed up a selection of poems that I admired, including Gary's poem on a *sesshin* at Shōkoku-ji, and mimeographed copies to hand out to the students.

The project was surprisingly successful. The students weren't much interested in Gary's poem, despite its Kyoto setting, as Zen practice held little attraction for young Japanese of that period. But they responded to most of the poems and, I hope, learned some English in the process. Denise Levertov's poem on the sharks was their favorite, its atmosphere of menace appealing particularly to the girls in the class.

I gave copies of my mimeographed selection to several of the younger professors in the English department, who scowled and puzzled over the texts. They had understandably never heard of any of the poets, and evinced little curiosity, though I suggested that one day they might end up teaching the works of some of them. In a way I don't blame them. As I know from experience, if you are struggling to read literature in a foreign language, it can be just as difficult and time-consuming to read new and unknown writers as it is to read those whose reputations are established, and afterward you're never certain if it was worth the effort or not. I therefore couldn't really criticize the Japanese professors for electing to stick with T. S. Eliot, as their predecessors of an earlier generation had stuck with Wordsworth. I hope that by now there is a younger generation of Japanese academics who are reading the works of Gary and other American poets—such as Cid Corman, Philip Whalen, and Clayton Eshleman—who lived in Kyoto in the fifties and sixties.

"In the sound of the bell of the Gion Temple echoes the impermanence of all things," declares the opening of *The Tale of the Heike,* a statement equally true whether one is thinking of the Gion of Shakyamuni's time or the Gion of latter-day Kyoto. Mrs. Sasaki was forever telling us how delightful Kyoto had been when she first lived there in the thirties, and how much of its appeal had since been lost. On the other hand, Gary in a recent letter mentioned that his son Kai, while studying in Okinawa, had visited Kyoto in the summer of 1988 and been greatly taken with it. Henry James's Florence, Hemingway's Paris—whatever the city, doubtless we think of it as at its finest the way it was when *we* first knew it, and as declining thereafter. In that sense, everyone who has lived there will have his own Kyoto, depending upon when he was there. I have tried to describe the one Gary and I had.

Of that Kyoto, I recall how, when the streetcar rounded a corner on a hot sunny day, people leaped to pull down the shades so no ray of sunlight would fall on them. How we swam in deep places in the Takano River and then all evening scratched the angry welts raised by sandfly bites. How someone was always toasting things over the hibachi—dried sardines or slices of rice cake—or playing in the ashes with the fire tongs. The time I was hiking on Mount Hiei and, hoping to take a shortcut, got caught by the sudden dusk and had to spend the night shivering on the mountain, the lights of Ōtsu twinkling enticingly at my feet.

I remember the old woman, in some world of her own, who stood every day at the Hyakumanben streetcar stop waving a flag and singing war songs; the girls from Ohara in the country who went through the streets selling homemade sweets and pickles; the feel of icy bedding when you came home late in winter, cursing yourself for not having put a hot water bottle in it before you went out; the smell of grilling fish at evening as women squatted outside their doorways, fanning their cooking braziers with big red paper fans—these were some of the sights and sensations of Kyoto in the fifties.

—*January 1989*

Philip Yampolsky:
KYOTO, ZEN, SNYDER

I have been asked to write of Gary Snyder in Kyoto in the mid-1950s and early 1960s. We worked together, we drank together, we knew each other well. But Gary had come to Japan for a definite purpose— to study Zen—and this endeavor was, I believe, the primary focus of his life in Japan. The serious study of Zen, the activity of the full-time Zen monk committed to the successful completion of his study, requires an all-consuming devotion to its practice. Few are capable, prepared, or in a position to engage in such a total commitment. Indeed, one famous priest at the turn of the century is said to have had five thousand students come to study with him during his career as Zen Master. Of these, eight completed their training and five were given sanction to teach. The vast majority of monks in Zen temples today are the sons of priests who serve in temples scattered throughout Japan. They study at most for three years, usually after having completed high school, and then return to their home temples, eventually to succeed their fathers in tending to the needs of the local parishioners. Some Zen trainees are laymen; a few may live within the temple compound, while others come in from the outside, engage in training periods, and return home in the evening, except for the extended meditation periods. This is the category to which Gary belonged: a serious and conscientious Zen student, but with a life and interests outside.

But rather than speak specifically of Gary, I will speak briefly of the Kyoto in which he and others found themselves, and of the Zen milieu—at least the American version of it—with which many of us were involved.

THE SCENE

Kyoto in the mid-1950s: relatively quiet, a city of temples and shrines and tourists, many of them schoolchildren on excursion. Many colleges and universities with uniformed students; countless bars and drinking establishments, some elegant, others simple stalls.

The pleasure quarters, scattered throughout the city, are still active; the government has yet to succumb to Western pseudo-morality. Occupation troops are about, but they are in the southern part of the city and in a base to the north. Westerners are here, but not in great number: They are students studying at the universities, would-be Buddhists, potters, artists, flower arrangers, and tea cultists. Western travelers, mostly elderly men and their wives with blue-dyed hair, congregate in the hotels and wander the streets in search of treasures, real and imagined. It is a busy city but it closes early; the streetcars and buses stop running and revelers rush to catch the last train. In these years things are not expensive; the exchange rate is 360 yen to the dollar.

I came to Kyoto in September of 1954 as a Fulbright student assigned to a Buddhist university, with the intention of gathering material for a dissertation. I spoke little Japanese, although I had some knowledge of the written language. In order to communicate I tried to keep away from my fellow Westerners as much as possible so that I would be forced to learn to speak. To this end I rented a small four-mat room on the second floor of an apartment complex above a market known as the Ebisu Ichiba, with about twenty stores, each specializing in a different variety of food. It was located on Nawate-dori, just around the corner from the Minami-za theater and adjacent to Kennin-ji, an important Zen temple; it was one block west of the Gion Kōbu, the most elegant geisha district, and one block east of Miyagawa-cho, the most respectable (if such a term is appropriate) red-light district. The establishment was owned by the head of what was known as the Shinohara-gumi. He was the *oyabun*, and all the store owners were his henchmen. Shinohara owned various buildings throughout Kyoto, some extensive structures filled with small drinking places that could accommodate only a few customers at a time, some brothels, some hotels of dubious respectability. Shinohara was also known as the King of the Kyoto Gamblers, and he would hold high-stakes one-on-one card games, such as *hanafude*, in one of the empty apartments, always with graceful geisha sitting in attendance, serving him drinks and catering to his needs. But this sort of gambling was (and still is) quite illegal, and the games were guarded by lookouts and never held more than once in the same place. This is where I learned to speak Japanese, mostly dialect and not of the highest elegance. I still suffer from an inability to speak the language properly.

ZEN

I held a Fulbright grant for two years, managed to stay another year on my own, in not inconsiderable poverty, and still could not bear to leave Kyoto. I was then fortunate to be employed by Mrs. Ruth Sasaki, who had established an institute for the study of Zen on the grounds of Daitoku-ji, a temple in the northern part of Kyoto. Known as the First Zen Institute of America in Japan, it was at the time the only center established by a Westerner for Westerners who had come to study Zen Buddhism. Mrs. Sasaki, originally Ruth Fuller, later Ruth Fuller Everett, had first come to Japan in the 1930s under the guidance of Daisetsu Suzuki, and had spent considerable time studying under the head priest of the Nanzen-ji. She came from what was originally a modest family, made wealthy by fortuitous dealings in the Chicago grain market; then she had married Mr. Everett, a distinguished lawyer some twenty years her senior. Returning to New York before the start of World War II, she had established the First Zen Institute of America in an elegant town house in the east 60s, and together with a group of interested Americans had made an effort to study the intricacies of Zen Buddhism. Their teacher was Sasaki Sokei-an, a Zen Master who was an heir in a distinguished line of Rinzai Zen. Sokei-an lectured in English, translating important works, and his disciples (in the established Zen tradition) took notes on his talks and recorded them faithfully.

The activities of this small band of Zen students were abruptly halted with the Japanese attack on Pearl Harbor. Sasaki Sokei-an was interned as an enemy alien. Ruth Fuller Everett, now a widow, rescued Sokei-an from his enforced imprisonment. She married him; five months later he was dead. After the war ended, Ruth Sasaki was determined to continue her Zen studies and to prepare for publication the writings of her husband. To this end she went to Japan, establishing her Institute and continuing her studies under the Zen Master Gotō Zuigan. She took up residence in a small temple known as Ryōsen-an on the grounds of Daitoku-ji.

Major Zen temples are composed of the main temple and its several important buildings, together with a host of smaller, affiliated temples, known as *tatchū*. These temples have their own priests, and some are repositories for important works of art, or have gardens and buildings of note. Ruth Sasaki took over a small, unpretentious temple, and over a period of years improved its facilities to make it more acceptable to western, convenience-oriented tastes. In addition, she added a small building, designed as a library and research center, and later a small, exquisitely-appointed zendo to provide a place for Western students to practice Zen meditation.

Ruth Sasaki's principal interest, aside from her Zen study and the desire to assist western students, was to prepare for publication the works of her late husband. To this end she assembled a small research staff; I do not recall who guided her selection, but it was in all respects brilliant. Oldest, in terms of tenure, was Hisao Kanaseki, an English professor of great good humor, wit, and competence, who helped Mrs. Sasaki in assorted ways. Mrs. Sasaki was not distinguished for her tact and at times assigned him, much to his annoyance, trivial tasks beyond her own competence to perform. Chief of the research staff was Professor Yoshitaka Iriya, a distinguished specialist in Chinese literature and an expert in the colloquial language of the T'ang dynasty in which many early Zen texts were written. A graduate of Kyoto University, he taught there and later became dean of the Department of Literature at Nagoya University. Professor Iriya is a scholar of formidable competence, and his knowledge of Chinese language and literature surpasses in many respects that of native Chinese specialists. Also on the staff was a younger scholar, Seizan Yanagida, an expert on Chinese Zen, who had an unparalleled knowledge of its texts as well as Buddhist texts in general. Today Professor Yanagida, recently retired from the Research Institute for Humanistic Studies at Kyoto University, is recognized as the foremost scholar of Zen Buddhism in both China and Japan. He is a prolific writer and has guided many American and European scholars in their studies. It must be remembered that this was some thirty years ago, when these professors had yet to attain the eminence they hold today. But this was a different Japan and the salaries university professors received were extremely small, so by working for Mrs. Sasaki they were able to supplement their meager earnings substantially.

Also employed, on a part-time basis, was the eminent translator of both Chinese and Japanese, Burton Watson, who has rendered into English countless works of literature, history, and poetry. Gary joined the staff shortly after his arrival in 1956, and I was employed on a full-time basis to care for the library, work on translations, and assist in the various publications that the Institute issued. There were secretaries whose term of employment varied with Mrs. Sasaki's whims, among them the beautiful Yōko Manzōji, a Kyoto University graduate in English studies, whose boyfriend was a leader in the student revolts that were closing the universities at the time. Her English was excellent, her attractiveness disconcerting to the uncommitted males at the Institute. She did not remain employed for very long.

One of the principal tasks of the research group was to prepare an English translation of the Chinese Zen classic, *Lin-chi Lu* (*Rinzai-roku* in Japanese), the recorded sayings of the T'ang dynasty Zen Master who has given his name to the Zen sect known as Rinzai. Mrs. Sasaki had at first intended to use the translations rendered by Sokei-an and recorded by the Institute members in Japan; however, it soon became apparent that they were inadequate, for they reflected later Chinese interpretations and failed to take into account the T'ang colloquial language in which the original text was written. The research group proceeded to redo the translations and render them into a correct but colloquial English. This was an excruciatingly time-consuming experience, made increasingly difficult by Mrs. Sasaki's rather primitive knowledge of both Chinese and Japanese and her self-acknowledged certainty of her own understanding of Zen. Adding to the time-consuming nature of the work was Mrs. Sasaki's insistence that the whole text be romanized, and the romanization checked and rechecked, an utterly unproductive and useless endeavor embarked upon because of her conviction that this would help the student just beginning his studies. Yet no matter how exasperating this whole procedure was, the presence of these Japanese scholars made for an exceptional educational experience for the Western participants. In many respects it was as though we were able to take part in a high-level seminar on Zen texts and to gain from the knowledge of these exceptional teachers.

Gary had arrived in late May 1956 determined to pursue his Zen studies in earnest—but as a layman. He lived first at a small temple within the precincts of Shōkoku-ji, sharing quarters with Walter Nowick, a pianist who was engaged in Zen study as a protégé of Mrs. Sasaki's. Although Gary was a devoted Zen student, taking part in the monastery *sesshins* and studying directly under a Zen Master, he allowed ample time to devote to his writing and to indulge in the diversions Kyoto had to offer: drinks at a jazz coffee shop, the Bel-ami, which played the records of Chet Baker; visits to tiny drinking establishments that served quantities of sake, including the delicious unrefined white milky version known as *doburoku*, which was splendidly inexpensive. I think we hit it off quite well, although I am afraid that I was a little harsh with him in my comments on his competence with Japanese. Gary's reputation had preceded him through the writings of Jack Kerouac; he made no effort to conceal his past experimentation with various mind-altering drugs and the innocent marijuana. He was tough and witty and sure of his opinions and attitudes, yet eager to learn of Japan and quick to adapt to new ways of doing things. He took pleasure in visiting mountains and monasteries, observing and commenting in poems and prose.

Sometime in the spring of 1957 Gary made acquaintance with some of the young ladies studying at Kyoto Women's University through his friend, the artist Will Petersen, who was teaching English at that institution. This university, run by one of the major Buddhist sects, had a reputation for strictness and conservative education. It had been the subject of a very successful motion picture, *Onna no Sono,* or *Garden of Women,* which had gained great critical acclaim but had also evoked a certain dissenting outrage on the part of the university authorities. One day that summer Gary arranged an outing with a young student, Yuiko Takeda, who brought along her great friend Etsuko Meiji, and the four of us set out for a day at the beach at Omi-maiko on Lake Biwa. It was a pleasant but uneventful excursion; I remember Gary earnestly casting pebbles at the cleft in Etsuko's somewhat ample bosom and exulting rather boisterously when a pebble finally achieved its mark.

Toward the end of August that summer Gary renewed his seaman's papers and shipped out as an engine-room hand on a tanker, the *Sappa Creek,* that was to take him to the States; unfortunately, the ship's owners did not provide for a direct voyage home and Gary spent almost eight months wandering several oceans and visiting unfamiliar ports of call. I have several letters from him, detailing the exploits of his drunken, whoring shipmates, and describing the books he read and his determined continuation of his meditation practice at a selected spot on deck. In the meanwhile, Miss Yuiko visited me at my rooms to inquire about Gary and then to ask for help with the English essay she was obliged to write as a graduation thesis. She came on several occasions; we took to going out for drinks (although she was no drinker), always returning to the school dormitory by the ten o'clock curfew. Will Petersen scolded me for paying her too much attention, but I could not assent to his cautionary remarks. The Japanese school year ends in March; Yuiko was to return to her home in Wakayama shortly. I abruptly realized that I should not see her again; the thought was too painful and, without previous calculation, I asked her to marry me. She agreed; we were wed in June of 1958 at the consulate in Kobe. For thirty-one years we have been together and I am ever grateful to Gary for having brought us together, and perhaps to the *Sappa Creek* for having furthered our acquaintance.

Gary came back to Kyoto in 1959 for a stay of several years. He returned to his Zen studies and his work at Mrs. Sasaki's, and moved to a charming rustic house in Yase in the northern part of Kyoto, somewhat isolated but readily accessible by his cherished Honda motorcycle. In February of the next year Joanne Kyger, his wife-to-be, arrived in Japan. On the day she arrived in Kyoto Gary brought her to our place for dinner. Before eating, they repaired to the bath for a leisurely cleansing. Since the door to the bath was semitranslucent, Yuiko was reluctant to go to the adjoining kitchen to complete the dinner and it was much delayed. When eventually they emerged I could not resist commenting: "You might at least have waited until you got home." I do not think the remark went over too well.

Judging from the diary Joanne kept and later published, she had great trepidation about the proposed union and was outraged that Mrs. Sasaki insisted that they be married at once. Joanne was handsome, blonde, and tall, conscious of how greatly she differed from Japanese women, terrified of the thought of going to a public bath to be stared at, self-conscious of her inability to converse in Japanese. Gary was not the most tolerant of persons when judging the behavior of others. He was far too demanding, too insistent on requiring conformity to Japanese customs, too much away during his Zen practice. It was not a marriage for which a prognosis for durability could be made. But still there were many happy times, good parties, people to delight in, people to despise.

Westerners came to study Zen, to make pots, to learn to carpenter, to arrange flowers. Many of them found their way to Mrs. Sasaki's;

some were celebrities, some noted scholars; others were would-be Zen students of varying sincerity of purpose. Among them was Janwillem van de Wetering, a handsome Dutchman who found his way to Kobe because of a vague desire to study Zen. He was taken in by Mrs. Sasaki and sent to the monastery at Daitoku-ji, where he lasted almost a year before being expelled for some egregious indiscretion. He wrote two books about his experiences and later became a detective-story writer of note. Ladies came from Egypt and Switzerland to practice, if at times only briefly. The Swiss lady played out her sexual fantasies, taking physical delight when struck by the cautionary stick wielded by the supervising monk who patrolled the Meditation Hall. Wealthy, aged ladies sought for spiritual salvation with indifferent success.

No one lasted very long as a student of Zen. Of more interest to Gary were the potters and artists and poets who had come to Kyoto for study and work. Splendid parties centering on food and marijuana and sake were held at frequent intervals—and through it all Gary continued his Zen studies assiduously, obviously making progress in his practice. But this is not a proper subject of discussion among Zen practitioners; one's progress is one's own private affair. All these were but a few of the Westerners who made Kyoto their home.

Japanese Zen Masters, in their writings, make frequent mention of the Zen Disease, the tendency of those who have moved only partly in their studies to become convinced that they know all that they need to know, that they no longer have need for further study. This disease afflicts many Japanese students, but often is overcome. But it seems to afflict almost all Westerners who are somewhat advanced in their studies. Some will even claim to have achieved sanction from their teacher when they have not. Others, convinced of their superior understanding, will set themselves up as impeccable authorities. In most instances the Zen Master will become aware of this aberration and simply cut off the student and refuse to have further contact with him or her. Gary, it must be strongly emphasized, is an exception to this rule.

But Mrs. Sasaki, convinced of her own infallibility, went against the instructions of her teacher, Gotō Zuigan, by insisting on building a dormitory for Western students. When her teacher cautioned her against the undertaking, she ignored him. He cut her off and summoned Walter Nowick, Gary, and me to the small temple next to the famous Ryōan-ji, at which he resided. There he detailed the reasons for having determined to cut off his relationship with Ruth Sasaki and to no longer accept her as his student.

Mrs. Sasaki must have been well upset by these developments, but she scarcely showed it or spoke of it. Things did not go too smoothly at the Research Center, as everyone's energies were frequently diverted from the studies at hand to other projects and books. A work entitled *Zen Dust* was prepared, an enormous, sumptuous work that described the Zen koan and contained exhaustive background information on Zen texts: a most useful book, if what you are looking for happens to be in it.

But the work at the Institute occasioned many complaints from those who were carrying it out. Little of substance was being accomplished; the atmosphere was becoming oppressive. Ruth Sasaki had the reputation of invariably quarreling with those with whom she was associated. This reputation was substantiated; she decided that I was no longer fit to be employed by her. But instead of simply dismissing me she hit on a plan designed to disgrace me. Summoning her lawyer and all the members of the staff, she accused me of having stolen the manuscript of the *Rinzai-roku* with the intention of taking it to New York and publishing it as my own work. She had reached this morbid conclusion because, in going through my desk drawers, she could not locate the copy of the manuscript that I used during the research sessions. Because of its bulk it would not fit comfortably into the drawer in which I customarily would have kept it and I had put it for safekeeping into a file cabinet in a corner of the room. A dramatic moment: I went to the cabinet and handed the "stolen" manuscript to Mrs. Sasaki.

But she did not relent; my dismissal stood. Gary quit, as did Burt Watson. Others stayed on, I like to think for economic reasons. I did receive enough money to remain another year in Kyoto so that I might do work on my long-delayed dissertation. Gary and Joanne went off to India in December, returning shortly before my family and I left for the States. Eight years in Kyoto were at an end for me; Gary was to stay several more.

Gary was and continues to be a serious student of Zen. But his knowledge and interests were and continue to remain wide and not confined to the Zen scene. A love of hiking and travel to temples and unspoiled scenes, a desire to know of other forms of Buddhism, an instinctive wish to help and educate others, a genuine love of Japan: All informed his character and his talents.

Mrs. Sasaki's Institute continued in a rather truncated form for several years until her death in 1967. The *Rinzai-roku* appeared after several years in abbreviated and not-too-happy form. The elaborate notes Professor Iriya had prepared were never published; Professor Yanagida's highly technical introduction was never rendered into English. The Institute that was to last for twenty-five years after her death was closed, the valuable library locked and unused. Mrs. Sasaki, in her later years, sought to regain the acquaintance and friendship of the many she had alienated and in this, to a large extent, was successful.

Hisao Kanaseki:

AN EASY RIDER AT YASE

I seem to be one of the few people who can attest to how seriously Gary Snyder studied Zen in Japan when he was young. So far as I can remember, it was in May of 1956 that we first met. It was in Kyoto, just about a year after the famous poetry reading in San Francisco where Allen Ginsberg read his *Howl* for the first time and where Gary, Ferlinghetti, and others also read their poems. Not that I knew that these things were significant literary phenomena at that time. I had never heard of Ginsberg, or Kenneth Rexroth, or Jack Kerouac until sometime after I met Gary, who educated me on such matters. My knowledge of American poetry was still rather limited, not going beyond Ezra Pound and his friends.

I think when Gary arrived in Japan that year he was twenty-six, while I was already pushing forty, though I considered myself much younger. My chief job then was teaching English at Doshisha University (I later taught at Osaka City University and Kōbe University), but I was also helping Ruth Fuller Sasaki, widow of the late Sokei-an Sasaki, a Zen Master who founded in New York the First Zen Institute of America. I would go to her residence two or three days a week to do all kinds of chores for her, from translating scholarly materials written in Japanese into English to making up rather idyllic quarrels between maids.

Ruth F. Sasaki had come to Japan soon after the war and the death of her husband, Sokei-an, in 1945 to complete her late husband's unfinished work, particularly the English translation of the *Lin-chi lu* (the record of great Zen Master Lin-chi, founder of the Lin-chi or Rinzai school of Zen), and also to resume her own Zen studies, which had been terminated by Sokei-an's death. Ruth Sasaki was 100 percent Caucasian and had enough means and power to receive from Daitoku-ji, one of the most prestigious Rinzai Zen temples in Japan, permission to restore a Daitoku-ji subtemple, Ryōsen-an, as her residence. Later she added a zendo and a library, mostly for use by non-Japanese students and scholars. I think it was around 1950 that she organized a small working group of Japanese and American scholars, including Professor Iriya and Professor Yanagida from Kyoto University and Dr. Philip Yampolsky and Dr. Burton Watson from Columbia, all eminent scholars of the Chinese language and of religion. As I remember, Gary was also included in this study group sometime after his arrival, for he was picking up the language remarkably fast. His chief aim, though, was to practice Zen with real monks.

Anyway, Gary arrived in Kyoto and started his practice at once under Isshu Miura Roshi. Miura Roshi was originally the priest of Koon-ji, near Tokyo, but had been persuaded by Ruth Sasaki to come to Kyoto to live in a subtemple in Shōkoku-ji, another great Rinzai Zen temple in Kyoto, where he could teach foreign students. Roshi liked Gary, for he was very intelligent and as hard a worker as any of the Japanese monks, obliging, bright, and fast to learn, doing zazen, sweeping, washing, and cooking. I heard only one complaint from Roshi about Gary at that time: "The meals Gary cooks for me are great, but sometimes I find sand in the vegetables. He must learn to wash vegetables more carefully, but a little sand in the stomach won't kill you, will it?"

When I remember Gary as a Zen novice in Japan I can't help but think of him as remarkable among those American writers who have shown an interest in Oriental philosophies. Since Emerson and Thoreau, there have been a good number of influential men of letters who have been interested in Oriental religions, including Buddhism—notably Aldous Huxley, T. S. Eliot, Kenneth Rexroth, and J. D. Salinger—but their interests rarely cut deeper than the intellectual level, and I think it very significant that Gary Snyder was the first to try to *experience* Zen by actually becoming a monk, though now a considerable number of writers are following Gary's example.

Everybody who was connected with the First Zen Institute at Ryōsen-an liked Gary when he arrived, finding him intelligent, earnest, good-natured, and full of vitality. I was of course no exception, but looking back to those days I think it rather amusing that, despite his reputation as a promising poet, I didn't particularly find him like a poet. The young man from California I met then was no doubt terribly intelligent and likeable, but he looked too much a "redskin" for my comfort to be called a poet; he hardly fit in with that much-caricatured image of the poet I seem to have had in those days, the *poète maudit* type, a palefaced and agonized martyr in a philistine society. If Gary was not a poet to me, he was an educated lumberjack from the Sierra Nevada—and this he really was, too. (He also looked like a younger version of Van Gogh in one of the artist's self-portraits.) You must remember that this was in the middle of the 1950s, only ten years after the end of the war, when the French Symbolist tradition was still admired among the intellectuals here and the latest literary fashion from the West was Sartre's existentialism.

Even Ruth F. Sasaki, an upper-middle-class Victorian to the marrow of her bones, was charmed by Gary's personality and impressed by his shrewdness as a Zen student. Though adamant in his unconventionalism, he was by no means obdurate, but reasonable and tactful enough, for instance, to remove his earring before he came to see Ruth Sasaki.

In the spring of 1957, a year after I met Gary in Kyoto, I visited New York (my first trip to America) to study at Columbia for a year. A few days before I left Japan Gary handed me a $20 bill and told me to spend it in America in the most foolish way I could think of. It was a few days later on the ship that I realized that there could have been a Zen catch in Gary's advice concerning the spending of the bill. But I soon forgot about it entirely, and though I now try to remember, I haven't the slightest idea how I spent the money.

I was coming from a country still suffering from the after-effects of the war, and New York in 1957 was to me like a paradise. Greenwich Village, where I was staying, was still quiet but exciting, with rows of attractive restaurants, bookstores, and little theaters. Senator McCarthy died that year, and where culture was concerned, elegant Baroque ensembles or cool bebop were the things you *had* to hear if you wanted to be sophisticated. J. D. Salinger had just published *Franny* in the *New Yorker* and was regarded as a demigod by the majority of the reading public.

And at Columbia everybody was still talking reverently about Eliot's *The Waste Land* or the Metaphysical poets, and during the entire year I was there I don't remember any occasion at which people mentioned such names as Ginsberg or Snyder or even Kerouac. Was I in a wrong corner of the campus? It was a long time after I returned to Japan that I first heard of the San Francisco Renaissance and the beatniks.

The next thing I remember about young Gary was when he got his first book of poetry, *Riprap*, published. This made me accept him more readily as a poet. That was in 1959. The poems were difficult for me, but I liked their granitelike texture and instinctively felt them to be first-rate achievements. But it was still hard for me to believe that this lean, tough-looking young man who rode on a huge motorcycle was a poet. At one time, when he lived in Yase, a northern suburb of Kyoto, he used to come to Ryōsen-an, our workshop (the literal meaning of the temple's name is "The Dragon Fountain Temple"), heralded by the great roar of the bike. It was really like a dragon descending into the fountain.

And I remember that Joanne Kyger, a very attractive young poet, joined Gary around that time. Gary, in the meantime, moved from Yase to Murasakino, only a five-minute walk from Daitoku-ji, to live with Joanne in a small Japanese house. I was invited to their house several times to join their informal parties, where I invariably saw colleagues like Watson and Yampolsky from Ryōsen-an. (I also once met Philip Whalen there; he was the kindest-looking man I ever met: a bodhisattva.)

Gary and Joanne were perfectly happy living together without getting married. But Ruth Sasaki couldn't tolerate this arrangement. She thought it a complete breach of social decorum. Gary could remove his earring before he came to see Ruth Sasaki, but not Joanne. So they had to get married—but for some reason they were unable to live happily thereafter, except for the first few years. They went to India together in 1962 and I presume it was a good trip for both of them. But in 1964, if I remember it correctly, Joanne left Gary and went back to San Francisco by herself.

In the meantime, Gary kept at his Zen studies by himself until later in 1964 when he went back temporarily to the States to teach at the University of California at Berkeley. Before going back to California, he had produced two impressive works of translation. One was *Cold Mountain*, poems by a mad Chinese hermit called Hanshan who had lived under the T'ang dynasty. This splendid translation was done from Chinese, which Gary learned very quickly, coached by Professor Iriya. Then he did an English translation of the great modern Japanese poet Kenji Miyazawa, who died in 1933. Gary's Miyazawa translations were excellent, but the thing that impressed me most was that Gary had done them guided by his instinct, recognizing his own strong affinities with Miyazawa. One might say, if I may use a Buddhist cliché, that Gary is Miyazawa reincarnated as an American poet, for the two poets are very much alike in more than just one way. Both poets are nature lovers and ardent ecologists (Miyazawa was one all his life without knowing the word), as lines like the following from Miyazawa's "The Pleiades" might testify:

After cutting trees in the mountains one comes home
feeling mighty miserable . . .

And both are Buddhists, though Miyazawa was a member of the Hokke Sect. You can recognize the spirits of the two poets Han-shan and Miyazawa amalgamated in Gary's lovely poem "As For Poets." I think literary historians in both countries should pay more attention to these translations because they were the results of the beautiful meeting of different poets from different cultures, reminding one of what happened between Poe and Baudelaire, and Li Po and Ezra Pound.

Gary came back to Kyoto in 1965 to resume his studies, this time under Sessō Oda Roshi of Daitoku-ji, whom he liked very much. Gary and I were still seeing each other at Ryōsen-an almost every week, doing our *Lin-chi lu* translation, which went on interminably. (The book was finally published in 1975 by the Institute for Zen Studies, long after Ruth Sasaki's death.) By then Gary was already a well-known poet and an avid participant of Zen training. In addition, despite his Bohemian appearance, he was a great scholar in his own right. I think it was during this period (1965–1968) that he studied the Mahayana-Vajrayana line of Buddhism and other Eastern religions as well.

One of the things that makes Gary Snyder trustworthy as an Orientalist is that he never romanticizes the Orient and Japan, as so many of his predecessors have done. Lafcadio Hearn, I think, was the real villain of the piece: He did much to make Japan and her culture sound mysterious and esoteric. Even Rexroth sounded a bit sentimental whenever I heard him talk about things Japanese. Gary, on the other hand, knew all about the human frailties and corruptions of institutionalized Buddhism, and on that basis he tried to see and assess our culture. But while I'd simply despise an avaricious priest who moved, under the cover of night, the boundary stones on the far side of his graveyard to expand his property, Gary, knowing all this, would still try to see hope for the enlightenment of such a man.

Around that time, I was teaching in Kobe and living in a small town called Takatsuki near Kyoto. One evening my wife and I decided to invite Gary and a few other friends to dinner at our apartment. It was perhaps my wife's idea to include in the party Masa Uehara, one of my students at Kobe University, the brightest and most vivacious girl in all the English Department. Masa came, and she and Gary seem to have been attracted to each other almost at once; after that evening they started to see each other regularly. Of course I hadn't had the slightest intention of making the occasion what we call in Japan *miai* (an arranged interview with a view to marriage), but as their relationship began to be more serious, Masa's father, Mr. Uehara, got very upset, thinking that I had planned everything with the aim of making his precious daughter fall victim to a foreign devil.

I was very happy when, after returning from our one-year stay in New York in the summer of 1967, I learned that Gary and Masa had recently married on Suwanose Island, a small island off Kyushu, where there was a little commune at that time. By then Gary, together with Nanao Sakaki, founder of the Suwanose commune, had a considerable number of young followers.

I don't remember exactly what year Gary and Masa went to California to settle in Nevada City, but it must have been around 1970. After that I visited them twice at their place, Kitkitdizze, and they came to see us here in Tokyo once in 1980. Sometime in 1988, however, I received a long letter from Gary, telling me that Masa and he had separated, that each was living with a different partner, and that it was altogether a satisfactory arrangement for both of them. Then sometime in February of 1989 Kai, their elder son and then a scholarship student at Ryukyu (Okinawa) University, came to stay with us for a few days. Kai was just twenty that year and almost ready to start life on his own. The day he went back to Okinawa, we saw him off in front of our house, and as he waved good-bye, I felt as though I were watching Gary, forty years younger, still an "axe handle to be shaped," walking away on his sturdy logger's legs. Now the time for the second generation has just started, but at only sixty Gary Snyder, the axe, still has a long way to go himself. The dragon must descend into the fountain many more times.

Will Petersen:
SEPTEMBER RIDGE

September

my favorite month
when the climate & spirit of Washington
San Francisco & Kyoto are the same & hang in the same
Indian summer haze

Gary to Pete, 1959

October, East Bay: 1955

You need a goddam passport, Rexroth complained,
but nonetheless crossed over from The City, served
as MC, as Coach bringing on the rookies.
Black walls. A dark space packed full. Converted
auto body shop? Co-op gallery? Mistaken memory?
History speaks of a momentous occasion at
Six Gallery, San Francisco. But I still feel
Jack passing jugs of dago red, Phil shy, Gary
reading straightforwardly, McClure insistent—

      light   *light*   *light*

In a time of blue suede shoes, of Elvis and rock & roll,
Canute against the tide

      light   *light*   *light*

—almost booed off. Expressionists impatient,
wanting wantonness, long before Minimalism,
Michael's poem, I hear it now, listening
to melting snow

               & then the tidal wave, Allen, new in town,

clean shaven, in charcoal grey, white shirt & tie, first time we
met, at Gary's, now in blue jeans, rousing all, hooping &
hollering, like a black baptist church's mass, all responding
to *Howl!* out of a dark space, transported——

"Save the invitation," Gary confided: "Some day
it will be worth something."

●

He was somehow certain of immortality, back then.
In an impoverished Taoist unpublished poet sort of way

leaving poems
in fire-watcher shacks, way up above
the timberline

May 1956

. . .
I am about reduced to a rucksack again,
a bundle of books.

Out under the Golden Gate
Aboard the *Arita Maru*
Gary's gone

1956: June

As a matter of fact I am riding my bike up
to Daitoku-ji & the Zen Institute this very morning.

. . . Sunday I am to attend my first Nô.
After the first of July I begin serious Zen training under
Zen Master Miura Isshu.

August

Dear Pete Oh nobody told me how hot it gets in Japan, nobody;
& a Sanfrancisco-mountaineer like me never knew weather could

be so warm . . .

*However: I spend my days studying Japanese
& (at the moment) memorizing sutras & waiting on Miura Rôshi.*

*Just got back from a five day hike in the Northern Japanese
Alps . . . Nice mountains to look at, but not the best sort for
wandering. I imagine the best wandering mountains in the world
may be the high sierra—no bugs, no rain, no people, clear
cool sunshine & hundreds of square miles of alpine terrain—
11,000 ft <u>level</u> or rolling land with lakes & rockpinnacles &c.*

. . .

*The ZI is just finishing a new building, a library &
zendo-for-hakujin, in Japanese mountain-style arkitekter that
will be very convenient. Number of loose hakujin floating in
& out want a place to study & zazen: I guess my old shave-
head Rôshi will give zazen to them as interested.*

. . .

*Are you going to be doing the artwork for next Bussei?
I'm considering submitting Kanzan translations.*

*<u>Needle</u> just came out with a poem of mine. Also in September
<u>Ark II Moby</u> is happening, containing Phil, Jack, me, Rexroth,
Patchen etc. etc. —a big manifesto of anarchist-buddhist-
west-coast young poets.*

September 56

*. . . was bowled over by wooden bosatsus from long ago.
I have gotten an unreasonable passion to learn woodcarving now.
If we ever build us a real <u>tera</u> in Amerkha we'll have to make
our own figgers & get cats like you to paint big Ajanta type
Buddha mural, but in whatever in now style. i.e. most now
sincere.*

*. . . Well now Japan's just fine, I reckon you could get
enlightened here just as well as anyplace else. But Buddhism
is sure a dead duck as far as the people go. I guess they'll
have to become real occidentals before it will mean anything*

to them again.

     . . .

          we will build fires
            under their zazen seats

Oakland

Still at Montgomery Ward's loading dock, working overtime,
saving all for boat fare, I room across the street. Christmas
rush—Hiroshi gets hired, moves in; all he
possesses packed into one duffel bag.

On a wall, a scroll.
In a bowl, five oranges.

Kyōto

*As far as Z goes I mize well be in America, where I had
plenty spirit for zazen and leading suitable life. Z bonzes
here are all (mostly all) obsessed with snobbish aristocratic
& insular self-esteem, & no sense of art except as "traditional
Japanese art" & no sensibilities for the wide world of people
& nature as it is now . . . Ikkyu, founder of Daitoku-ji, said
exactly the same thing in the 13th century, so it's nothing
new*
    *. . . Anyhow I got faith in me own Buddha-nature so.
& have come to realize that I am firstmost a poet, doomed to
be shamelessly silly, undignified, curious, cuntstruck, &
considering (in the words of Rimbaud) the disorder of my own
mind sacred. So I don't think I'll ever commit myself to the
roll of Zen monk, as free as that role seems to be.*

                        . . .

At sea

a vision of back-packing companion,
a dream of high sierra meadow, cool lake,
a dream of dust-free air, in September,
the favored month of Noh, the time

of recurring ghosts, of attachment
& release

•

January 1957

Yokohama. After twelve days humping the icy Aleutian route,
riding the *Sea Dragon,* headed for Kyoto Women's U, Pete
disembarked: shave-head with naught aught but what one foot
locker held, with pride in torn T shirts, Reverend Imamura's
brother's suit, five-year-old Mari's photo in my pocket. My
old baseball mitt passed on to chubby Ryo.

Back again! old haunts——It was not immediately I
hunted him up, north, neath gnarled pine

down off the raw veranda wood
Tiger pounced upon me, exuberantly
embraced me, you must
know, no tigers ever existed,
not ever in Japan, only on

tourists' backs, on GI jackets, on
paper-panelled screens
of temple entranceways
ferociously silly, rendered in a cat's dream,
intensely whiskered eyebrows
prefiguring twinkle-eyed

bonze

cup of
tea

Rinko-in

Gary, Walter, & Walter's piano, dark, looming high, heavily,
on low horizon tatami, co-exist
within "somewhat rundown" ancient pine, gravel path

& wet moss temple compound, Shôkoku-ji

Since 1392

Quakes   Fires   Wars   Rebuilt countless times Past its prime

All the junk that goes with being human

stashed
in the tokonoma,
Zen's
altar

hard rock wavers
tour buses crowd Ryôanji

Even the heavy present seems to fail
This bubble of a heart

highways creep up
the mountains
tour buses

Stashed in the tokonoma, Zen's true altar—Skis.

Temple spaces rented to Christian College Boys
from red-brick University neighbor. South,

across bicycle congested ox-cart pushcart scooter
three wheeler honking truck trolley Main Drag the
Ancient Imperial Palace Grounds: a vast
rectangular breathing space.

Stupa

Off the path, in the moss, a tumble of stone.
We set the stones once again one atop the other.
Good karma, Gary smiled. We hiked on.
Upward. Past fern.

•

They approach us

barefoot on worn wooden clogs, in frayed academic uniforms,
caps & brass buttons signifying what college, "A chance to

practice English," one says. "No, they don't look American,"
the other says; they pass us by

> ——Gary's impish smile,
> residue of the cat, lingers.

Yuiko [23 June 1957]

college girl, she climbed with us to the top,
sighed, reclined in a glade, in shade. Taking up rotted
fallen branch, assuming heroic stance, I engaged my rival
in mock samurai battle, bark flying, wood splintering, we
were stags, reduced to a stub & a stump, we sweated, we
went on down, Gary & I, and She, down to Lake Biwa,
to cool

●

All those years

we licked roadside trickles, dropping down, cold, clear.
Up on Mount Hiei we lay on our bellies,
lapping rivulets between moss.

●

Yuiko's friend

on a river island, mere sandspit
just outside Kyoto, we spend the night
the three of us

> geta strap snapped
> hobbling back

> I marry her
> Gary goes to sea

As he leaves

Gary hands me a letter from Italy,
"Pete, see what you can do. Be good to have him here.
Great editor. His mag first rate—Olson, all those guys . . ."

Poet Corman does indeed sail in, under a French flag. *origin,* second series does occur; *Riprap,* Gary's first book, Origin-published, does appear. & more poets arrive.

Proofreading Berkeley's *Piute Creek* in Kyoto: the printer marks the top of the sheet *heaven;* the bottom edge, *earth.* Same as arranging flowers: heaven above, earth below; human in between

> *Always carry a rucksack.*
> *It's one of the 32 marks of a Buddha.*

> *one small poem also*

> *eros & agape*

> *Did you get bicycle from Rinko-in?*
> *it's waiting for you*
>
> **G**

6 September 57
just off Singapore

Dear Pete, I discover that I'm on a rusty old tramp tanker.
It seems I signed a thing called ship's articles which means
I am supposed to stay on this ship until it goes back to
America—which won't be for another five months, unless the
engine breaks down or the crew goes totally mad, which it
may well do.
> *. . . if I'm going to be on this tub for a*
long time I think I better lay in some reading matter.
I rely on you . . .

8 September
Bay of Bengal

Forget all that shit about books for the time, we just got
new orders to go to Trincomalee Ceylon and then to Colombo,
& after that nobody knows

> *. . .*

10 November
Red Sea in the narrow place just south of Suez
heading Northwest

. . . it sounds so beautiful & fragile & impossible & maybe
when you get this something awful will have happened &
everybody will be catapulted back into little lonely rooms
again. But DON'T let it because you are the best scene in
this whole gloomy world . . .

 all the long way southwest the southern coast
of Arabia never out of sight of what is really an enormous
thousand-mile scarp with stratification clear to view, a
straight cliff well over a thousand feet high,
not a sign of life not even one
spit of a seed
 . . .

 Crew madly talking Italy, world of quick fuck.

The Classical world

hit me like bricks in Byzantium, to which I have
journeyed & returned
 . . . Iranian & Turkic long-mustache &
leather-stocking world: the real bridge between east & west
those people; minarets, desert capitals now dust & ancient
Buddha-days in Turkestan before Mahomet heard the dove;
& the terrible silence of Hagia Sophia that has been Christian
& Moslem & is now void, who knows what temple next?—its
hanging lamps & tile high figures that are any sacred couple

in the world, & any sacred baby be coyote jesus gautama
or quetzalcoatl . . .
 In the little poems & long epics back then
there is the same wire twanging that we hear in DHL.
& old crackerbeard.

Wow, an image; poetry like a guitar string—
one end anchored to the void that makes it hum,

the other to busy old finger world that picks a tune.
I'm tired of images like that.

. . .

Just went topside & saw the Southern Cross & bummed a sip of
vodka off the cook.

Aegean Sea: 22 December 1957

Dear Pete, well about 35 days ago it seems an age I did get
two letters

. . .

From my last letter-place, Bahrein Persia, went to Augusta
Sicily—through sandy old Suez & hashish-smoking Egyptian
boatmen—Crete at dawn one morning 10 miles north, & Sicily
foggy & windy with white-blown olive trees & rocky hills &
pastel houses with red tile roofs, good wine & good bread,
a dreary whorehouse scene of nothing-but-blowjobs & too much
expense; & whole drunken crew barely finding its way back
to ship; then on through straits of Messina & up to Pozzuoli
which is a suburb of Naples & at Naples I stayed sober &
spent a day at Pompeii & journeying up Vesuvius. Pompeii a
most impressive town & images of another life entirely——
civilization is a matter of proceeding from one mass kick to
another, & when the kick is forgotten the civilization it was
is as unavailable to our minds as a half-forgotten dream, &
as weird; as complete & self-contained, & as transitory;—
not an expression of Buddhist sentiments, but a comment on
the nature of a high culture to be a sort of obsession &
delusion so that those under its influence may stick to tri-
angles & never imagine circles, paint in red but never
conceive of blue, & consider themselves (as we do) to be com-
plete humans missing no possibilities—when another equally
consistent, logical, self-contained little cosmos of thought &
action which is utterly inconceivable to us lies just around
some historical corner. From Italy back to Persian Gulf &
then out around the Indian Ocean (enroute to Pearl Harbor

WILL PETERSEN 85

our orders get changed & we alter course back to Red Sea
& Suez) & again Mediterranean, this time Turkey.

. . .

This damned ship

just goes on & on like the Flying Dutchman, I sort of begin to
believe it will never go home or stay anywhere more than a
day, until the last drop of deep-down Arabian oil is drawn &
the last gearbox oiled & the ultimate airplane wrecked & all
the paint gone & the Sappa Creek just floating around in its
own rust & ruin with its hoary white-bearded crew re-reading
the ten thousandth time the same magazine & wondering when
we'll ever get home.
                This is the sea where heroes sailed.
& goddesses came to shepherds on mountaintops, & the
dawn is REALLY rosy-fingered, the sea wine-dark, & I
intoxicate myself with Classical memories & look about
for pagan deities & long-prowed galleys.

Wrote longe poeme called "Tanker Blues".
Also this short piece amongst others:
        USNS SAPPA CREEK
                    . . . rags in bales,
        the final home for bathrobes,
        little boy bluejeans & housewife dresses

                    . . .

On these long runs

after a certain time you flip & get happy & quit figuring
how much you're making & how long til you get home & just
amble about hollering & laughing covered with grease &
loaded with silly wrenches & generally being a sort of
Bodhisattva of machinery without any past or future,
I got a full beard & wornout shorts & no shirt &
old bandana on my head which is shaggy.

                . . .

March 1958

near the
gilbert islands
in the rainy
dark
a heavy swell
ten p.m. drinking tea

this is the last time this hoss'll write from sea I suppose,
unless we are mysteriously sent back to Arabia to go on and
on—til the oil runs dry under the big shale hills and the
sheiks go back to goats and mares and Aristotle Onassis is
dry bones in greek richman's graveyard, when the oil is gone
and ball-bearings finally creak rusty & shuddering to a final
stop and little boys with tallowpots have to run alongside
covered wagons greasing the axles by hand again, juice gone
from the ground & the sap dried up in the machinery & we'll
put cowbutter on our hands—& the only tankers will carry
oil and wine.

      . . .   *we are coming leisurely by way of the south*
seas home; passing south of mindanao through the sulu sea,
through the celebes sea, over the equator and under the southern
cross, we drew in 22 March to volcanic green flowery hills of
steep pago pago bay, tutuila a little island in samoa, and for
thirty hours lived in lotus-eater land, a buddha-realm of flowers
and delight which is really like old captain cook and herman
melville and everybody says, ravaging modern society seems a
joke when you walk around where people nap in the daytime and
make love at night and care for naught because nobody's jealous
or scared, if babies get born they are raised up, when girls
reach puberty they make love, when men feel energetic they take
torches at night and go fishing—big-thighed long-haired samoan
girls & our mad tight crazy rich crew; drinking can beer in
bungalow screen-walled bar & dancing to samoan drum records,
samoan men & women in flower-color lava-lava skirts on happy
haunches, or cadging beer from sappa creek crew, or talking
away, the policeman says to me "I feel silly in this policeman

WILL PETERSEN   87

shirt"—because he didn't like being the samoan policeman when everybody is having fun—so I took off my shirt and gave it to him; later a girl took my zoris away too, so I was dancing in bar shirtless and shoeless—we all went to the seaside and had bonfire and picnic and swimming and ate breadfruit—a robust girl latched on to me & said she was my girlfriend til the ship left, and wouldn't let me look at other girls, but she looked just fine, and we did it one time swimming in the water like seals or whales do I suppose—and when they get away from town they do like old times and villages, take off things above the waist & let bare breasts swing & smile in the light—all night at the beach—somebody took $20 out of my pocket while swimming & lots of other guys lost money too, but it's all so good-natured nobody even cared—there was a horse walking around too, eating flowers, just like a weird gauguin—the hills they say have wild pigs; there are americans there too, maybe fifty, and they are all sleepy samoans now. Then in the afternoon we had to go, & we strolled back in couples to the ship which blasted go-away whistle, & up the gangplank to take in mooring lines, the girls waving, & my girl Miss Afuvai whipping off her lava-lava to wave it like a great flag in the wind, & then bending over to show her bare bottom to the crew, a great roar of laugh & approval, as we pull to the sea, & now 2 more days we get to Kwajalein to unload more oil, & then to Hawaii to finish off discharging, & we hope back to west coast.

22 April 1958

Ah, Pete, we came through.
Made it back to white clean sea-air San Francisco unrolled
or robbed . . .

    Can't find it.
    It's in the dust, in dew, in
    moon, in shade of tree & flow of
    stream;

        in my kitchen
        in a jar

tokonoma.
Wherever. Anywhere.
Staying overnight with Gary, 1969,
in Midwest college town motel
he makes of dresser top, a shrine

places with casual precision a hand-hidden carved wooden
bear; three, four other discrete objects, making
of this careless space,
his world.

Open the sacred medicine bundle,
unroll the sleeping bag

  no one loves rock,
but here we are

under stars
at ease

   •

(*September Ridge* is a chapter from a work-in-progress.)

The Wide Pacific
1959–1969

Katsunori Yamazato:

SNYDER, SAKAKI, AND THE TRIBE

During his Japanese years (1956–1968) Gary Snyder met and cultivated friendships with many Japanese. Among various men and women that he met in Japan, Zen monks, working men, and a group of people whom he calls "Japanese cultural radicals," were the "three interesting types of people" for him.[1] These three types especially receive Snyder's poetic attention in the *Far East* section in *The Back Country*. "March" in the *Far East* section, for example, depicts the poet investigating "marginal cultures" (Korean food and an Okinawan *awamori* bar, for example) with the "cultural radicals":

> Up in dirt alley
>   eat korean food
> drink white doburoku out of bowls
> broil strips of beef & liver over coals
> finish off with raw cow's womb
>   in sauce, jade-white and oyster smooth
> piss against the slab posts of the highways
>   overhead,
> bar girl girl-friend with a silver trinket cup
>   hung on a neck-chain, she, gives us,
>   all beer free.
>
>
> sift through night streets,
> Kato, Nagasawa, me, Sakaki,
> okinawan awamori bar
> clear glasses full up to the brim
> like flavord gin — must millet —
> with choppt onion.
>   whirl taxi by
> glass door opening sharks, their,
>   eyeballs to the sky —
>   in coffee, tight butt tress;

to station where the world trains meet
I south around the loop
yellow writhing dragon full of drunks
& hall the windy concrete of
Zojoji.[2]

Mamoru Kato, Tetsuo Nagasawa, and Nanao Sakaki represent the third group of interesting figures. These cultural radicals rebelled against a tightly regimented, class-conscious society, and sought (and continue to seek) an alternative way of living. They were Snyder's "teachers about Japanese marginal culture,"[3] and, from them, he learned about Korean food, *doburoku* (raw sake), and Okinawan *awamori* (a white distilled liquor made from rice, not yet well known among Japanese people at that time). These cultural radicals later formed a loosely organized group called *Buzoku* (Tribe), and Snyder briefly lived with them at the Banyan Ashram on Suwanose Island in the summers of 1967 and 1968.

Snyder and Sakaki have struck up a lifelong friendship, and Snyder honors Sakaki not only as his friend but also as his teacher: "Sakaki was my teacher about what it was like right after the war, what it was like to live under the bridges after the war in Tokyo."[4] Although he met and talked with Japanese intellectuals who were "poets, socialists, and Marxists," Snyder was not comfortable with them: "Poetry was not very interesting, was pretty much derivative from French surrealism still; politics was too doctrinaire. . . . I was interested in anarchist politics. . . . I was not comfortable with poets for three, four years, and then I met Nanao and others."[5] Snyder's friendship with Sakaki and the members of the Tribe, thus, is indispensable in considering his development as a poet and thinker. What follows, then, is an attempt to recount the origin and development of Snyder's friendship with Sakaki and the young Japanese cultural rebels.

On December 10, 1961, after the *Rōhatsu sesshin* (an intensive meditation week: December 1–8) at the Daitoku-ji monastery, Gary Snyder left Kyoto with Joanne Kyger for Tokyo. They stayed in Tokyo for two days and, on December 12, took a train from Tokyo to Yokohama, passed through immigration and customs, and "walked down this long dock to the *Cambodge* where it was moored alongside—a pretty big ship, all painted white."[6] By then Gary Snyder had lived in Japan for several years, and he had decided that it was time "to see the hearth-land of the Buddha's teachings."[7]

Aboard the *Cambodge* on his way to India, Snyder met a fellow traveler who attracted his attention:

An Australian named Neale Hunter had done French, Chinese, and Japanese literature at the University of Melbourne, then went to work in the bush for a year or so, took the money and went to Japan, Tokyo—lived for about four months in Shinjuku, Tokyo (a kind of bar and underworld hangout zone of enormous dimensions) then took off for India—fellow who knows about literature, wild life, and for some reason became a converted Catholic and is now trying to reconcile Catholicism and Buddhism to suit himself.[8]

Hunter also impressed Joanne Kyger, and she wrote in her journal: "Neale Hunter, Australian, short with black beard, very sharp."[9]

Arriving in Hong Kong, Snyder, Kyger, and Hunter went into town. While Kyger went shopping for a raincoat, the men went into "an old style wineshop" where they talked to "the old men" in broken Chinese and enjoyed wine. The next day Snyder, Kyger, and Hunter took a bus to the border, climbed a hill, and "gazed out through pine trees at the Chinese People's Republic—spread out before us, a watery plain with houses here and there—a barbed wire fence along a river at the foot of the hill showing where the actual line is."[10]

As Snyder writes, Hunter had lived for about four months in the Shinjuku district of Tokyo. It was in Shinjuku that Hunter met Nanao Sakaki, who had drifted into this area, and, striking up a friendship, they co-translated Sakaki's poems into English; these translations are included in Sakaki's book *Bellyfulls*. The first edition of the book was printed in Tokyo in 1961, and Neale Hunter carried a copy of the book with him. He showed it to Snyder during their trip to India and told him to find Sakaki after his return to Japan, which Snyder did.[11]

Nanao Sakaki was born in Kagoshima Prefecture on January 1, 1923 (the Year of the Wild Boar).[12] His parents ran a dye house, and it was built on the Sendai, the second-largest river in Kyushu, which often flooded the area. After finishing his compulsory education, Sakaki worked as an office boy in one of the prefectural offices in Kagoshima.

During the war, he was drafted into the Japanese Air Force and trained as a radar specialist. Just before he left Kyushu for an island in Southeast Asia to build a radar base, the transport ship that was supposed to take him there was hit by a U.S. submarine and sank near Sasebo, Nagasaki. Sakaki was then sent to an airfield near Izumi City, Kagoshima, where the Air Force was building a new radar base. He watched kamikazes leaving for suicide missions, and secretly read, when he had time to do so, such thinkers as Nietzsche, Schopenhauer, Kropotkin, Marx, and Engels.

When the war ended in August 1945, he returned home briefly. But then he immediately left for Tokyo, where he lived in an underpass near Ueno Station. According to Sakaki, this was how the postwar homeless lived in Tokyo. Moving out of the underpass, he worked in a foundry located in Amagasaki near Tokyo. The work, however, was physically too demanding for him and, after two months, he quit the foundry. After leaving, he worked as a turner for about six months, which he never enjoyed wholeheartedly.

Quitting his second job, Sakaki started working in the office of Sanehiko Yamamoto (1885–1952) as an unofficial secretary. Yamamoto, known for founding the publishing company *Kaizōsha* in 1919 and publishing the magazine *Kaizō*, was at that time purged by the American occupation authorities for his political activities during the war. Born in Kagoshima Prefecture, Yamamoto knew Sakaki's uncle, and thus hired him for running errands. He worked for about two and a half years at the office, and then completely lost social interest.

In 1952 or 1953, Sakaki moved into the Sanya district in Tokyo, an area crowded with cheap rooming houses used mainly by day laborers who, hitting economic bottom, struggled to survive from day to day. He lived in "a strange world of day laborers, sneak thieves, prostitutes, and gays," and he never worked while living in this skid-row district. All day long he studied English and read books, and his neighbors shared food with him and what was minimally necessary for survival at the bottom of the social and economic strata. All he needed was "time to think, to feel, and to create something."

After two years in the Sanya district, Sakaki drifted into one of the flophouses in Shinjuku. He became interested in art and in paintings by Australian aborigines. Modernist art never interested him; instead he was very much attracted by primitive art. Later, in a book about Bushmen that he checked out from the British Council in Tokyo—*The Lost World of the Kalahari*, by Laurens Van der Post—he discovered a line that was to become the philosophy of Japanese hippies: "There is a dream dreaming us."

Among the young artists he met in Shinjuku at this time was a talented sculptor who needed imaginative guidance. Sakaki often gave him advice, and, in 1955, the two started traveling throughout Japan. Since the young sculptor carved Buddhist images in wood, they searched for suitable material. Their search for wood and inspiration took them up to the forests of the Shiretoko peninsula in Hokkaido, and down to those on Yaku Island, between Kyushu and Okinawa, where they carved images using the renowned Yaku *sugi* (cedar).

Sakaki and the young artist traveled together for three years, visiting virgin forests scattered all over Japan. During this wandering, Sakaki became conscious of his relationship with forests in Japan, and he began to write poems that reflected his ideas and feelings about them. His feelings about the woods were clearly ecological, and he became aware that his aesthetics were deeply rooted in his experiences in the woods and mountains. The two wanderers found themselves productive and, combining poetry and sculpture, Sakaki and the artist held two exhibitions, one in Kagoshima in 1955 on their way back from Yaku, and the other at the Mitsukoshi department store in Ikebukuro, Tokyo, in 1959.

When their wandering ended, Sakaki and the young artist chose to go separate ways. While the artist became successful and attracted wealthy patrons, Sakaki returned to Shinjuku—to the world of young artists, poets, musicians, and dropout students who would soon organize themselves into the Bum Academy and, later, the Tribe. As Snyder writes in his brief introductory note in the American edition of *Bellyfulls*, Sakaki at this time in Shinjuku became "a gentle breeze-like force for the foot-loose generation—under twenty-five—of poets and 'students' floating thru Tokyo's Shinjuku district."[13]

It was here that Neale Hunter met Sakaki and they became friends. Without home or money in the chaos of Shinjuku, they moved daily from place to place. They never slept in the same spot twice, and this was the game that they played for about four months until Hunter left Shinjuku. They slept in a park, they sat in a coffeehouse until dawn came, or they simply stayed all through the night in stations talking or reading. Sometimes Sakaki's friends, both men and women, invited them to stay for a few days at their apartments, but most of the time they floated through the Shinjuku area. They had both studied each other's language—Sakaki had been studying English and Hunter Japanese. Their mutual interest resulted in the translations of Sakaki's poems into English. The book, printed in Tokyo in 1961, was entitled *Bellyfulls*, and it was a copy of this book that Snyder saw aboard the *Cambodge*.

Snyder and Kyger returned to Japan on the *Cambodge* on Snyder's birthday, May 8, 1962, with "minds deepened, widened, and saddened by the lessons of India."[14] The question now arises as to when and where Snyder and Sakaki found each other for the first time. According to Sakaki, he met Snyder in Kyoto through Gavin McCormick, an Australian and a friend of Neale Hunter, who was living in Kyoto at that time. Sakaki remembers meeting Allen Ginsberg at the same time that he met Snyder. Snyder's account of the first meeting, however, is contradictory. According to him, they met "one spring," and "spent a week walking or talking through the streets of Tokyo. Linguistics, Bushman ethnology, Sanskrit studies, Japanese archaeology, Marx, Jung, Nagarjuna—and above all, Revolution."[15] Be that as it may, it is very likely that they met for the first time in 1963, either in Tokyo or in Kyoto, in early summer when Allen Ginsberg was staying with Snyder upon returning from India.

Through Sakaki, Snyder met certain young Japanese—Tetsuo Nagasawa, Sansei Yamao, Mamoru Kato, and Kenji Akiba, to name only the representative figures—who were seeking alternative ways of living. They had much in common, and for the first time in Japan, Snyder found like-minded poets and intellectuals who sought ways to go beyond conventions imposed by modern society. Although the young Japanese poets and intellectuals had administered no impact whatsoever on Japanese society, they deeply impressed Snyder by sharing the same concerns with him, and he wrote sympathetically about them: "These concerns may seem obvious to us, but in Japan—where even the 'communists, artists, and poets' are square beyond belief—this is a real step."[16]

These young people, who later gathered around Sakaki, became the central core of the loosely organized Tribe. Having wandered all over Japan with their rucksacks, they eventually drifted into Shinjuku and gradually formed a group around Sakaki, who was then staying in this district. The impression that they made on Snyder was such a deep, lasting one that, in an interview that he gave immediately after returning to the United States in 1968, he talked highly of them:

> The "tribe" people have lived so much closer to the economic bottom than anybody in this country ever knows that in some ways there's no comparison. Now what they have is the real strength of hitting the bottom and surviving.
>
> What they have all done is each one of them separately hit the bottom and survived and then discovered there were some others who had hit the bottom. And from that they have formed a little subculture of their own. . . .
>
> Now here's a group of people who have literally dropped out so thoroughly that they have to learn how to make it together. Because they have to learn how to make it together, they don't cheat each other. They're reliable with each other.
>
> And they have hit their own level of independence and individual freedom, which is rare in Japan because it's not a society which creates individuals or individualism. And then they've been able, on top of their individualism, their sense of individual personal destiny, to add a discipline of cooperation and living and working together.[17]

What Snyder saw in this group of young people led by Sakaki was a possibility of an independent subculture entirely free from materialistic drive and able to support itself by a natural tribal spirit.

Initially, the members of this group half-jokingly called themselves the Bum Academy, and it *was* an academy that consisted of remarkably curious young people who were seeking and continue to seek an alternative culture by fusing Far Eastern practices with some European and American models. With financial support from a sympathetic patron, they published a magazine entitled *Psyche,* which, however, did not survive beyond the third issue. The activities of the Bum Academy gradually extended beyond Shinjuku, involving young people who envisioned a liberated Japan in the late sixties. And, according to Sansei Yamao, the Tribe was finally born when the group obtained communal land both in Nagano Prefecture in central Japan and on Suwanose Island, which lies between Kyushu and Okinawa.[18]

Sansei Yamao dates the birth of the Tribe from the first issue of the newspaper *Buzoku* in December 1967, although some members of the group continued to use such former names as Bum Academy or Harijan.[19] (Snyder, for example, refers to this group as Harijan in his essay "Suwa-no-se Island and the Banyan Ashram"; according to Sansei Yamao, the name was first proposed by Tetsuo Nagasawa.)[20] According to Yamao, the Tribe as an organization had no self-imposed bylaws; one became a member at the moment one felt he or she belonged to the group, and could leave at any moment. Yamao estimates that by 1970 a few thousand young people could relate to or regard themselves as members of the Tribe.[21]

The Tribe had some branches. In his essay "Buzoku ni tsuite no shikō" ("A Poetic Reflection on the Tribe"), Yamao mentions three such branches: the Dream of Banyan (in Suwanose), the Thunder Red Crow (in Fujimi, Nagano), and the Emerald Breeze (in Kokubunji, Tokyo). Although Yamao (a member of the Emerald Breeze) in his essay envisions such "small tribal communities emerging in the cities and in the country," the Tribe could not establish many other branches beyond these original three.[22]

Snyder was basically regarded as a member of the Tribe, and his presence to a considerable extent stimulated the group both intellectually and spiritually. For example, the year of publication of the first issue of the newspaper *Buzoku* is "40067." This was how Snyder dated his writings at this time—"reckoning roughly from the earliest cave paintings" (as he did in "Suwa-no-se Island and the Banyan Ashram" in *Earth House Hold,* for example). The group was also interested in the developments of the countercultural movement in the United States and other countries. They read the *San Francisco Oracle,* for instance, and Snyder naturally became their teacher in this area. He spoke Japanese fluently, and thus members of the Tribe could discuss with him the latest developments of the countercultural movement in the United States. He was well informed on this matter. He returned, for instance, to America in 1966 to give poetry readings on college campuses and came back to Japan the following year after witnessing the surge of the "tribal" movement on the West Coast. Later, when Sansei Yamao visited Snyder at his home in Kyoto in 1968 to celebrate the birth of Snyder's first son, Kai, they discussed at length the "long hairs" of San Francisco.[23] Thus Snyder was again a major source of information for the Tribe on the latest developments in the countercultural movements outside Japan. Moreover, Snyder undoubtedly stimulated the members of this group when his essay "Why Tribe" (later included in *Earth House*

Hold) was first published in the first issue of the newspaper *Buzoku* (No. 1, 1967). Tetsuo Nagasawa's essay, "Hitotsu no jiko hitotsu no karada" ("One Self, One Body"), printed in the second issue of *Buzoku* (No. 2, 1968), clearly echoes some passages in "Why Tribe." But perhaps the influence was sometimes mutual; Yamao thinks that Snyder's essay is partially based on his observations gained while he was participating in the activities sponsored by the Bum Academy and the Harijan.[24]

In mid-April 1967, soon after his return from the United States, Snyder went to Tokyo to participate in a march and a poetry reading sponsored by the Bum Academy. On April 16, Snyder, Sakaki, and the members of this group marched through part of the Shinjuku district to Shinjuku Station. Some of them bore banners that stated: "We are primitives of an unknown culture." Masa Uehara, then a graduate student in English at Ochanomizu Women's University in Tokyo, also participated in the march. (Snyder had met her in Osaka in 1966 through Hisao Kanaseki, Masa's undergraduate professor at Kobe University and a colleague of Snyder's at the First Zen Institute of America in Japan, in Kyoto.) Next day, on April 17, a poetry reading was held at the Yasuda Seimei Hall in Shinjuku; eight or nine poets, including Snyder, Sakaki, Sansei Yamao, Tetsuo Nagasawa, and Kenji Akiba, participated in the reading. Gary's poem in *Regarding Wave*—"By the Tama River at the North End of the Plain in April"—partly reflects this gathering of "friends and poets" in Tokyo:

> Round smooth stones
> > up here in the weeds
> the air a grey wet,
>
> Across the Tama river
> > a screen drum turns sorting gravel:
> > > dumping loads in
> > dump trucks one by one.
>
> Deep in the hills
> > the water might be clean
>
> Grilling raw squid over smokey twigs
> > a round screen perched on broken bricks

Masa bending on the rocks
Staring close to the water,
Nanao and Nagasawa
    with their lifted cups of shochu,

Friends and poets
Eating, drinking in the rain,
    and these round river stones.[25]

As we have seen, Snyder's cultural interest in Japan clearly extended beyond the Zen circle in Kyoto. In the sixties, he also became deeply interested in the *Shugendō* (or *Yamabushi*) tradition in Japan. *Shugendō* originally was a nature-worship religion that borrowed its theoretical basis from the *Shingon* school (also known as *Mikkyo*: literally, the secret teachings). Although Snyder's penchant for the *Yamabushi* tradition had manifested itself earlier in his essay entitled "Anyone with *Yama-bushi* Tendencies," printed in *Zen Notes* in 1954, it was after his arrival in Japan that he directly experienced this tradition. He visited Mount Omine, a sacred mountain in the *Shugendō* tradition, and was initiated a *yamabushi* (a mountain priest) in 1961. Sansei Yamao remembers a short trip that Snyder and some members of the Tribe took to the sacred mountain in the late sixties. As an initiated *yamabushi,* Snyder guided his friends onto the mountain, and, coming across a rest station that looked neglected, suggested they clean it. Other members willingly accepted his suggestion, and they spent some time cleaning it. When they reached the top of the mountain where the main temple was located, they were greeted by a high-ranking priest who gave them a memento to commend them for their good act; they realized that word spread quickly on the sacred mountain.[26]

Suwanose is a tiny island with a population of about fifty. Walking through the Amami Islands in the early sixties, Sakaki first heard of Suwanose, and a friend he had met while working as an office boy in one of the prefectural offices in Kagoshima Prefecture introduced him to the mayor of Toshima village, to which Suwanose belongs. The mayor gave Sakaki permission to take the village boat without charge so that he could study the archipelago freely. On the boat he met a man from Suwanose, who took him home. After a week on the island, Sakaki returned to Tokyo and spread the news of the availability of land on Suwanose. Several members of the Tribe, led by

Sakaki, first went to the island in May 1967 and started building the Banyan Ashram. Masa and Snyder followed them in July, first going to Kagoshima, the southernmost city of size in Kyushu, and then taking the *Toshima-maru* to Suwanose. On the island they participated in the communal life in the ashram.

Snyder's relationship with the members of the Tribe culminated when, on August 6, 1967, he and Masa Uehara had their wedding rites at 6:30 A.M. on the edge of the crater of the volcano on Suwanose. Through early morning mists, the members of the group living at the Banyan Ashram and some villagers climbed the steep hill to the edge of the crater that rises about 1,800 feet above the sea, and there they celebrated the wedding.

The members of the Tribe then staying on the island worked hard preparing for the wedding. During the wedding rites, Sakaki acted as priest; the group offered *shōchu* (sweet-potato alcohol) to the gods of the volcano, the ocean, and the sky; Masa and Snyder exchanged the traditional three sips (nuptial cups) using a Sierra cup; and then everyone recited the Buddhist "Four Vows" together. Below I quote the "Four Vows" that are currently recited at the Ring of Bone Zendo where Gary now resides:

> Beings are numberless: I vow to enlighten them.
> Obstacles are countless: I vow to cut them down.
> Dharma gates are limitless: I vow to master them.
> The Buddha-way is endless: I vow to follow through.

By giving three blasts on the conch, they ended the rites and ate lunch, which they had carried up in their rucksacks. From the edge of the crater they saw its red lava. Then they descended the narrow path to have a wedding reception at the Banyan Ashram.

After the wedding and the birth of their first son, Kai, Masa and Snyder decided to take their household to America, and the wedding and the brief, semiprimitive life on Suwanose, a subtropical, isolated island swept by the powerful Black Current, became an overture for *Turtle Island*. Snyder wrote as follows at the end of his superb essay, "Suwa-no-se Island and the Banyan Ashram":

> It is possible at last for Masa and me to imagine a little of what the ancient—archaic—mind and life of Japan were. And to see what could be restored to the life today. A lot of it is simply in being aware of clouds and wind.[27]

Prior to his permanent return to America with Masa and Kai, he had bought some wild land—which he later named Kitkitdizze—in the foothills of the Sierra Nevada. The life on Suwanose led to a new life in the foothills where it was necessary to be profoundly "aware of clouds and wind" to establish a household among pines, oaks, squirrels, deer, and coyote.

Snyder's relationship with Sakaki and the younger members of the Tribe did not come to an end when he left Japan with his family in December 1968. After his return to the United States, Snyder invited Sakaki to California by sending him an airplane ticket in the summer of 1969. Feeling a journey by plane too luxurious, Sakaki took a freighter to Seattle, and from there went down to San Francisco, where Snyder and his family lived in an apartment. Since then Sakaki has visited America several times, traveling, exploring deserts and mountains, writing and reading poetry. Snyder has helped Sakaki's works become known in America. The English translations of his poems, entitled *Bellyfulls*, were reprinted by Toad Press in Oregon in 1966. Snyder not only introduced the poet to the publisher but also wrote a note briefly depicting the Japanese poet's life. In 1987, Sakaki's first major collection of poetry in English—*Break the Mirror*—was published by North Point Press, which has been Snyder's publisher since *Axe Handles* (1983). Other members of the group have also visited the United States and, needless to say, Masa and Snyder have given characteristically warm hospitality to their old friends.

Snyder's sojourn in Japan may be regarded as "a provisionary stage" in which he studied and disciplined himself, writing poetry and creating a vision of an alternative culture. In Japan, he developed into a mature poet, trained in the rigorous, orthodox Rinzai Zen, and emerged fully armed with a deep, balanced view of Buddhism, and with the vision of a new, alternative culture. By 1968, he had found tentative answers for the problems with which he had struggled since the 1950s. He was ready to return to America, to Turtle Island, the place of his true roots, to test and incorporate his insights gained in Japan into everyday life.

His meeting with Sakaki and the younger cultural rebels of the Tribe enabled him to experience Japanese subculture fully as it began to manifest itself in the early sixties. It may not be an exaggeration to say that Snyder's Japanese years became complete and well balanced after he established a close relationship with Sakaki and his circle. Although Sakaki and other members of the group practiced Zen meditation, their world was fundamentally different from that of orthodox Zen as Snyder knew it in Kyoto. Snyder, who sometimes felt skeptical about the patina of Zen and Far Eastern culture—as expressed in "Dullness in February: Japan," included in *Left Out in the Rain* (1986), for example—thoroughly enjoyed his relationship with these unpretentious people who were seeking a new culture. He knew the limits and weaknesses of an institutionalized religion, and thus in Japan he sometimes distanced himself from the ambient culture. His relationship with Sakaki and the younger poets and writers enabled him to have new insights into Japanese society, which might not have come to him if he had chosen to stay within the Zen circle alone in Japan. By meeting and living with the members of the Tribe in the sixties, Snyder added the last touch to his Japanese experience. The members have shared with him an exciting friendship, which has enriched them intellectually and spiritually, and the vision that they shared more than twenty years earlier has since been deepened, elaborated, and spread on both sides of the Pacific. It has indeed been a rare friendship.

NOTES

1. Gary Snyder, conversation with Katsunori Yamazato, March 29, 1981.

2. Snyder, *The Back Country* (New York: New Directions Publishing Corp., 1968), 56.

3. Snyder, conversation with Katsunori Yamazato, March 29, 1981.

4. Snyder, conversation with Katsunori Yamazato, March 29, 1981.

5. Snyder, conversation with Katsunori Yamazato, March 29, 1981.

6. Snyder, *Passage Through India* (San Francisco: Grey Fox Press, 1983), 1.

7. Snyder, *Passage Through India*, ix.

8. Snyder, *Passage Through India*, 3.

9. Joanne Kyger, *The Japan and India Journals* (Bolinas, Calif.: Tombouctou Books, 1981), 13.

10. Snyder, *Passage Through India*, 4.

11. Snyder, "Nanao Sakaki," in Nanao Sakaki, *Bellyfulls* (Eugene, Ore.: Toad Press, 1966).

12. Nanao Sakaki, interview with Katsunori Yamazato, November 11, 1987. The information on Sakaki, unless otherwise noted, is based on this interview given in Davis, California.

13. Snyder, "Nanao Sakaki."

14. Snyder, *Passage Through India*, ix.

15. Snyder, "Nanao Sakaki."

16. Snyder, "Nanao Sakaki."

17. Snyder, *The Real Work: Interviews & Talks, 1964–1979*, ed. Scott McLean (New York: New Directions Publishing Corp. 1980), 11–12.

18. Sansei Yamao, letter to Katsunori Yamazato, January 17, 1989. Yamao—poet, essayist, and a former member of the Tribe—met Snyder in the 1960s. With his family, he moved from Tokyo to Yaku Island in 1977, and since then has published several books.

19. Yamao, letter to Katsunori Yamazato, January 17, 1989.

20. Yamao, conversation with Katsunori Yamazato, February 4, 1989.

21. Yamao, letter to Katsunori Yamazato, January 17, 1989.

22. Yamao, "Buzoku ni tsuite no shikō" ("A Poetic Reflection on the Tribe"), *Buzoku* 1 (December 1967): 27.

23. Yamao, letter to Katsunori Yamazato, January 17, 1989.

24. Yamao, letter to Katsunori Yamazato, January 17, 1989.

25. Snyder, *Regarding Wave* (New York: New Directions Publishing Corp., 1970), 7.

26. Yamao, letter to Katsunori Yamazato, January 17, 1989.

27. Snyder, *Earth House Hold* (New York: New Directions Publishing Corp., 1969), 143.

Nanao Sakaki:
DUST FROM MY OLD BACKPACK

(1) THE FIRST STAR   •

One evening, probably in early summer 1965, Gary Snyder & I are rambling on one of the long and narrow lanes in Kyoto, just after a brief rain.

Several Japanese gentlemen are walking behind us. We hear them speaking of us as "Gaijins" (outsiders). Looking back at them Gary shouts in Japanese: "We are Naijins!" (insiders). Leaving them open-mouthed we keep on walking. Soon we see the first star in western sky.

(2) SEA OTTER

1. We are on a coral reef of the Tidal Point, the southernmost point of the Suwanose Island in the East China Sea. As the solar system revolves ceaselessly, it's now the summer of 1967. Excited about their first dive into a coral reef, about ten young people wearing snorkels, diving masks, and fins stand on the beach in a calm cove of the Tidal Point. Gary Snyder is among them. Soon we discover that he is a surprisingly good swimmer. "Sea otter, isn't he?" somebody shouts. He sometimes pushes up his head above the waves, then dives again into the coral garden. He moves further and further away from the shore.

2. By chance, the chief elder of the island passes by. He makes a sign to me to come ashore. "That American is going too far. It's very dangerous to go beyond the reef. Call him back, please!"

"You think so?"

"The Black Stream washes there the Tidal Point. You know it very well, don't you?"

3. Three days before Gary's arrival on the island, I rowed the small fishing boat with six islanders against the current of the Black

Stream. The great oceanic river runs three nautical miles per hour at the Tidal Point. My hands still remember what a hard rowing it was even for seven men.

4. Anxious and irritated the elder almost scolds me:
"Bring him back quickly! If not, who knows what will happen to him?"

"Gary, come back! Come back, Gary!" Wind and waves blow away my voice. Now he changes into a sea otter completely. His head shows above the waves one second or two, then instantly disappears into the blue water. Under the scorching midsummer's sun we see him again at another unexpected spot.

5. Surprised by my shouting, with confused faces everybody gets out of the water. The elder's half crying voice moves me. At that moment I catch a glimpse of the Sea Otter's head near the Tidal Point. From rock to rock, like a flying goby, my body runs, jumps & flies to the Tidal Point. I signal him, using my red loin cloth as a flag. At last the Sea Otter gets my sign & swims up to me.

6. "What is the matter?"
"Are you going to swim all the way to the West Coast?"
"Should I try?"
I point to the sea. "The Black Stream runs right here. Everybody on the beach is worried about you. Let's go back!"
"O.K."
Now, two sea otters swim back toward the beach, fighting against the ebbing tide. When we land at last, the elder smiles at us approvingly.

7. A couple weeks before that, Banyan Ashram was born at the foot of a volcano. Everybody in the ashram was joyous and trusting each other. At that time we knew very little about the ocean or the volcano. During those few weeks the usually so active volcano remained silent. But the cicada's song was roaring in the bamboo thicket day after day.

8. In the evening after the first diving we enjoy our humble but delicious dinner under the Banyan tree. Here comes a firefly, then

the elder with presents of a bottle of homemade sake & a big Spanish mackerel. The elder teaches us many magical tricks: for example, how to locate the direction of a typhoon without any weather report. And then he tells about several sea accidents that happened on the island. Once, at the Tidal Point, a student from Osaka was carried away by the Black Stream & never seen again. A few islanders were on the beach nearby but they had no way to bring him back to the shore.

9. The next day, first passing through a semitropical woods—camellia, Fatsia japonica, palm . . . we all dive again into the water. The Sea Otter heads straight for the Tidal Point. He holds the elder's advice in his mind. But the coral garden lures him further & further into the ocean. At the end I see him swimming on the reef's edge.

10. Our third day of diving, the Sea Otter goes beyond the reef with a spear. A couple of hours later he comes back to the ashram with three sea breams & a huge octopus.

—*Mt. Akaishi*
February 1989

Shasta Nation / Turtle Island

1969—THE PRESENT

Rain-rain-and deer
browsing daily by the
house. burning a few
piles of brush — with
the road so muddy no
one comes to call—
how pleasant!

隠者の着目

Michael Wm Corr .Ph.D.
北京都,大徳寺　1973

Doc Dachtler:
TRUE ENLIGHTENMENT

It was 1969. Gary and Masa were building their house way back in the woods. I was teaching school and living on the main road. School was one room, grades 1–8 with outhouses out back. We did have phone and power. That's how I met Gary; he needed a phone that was closer than North San Juan. We worked it out so he just wrote down his calls from our house and I billed him at the end of the month. He always wrote the numbers so I could read them and he always paid the bill. So I knew he wasn't a flake. Then I heard he was a famous poet. I told Jimmy Coughlan, my landlord, about this poet who was building a Japanese farmhouse across the diggings and one summer morning Jimmy says,

"Let's go see where that Snyder fella is buildin'."

Jimmy was eighty-five years old and didn't drive anymore. He was born in these woods in 1885 and knew them better than any man alive at the time or since (except maybe his brother Mick who was the cowboy of the family and knew it by horseback in his bones, but Jimmy's memory was better at the time so who knows now?), and when we got to the house site Jimmy got out of the truck, leaned on his cane, rearranged his felt hat, looked around, took his time, then pointed with his cane to a clearing down from the house and said,

"Ha! This is Little Bull Flat! Yessir. Years ago we ran our cattle over here and Mickey once found a little bull calf living here all by himself and so they roped him and cut him on the spot and so we called it Little Bull Flat."

We all sat down in the pine shade and Gary offered us some water from his new well. Jimmy tasted it. We waited. He said it was fine water and that most well water on the Ridge had too much iron in it. We talked about the weather. We talked about the house. Jimmy looked around at the north slope bowl we were in and said,

"Boy, she's gonna be cold here in the winter!"

And she was but when I would ride horse over to visit with a little snow on the ground Gary would be walking around the house barefooted so I said you're a tough son of a bitch and he said not really but had I heard the story of the People of the Inner Heat? No, I hadn't, so he told it: which was of being in New Delhi in the winter in the sixties sometime and it was raining and cold and down the street came a tribe of people marching tall and proud with no clothes on. The men carried long spears with rings attached. Every ten steps or so they jabbed the butts of the spear shafts onto the street and the rings would jingle and then they walked on. The women had rice pots tied around their waists and a few supplies. Gary asked who these people were and was told the People of the Inner Heat. Very respected. He followed them to see what was up. The tribe marched and jangled their way to the House of Parliament, which was in session, very British with coat and tie, and up the steps, through the doors down to the floor where the laws were being made. The proceedings stopped. The tribal leader made a speech, the spears pointed straight up. Parliament listened. The tribe had a gripe, which they expressed and then marched out. The matter I'm sure was looked into since any group that wears nothing ever does not just bullshit whine. Over the years I've gotten a lot of warmth from Gary's story and tell it myself when I hear complaints of how cold it is.

I remember putting a roof on Steve Sanfield's woodshed one fall day about fifteen years ago. Steve was sick. Gary was working the corner of the roof near a black oak and his hammer swing hit the rubbery bark of the tree instead of the nail, bounced back, and hit him right above the temple. I laughed because that's what you do in the trades to ward off pain. Gary rubbed his head, looked at the cold steel of the hammer head, and muttered,

"True enlightenment!"

When I ran out of money in '72 building my house, Gary heard about it and gave me $500 to put the roof on. Someday when I'm rich I'll pay him back.

I've heard him read his poetry and I've heard him when he gives talks about how art and life and the world meet and that is what impresses me most about the man: the range of his grasp of things.

Bruce Boyd:

AN ENCOUNTER AT KITKITDIZZE: SUMMER OF 1970

By way of a preface, I was part of the crew that built Gary and Masa Snyder's house in 1970. There was a core of ten of us, all very young. I had some experience and was hired as job boss. All of us were mentally open for anything, but short of the skills necessary to build a home of poles. We managed, and had a wonderful time doing it.

•   •   •

There is a photograph taken the summer Kitkitdizze was built of a young western fence lizard sunning on a black zafu amidst the stiff, bent, sun-dried grass and pine needles of the outdoor zendo: a line of pines on the edge of the meadow where we camped, where some of us would sit each morning in meditation before work began.

Days were long and the nights were long. The work hard, dusty, and hot. It wasn't often that I got up for zazen at 5:00—perhaps because of lots of responsibility for the work, or the tiring combination of learning while doing, or the youth of all of us, or the enormous imperative I felt to finish the house before winter set in. I was there to build a house. Yet, sitting zazen, listening to Gary and visitors talk on Buddhism, the East, and ecology, hearing great poetry—that talked of our daily lives in the woods—read aloud, while sitting by a campfire under an open sky, were the perks. A whole new world consisting of equal measures of communal camp life, Zen, Blue Sky, stars, forest, swimming the Yuba River, new friends and comrades, red earth, Coyote, and building from the very ground up, by hand, with stone, cedar, and pine logs. So I tried to make it to zazen even if I did bring all the problems of work with me.

One clear morning when I did make it to zazen: We sat in our forest temple without walls, in the meadow as it filled with morning light and birds, chilled by the dew, looking (not looking) at our hands. I was counting breaths. During the week we had been talking about Sanskrit and seed syllables. Mixed into the discussion were asides into demons, shamanism, and the spirit world. Sitting, every once in a while coming back to count more breaths, drifting off again not really knowing my thought, I became vaguely aware of a growing rumbling sound that seemed to swirl around us, coming nearer with every circling. The rumble became a buzz invading my mind. As this whorl brought me to consciousness, Gary, sitting two pillows down, rose on his haunches and gave a mighty *phat!* and sliced the air with his arm.

I saw this out of the corner of my eye and thought I heard him. The buzzing moved off into the sky and disappeared. The meadow sounds returned and I went back to counting my breaths until the bell rang and zazen was over.

Breakfast, then work resumed and other wondrous challenges filled my time. I've never talked to any of the other sitters about this, but I've always thought that one of us, with our naive, ignorant, but powerful open minds had attracted some malevolent thing from someplace else, and that Gary, as he has done in so many countless ways for so many students and seekers, cut down the demon that stood on the path about to harm or lead one of us astray.

—February 14, 1989

Steve Sanfield:

AS IT IS

A quiet day with friends.
No better way
to see the old year out.
        —for Gary & Masa

So caught up in ourselves
friendship only by accident.
How I miss him.
        —for G. S.

Between these hoops lie two decades of a multifaceted friendship. The first was written almost twenty years ago when we were still new to this place, the San Juan Ridge. Our families, our reinhabitation only just begun, we celebrated everything: the land, the children, the flora, the fauna, each other. We would join together in varying combinations of old and new ways to commemorate the New Year's (both Eastern & Western), Passover, Buddha's birthday, the Bear Dance, May Day, Halloween, and the solstices and equinoxes. Ofttimes we heard ourselves called "Buddhist-Jewish-Hopis," and for a while it seemed a proper appellation. Life itself was a celebration, and we embraced it fully and fiercely.

But we did much more than observe and play. We also built our homes and schools, raised our children, tried our hand at homesteading (some more successfully than others), and studied and practiced varying disciplines, each according to particular needs and inclinations. We found ways to support ourselves, some as carpenters, builders, mechanics, some as farmers and orchardists, others as teachers, artists, writers, and craftspeople.

In the process of all this living there grew an intimate awareness and love of the place where we'd chosen to settle. We tried to speak not only for our own interests but for those of the land, water, trees, and creatures that didn't seem to be given a voice. Of course, there were other interests as well, those of loggers, gold miners, developers, and just plain folks, and because these people did not always agree with us, or we with them, there was a reluctant but necessary plunge into the politics, mostly local, that many of us felt we'd left behind forever. Quite a surprise, all those committees and meetings, fund-raisers and lawyers, but we persevered and even managed to win a few of the battles.

In the end, the result was the natural emergence of a community without a center or a leader, a community that doesn't need a name but one that just about everybody, at least those of us who live in it, recognize immediately.

We grew up together along with our children, and as we became more comfortable, both collectively and individually, we began to turn more to ourselves, our own families, our own careers, our own particular work. A daily busyness became a part of our lives, and thus, sadly, the second hoop, written only last year.

Nothing is ever really lost, however; it simply changes and then changes again. But because friendship for me remains as profound and complex a mystery as love, methinks this is probably not the proper forum to examine it in all its manifestations.

Instead, let this become a *Hakarat ha-tov*, the acknowledgement of kindness or favors received from others. The sense of gratefulness is cultivated in the Jewish tradition and is not limited to powers beyond ourselves. Rather we are enjoined to openly thank our fellow beings for the beneficence shown to us. It becomes an honor and a high moral duty in our relations with others.

And so let me publicly thank Gary for his original and continuing support to me as a writer and an artist, as well as a friend. His early critiques, appreciations, and encouragement were vital and important stimuli for me to continue to court the muse at a time when I was about to leave the quest (or it me) behind forever. His introductions, on paper and in person, led directly to readings, publications and, most important, friendships and working partnerships that are still very much alive. No one else has been more generous with his time and energy. I also know that it certainly wasn't to me alone that Gary so unstintingly gave his help but many other poets and writers as well.

For all that and more, a simple and deep bow of gratitude.

•

ADDENDA

Question: How do all these varied aspects, the respected poet, environmental thinker, local activist, good neighbor, come together?

Consider: In 1975, over the strong objections of state and local officials, the community on the San Juan Ridge was in the process of building its own school. We wanted it to reflect our lives, our feelings, our visions. We wanted it to be *our* school, our children's school. To make that possible, a large work force of volunteer labor was established.

That same year Gary won the Pulitzer Prize for Poetry. Along with the award and the resulting prestige ("At long last they'll have to call me something besides a 'Beat Poet'") came a check for a thousand dollars. Gary quietly turned it over to one of the volunteer organizers and asked that it be used to help build the school.

The organizer said most of it would probably go for beer. It did, and though none of us knew where those beers came from at the time, they sure did taste good.

—*Montezuma Hill*
San Juan Ridge
Winter '89

Will Staple:

THE ONE AROUND THE CAMPFIRE

I have known Gary since Berkeley in '64. I helped build his house and have built one for myself a half-mile away. From the very beginning, we have shared the Ring of Bone Zendo. No one has dared to abuse him good-naturedly to his face (or receive his good-natured abuse) to the degree I have. I was one of the last to ask to contribute to this book. I know where the bodies are buried. I was there when fights broke out. I know what was said by both parties and saw both points of view.

Could I make a million with a kiss-and-tell book? Some loyalties supercede the public's right to know. Some loyalties are stronger than that to any government or state. Gary is part of my primary male kinship group. My secrets follow me to my grave.

Why? Peter Coyote and I recently discussed this. As we emerged as youths, each with our unique, fragile vision, Gary accepted us. Not praised, promoted, or advised, but as an older male he accepted and included us with his life, his group, his thoughts. I was a Taoist anarchist; he had recently done his Buddhist Anarchism piece for *City Lights Journal*. He took me on his motorcycle to see the great Catholic anarchist, Saint Amon Hennessy (the only man to be a C.O. in three wars). He included me at Beat parties, introduced me to Rexroth, commiserated from Japan about my disappointments with women ("it is the pain they give us that is worth much more than the pleasure"), and later advised me to send my work to *Caterpillar*, which established (suddenly) my career.

From Gary I learned that to get ahead I needed to get up earlier. I learned that all great men have feet of clay, that the grass is never greener on the other side, that insults are workingmen's way of showing affection. I learned that the best minds are right sixty percent of the time. I learned the joy of hard work well done, the joy of selfless service, of being one's own man.

Gary's accomplishment was to bring the nobility of the animal in man to light. This is what comes out on the trail riprapping, comes out in sheer sweaty exhaustion, comes out when zazen wipes away conceptions and one is one with all beings. My favorite Gary is the one around the campfire, on the trail, the one laughing at his own gross human folly.

Gary's personality has taken many changes through the years. This last decade of zazen has mellowed him considerably. I suppose his recent divorce was the final rite of passage into the full humility of manhood. True men (anarchists) long for work that benefits the entire community (not only the human dimension), and true women are not excluded from that longing. It is Gary's activity as a cultural worker that has made him realized. Zen has lent the concentration, the access to powers including memory. All humans are sometimes rude to one another. It is a measure of Gary's Zen and manhood that he can realize his faults and apologize for his own acts of over a decade ago. This is attention to detail. This indicates a transcendence of pride (the chief male weakness) and a recognition of human kinship. It would be easier for a cultural hero to omit this degree of thoroughgoing wayfaring. Gary doesn't.

Gary Lawless:

MY APPRENTICESHIP AT
KITKITDIZZE: SUMMER OF 1973

I grew up in a small town on the coast of Maine. As a teenager in the 1960s I felt pretty removed from any literary or cultural excitement. There were no clues that anything was happening. There were no new books, no poets, little music. Local excitement centered around football, basketball . . . If you weren't playing sports and weren't interested in them, there was something wrong with you. Teachers were not recommending new writers, new artists, new ideas. Nothing was happening.

In 1967 I found a book on the rack at Palmer's Stationery. The cover blurb claimed that it was "The book that turned on the hippies—by the man who launched the hippie world, the daddy of the swinging, psychedelic generation." The book was, yes, *The Dharma Bums*. I had not heard of Jack Kerouac and didn't know what the dharma was, but from the first page I had a new community, a new identity. I had joined the "rucksack revolution."

This was new information, new territory. What this book gave me was a great gift. I had never read anything like it. I read about Japhy Ryder and heard things that no one else had told me. Boundaries dropped away. The world widened. This may sound dramatic, but I'm not exaggerating. That's really how it felt. Kerouac's book, and Japhy's example, were saying to me that it was okay to like poetry. It was okay to love the woods and the mountains. You could be interested in plants and animals, myths, Indians, Asian religions, and you could have fun. You could write poems and stories out of your own experience, in your own language. There were people out there doing just that, and it was okay. This was a new attitude. It gave me a new sense of my own life, new possibilities. I didn't have to feel sad, incomplete, inferior because I wasn't athletic, because I read too many books, because I liked poetry. I no longer felt suspect, and I had a new hero, Japhy Ryder.

It was another two years before I found out that there was a real Japhy Ryder, a poet named Gary Snyder. I started searching Maine bookstores for copies of his books, usually having to order them. I now know (or suspect) that there were many other young people like myself, discovering *Riprap* or *The Back Country*. The poetry changed our lives, dazzled us, inspired us, spoke to us. Gary's work encouraged us to read on into the various traditions from which he was drawing. We were led to Gary's contemporaries (like Whalen, Welch, Ferlinghetti, Ginsberg, Kyger, diPrima, and Rexroth). The Han-shan translation led us on to Chinese and Japanese poetry. Reading *Earth House Hold* led me to read the work of Jaime de Angulo. It seemed that every book of Gary's led me to something new: a rich, vital territory whose existence I had had no previous clues about. This was not blind guru worship. I wouldn't run to every reference Gary made. Rather, this was a whole new world of possibilities, in which I was (and remain) very interested.

In high school the poets we were given to read were long dead, and did not speak from any tradition with which I felt much connection. Gary led me to a generation of poets alive and well and writing very exciting work. Now I had the courage to listen to my own voice.

By then I was in college, and had changed my major to East Asian studies. In 1971 I helped coordinate a reading tour of Maine colleges for Gary. I had a chance to talk with him, and rather boldly suggested that I come and live with him in California, as his apprentice. I felt that it would be more useful for me to go and learn from a poet whose work I admired than to go on to graduate school or some dreary writing program and study with some poet whose writing I didn't even like. Gary advised that I finish my B.A. and stay in touch. The reading was successful enough that we were given money to bring other poets to campus. During the next two years we brought James Koller, Ted Enslin, Joanne Kyger, David Meltzer, Michael McClure, and others to Maine. The English professors didn't quite know what to do with us. One professor tried to block Snyder's visit, saying that he wasn't really a poet. Another professor, at another college, denied funding saying that Snyder and Ginsberg would never read at his college. These weren't the people we were supposed to be reading. But the word was spreading. People were coming to the readings. People were publishing little magazines, writing and reading poetry. Something was happening.

On the day of my last college exam, in May of 1973, I left Maine for California, to spend the summer at Gary's. I had never been more than 200 miles from home. After driving and hitchhiking for several days, I arrived at Gary's on a sunny Sunday afternoon. To get to his place, Kitkitdizze, you followed dirt roads through a desert moonscape left over from hydraulic mining practices from the preceding century. You then passed through the adjoining Ananda Meditation Retreat, and followed a footpath through the woods down the ridge. As I came closer to the house I could see a group of naked people sitting in the shade. Others were dumping buckets of cold water over their heads. An archery target was set up. I had come at the right time. Sunday was sauna day, a day of relaxation, a day of community. I was nervous and tired from the trip, and I didn't know anyone. Gary and Masa suggested that I put down my pack, take off my clothes, and go sit in the sauna.

I pitched my tent under a madrone tree (after learning to identify poison oak), unrolled a mat for sleeping outside, and settled into the rhythm of things at Kitkitdizze. That summer the daily schedule was pretty well established. On weekday mornings we would rise early and make our way through the woods to a hilltop clearing used as a zendo, for morning meditation. After breakfast we would work on the day's chores, with a noontime break for lunch and siesta. We would work again in the afternoon, until the evening meal. Quite often there were guests for supper, so the evenings would lengthen into talk, poems, songs. This was a very important part of my learning process. Visitors would share in the daily work, and at night would share their own current interests. Gary had a way of easily drawing out useful and exciting conversations. I was learning how to listen. I was also still trying to get over the fact that here were people whose books I had read, just sitting down to supper and talking. For a long time that just didn't seem real. In Maine I really hadn't been able to connect real people living their lives with the poems and the novels.

On Saturday mornings we would have a dharma discussion at the outdoor zendo. I was now sitting zazen on the days when I wasn't cooking breakfast, but I had very little idea of what I was doing (or not doing). Dharma discussion centered on practice, and gave me some guidance. Saturdays were community work days. Someone would announce a project requiring a number of people, and we would all show up to help out. (Notes were left in mailboxes to coordinate this, as there were no CB radios or phones.) Usually an evening meal would be provided by whoever you were helping. Sunday was a social day at Kitkitdizze. The sauna would be hot for most of the day. There would be a fresh batch of Will Staple's homebrew, and people would gather to visit and relax. This was also like a day off for me, a little private time.

Gary has spoken of the apprenticeship experience as expanding the relationship between teacher and student into "something more personal, more menial, more direct." At Kitkitdizze I was part of the extended family. We worked together, ate together, traveled together. I helped take care of Kai and Gen, who were small then. I was made to feel a part of the daily routine. My presence helped to free Gary from some of the daily work, giving him more time for his writing projects. (Among other things, he was finishing poems for *Turtle Island*.) We rarely discussed the "how-to" of poetry directly. Poetry was there every day, in Zen practice, in daily work, in conversation, and in each day's mail and visitors. I was listening, watching, learning. I wasn't trying to write much. The poems would come later. (Gary would refer to traditional Japanese apprenticeships, where years would be spent learning how to sharpen and use the tools properly.)

It was a busy summer. There was a chicken coop to build, postholes to dig, firewood to cut, gardens and bees . . . The San Francisco Zen Center was putting up a temple in the woods behind us (brought across the Pacific in pieces from Kyoto and reconstructed by Japanese temple carpenters). Bioregionalism was a new topic of conversation, and one day a group of neighbors took the day off and we all drove around the watershed, tracing its sources. We went for hikes in the mountains and for walks to the Yuba to swim. We had dancing, music, readings by visiting poets, fantastic meals. . . .

I remember a day traveling bent over through manzanita, following Nanao down deer trails to the river. I spent a week in Berkeley, working on early *Planet Drum* issues with Peter Berg and Judy Goldhaft (Gary had given me his Hokkaido journals to edit for the North Pacific Rim Bundle). There was one day of fighting a forest fire, and many Sundays singing in the sauna. I remember Masa, beautiful, calm, strong.

It was the most intensely lived time of my life. At the center of it was Gary, holding it together, creating poems out of his life, and showing me how that might be possible for me as well. Gary convinced me that there was a need for poets who stayed "at home," learning the language of their specific places, the rhythms and cycles, and writing from that experience, trying to let the voice of place speak through the poems.

Living here in Maine I seldom see Gary. I think of him often, and I go back to the poems. It is true that poetry can change your life. My life was changed by finding *The Dharma Bums* and, from there, Gary's poems. My life changed even more when I went to live with Gary in California. The life I am living now owes much to Gary, and I know that there are many of us whose lives have been changed by his poetry, his example, his showing us a new way to see, to live. Poetry does help us learn how to live more fully, more completely in the world, and Gary's work is a great example of that. I cannot imagine who I would be if Gary's work had not touched my life. Gary brought me,

> To the real work, to
> > "What is to be done."

I can never thank him enough.

—*Chimney Farm*
Nobleboro, Maine

Scott McLean:

"THIRTY MILES OF DUST: THERE IS NO OTHER LIFE."

I

I first heard Gary read in Santa Barbara. It was May of 1973, I had just taken my doctoral exams, and my head was full of German Romanticism and Goethe. But I had also been reading a lot of contemporary American poetry in the hours away from German literature. Kenneth Rexroth was still teaching at UC Santa Barbara then and I had spoken once or twice with him that spring. I said one day I would like to talk with him at some greater length during his office hours, and he told me that would be Sunday at the beach. I never got down to the beach for those hours, but when Lawrence Ferlinghetti, Allen Ginsberg, and Gary came to campus to give a benefit reading in support of Rexroth's teaching beyond the mandatory retirement age, I went. And, above all because of the closing lines of one poem ("that quiet meeting in the mountains / cool and gentle as the muzzles of / three elk"), I carried a copy of *The Back Country* tucked under one arm.

It is now almost twenty years since that May evening, and I start this homage to Gary in recollection of that occasion because my life and my course of study took a different direction that night. For what I heard that evening in Gary's reading was a poetry that moved into territories and realms that were both familiar and yet breathtakingly, scarily new. I had grown up in backcountries, in the woods of northern Minnesota and the scrub chaparral of southern California. But I had never heard a poetry that addressed the larger realms we awkwardly call "nature" with the kind of precision that echoed in the sharp meters and images of Gary's lines, and I had never really faced it with the absolute, hair-raising acceptance of its laws that Gary was speaking of and to. Gary's poetry, heard in the context of the German idealistic philosophy and literature that I was studying, literally took my breath away and turned me around. When I packed my things for a year in Germany, I took with me those texts I needed for my dissertation work and every book of Gary's I could get my hands on.

In my readings on European Romanticism I had stumbled on what perhaps was an apocryphal story; it was said that Coleridge, speaking later in his life of Wordsworth's work, said that Wordsworth had lifted up the skirt of nature and promptly dropped it, running back in terror. Whether true or not, the story captured a good bit of the problematic state of European Romanticism's complex relationship with nature, and Gary, it seemed to me that night, had cut to the quick of this problematic, for "nature" in his poems had the tone and tenor of fundamental truth, resounding with, as he wrote in "Hymn to the Goddess San Francisco in Paradise," a kind of naked sacredness. It was a trail I wanted to be on, and I have followed along all these years—not on the same path, but on one to the side of his and heading the same direction.

For what I heard that night and only many years later recognized was a poetry that held two realms in a delicate balance. The first of these was the realm of wild nature and of a poetry on the wild edge, bent on discovery and exploration and on finding the condition of the wild, both within and without. And the second was the realm of community, recognizing the connections and bonds of lovers and family and children and neighborhoods and their relations to the spheres of wild nature. These were the two threads in European Romantic thought that most interested me at the time; and although I certainly would not have formulated my response to Gary's poetry in these terms that night, what I sensed immediately was that Gary's work spoke to what I felt were the most fundamental questions of our lives.

It was the wild edge of Gary's poetry that first pulled me into familiar territories that were turned about, into "forests covered with mud and asbestos," "kissing the lover in the mouth of bread: / lip to lip." And when he asked his friend Nanao to come forward that evening and read a poem, what Gary called forth was an elegantly zany poem about pumpkins and rattlesnakes read by a wiry and sage-looking Japanese. I have it still, scribbled in the back of that copy of *The Back Country,* and it reads:

> rattlesnake is the seed of meditation
> meditation is the seed of the pumpkin.

It has been a long time since that evening, and Gary and I have been close friends now for the better part of fifteen years. There have been long walks and talks in the woods, early mornings sitting zazen in the barn, and coffee in the dawn light by the fire. We have lived in the same county the last ten years, with our friends have built a zendo, and now work and teach together at Davis. But the seed of the meditation has indeed been the kind of quick, sharp turnaround that the rattle of the snake demands when you hear it, and the meditation deepens in the fall harvest and the time of pumpkins when we all gather in the season of "seeds-to-snow." So I'll fast-forward these reflections to 1989, to our life here along the San Juan and the other ridges of the South Fork of the Yuba River, and pursue in what follows one fundamental thread in Gary's poetry—the bonds of community life.

II

Each year at Halloween we have a ceremony in which Tibetan-masked Figures of the Four Directions dance and feed the hungry ghosts. On a hilltop meadow friends and neighbors gather together for the day and in the late morning stand in a large circle at the center of which is an altar with a small Buddha figure and with dried husks and beads and bones. The four dancers enter, ponderous with heavy wooden masks, bow to the directions of the compass and to the altar, and the ghosts, strung with bones and with faces painted white, run into the circle, shouting and demanding to be fed.

This year after they had danced out of sight I came back and stood next to Gary at the circle's edge, shaking off the cold night air in the late morning sun. Standing there I thought of another poem of Nanao's, "A Love Letter." The poem traces circles within circles. Nanao begins his meditation in a circle one meter wide, in which "you sit, pray and sing," and he extends the meditation in ever-increasing arcs: to circles "ten meters large" (where "you sleep well, rain sounds a lullaby"), to forests ten kilometers across, where one plays "with racoons, hawks, / Poison snakes and butterflies," moving then ever deeper into the circles of the cosmos, where in a circle "one hundred thousand kilometers" across one is "swimming in the sea of shooting stars," and Andromeda (at "one billion light years large") melts "away into snowing cherry flowers"—to come finally to a circle "ten billion light years large" where, as Nanao says,

There again you sit, pray and sing
You sit, pray and sing.

For we all move in many circles out and away from the small-self of one meter, and if we are lucky we see, at times, into the wider reaches of the circles that are the ground of our being, the reaches of the stars at "ten billion light years large"—finding there, as Nanao's title ("A Love Letter") implies, the "Love that moves the Sun and the other stars." But we first glimpse those farther distant reaches, I would argue, in the circles of community life, of family and friends and neighbors, and in gatherings like these at Halloween and on May Day. These gatherings celebrate our common lives, the valleys and ridges where, as Nanao says, we "gather firewood, water, wild vegetables and Amanitas," "play with racoons, hawks, / Poison snakes and butterflies": the life that Gary celebrates so eloquently in his poetry.

I see the interwoven reaches of the circles everywhere, and they begin for me in Gary's house. He built it, following Japanese-farm and Native-American traditions, with a fire pit in the center, a circle of fire in the middle of the home. As he told the readers of *Fine Home-building* in 1982, "I wanted a house where we could sit around the fire. . . . in spite of the occasional smokiness, the firepit has been magical and right. Children have listened to songs and tales, and drifted off to sleep by its flickering light. This is the archaic beginning and the sophisticated completion of the transmission of culture." It can be smoky, but I've always liked the smoke; winters my clothes smell good and later remind me of the nights around the fire. And when the library was in the main house and one borrowed books, they all smelled like smoke and talk and songs and jokes, and this lent a rather special frame to the reading.

But, more importantly, those evenings have been a genuine part of a transmission of culture: telling stories in the circle, enacting scenes of plays, listening together to tapes of new songs from distant friends; the circle of fire at the center of the house has been archetypal for life on the Ridge. I remember Peter Coyote singing to the kids there, lots of poems being read, and raucous, intense conversations about anything and everything. Lots of children have played at the edge of the fire and stared over its edge, and winters in the afternoon it is a wonderful place to sit and drink green tea. The governor sat around that fire, as have poets and writers from all parts of the world. And what we discovered around that ring of stone was a local culture that was and is authentically ours, fueled by a wide range of poetic forms that Gary encouraged and fostered and drew upon himself.

But the heart-and-core of it all is in the small encounters, the meetings along the road, at Ma and Pa Truckers' or in town, to then get together again, for work and for play. In the summer, riding down the road on his motorcycle to "see what the neighbors are up to," introducing Doc or Steve or visiting poets and artists at the North Columbia Cultural Center, or in his orange hard hat going over finances during the building of the zendo: I always see Gary in the middle of us all, helping out, quietly aware of people's problems or difficulties and seeking to lend a hand. It's a pleasure to work with Gary; he has an especially loving regard for old tools that is endearing, and a pragmatic, work-hardened attitude toward new technical developments. Like Gandhi, he finds the sewing machine and the bicycle to be wonderful technologies, and would add to that list his Macintosh. Moreover, Gary has a precise, sharp presentness of mind, he quickly turns the right word in funny and playfully insightful ways, and it is a delight to be around him. I remember one winter he and I came back over the Donner Summit in a snowstorm to a party at his house. Later on the trail it was pitch black, cold, and I didn't have my flashlight. Heading for home my wife Patricia held my arm and I said, "Don't worry. I know this place like the back of my hand," and promptly walked us not up the hill but straight into the pond next to Gary's house. One of the members of the zendo got the story a few days later and sternly said to Gary that he felt some of us were drinking or smoking too much at times, that one of our friends, he had heard, even walked into the pond the other night. And knowing full well that I hadn't had anything at all, Gary turned to him and said only: "the sober man / walks into the lake."

But aside from casual haiku and poems that speak to local political concerns, Gary's work has exerted along the Ridge the kind of centripetal force that Wendell Berry speaks of when he says that there must be such a force in a community to hold "local soil and local memory in place." I remember buying buttermilk on a hot July day (it must have been 1978) at Peterson's Corners, driving in the Willys down to Burt Hybart's for a visit. Burt had dug Gary's pond a few years back, and Gary wanted to visit Burt as he had been sick for some time. It was years later, after Burt had died, that I thought back to that day and to the man and his rough voice and gnarled hands. Reading through *Axe Handles* I came to a text that holds a bit of that memory in place, with lines that reflect the kind of tough sentimentality (or sentimental toughness) that Gary most often brings to his friends and those he loves. And I came to understand a bit of the conversation we had had that day and the man who had spent a lifetime with difficult machinery and who knew how to shape the soil for generations to come. For Gary spoke profoundly of what Burt truly embodied and handed on when, at the end of the poem "Removing the Plate of the Pump / on the Hydraulic System / of the Backhoe" Gary caught, "through mud, fouled nuts, black grime," "a gleam of spotless steel":

> relentless clarity
> at the heart
> of work.

Poems like this one, and there are many, remind me that one cannot read Gary's poetry from the past fifteen years without being constantly made aware of how much it is an expression of community life, and how it must first be seen within the context of the community of the San Juan Ridge. This is not to say that the poetry speaks only to a small circle of friends; it is to say that Gary's poetry has the authenticity and currency it does because of his profound rootedness in place, and his work argues that if one wants to touch the deepest levels of our humanity, one must learn within the relationships of responsibility that bind family, community, and place. I do not want to glorify community life on the Ridge and paint it in hues that would suggest all is inherently good and forever imbued with the virtues of selflessness and harmony; as in all communities, people fight, sometimes violently, and we have our proper share of bitchiness and quarrelsomeness, and people break up and suffer the same emotional unravelings and losses that people suffer everywhere. But such a commitment to place and community brings with it an overriding spirit of concern and care and less of the small-mindedness and selfishness that characterize much of what we call modern experience.

The culture of the Ridge moves in funny, pragmatic-American, backcountry ways. But the circle of family, friends, and neighbors is the very heart of it, and has become the bedrock of Gary's poetry the past twenty years—a fact the dedication of *Axe Handles* ("This book is for San Juan Ridge") makes explicitly clear. Community life sustains the knowledge of connection and responsibility, and that knowledge, as Gary once noted in *Earth House Hold,* is the very basis for any spiritual practice and discipline. Just how deeply this is ingrained in Gary's practice can be seen with reference to a statement he made in a talk titled "Poetry, Community and Climax" in 1978. "Poetry is written and read for real people," he said then,

> It should be part of the gatherings where we make decisions about what to do about uncontrolled growth, or local power plants, and who's going to be observer at the next county supervisors' meeting. A little bit of music is played by the guitarists and five-string banjo players, and some poems come down from five or six people who are really good—speaking to what is happening *here*. They shine a little ray of myth on things; memory turning to legend.

I began to understand this in the late seventies as I first joined in with the work, helping one community workday to put a porch on the temporary school. And in the days of the CB network the relations of community and culture and spiritual practice became, for me, ever more sharply defined. Those CB days are now gone, but they offer a kind of palimpsest for the ways of community life, and a look back on that neglected history is instructive.

III

In the late seventies, when Patricia and I first came up to the Ridge, most people did not have phones. Everyone depended on the mail more, it was hard to set dates on short notice or to deal with any sudden change in plans and, what was worse, there was at times a critical lack of gossip and new jokes. The solution to these problems was found on an early weekend in September of 1977 when, everyone having purchased the necessary equipment, a CB-radio communications network was established.

It was genuine decentralized, community-based enterprise in action. At specified times, and on a little-used channel, everyone would get together on the airwaves and take care of business, gossip, listen in, and learn how it was with the neighbors over the hill and across the ridges. Now that everyone has phones, a lot of us miss those days and the names we had. They were wonderful names, and the mere mention of the Blue Sky, Oak Leaf, Dr. Flash and the Firecracker, of Luz Morales, Bear Scat, Tangled Skein, Rose Hips, Popeye and Olive Oyl, the Golem, Jimson Weed, or of Snakey, Cloudberry, Little Apple, the Flying Shuttle, Old Man Rattlesnake, Plymouth Rock, the Blonde Corvette, or Hardscrabble Farm can, for those of us who remember those days, recall a small world whose names spoke with some greater precision, to who we were, or wanted to be, or to how others saw us. It was a simple kind of poetic naming that delighted in the play of the names and in the play of relationships that the names called forth.

That first September evening Tarweed (Gary's handle in those by-gone CB days) sat by an antenna-crowned ponderosa, microphone in hand, reading to the Frog Wizard, seven miles and seven hundred feet higher up the road. All who were listening in heard passages from a letter Michael McClure had just sent. Michael had hiked for some days into the recently fire-ravaged Ventana Cones Wilderness Area in Big Sur. After Gary read from Michael's letter, I remember hearing his last comment to Dale: "All these people say, 'God, there's been a fire there, let's go to other mountains.' Not Michael McClure. He goes backpacking right into the fire area, to see what's happened, what's at work. There's the poetic imagination at work."

Listening to Gary read from the letter, I thought back to news-paper accounts of the fire, and pictured Michael crossing blackened and charred paths. But as we sat by the dying embers of the cook-fire that night I realized Gary was himself at work—talking in the evening hours with his friends, sharing the news, finding in Mi-chael's trip details emblematic of a life of the mind lived fully in the tough world of earth, water, wind, and fire. He wanted Dale and the rest of us to wander across those burned-over landscapes of the Ven-tana Cones, and he was going to push us out into those territories along some wilder edge of the poetic imagination.

For Gary had found that late summer evening an eminently prac-tical tool in the populist CB radio—in the network of community relations it was fun and, he immediately grasped, profoundly useful. Not just useful for setting meeting times and such, but useful in es-tablishing a kind of daily, playful, poetic chatter that nurtured com-munity bonds and fed into the many types of poetic discourse Gary was pursuing. The relations of the CB network fostered, I see today, a deepening of the creative context of community life, a life that, as Wendell Berry recently noted, offers the necessary "continuity of attention and devotion without which the human life of the earth is impossible"—and without which the world can snap us in two like brittle twigs.

In the years that followed I often saw Gary's great delight in the radio talk. It was like a big community circle, an electronic gathering one sat at mornings and evenings, providing another dimension to the community dialogue, a dialogue that grounded Gary's poems in the present circumstance and that framed the very fundamentals of his poetic enterprise. With the CB Gary had daily access to his greater circle of friends in the community, and he would use it, in different ways, to push us out into those territories where, as he said that night to Dale, the poetic imagination was at work, "shining a little ray of myth on things; memory turning to legend."

One can see how Gary's understanding of this community dialogue found its expression in the great variety of poems that his later volumes contain. For community life generated early on a wider range of poetry, and one can say, in the simplest terms, that Gary basically began writing different kinds of poems that do different kinds of work. It was not a feature that all critics warmed to. *Turtle Island* was Gary's first collection after he built his place at Kitkitdizze, and scholars lamented his departure in this volume from the purely imagistic lyric for forms that were too overtly political or were too centered on one locality and that, in the reviewers' eyes, oversimplified complex issues in imprecise generalizations. But what one sees, especially in hindsight, is that these poems represented for Gary a series of notes in an open scale, a range of poetry that community life and involvement demanded. For when the mining interests or the developers are right there at a neighbor's property line, and she comes to you and you try to work out a response, it is important to have a poem that ends, "And here we must draw / Our line."

But it is here, too, in poems like these, that the reach of the wild enters Gary's work. For those practical calls to draw a line, to protect the backcountry and "the forest that goes to the Arctic," are calls to protect the territories of the wild that are our sources—and to note this is to see how deeply the realms of community and what Gary calls "the practice of the wild" are intertwined. Wild nature is not some *terra incognita*, and there is no neat boundary you cross over. The backcountry is right there, out your door, literally and figuratively, and a part of what Gary does is to erase neat, arbitrary boundaries that separate us from the wild. In that erasure we come to another "nature," both without and within, a nature where we are, indeed, more at home; for as Gary said once at a San Francisco seminar on nature writing in the West, "life in nature is familial, and not heroic."

IV

When Gary gives a reading on the Ridge these days it is usually at the North Columbia Cultural Center, housed in the old North Columbia Schoolhouse. The cupola and bell are still in place, but the bell is rung now only to call people back after breaks at outdoor events. Inside on one wall hangs a broadside of Gary's poem "For All." Upstairs, where Bruce Boyd has his architectural office, hang pictures of Gary's house, the first house Bruce, as a young student out of Berkeley, worked on. Poets and storytellers, both local and from as far away as Maine, regularly give readings and performances, and local artists mount their shows at the center. Across the street from the center is the Coughlan house, built in the early twenties, the prehistory of which was recorded by our friend, the storyteller/poet/songwriter Doc Dachtler, who always seems to have his eye on the telling details:

Jimmy and Francis Coughlan and their Dad were picking apples below the hill. They saw the cloud of smoke rising fast and mean. They started up the hill toward the house. Francis still had a full gunny sack of apples slung over his back. His father stopped running and said, "Francis! Now just put those apples down! You're not going to have a place to put them when you get there."

There have been a good number of readings now at the cultural center. Mary Joan Campbell, Jimmy and Francis' niece, lives in the house built after the fire, and she came over one night a few years back and listened in. Her only comment, a friend later told me, came after one of our neighbors had read from his latest work. "A grown man," Mary Joan said, "three lines, and he calls it a poem."

But Mary Joan keeps coming back to the center for events, especially when Doc reads and sings. For artists like Doc draw deeply upon the spirit of the place and community, and they bring their work to their audiences as a day-to-day part of life, a reflection and intensification of the luminous details shared by all within those small walls. The Campbells and Coughlans still tend the trees, some planted more than fifty years ago, at their home across from the old school, and the cries of their peacocks, raucously interrupting every event in the spring and summer, are as much a part of our lives as they are of those at the Coughlan homestead.

One of my most vivid memories from the cultural center is of an evening in the spring of 1986 and of a reading Gary gave to celebrate the publication of *Left Out in the Rain*. The center was packed, people were jammed into every corner, Bruce Boyd and Jeff Gold had opened their upstairs offices so that people could sit above in the loft, the doorways were full, and people were sitting on the ledges of open windows. It was Gary's hometown, the people knew all the little references, and each word here had a particular charge and resonance because the audience heard and responded strongly to the subtlest associations.

Stepping out into the night sky after the reading under the cold stars, talking with friends as we made our way to the cars and home, I looked across to the Coughlans' and the line of trees in the orchard, stopped for a moment, and clearly heard and saw again lines Gary had read that evening:

> I walked the Great Wall today,
> and went deep in the dark of a tomb.
> And then found a persimmon
> ripe to the bottom
> one of a group on a rough plaited tray
> that might have been drawn by Mu Ch'i,
> tapping its infant-soft skin
> to be sure that it's ready,
> the old man laughing,
> he sees that I like my persimmons.
> I trade him some coin
> for this wealth of fall fruit
> lined up on the roadside to sell to the tourists
> who have come to see tombs,

> and are offered as well
> the people and trees that prevail.

Coming down from the Great Wall, descending into "the dark of a tomb," returning, Gary finds in the circumstances of the market our essential nature. It is not defined by the heroic gestures enshrined in great walls or by the trip to the tomb; it is closest to us in the life of the people and the trees that we oftentimes pass by, bound for the wonders of civilization. And thinking back to that moment today, I see how in his loving attention to these scenes Gary has, these past thirty years and more, turned us ever more to this our actual world— to the reaches of the wild, to the connections that bind our worlds, to the people and the trees that prevail, and the communities that sustain them. Nine Bows, Nine Bows, dear Friend.

Kai Snyder:

HAVING A POET AS A DAD IS KIND OF LIKE HAVING A FIREMAN AS A DAD

There are two questions that people have asked Gen and me ever since we were able to talk. "Are you going to be a poet when you grow up?" and, "What's it like having a famous poet as a father?" I've always thought that these were pretty stupid questions, because I can't see the future and I've never had a dad who was anything other than a poet, and furthermore because these questions were never asked in a context in which I could really be expected to give a serious answer. It's as though I ought to be able to answer in a simple, light one-liner, like, "Oh, sure, I'm going to be a poet. Having a poet as a dad is kind of like having a fireman as a dad."

When I think of Gary, a flood of various images, memories, and strong feelings come across me.

Mom and Dad always read stories to my brother and me at bed-time. It was a real treat, one of those things from childhood that I miss the most. As I drifted into sleep, the stories ended each segment in a dream, frayed into a million different stories. The warmth, calm, and comfort from those stories is something that has stayed with me, radiating the safety of childhood like a woodstove on a snowy day.

One of my favorite books was *Ishi, The Last of His Tribe*, an amazing story about a California Indian who lived near Oroville in the early part of this century. One of the scenes from the book that has always stuck with me is that in which Ishi and his sister, making animal sounds, call a multitude of critters into an open meadow, until it is all shattered by the appearance of a bear.

After reading this book, we and some friends of ours who had also just read the book decided to go to "Ishi country," the actual area where Ishi lived. It wasn't too far from our house: a few hours by car down into the foothills. We drove down Highway 20 toward Chico, which has always been one of my favorite drives, because there's this dip in the road that sends a shiver up your spine like a roller coaster.

High school is a difficult time for just about everyone, I suppose, but it was a bit more of an ordeal for us "ridge" kids, coming in from so far out. I had to ride my motorcycle out the three miles of dirt road at six in the morning to catch the school bus going to Nevada Union High School. I remember Dad's words clearly, "If it gets below 28 degrees, I'll drive you out." I wasn't the only one, though. Brennan Ryan and John Tecklin both rode motorcycles out to catch the bus too.

One of our favorite games when I was about six (and Gen four or five) was wrestling with Gary in the tatami room. He'd crawl around on his hands and knees and growl like a bear, while we tried to tackle him. We'd get a running start and leap onto him, trying to pin him down. He'd scoop us up and send us flying back into the corners of the room.

Gary has this long stride; he takes large steps, allowing himself to walk fast without moving so fast that he tires himself out. I remember walking down from the garage to the house in the snow, trying to keep up, stepping in his footprints.

Backpacking. We drove long hours down 395, talking about drugs. I asked him all about hallucinogens, and he gave me honest answers; when I finally did them later, I was responsible. He pointed out the restaurant that he and Jack and John ate at after climbing the Matterhorn. We hiked up a trail of fallen logs and scattered granite boulders, in a light drizzle. Looked around the beautiful alpine lake, a teardrop from the heavens. Scoured basin, gnarled trees, the emptiness and space of mountaintops.

Five Lakes Basin. Grouse Ridge. Black Butte. These were our stomping grounds whenever we went backpacking in the Sierra. A close-by, accessible, medium-high portion of the Sierra crest.

Hiking through fields of mule-ears, the cows.

Collecting mushrooms, the way he notices things, sharp pointed, focused with a specific interest.

Long discussions around the kitchen table about the history of China, the difference between capitalism and communism, and so on.

He did many of the things that a father is stereotypically supposed to do in the tradition of the American wilderness: He took us camping and fishing.

I always trusted him to listen to what I had to say when it really came down to him, and I knew his judgment would be fair. Except when he loses his temper, which seems to happen a lot more often when he's writing one of those damn books, I've always thought of him as being a very sensible, reasonable, and fair person. He has a very different temperament than I do, however. He is one of those people who can get very angry quickly, and have totally forgotten about it twenty minutes later. I'm not really that way. I don't get angry too often, but when I do, it tends to smolder inside of me for quite a while longer.

He's given me a lot of respect and trust in my judgment over the years, which I truly appreciate.

It's kind of funny, looking back on how I thought of us going out to the wilderness to go backpacking with our family, when now, when I bring my friends to visit, they think that we *live* in the wilderness. (We really don't—by my standards, anyhow.)

Gen Snyder:
WHAT I HAVE LEARNED

I remember Gary always doing things with me when I was little. Whether he was fixing the chain saw or pruning fruit trees, he always explained what he was doing. I never saw the point of this, and sometimes felt I was just wasting my time. Now I realize that I learned an incredible amount just listening to what he said.

What is important to me as a son is the amount of confidence and patience he has shown my brother and me—telling us about his views of the world, but not oppressing us with that which we might otherwise reject. This approach reveals that he trusts the powers greater than himself and lives as one who has explored and respects them. What I have learned is his particular worldview—to be dedicated and open to the sounds of nature—which is something that will always be with me.

Jim Dodge:
TEN SNYDER STORIES

SOME ZEN THING

I first met Gary Snyder in 1969 at a reception following his reading at the University of Iowa. I was there with my friend Steve Shrader, who had a question for Gary: What did he think about Kerouac's portrayal of him (as Japhy Ryder) in *The Dharma Bums?*

To my ear, Gary replied by rote, making the diplomatic point that fiction's accuracy isn't necessarily served by fact. He praised Kerouac's sharp eye and intuitive rhythm, concluding (this I remember well enough to quote), "And *Dharma Bums* is a fair portrait of what we were into then."

I'm extremely shy, so was astonished to hear myself ask, "What are you into now that's any different?"

Gary turned to me, pressed his hands together under his chin, and made a strange little bow.

Bewildered, I was just mustering enough wit to inquire what the hell that bow was supposed to mean when some other folks joined us. On the principle that silence seldom betrays ignorance, I shut my mouth and listened as the conversation shifted to other concerns.

Walking home later with Steve, I asked him about Gary's weird bow, what it meant.

Steve said, "I don't really know. Traditionally, it's a gesture of respect, or gratitude, or an acknowledgement. But Snyder's a Zen Buddhist, so it might be some Zen thing."

Being your basic blue-collar jock WASP boy, I'd never been much for mystic hoo-ha of any stripe, and even though Eastern religion was getting some heavy counterculture play at the time, I assumed it was the same old salvation hustle. I'd had some bad experiences with Southern Baptists in my prepuberty youth, and was seriously committed to heathen sinning as a spiritual model, figuring redemption might be a better project for my old age, when I had more material to work with.

But I kept thinking about Gary's goofy bow, so a few weeks later I bought a couple of books on Zen Buddhism (by Alan Watts and Paul Reps, I think). I couldn't get much traction on either book, but as near as I could tell Zen monks gave the same sort of bow when their masters showed them what was what, even if what that was absolutely eluded me. He'd mistaken my question, which was meant to solicit his perceptions on cultural changes between the fifties and sixties, for some metaphysical challenge on the nature of comparative distinctions. In compensating for my shyness, perhaps I'd been too aggressive.

Since I was twenty-four years old, my musings required conclusions. I came to three, and in retrospect they weren't too far off. I'd enlightened Gary Snyder. Gary was easy. And he owed me.

THE INTEGRITY OF MOUTH AND FEET

A few months later Gary gave a reading in Arcata, California. I was working on a sheep ranch fifty miles inland, and since it was lambing season I couldn't get away to hear him. A few weeks later, on a supply run to town, I stopped to see Jeremiah Gorsline, an old friend who'd introduced me to Gary's work. Jeremiah reported that Gary had given an exceptional reading. What's more, he'd quietly slipped Jeremiah a portion of his reading fee as a donation to the community, leaving the choice of the exact recipient to Jeremiah's more knowledgeable judgment.

As I assumed then and later confirmed, Gary often donated part of his fee to the local community defense fund—more precisely, to the revolutionary elements seeking a wilder sense of both locale and community, and thus needing defense funds. Since Gary was talking the talk—revolution starts at home, less is more, enough is plenty, mutual aid, give something back—I was glad to see he walked the walk. Showed class.

A ROAD-KILL ON THE HIGHWAY OF KARMA

In late autumn of '70 I hooked up with Jeremiah Gorsline, Ponderosa Pine (still Keith Lampe then), and Mark Wilson for a ten-day trip through southern Oregon and northern California to check out the action in the back-to-the-land movement. Our loose itinerary included a visit to Kitkitdizze, the Snyder homestead on San Juan Ridge.

When we pulled in, the place was bustling with winter preparations. A dozen shiny-eyed youths were putting up berry jam in the outside cooking area. Considering the task and the cold wind, they seemed inordinately cheerful. We soon learned they were Goddard College students involved in some sort of experimental work-study/master-apprentice program. They were evidently studying the principle of hill-people hospitality: If you eat, you work. And Master Gary obviously understood that free and eager labor on a new homestead presented an ideal pedagogical situation.

Gary greeted us at the door of the family's recently completed dwelling, an architectural blend of Mandan hut and Japanese farmhouse. I'd never seen anything remotely like it in the hills before, but beyond the immediate shock of its novelty, its clean lines and subdued colors meshed flawlessly with its surrounds. Solid, functional, a general feeling of humble elegance—Gary was well situated.

When Gary and I were introduced (my companions were old acquaintances) he didn't seem to recognize me, so I mentioned that we'd met after his Iowa reading and talked briefly about *The Dharma Bums*. Gary cocked his head, shook it, and said with a smile, "I don't remember you, but I hope that doesn't make you feel less welcome. Come on in."

I admire honesty, especially when cushioned by tact, but seeing as I'd enlightened him, I'd expected another one of those bows at least, maybe even one a little deeper, and was disconcerted by his failure of recollection. Perhaps I'd wildly misconstrued the bow. Maybe it was a Zen gesture meaning, *Get outa my face and go eat shit, dharma jerk*. As we shed shoes and filed into the house, I found myself in a state of mind that Gary's presence always seems to inspire: alert.

After tea and some quick catching up, Gary put us to work. I was assigned to split stove wood. I passed the tool room/shop on my way to the woodshed. Since I was curious about what sort of man I was dealing with, and experience had convinced me that how one cares for tools and equipment offers a good rule-of-thumb read on character, I checked out the tool room. Neatly arranged, clean, spare parts boxed and labeled, the tools put away and well maintained. The tool room was a lucid expression of a person who understands that organization is freedom, that good maintenance saves time, money, and fits of cursing frustration, and that keeping your shit together takes less energy than constantly gathering it back up, assuming you can find it. My kind of guy. (A kind, fairness prompts me to note, that others often call "fastidious," "meticulous," and, if they fancy themselves Freudians, "anal-retentive"—as opposed, one presumes, to anal-expulsive.)

As we were saying our farewells the next morning, preparing to mount up in Ponderosa's van, I happened to glance up the hill just as eight men in white robes and sandals crested Gary's driveway in an oddly clustered formation and headed toward us with both a sense of solemn purpose and what appeared to be a large dead doe (pregnant, by the swell by her belly) lashed upside down by her feet to the long pole supported on their shoulders.

It was the sort of sight one prudently verifies with other observers before believing, and I was trying to think of a casual way to mention that either a herd of swamis on safari was bearing down on us with a dead doe or I was giving up drugs for good, when Gary seemed to sag beside me, moaning, "Awwww shit."

"You sure have a fascinating life," I consoled him.

"Road-kill," Gary muttered. "I've got to catch a flight this afternoon for a reading back East, and every time I'm running late they show up with a road-kill. They think I'm some sort of blood-thirsty troll always sharpening his knife for slaughter." Hunching his shoulders and lolling his tongue, Gary wildly pantomimed stroking a blade on a whetstone. Looked just like a blood-thirsty troll.

As they continued their solemn advance, Gary explained they were neighbors from the nearby Ananda commune, which was strictly vegetarian, and since Gary was a notorious omnivore, they brought him all the local road-kills. I gathered from his tone that they did so with that in-your-face delight of the righteous. Eat this, infidel.

Gary graciously accepted the dead doe and thanked them for their thoughtfulness, but his gratitude, by tone and gesture, seemed more ceremonial than heartfelt. I was wondering why they hadn't just rolled her over the embankment rather than tote her down to Gary; I'd lived in the hills long enough to figure out Nature wastes nothing—grub is grub, and from microbe to human there are lots of hungry critters on the planet. Lugging it to Gary meant he'd have to do the work of their mindfulness. Gary was running late already and the Goddard folks were off picking more berries, so I volunteered to gut and skin the doe. Seemed a fair way to reciprocate his hospitality, and I'd been dressing-out deer and other mammals since I was twelve years old.

Gary gave me a semi-bow and said, "I appreciate the offer, Jim, but I don't want to hold you guys up."

"Only take twenty minutes," I said.

Everyone looked dubious.

With a confidence that I hoped I wasn't mistaking for vanity—a confusion to which I'm particularly susceptible—I said, "Just point me to the skinnin' tree."

"Have at it," Gary said.

The Ananda communards accompanied me to the skinning tree, the doe still slung on the pole in that Great-White-Hunter-on-safari style. They unlashed her stiff legs and gathered around ceremoniously as I opened my pocketknife and knelt to gut her. I had a moment of apprehension over her swollen belly and what I assumed would be the fetus inside. I was struck by the realization that a doe wouldn't be pregnant in October a moment before I was struck full-face by the vent of gas from her abdomen as I inserted the knife blade. Holding my breath (if gagging can be considered a voluntary activity) I shifted my position slightly and pressed my knee against her paunch, aiming the stream of death-bloat gas at the Ananda folks in a generous effort to share the olfactory dimension of the ritual conversion of death into dinner. They didn't crowd closer.

Once past the gas, the rest went quickly—maybe not twenty minutes to the tock, but close enough for government workers and us Okies.

When I was washing the blood off my hands at an outside faucet, Gary came over and thanked me for the help. But there was a gleeful twinkle in his eyes that wasn't connected with gratitude. Sensing I'd noticed, Gary explained, "My friend Zac killed a buck last weekend—took him most of the afternoon to skin it out. You were a whole lot faster. I can't wait to give him a bad time."

"Naw, don't do that. Wouldn't want to think doing good would make somebody else look bad. Besides, I've had tons of practice."

"No," Gary grinned hugely, "I'm really going to give him some shit."

And I remember thinking, *Now here's a man who enjoys his friends.*

KNOW THE PLANTS!

Gary and Masa were bringing Gen, their younger son, to the Cazadero Music Camp and then coming on out for their first visit to our place, an isolated homestead on a ridge above the South Fork of the Gualala. I was delighted by the prospect (not only Gary's good company, but Masa's, whom I didn't know as well but liked immensely), yet my anticipation was tainted by a certain dread. For five years I'd been hearing Gary claim and constantly reiterate, lecture, and hector, that the most crucial step toward understanding where you live is a solid knowledge of the local plants and plant community. While I absolutely agreed, loudly and in public, I'd never quite gotten around to mentioning that I personally didn't know diddly-shit about the flora where I lived. (Well, I did know half the trees, two edible mushrooms, and a handful of wildflowers. In my feeble defense, I submit there is a distinction between "knowing" and "identifying." I felt I *knew* the plants beyond the superficial distinctions of category and name. Further, my personal notion of hell is a roomful of taxonomists on speed.)

I'd hiked around other places with Gary enough to know that he was an inveterate botanizer, always stopping to fondle foliage and peer into flowers. He'd even mentioned that he was looking forward to the visit as an opportunity to learn more about west-slope Coast Range ecology. As sure as self-serving deceit is eventually exposed, I knew the first thing he'd want to do was go on a nature walk, and he'd expect me to identify unfamiliar species.

I had three hopes to avoid the shriveling admission of deceit or, should I choose to bluff, the pathos of desperate pretense. My three hopes were Vicky Stockley, Leonard Charles, and Lynn Milliman, the other founders of Root Hog Ranch, true friends all, who'd made it a point from the beginning to learn the plants—and, even better, had. At least one of them, I prayed, would go along on forays into the flora.

Gary and Masa arrived just before dinner, and by the time our *après chow* conversation yielded to the exigencies of dishwashing and other evening chores, there was barely a half-hour of daylight left. Gary and Masa wanted to see how our coop was set up, so they accompanied me out to secure the chickens against coyote cunning and the brilliant persistence of 'coons.

The chickens were already roosted, so it only took a few seconds to shut and latch the door. Gary, I noticed, was checking the lay of the land, looking restless. Sure enough: "This place isn't what I expected. We'll have to take a good, long walk in the morning. Maybe pack a lunch. But since we've still got some light, let's see your studio."

We were walking back to the ranch house when Gary suddenly stopped and peered heavenward. We were in a small grove of trees, but I wishfully assumed he was looking at a bird.

"What caught your eye?" I said.

Gary looked perplexed. "I've never seen a bay laurel like this."

I followed his gaze, then gladly offered an explanation: "No wonder, Snyder, you dumb shit—that's a tan oak."

Gary's peer intensified. "Why, so it is."

I wagged my finger at him, admonishing, "Know the plants."

"Wise advice," Gary muttered.

It was the perfect opportunity to mention, consolingly, that I, too, was still learning the plants, and thus prey to similar errors. I boldly scorned the opportunity, choosing instead to assume a haughty air, just the right balance of disdain and disappointment. I was testing my theory that if one truly embraces folly, it inspires the gods' compassion. Tests have proven inconclusive, but I can say with certainty that sometimes the theory seems true.

The next morning, for example, Vicky decided to take the day off so she could join us on our walk, a decision encouraged by my cash-up-front reimbursement for lost wages. Just because a fool has to trust the gods doesn't mean he shouldn't cover his ass. And though I've presented it here as a sleazy act of self-aggrandizing deceit, the truth is I did it for Gary.

I know Gary would understand. As he's told me more than once, "Jim, your biggest problem is that you're a nice guy."

HELP ON THE WAY

Gary, as he makes abundantly clear in his work, reveres high-quality information. Though the old alchemists would cringe at the crudity of the following description, the basic process of making sense is the transformation of information into knowledge, the conversion of knowledge into understanding, and the refinement of understanding into wisdom. Therefore, accurate information is fundamental: no roots, no flower. It seems tediously apparent, even insulting, to say Gary Snyder has a firm grasp of the obvious, but I think it is the source of his powers. Naturally, I inquired.

"You're always singing paeans to quality info—where do you find it?"

He said, "You mean beyond the direct perception of your own five senses and gut, breath, and brain, tempered by experience and honed by scholarship?"

"Yeah."

"Good teachers and smart friends."

And so one summer day in the early eighties, having provisionally decided (provisional decisions being a specialty of the house) that I needed a traditional practice to focus and perhaps clarify some spiritual impulses that were besetting me, I gave Gary a call. I was specifically interested in Taoist meditation practices and, as I explained to Gary, "I mean the raw original—you know, nothing later than the *Tao Te Ching,* Lao-tzu style; before temples and priests."

"Well," Gary said, using that thoughtful, impeccably considered tone he reserves for questions demanding judicious scholarship, "I'm not exactly sure. I can give you *my* sense of it, but I can't insure its accuracy."

"Whatever you got."

"Well, from what I understand, they just sort of sat down somewhere—a rock on a hillside, under a tree in a meadow—and did some thinking."

I said, "No torturing postures on cold floors before sun-up with special breathing and trying to empty the mind and stuff? Just plunk your ass down and think it over?"

"As far as I know, yup, that's basically it."

Sounded good to me, so I announced, "Gary, I'm converting to Taoism."

"Jim," Gary said with great solemnity, "I'm not surprised."

And we both started laughing like loons. Personally, I was laughing because one of the sweetest joys of friendship is being understood. I can't speak for Gary's glee, but I assumed it was his perverse delight in knowing that the easy way is hard enough.

CURE BY IMMERSION AND MODEL

In 1983, after many years devoted to poetry, I tried my hand at fiction. Having no idea what I was doing, the result was a seventy-page work called *Fup*—far too long to be considered a short story, yet too short to qualify as a novella. I called it a story, and assumed its unusual length would discourage publication. But Michael Helm, the publisher and entire staff of City Miner Books, in Berkeley, felt like gambling. The first printing was twelve hundred or so. A few good reviews led quickly to a larger second printing and, thanks to Michael's acumen and willingness to court bankruptcy, *Fup* began to appear on a few regional best-seller lists. Though I didn't know it, I was about to receive my fifteen minutes of Warholian fame.

Looking back, I think Gary anticipated the glut of attention about to descend. He knew that readings and public appearances were a struggle for me, not only because the podium had better stage presence (and perhaps more to say), but also because I felt like a shrinking rawhide knot of neurotic anxiety beginning a month before a scheduled appearance, and toxic scum on the Slough of Despond for two months afterward. At any rate, without so much as a flicker of hidden purpose, Gary called one day and asked if I'd like to accompany him the following week on a brief Bay Area promotional tour for *Axe Handles,* which North Point Press had just released. Do a couple of intimate little readings, a few bookstore appearances, talk to people . . . all real low-key, no hassle, no stress.

I hesitated. My nervous system was already starting to twist at the thought of public performance; I feared that two in the same week might kill me outright. Or just as bad, Gary would have to suffer a traveling companion whose unraveled babble would only be relieved by bouts of catatonia. However, three considerations tipped the balance toward acceptance. The heaviest was my ego, already beginning to bloat with *Fup*'s modest success; I could decline the invitation, but not the honor. Nor could I refuse the intricate kindness informing the offer. Gary knew that Michael, like most small publishers, didn't have the bucks for promotional tours, and *Fup* was at a point where a nudge of exposure might kick it loose. To refuse would insult Gary's thoughtfulness, betray Michael, and deny my ego a wallow in honey. "Sure," I told Gary, "let's do it. But I want you to understand that I'm already terrified."

"Well," Gary said, "be terrified. I'll meet you Sunday night at Lee Swenson's place in Berkeley."

We left Lee's early Monday morning and returned four days, five readings, a dozen bookstores, and assorted interviews later. The smallest audience for the intimate public readings was two hundred, and since I was an unadvertised addition to the program, my ego couldn't honestly indulge its usual self-ravishings. Further, one of the readings collected cash admission at the door, of which Gary gave me a generous chunk. In fact, it was more money in one night than I'd made *total* in twenty years of writing poems—enough to cover the trip's expenses with plenty left for play. (I'd always adhered to Jack Spicer's injunction to "hold on as long as you can before you sell out." There's nothing like two decades of austerity to sweeten corruption.)

Given Gary's spectacular notion of intimacy, I wasn't surprised that his sense of "no stress" was my idea of "frenzy." We signed books, socialized, read, drove, did it again. When the tour ended, Gary was coming down with a cold and I was still rising on a new-found, solid, magically real rush of self-confidence, so high—as my brother puts it—that I could hunt ducks with a rake, my dread-o-rama stage terror cured for good.

Magic sometimes eludes explanation by taking sanctuary in the obvious. The rapid succession of public appearances clearly didn't allow me the voluptuous leisure necessary to ripen morbidity. Up to your ass in alligators before you realize you're in the swamp.

No doubt either that the acknowledgment of my work, implied in Gary's invitation, bolstered my confidence. Recognition is relaxing, especially from someone whose work you admire.

But I think what really turned the trick was a direct-force vibe transfer of confident professionalism accomplished through sheer proximity to the power of Gary's model. The pattern of transmission, however, is always complex. To cite Gary's citation of Lu Ji's Preface to *Wên Fu* in the title poem of *Axe Handles,* "In making the model of an axe by cutting wood with an axe, the model is indeed near at hand." And if you're not making another axe handle, you can always use the axe in hand to cut through bullshit or pound some sense into a fool's head.

As I've told him many times, Gary's big problem is he's a natural teacher.

MANIFOLD KNOWLEDGE AND ITS
FOUR-SPEED TRANSMISSION

I'd gone over to Nevada City to appear with Gary, Doc Dachtler, and Greg Keeler at a benefit to help fund the local battle against a grubby gold-mining proposal. The next day there was a community potluck at Tony Mociun's place and a bunch of us were sitting around the table discussing the omnipresent and ever-burning rural question of the local school and, more generally, the education of our young.

As Gary's work makes clear, in his judgment human social progress ended in the Neolithic, and since then civilization has been pretty much coterminous with the degradation of enlightened values and, inextricably, the planet. He's such a wild-assed conservative that he sounds radical (and is, in the sense that "radical" denotes "root"), so no one was surprised when he opined, with a trace of impatience, "I still think the best education is simply kids hanging out and working with adults—they learn a lot that way."

His son Gen was sitting beside him and immediately said, in that tone of exasperated scorn endemic to sixteen-year-olds dealing with doltish elders, "Yeah, but you never tell us the stuff we really want to know."

Gary's head swiveled. "Such as?" he challenged.

Gen was prepared. "Such as how do you figure sixteen-point-nine percent APR financing on a new Camaro?"

While I and everyone else roared into laughter, Gary sagged till his head touched the table. And then he beat his head on the table, weeping. Then laughed. Then pounded his head on the table some more.

THE PRACTICE OF POETRY

In October '86, Gary and I, under the aegis of the Vermont Arts Council, made a week-long tour of the state, appearing in a different city each day for an afternoon workshop and an evening reading. We'd specifically requested the October date to afford ourselves the

sensual indulgence of Vermont's autumnal foliage, which coopera-
ted gloriously. To make the trip even better, Geof Hewitt—an old
friend and fine poet—served as the Arts Council's liaison, road show
impresario and, happily, our personal guide and chauffeur.

I had so much solid fun and sweet high-times on the Vermont tour
that when my work is going shitty, when it seems a pointless exercise
in dumb endurance and an unnecessary stain of silence, I remember
Vermont and take heart. Especially driving between gigs through
that dazzling landscape, three guys who enjoy conversation sound-
ing each other's opinions, speculating, commiserating, gossiping,
and generally shooting the shit.

The moment I recall most vividly was sparked by Gary's comments
on the practice of poetry, delivered in the mock professorial voice he
adopts for serious play, and to the point that young American poets
had a scanty knowledge of prosody, a contempt for scholarship, a
constricted appreciation of their own traditions and virtually none
for others, and so on. I'd heard it before and generally agreed. Geof
wanted an example.

Gary was delighted to provide one. "The limerick, for instance.
How can you call yourself an English language poet if you can't
write a decent limerick? Poesy should soar—yes; take mad lyrical
plunges at the meaning of it all—of course; present glorious seizures
of the self o'er leaped—indubitably; make private woes public issues
in clear, passionate language—by all means. But what of poesy's
playful dimensions? Where's Eliot's limerick? Pound's? Williams'?"

"Where's yours?" I'm a good straight man.

Gary replied archly, "I have nothing worthy as yet. However, I
haven't given up, either. And I *am* familiar with the canon."

So was Geof. Me, a little. And for thirty miles of flame-leaved
countryside, in trimeter and dimeter anapests, we took turns paying
bawdy homage to the limerick and its more memorable characters—
the young man from Nantucket; the elastic miss of Tangiers; the in-
ventive Doctor Zuck—until our sides ached with perfect practice.

GIANT ZAZEN

Come to think of it, the Vermont jaunt wasn't completely without
annoyance, at least for me. The Giants were playing the Cards in the

League Championship Series at the time, and I'd missed a few games in the press of professional obligations. I mentioned my dismay to Gary after we returned to Berkeley. "What a shame," he said, utterly without sympathy. Coldly, in fact. And the look he gave me—as if I'd just announced that I fervently supported damming every wild river in the country as soon as the last old-growth forest was clear-cut.

I was hurt and confused. We were just pulling into the motel parking lot after a late dinner with Jack and Vicki Shoemaker, still floating on the sweet conviviality of the evening—I didn't understand what was happening. And then I got it: In the years I'd known Gary, I could not remember a single instance of him mentioning sports. Real sports, anyway, like football and baseball; not stuff like kayaking or rock climbing. *Ergo* and *voilà,* Gary didn't like sports. Gary Snyder did not like baseball.

"Gary, you ever been to a Major League ball game?"

"No," he said—rather primly, I thought.

I consider Gary a friend. I take the obligations of friendship seriously. "Gary, next year I'm going to take you to a Giants game. My treat all the way."

"No thanks. But I appreciate the invitation."

I tried to reason with him. "I'm appalled. You are an American male, an anthropologist with pretensions to understanding this culture, a man of eclectic tastes who values diversity and therefore abhors snobbery in all its prejudicial manifestations, a man who appreciates excellence, simple pleasures, ritual and ceremony, grace under pressure. Didn't I just hear you in one of the Vermont workshops cite the creative necessity of 'mind open to moment'? Sweet Jesus, Gary, *how* can you *call yourself* an American poet if you've never been to a big-league game?"

Gary pursed his lips and thought about it, which meant I was in trouble. He's a good thinker.

After about ten seconds, he smiled. "Okay, I'll go to a ball game with you. *But,* to complete this little exchange of widened horizons, *you* have to come over to Ring of Bone Zendo and attend a *sesshin.*"

My jaw dropped. "You're kidding? A Giants game in trade for . . . What is it? three days? a week? of getting up hours before dawn and sitting cross-legged in a freezing room meditating or not meditating or some damn thing, and go see a roshi who whacks you with a stick or bites your ankle if you don't get one of those twisty Zen riddles . . ."

"*Koans*," Gary interrupted, ever the stickler for precision.

I returned to my point. "A *sesshin* for a ball game is not a fair exchange. Punishment is not fun."

"Anything as difficult and exhausting as a baseball game is fairly matched by a *sesshin*. Both are arduous, yet offer a unique opportunity to glimpse our true natures."

I changed my angle of attack. "Okay, you're on—with this provision: You can chant sutras at the ballpark; I can drink beer and eat hot dogs while I'm emptying my mind."

"That would contaminate the spirit of both," Gary said firmly.

And there it stood. And stands.

Like my Uncle Willie always said, "Takes a helluva dog to whip a 'coon."

ARTICLE OF FAITH

The last time I talked to Gary on the phone he mentioned some upcoming event at the zendo. I couldn't resist asking, "Are you still sitting on your ass trying to get totally and perfectly enlightened?"

"Yes," Gary said. Then, lowering his voice, he confided, "But you know, Jim, I've been doing it so long now that when I sit I can fall asleep almost instantly, and no one can tell."

It pleased me to hear that. Awakening cannot be far behind.

—*Summer & Autumn '89*

Peter Coyote:

GARY SNYDER AND
THE REAL WORK

There is an early photo of Gary from his student days in Berkeley in which he is sitting, Japanese-style, wearing a simple Japanese kimono. He is cradling a bowl of tea and staring at the camera in a reprimanding manner, as if he had been disturbed by the photographer. His face is boyish, tough and spare; finely featured with a sharp nose and high cheekbones. His eyes appear almost Asian, slightly hooded and piercing, but also sweet and soft. When I first encountered this photo in a book about the Beats, and before we had even met, I was impressed that he had *allowed himself to be photographed at home* while drinking tea from a small bowl, dressed in robes, with no evident suggestion whatsoever of being prepared for the photographer. Today, it might appear "a bit much" to wear Japanese clothing and live on a tatami-mat floor while pursuing Asian studies at a university, but at the time, I perceived his apparent total immersion in his subject as a form of exemplary commitment. I became immediately curious about this person who could meditate, read and write Chinese and Japanese, and still carouse with his Beat contemporaries. It occurred to me that perhaps they appreciated this breadth in him also. Jack Kerouac dubbed him Japhy Ryder in his novel *The Dharma Bums*. The dharma bums referred to by the title were a small band of friends who scorned socially ordained goals and wealth (being bums) to seek personally meaningful experience and knowledge (dharma), which led them to Zen, Nature, and various yogic traditions. Japhy, a mountain-climbing, logger-poet, student of Zen, was explicitly drawn from Gary's life. This character introduced American readers to the style and feel of a Beat ideal: a new kind of contemporary life that was spontaneous and authentic.

I had read *The Dharma Bums* as an adolescent, just as I was reaching the limits of the bourgeois suburban possibilities into which I had been born. As one of the new Beat crowd who appeared to be living a more autonomous and exciting life than my own, Gary was a seductive figure.

By 1968, however, I had traveled a great distance, physically and psychically, from those suburban possibilities. I was living on an old ranch near Olema, California, quite sure that I and my extended family known as the Diggers had transcended our Beat mentors in hipness, integrity, and appropriateness to our time.

My carousing and peripatetic roommate at that time was Lew Welch, an intimate of Snyder's and a poet with an authentic American-Zen tone to his work. In my own mind, I construed part of Lew's friendship as an acknowledgement of our hipness and a legitimization of the Diggers as rightful heirs to the title of spokespeople for our decade. It seemed only appropriate for Gary and I to meet, and Lew was happy to arrange the occasion.

Like myself, Lew was fascinated with Snyder-lore. Sitting cross-legged, holding a jug of Mondavi red wine, grinning loosely, the softness of his moist eyes contrasting with his sharp cheekbones and angular Irish face, he would spin out story after story about Gary, in a way which was sometimes incredulous, sometimes awestruck, and at other times tinged with a note of competitiveness. It was easy to see that Gary exerted a powerful hold on this singularly intelligent and talented poet, but it was not until I actually met Gary himself, and some time afterward, that I understood the real nature of that pull.

It's embarrassing today to recollect my first thoughts upon seeing Gary's pristine Volkswagen camper bump its way over the rutted road to our ranch house. "How could Gary Snyder be driving a *new* camper?" I thought. It was so bourgeois!

The camper came to a stop under the willow tree by the galvanized watering trough. Lew hopped out with his customary manic enthusiasm and I ambled over. Salutations were exchanged. Gary threw open the back door and invited me inside. Before I had climbed on board, he had already opened some peanut butter and a box of crackers and was in the process of just the kind of introduction that I had so often imagined.

Gary was wearing an old straw hat that shaded his eyes, and I remember him cocking his head to one side to look at me. His look was so clearly appraising, so without social camouflage, as to be startling. (The look might have had something to do with the fact that under Oshkosh overalls, I was stark naked, and I wore long hair that I could sit on, six tiny gold earrings with fox toe-bones tied to them, and a tiny Fu Manchu moustache cum goatee. Anyone would have been inclined to stare, but most people would have pretended not to.)

The rest of the visit was uneventful. We ate crackers and talked. Gary was not overweening, was full of interesting raps, and was obviously, in the parlance of the time, "together." His body was muscular and lithe. His eyes crinkled pleasantly when he smiled. His voice was cultivated and his speech very precise.

I was a little disappointed by this initial encounter. I had neither been congratulated for having carried the banner of sixties liberation onto new battlefields, been acknowledged as a peer, or even been questioned about my life-style and politics. All he had done was look me over as if asking himself, "What's this guy about?" He did not find it necessary to create a philosophical or political bond. In fact, he did not seem to find it necessary to define himself in relationship to me at all. I had shared some peanut butter and crackers and a pleasant time with him and that was that. After he had driven off, little remained in my memory except his straightforward visual estimation. His penetrating initial look had made me squirm mentally and I did not know why.

As I replayed the visit afterward in my memory, trying to analyze why I had felt so checked and inarticulate, subtle attitudes of competition, jealousy, curiosity, and remorse colored the event, making me confused about what had actually occurred. I can't remember now how this welter of feelings gradually metamorphosed into a friendship, but I know that the process began the first time I visited Gary's house, and that the house itself played a major role in that transformation.

In 1971, the Diggers were planning a truck-caravan to visit and link disparate communities and to organize trade routes so that people like ourselves could travel the seemingly hostile landscape without money and satisfy their needs by trading goods and services in an alternate economy we would invent. Peter Berg and I went north to speak to Gary about our plan and to seek his support.

Today I don't remember that first drive to Gary's house very well. I do know it took four hours to drive from San Francisco to where Gary lived, but my memories of this trip begin in the Sierra foothills, where his house is located. The last hour of our journey was made over progressively smaller and dimmer roads, until finally we were following a set of tracks through the woods to its end under a large oak in a small clearing used to park vehicles. The walk to the house was shaded by pines, oaks, and madrones, and the air smelled of witch hazel from the kitkitdizze bushes for which the place had been named. Except for the shushing leaves underfoot, there was total quiet. By the time I reached the clearing, the nervous acceleration of the auto trip and provocative conversations with Berg had evaporated. Perhaps it was this interlude of walking between the car and the house that enabled me to really "see" Gary's house.

From the hill just above the clearing, the house radiated a sense of unmistakable, timeless gravity. The thick, orange clay roof tiles were supported by heavy, hand-hewn lintels and posts. Between these, adobe walls or small-paned windows lightened the feeling of the house's massive construction. The house gave the impression of being fastened in place, as if the trees supporting it had not been cut down, but simply peeled and pressed into service where they stood, with their roots still gripping the soil. It seemed then, and still seems today, to be a house that is *exactly* right: no bigger or smaller than necessary, practical and beautiful. Built onto the end of the house, protecting the door and open to the hill at the front, was a small cubicle with a sink and a place to store boots and raingear. The main entrance was this door to the kitchen, exactly wide enough to admit a wheelbarrow-load of wood.

Beside the house was a narrow rectangular workshop attached to a wood-fired sauna, built in simple board-and-batten style. A tall, red, hand-cranked water pump stood beside it on which each guest was tithed one hundred strokes, that being the energy required to send a daily ration of water uphill to the cistern from which it could return to the house by gravity as needed.

The more I observed this house—built by a crew of friends and Zen students, many of whom later settled in the area—the more I saw how form and function combined in an absolutely perfect way. It was a simple but eloquent statement of Gary's philosophy of life, expressed without an excess syllable.

The flagstone kitchen was cool and dimly lit and contained a large wood-fired range, glass-fronted cabinet with black Japanese dishes and cups, and well-crafted oak table with benches, all of which seemed poised in their tasks. Adjacent and open to the kitchen was a raised, wood-floored living room, walled in on three sides to form a small rectangle. The spaces between these concentric inner and outer structures were arranged as a pantry, a children's room, a library, and a master bedroom.

In the center of the living room was an octagonal open fire pit rimmed with stone. Above the pit, all the ends of the log rafters formed an impressive vault under a small windowed cupola that completed the roof and served as a vent for the fire. The logs were blackened by pitch and felt ancient. The room smelled of smoke, incense, and oiled wood. Hanging over the fire pit, a log was cradled by two thick ropes hanging from the beams above. Anchored to that log was an adjustable iron device of obvious Japanese origin, which suspended a large cast-iron water kettle over the flames. These elements—stone, wood, iron, and fire—seemed utterly primal to me, descending as they did from any number of ancient cultures. And yet, somehow, they were not inharmonious with the modern ghetto-blaster sound system, Winchester rifle, banjo, Japanese pillows, Buddhist altar, and bottle of Jack Daniels. I was amazed to learn that the whole space totaled no more than nine hundred square feet. A house like this was the product of so much thoughtful, patient work that my own idle wandering through it felt frivolous.

My reaction to the house forced me to reevaluate Gary, who at the moment of our arrival was stark naked, wearing plastic thongs and throwing a boomerang with his children. His wife was cooking lunch over an outside fire pit beside a small, pole-framed ramada with a bamboo mat roof that sheltered some crude counters and an old refrigerator. Moving the family outside in the warm weather, they used this as a kitchen. Every time I asked myself what *he* was about, the answer appeared self-evident to me. He was *about* his house: part Japanese farmhouse, part log cabin, part Indian longhouse; highly civilized, elegant, refined, and comfortable, and obviously efficient. Its design and construction had been reflected upon over years of meditations in wintry Japanese monasteries, rolled around in Gary's mind until each detail had rubbed every other into a smooth, seamless fit. I liked being there. There was no city filth, no heavy revolutionary consciousness, no place into which I could insert ideological criticism or a wedge of radical chic. Everyone was stark naked, having a good time. Their skin was sun-browned and squeaky clean; hair, eyes, teeth, bright and shiny—quite a contrast to my own grimy, hepatic pallor. The house and grounds were shipshape. Gary laughed easily, and he and Masa, his wife, teased each other lovingly.

This impressed me as a very nice way to live, and from that time on, my glorious Digger vision of free food, expanding networks of communes, national trade routes, and depots of junkyards to service our fleets of pre-1950 vehicles lost some of its luster. It made me reflect also on how my own house, an abandoned cow shed covered with tar paper and old rugs, had no water or conveniences, and represented, whether I liked it or not, *my* vision of "the timeless present."

The facts and implications of Gary's house were an epiphany for me that demanded a reexamination of some of my personal beliefs and premises. In the body of this house, craft, family, community, and a host of attendant values were expressed without cant or didacticism, calmly attesting to the silent power of mindfulness, respect for particulars, and unremitting effort. Only a fool could ignore a dialogue with benefactors like those, and though I may have *been* a fool, I decided then and there that I was not going to *remain* one forever.

Gary loves to work. He loves tools and he loves taking care of tools. (For each tool he owns, he also owns one or several tools for taking care of that tool.) He would profess that his collection is simply practical, but he can barely contain his delight when he discovers, for instance, some ingenious attachment to power a Sony Walkman from an automobile cigarette lighter, or when he can demonstrate a CB radio tricked out with a special ridge-only wavelength so that neighbors might communicate without telephones. He has Finnish knives, Japanese hatchets, and German chain saws in several sizes, with tools to set the pitch and sharpness of the blades. He has a host of miniaturized technology as well: a tiny Casio calculator-alarm-clock-calendar and a slim Olympus dictating and transcribing machine. Hanging from assorted hooks and rafters are well-worn ice axes and multicolored mountain climbers' rope, saddles and skis, ornate brass kerosene lamps, backpacks, scales to weigh backpacks, and even containers to fit inside the backpacks to organize their contents. Gary's ex-wife Joanne Kyger once laughed to me about the amount of stuff that Gary had to store so that he could go off to Japan and live simply.

I found Gary's penchant for collecting difficult to deal with at first. The Diggers were decidedly minimalist when it came to "stuff," adhering to a vaguely Calvinistic bent that eschewed material comforts for more austere revolutionary and visionary values. Gary was unfazed by such concerns. He likes his stuff, calls it all "tools" or "gear," uses it lovingly and unsentimentally, always selecting for applicability and excellence. In fact, shortly after we met, while I was busy pontificating about some fine point of Digger philosophy, he challenged me with the following riddle:

> The first followers of Gautama Buddha said, "The problem is desires. Turn them off." They lived in caves as monks, with minimal possessions. About five hundred years after that, followers said, "No, that's not the problem, turn 'em on." And they went out into the world, married, became arrow makers and musicians, raised children. Why did they turn 'em off? Why did they turn 'em on?

It was easy to see which side of that riddle Gary had chosen. Even before I perceived an answer, I could see that he acted out his chosen role vigorously and that his gear was indeed an integral part of his life inasmuch as it multiplied the amount of work that he could accomplish. Each time I arrived, I discovered that something had been newly built: a barn, a solar-heated laundry, a twelve-volt electrical system, a deer fence surrounding some newly planted fruit trees with painted trunks, a black plastic irrigation system.

I began to understand that there was, in fact, a common underpinning supporting all these undertakings. It was obvious that Gary did things for the sake of doing them, but also that the act of doing them was informed by some quite enigmatic quality. It is this other quality that I have come to consider Gary's *real* work, and it strikes me anew each time we meet how consistently and with what detachment and good humor he evinces it.

The "it," or *the real work*, is his ability to sensitize the contemporary American psyche to more appreciative, less exploitative social and economic possibilities than are currently widely available within the strictures of Western worldviews and values. His point, as I understand it, is to nurture ways of life that are more consciously interdependent with other species and with ancient human traditions, whose efficacy in stabilizing sanity and joy, in restraining rapacious human excesses, is made evident by the study of many indigenous and preliterate people today. Such values reside within the realm of what Gary refers to as "the Great Underground"—the shamanistic, yogic, poetic wisdom tradition extant since the Paleolithic, forty thousand years ago. This perspective, which treats Mother Nature and human nature, wilderness and wilderness-of-mind (imagination) with the same respect, has been submerged but never vanquished by the "high civilizations" that have evolved from it. Aboriginal peoples, Buddhists, Hindus, Hippies, Yogins, mystical Christians, healers, and artists of all sorts are the manifestation of this still vital lineage. Gary's work, it seems to me, is nothing less than the tangible manifestation of viable cultural and economic possibilities informed by this tradition. This is the center around which the disparate expressions of his personality gravitate—the artist, homemaker, community member, and Buddhist.

The community religion around Gary's homestead is Zen Buddhism. Until this community gained Aitken Roshi and his dharma-heir Nelson Foster as their teachers, Gary functioned as a lay priest to initiate and nurture formal practice as well as the building of a nicely crafted community meditation hall. I am not suggesting that a discipline as ancient and deep as Zen practice centers around Gary, but it is fair to say that it might not have rooted in that stony ground without his persistent attention. Because of this attention, a community is actively inventing and discovering American Zen, and American Zen is transforming what was once an aggregate of singular rural families into a community. This is Gary's work.

Gary once suggested to me that if I served with him in Governor Jerry Brown's administration as an Arts Council member, it might be "a good opportunity to define the state." Since I understood this as an invitation to help design and administrate a governmental apparatus that might reflect values that we held in common, I could not refuse. That casual suggestion changed my life by affording me the opportunity to observe the "work" in the Byzantine political realm of Sacramento. This was an environment that Gary explored the same way he explored a new ridge while carrying a heavy pack on his back and carefully determining where to put the next foot. His method sometimes appeared stodgy (as did his mountain walk when I first saw the way he splayed his feet outward in a manner that made you expect a "splat" sound when they landed)—but his pace never faltered and he did not stumble. Despite the fact that he rarely chose the obvious paths of political expediency, he never created antipathy or enemies.

Our job was to serve the larger community of the state, and honoring that charge required probing public policy and often altering policies that had served a few quite well at the expense of the larger community. These types of judgment calls always draw hostile fire, which Gary persistently handled with unshakeable aplomb. He *enjoyed* being put on the spot and challenged in public meetings; he loved uncoiling his mind into a large inclusive loop and then expressing elegant formulations and solutions to meet these challenges. His methods evoked the design of his house: Things work when they are unpretentious, well crafted, authentic, and useful.

The superficial agenda hardly seemed to matter. The deeper agenda, "the real work," was the constant way he addressed each person, giving them unspoken assurance that he and they were, after all, on the same side (though I am sure that Gary's understanding of "sides," which really means "everything this side of Death," certainly transcended the narrow partisanship of most politicians).

It was sometimes amusing to watch Gary, with a red bandana around his forehead, his long braid tied up Navaho-style, wearing the Amish mail-order suit of which he was uncommonly proud, or his natty fishing vest with a hand-embroidered turtle on the breast, which represented Turtle Island—the reimagining of America rechristened with its ancient Native American name. He would speak from the dais, under the state flag, and cheerfully lecture the assorted fat cats representing the institutions of Western European high arts—opera, symphony, and ballet—explaining to them why it was important to make sure that scarce dollars served Asian, Latin, Native Californian, Micronesian, rural white, and black culture, as well as their own. He would disarm radical activists seeking to appropriate the monies dedicated to those same Western European high art forms, with minitreatises on excellence as a form of radical activity and on the necessity of cultural diversity. Restive as any partisans might be with his premises and conclusions, the explanations were always so interesting, informative, and articulate that I know of no one who ever took exception to the manner in which Gary considered their cause.

I perceived this quality as a form of subtle and beneficent magic that almost invariably defused animosity and created an atmosphere in which ideas could be exchanged calmly. The list of opponents we on the Council won over by following his example was impressive. Adhering to three basic principles—no lies, admit every error, and tell the truth—the Council slowly but surely won the respect of most state legislators.

After I had succeeded Gary as chairman, near the end of my term, I remember attending a final budget subcommittee hearing at which, just as I took my seat to testify, all the legislators present donned hippie headbands as a good-humored gesture of good-bye. The gesture was not, I felt, intended for me alone, but saluted the Council's consistently high standards of deliberation, lack of defensiveness, and respect for the political process. When it serves these ends, the political process becomes an extension of "the work," and the Council's success at this was Gary's invisible heritage, passed *through* him (I think he would say), as temporary spokesman for Great Underground insights and traditions, to the rest of us.

I've discussed the householder, the Buddhist, and the community member, but not the artist, and it is this aspect of Gary that, being simultaneously his first and last calling, completes the circle of his personality. For it is through his art that most people have come to know Gary's worldview and ideas; it is through his art that he has become a public figure. It is last for me, however, because it is also the most private and intensely personal side of Gary. But, in Gary's case, "personal" does not mean hidden.

There is a translucent quality to Gary's work that reminds me of an open pipe through which various qualities may flow. Usually we pay attention to the contents and ignore the pipe, dismissing it as a constant. But this constancy is worthy of note in Gary's art. *Because* his attention is so fixed, one feels that his poems never fail to harmonize somehow with the constant, drone note of his preoccupation with "the real work."

Reading one of his poems, I am rarely sure whether Gary has *constructed* something of elegant and evocative design, or *perceived* the world and simply articulated what for him is a quite normal perception. For instance, he writes of a peregrine falcon leaving its perch on a Manhattan skyscraper:

> —Peregrine sails past the window
> Off the edge of the word-chain

>   Harvesting concepts, theologies,
>   Snapping up bites of the bits bred   by
>   Banking
>   Ideas and wild speculations
>   On new information—
>   and stoops in a blur on a pigeon.

This passage makes connections between information and food, the behavior of a raptor and human beings, money and calories, and behavior and language. Are such connections the poet's assertions or his perceptions? The confusion may exist because Gary does not really differentiate between his art and other activities. Most men, especially those who are rewarded for particular artistic skills, treat their skills as special and lavish attention on them at the expense of other areas of their development. For this reason many artists are viewed as *prima donnas* or *enfants terribles*.

Gary does everything as well as he does anything. He builds a house, fells a tree, fixes a Jeep, with the same dedication with which he writes a poem. In Zen practice, fixing a Jeep is no more or less important than writing a poem. Gary's poems are also tools, wedges of insight, designed to crack rigid mental assumptions about ourselves and, consequently, the world we roam about in. These assumptions bind us so hypnotically that we forget that they are simply concepts and mistake them for reality. In this regard we are like a man who confuses the reflection of the moon in a pond for the moon itself. Liberating one's perceptions is its own reward, Gary might say, for it delivers one from the suffocating trance of self-absorption to the fluid possibilities of cloud formations, or the polyphonous arrangements and rearrangements and harmonies of a field of frogs and crickets. Because they are so functional in this regard, they "work," and therefore it is not inaccurate to refer to Gary's poems as another piece of his "gear."

In Gary's study, there is a large file box. It is a card catalog from a library, and it contains numerous small drawers for library cards. This file box contains the notes of twenty-five years of Gary's reading. It is organized into various subject areas—anthropology, Buddhism, and so on. The cards contain bibliographies and quotes, random thoughts and ideas, all indexed and cross-referenced to specific books and journals. It is a formidable archive, but it does not, I suspect, exist solely because of an appreciation for clarity and order. Gary's organization is really another art form that he practices invisibly and, I suspect, a foundation for everything else he does.

Organizing one's office is simply a matter of *imposing* an idea of arrangement on inanimate objects. Organizing one's perceptions of the world, whose vastness and complexity is unimaginable, requires *discovering* areas of order and then linking them in coherent patterns that can be recognized readily enough to be useful. Without intending to be mysterious, Gary has evolved this process one step further, I feel, by *identifying* with the patterns he perceives, merging into his perceptions of them as one merges into one's breathing when meditating. He might, for instance, feel that the back of his head opens onto the Sierra mountain range, and that that range is his spine. Tripping from ridge to ridge, therefore, or in larger steps from rainforest to high desert, is no more complex for him than exploring his body. Coursing through human epochs—caves of Altamira and Lascaux, Anasazi ruins, or vine-throttled temples of Ankor-Wat—is simply being intimate with different areas of his own psyche. The impression is that he uses his knowledge of Body and Mind as templates for his understanding of Earth and History.

The *suchness* of a Dall sheep, the windy sweep of tundra, roiling whitewater, grizzly, salmonberry, and 'coon are inseparable from his perception of them, and consequently are part of him. To know any one of these intimately is to know Gary and finally to know oneself. This is the point at which "the real work" becomes our own. The artist and Zen teacher lead us ultimately in the same direction, through the gates of our individual imaginations and perception into the realm of limitless possibilities, pure pregnant energy and its ceaseless transformations as the birth and death of matter. This is the *ground of being* that offers us a place to settle, outside our own personal or cultural loyalties and limitations, to identify with the universe. Gary reminds us, through the totality of his efforts, of the fundamentally sane ground that is readily available to each of us. He dives into this sane ground and returns to the surface with gifts of varying complexity and tangibility: his detachment and clarity, his art, his family, his community, and his spiritual practice. They are each, from one point of view, different. From another point of view, they are the same. They are the real work.

Gary Snyder:

HARRIET CALLICOTTE'S STONE IN KANSAS

From the 1985 Journal

Wes Jackson invited me to come to read some poems and give a talk at the Kansas Prairie Festival. This happens every year now at the Land Institute, the perennial ethnobotanical future agricultural research and teaching station that Wes and Dana founded. I asked Wes how far Salina is from Carneiro, Kansas, and he said not far at all.

Carneiro is a town from the telling of my mother's family's lore. Lois Snyder Hennessy, my mother, born Wilkey. Her mother was Lula Callicotte, born in Maryville, Missouri. Lula's mother, Harriet, died in childbirth in Carneiro in August of 1884. She was having twins, my mother says. She asked to be buried under a stone that one of her sons had played around, and had once traced the outline of his small hand in with a nail or knife. It was a solitary piece of sandstone in an isolated field on a hill outside of town.

I. VI. 85—Gen Snyder and I fly into Wichita and are driven to Salina. Two days of talks by handy farmers and agrarian intellectuals, a great presentation by Gene Logsdon, poems by Harley Elliott and Joe Paddock, and a play by Nancy Paddock. Beer kegs in the warm evening. Den Berry plays a fine guitar. Wes the impresario, the long view, the true scientist.

Kelly Kindscher has come up from Lawrence. He is a prime bioregional thinker, leader in the "Kaw River Watershed Council," scholar of agro-ecology and ethnobotany, the man who walked the width of Kansas to feel the watershed in his very bones. Kelly says he'd like to help Gen and me look for Harriet's gravestone after the festival.

A warm humid breeze blowing over the rolling grasslands. Far lookouts. This grassy growing smell. Salina 1200' elevation.

3. VI—Cool, with a cloud layer. The festival over, Kelly, Gen, and I then drive west on modest two-lane grassy-shouldered Highway 140

through Bavaria and Brookville to Highway 141, the Carneiro turn-off. The grasslands and wheatfields of central Kansas, Ellsworth County. Carneiro is a ¾ ghost town. There are a few occupied houses, but it is mostly vacant wooden buldings, vine- and brush-overgrown vacant structures. After cruising a bit through the small town grid we double back from the railroad tracks edge of settlement and again up the main street. A substantial two-story brick school building, closed and broken. The inscribed date is 1915. We stop and peer into another large building through the window. "Open," it says, but there are padlocks on the door. It is full of recent cast-offs, and outside along the wall are discarded stoves, washers, refrigerators.

Across the street a man is ambling about his well-tended mobile home. A collie trots toward us. We walk across the street to him. He asks, "Do you want to get into the store?"—I say, "I'm looking for a rock," and explain my quest. "I'm new here," he says. "I never heard of anything like that." But he says Mr. Sneath across the street (now out) might know. He has a purple pitted nose. And then he recalls: "There *was* a place like that I heard about east of here. Go back to-ward Brookville about 1 mile past where 141 crosses the road (Kan-apolis Lake and the state park) and turn right. About one half mile south the road takes a bend and you might find something there. You might stop and talk to Mr. Mullin."

We find our way down narrow gravel roads with fenced wheatfields or grazing on both sides. "Lots of holstein bulls," Kelly comments. At the bend we stop, park, and go through the fence to beat the grass and look. Gen spots a hollow square of stones, most likely an old cabin foundation. It is a little corner left unmowed and uncultivated. But there is no single large stone. So we drive on around the mud puddle road to the nearby farmhouse, pull into the driveway, and park by a double garage. The light's on, and someone is working in there. A tall thin elderly man with blue eyes and white hair comes out. Again I tell the story. "My great grandmother lived in Carneiro and my great grandfather worked on the railroad. She was dying in childbirth, and she told her family that she wanted to be buried up on the hill outside of town near the old emigrant wagon road where there was a big stone with a child's hand engraved on it. So they buried her there, and added her name to the rock. Later a little fence was put around it. My mother said that it was famous in town, and that anybody I asked could tell me where the gravestone was. My sister got somebody to take her there in the fifties. But so far I haven't been able to find anyone who knows of it." He says he's really sorry, but he never heard of it. Just as we're about to leave he invites us to look at the work he's doing in the garage. On the bench at the back, tools and a vise, he is making stainless steel spurs. "So blamed hard, it's slow work—uses up a lot of drill bits." They are clean simple designs, and very good looking.

Then he asks us to see his spur collection in the house. We go in through a screen door and a wood door and are greeted by his wife. I ask her about the gravestone. She says "I *heard recently* of something like that. Who from? A stone grave-marker I think. They said it was on the old Smith property." She gives Kelly instructions on how to find that piece of land. We then look at a case of fine crafted spurs, each stamped with a tiny "CCM." "Charles Christopher Mullin, that's me," he says. "I sell them at fairs and at rodeos. It's my hobby."

We head west again, down dirt roads that take us past the Mushroom Rocks in Kanapolis State Park. We walk a bit through these odd formations of resistant rock above, softer rock that has been cut away below, leaving twelve-foot-high "toadstools." My mother had spoken of these rocks, and had shown me an old color picture postcard of them.

The road turns north and goes over a gentle grassy hill. To the west there is a windmill. This is as Mrs. Mullin had described. We get out and push into the grass, but it is such a vast hill, such wide grass range, that we soon doubt we can find anything. We see that the road we're on loops right back into Carneiro, so we drive back in and up to Mr. Sneath's house to see if he's home yet. His wife comes to the side-porch door. Mr. Sneath, she says, is "out working some cows." I tell her of our search. She says, "That land used to belong to Smith. I lived up there until about forty years ago. There was a stone with a name on it all right. I don't remember the name." She tells us where to find her husband, by going back to the main paved road and then up a side road through some cottonwoods. Gen, Kelly, and I drive there, easing in and out of some water holes. It has started showering rain. We negotiate a saggy barbed-wire fence gate held by a levertightener stick. We walk around a bend into a muddy corral where two men are standing by a pickup. They don't notice us until we're almost up to them.

He hears me out. "It's there all right. East of the windmill about two hundred yards on the highest ground." The younger man adds, "Ola Shellhorn, in The Pines retirement home in Ellsworth, would be the one to know most about it."

We drive back again through Carneiro, cross the railroad tracks, and climb up the hill, which is a miles-long east-west running ridge about two hundred feet higher than the town site. We park off the side of the road and slide through the wire fence. Walking east, hundreds of yards, onward and onward, to the highest point on the ridge. I know we've come too far. All there is to see is grasses, this long ridge, and a shelterbelt of trees down the slope to the south. A good view north to the Carneiro basin. Longer views of far-off prairies rolling. The sun is near the edge, and the sky is darkening with more rain clouds and hints of further showers. We turn and start walking toward the car. Kelly notes a faint depression in the ground and a subtle change of vegetation within that—"A wagon road probably"—and wonders if this might be the ghost of the old Fremont wagon trail, which tends to follow high ground. We walk this faint trace, which goes downslope and runs parallel to the spine of the ridge. I see some rock poking through the grass. Closer, it's reddish tan, about two and a half feet wide, lying on its back. Then we are over it, and can see the lettering, HARRIET CALLICOTTE sure enough. Gen and Kelly catch up. Gen kneels down next to me, and we try to see if anything else is legible, but clearly the stone has been eroding away, and only these larger letters remain. No trace of the hand, or her dates. No fence, only an irregular circle of smaller rock chunks around it. We stand, and look around the sweep of the whole landscape, putting it in mind (as I did at Vulture Peak in Bihar the day I visited there, to remember it in future lives), and I tell Gen to remember the lay of the land so he can find it again someday. Specifically: It is up the hill south of Carneiro, about 900 feet east of the road, and about 80 feet north of the faint watershed divide of the ridge. I chant the *Prajnaparamita Heart Sutra*, the ceremony for the moments when realities roll out and up, like a seal or a whale surfacing, and then dive back again into the depths. I tell Gen, "Now you've touched the far ends of your ancestry. You've been to the tomb of the Ibaru clan in Okinawa and you've seen your great great grandmother's headstone in Kansas."

(Lula Callicotte met Rob Wilkey when she was 19. They were going out on a date, riding in Rob's wagon to a party, and a storm came up so that they lost their way. They crossed and recrossed several creeks all night. By morning they had found their way to the town of Ellsworth. They went straight to a preacher and got married, and then told Lula's father. Rob and Lula later went west to Leadville, Colorado, where he worked in the mines. Eventually they moved to Texas to work for the railroad. My mother, Lois, told me how she had been brought to see this grave by her mother on a visit from Texas when she was quite small. "She flung herself on the ground before her mother's grave and wept. Then she paid a man named Luck to put a fence around it. He sent her a photo of the fence to prove it had been done." I had seen that photo.) We walk back to the car in a slanting rain lit by the setting sun from under the edge of the clouds.

Kelly Kindscher has further rocks in mind: He drives us back on Route 140 to a place from which we walk a path along the edge of a wet field of ripe wheat for over a mile. We push through small brush, cross a creek, go by a field of young alfalfa and thru a sumac (Kelly pronounces it "shumac") stand, continue around a hillside, and find ourselves under a cave on the side of a rocky hill. Soft sandstone. There are the names of Euro-Americans of the last century scratched here and there, and higher up and deeper in the elder petroglyphs. One impressive glyph on the rock face above the cave mouth is about twenty feet long. Information traveling on rocks through time.

And heavy rain, really wet now. We return to the car with squishing shoes. Rain-heavy heads of wheat, singing meadowlarks, June evening rainclouds. Gen strangely good-humored in the wet. We drive back through Brookville to Salina for a celebratory Mexican dinner—the three of us—and then Gen and I meet Wes, who drives us through the night with talks and plans (and the many mysterious lights that appear in the dark on the Kansas plains) to Wichita. We catch our plane back to the coast.

Gary Snyder, seated center of first row, in fifth grade, Lake City Elementary School, Seattle, fall of 1939. Photo: Gary Snyder Collection.

Gary Snyder with his sister, Anthea Snyder, leaving for camp. Circa 1946. Photo: Gary Snyder Collection.

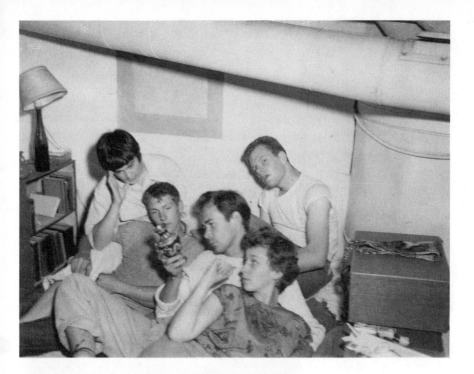

College days at Reed—basement room of 1414 Lambert Street house. From the left: Alison Gass, Gary Snyder, Bill Baker, Carol Baker. David Lapham in back. Photo: Gary Snyder Collection.

In an alpine meadow near Sourdough Mountain Lookout, North Cascades, summer of 1953. Photo: Gary Snyder Collection.

Spud Murphy rides at the head of his string of mules near Tuolumne Pass in 1960. Photo: Walt Castle.

Roy Marchbank stands proudly with a string of trout in a trail crew camp at Beehive in northern Yosemite in August 1956. Photo: Bob Barrett.

These trail crew folks are nearly finished with a long stretch of riprap on the Yosemite Falls Trail in 1983. Photo: Jim Snyder.

At the Marin County cabin in California, early spring, 1956. Photo: Harry Redl.

Oda Sessō Roshi. Photo: Gary Snyder Collection.

At Rinko-in, in Shokoku-ji, fall of 1956.
Left to right: unidentified man, Miura Isshu Roshi, Mrs. Kobayashi,
Gary Snyder. Photo: Gary Snyder Collection.

Ryosen-an library, the center of Ruth Fuller Sasaki's First Zen Institute of
America in Japan's research and translation activities. Kyoto, Japan, circa
1957. Left to right: Philip Yampolsky, Gary Snyder, Donna Lebowich, Ruth
F. Sasaki, Miura Isshu Roshi, Vanessa Coward, Miss Manzōji (secretary),
Walter Nowick, and Seizan Yanagida. Photo: Gary Snyder Collection.

Just north of Kyoto, setting out to walk to the Japan Sea, late April of 1961.
Photo: Joanne Kyger.

On an empatsu, "long distance begging" trip, with monks of the Daitoku-ji Sodo, Mie Prefecture, April 1963. Photos: Gary Snyder Collection.

Gary Snyder, Almora or Kausani, India, after visiting Lama Govinda's house, January 1962. Photo: Allen Ginsberg.

Joanne Kyger and Gary Snyder, probably in March 1962, astronomical observatory, Jaipur, India. Peter Orlovsky in sunlight above. Photo: Allen Ginsberg.

Allen Ginsberg and Gary Snyder doing calligraphy in the Snyder Kyoto house, summer 1963. Photo: Gary Snyder Collection.

Gary Snyder resting, trip to Japan Sea, July 1963. Photo: Allen Ginsberg.

Nanao Sakaki in the Snyder Kyoto house, 1965. Photo: Gary Snyder Collection.

An all-afternoon "protest meditation" at the Oakland Army Terminal, in the spring of 1965, organized by Gary Snyder and Richard Baker. Gary Snyder was jikijitsu. Philip Whalen is to his right. Photo: Gary Snyder Collection.

Gary Snyder and Philip Whalen at the summit of the 12,524-foot peak east of States Lakes Basin in Kings Canyon country, July 5, 1965. Photo: Drummond Hadley.

Gary Snyder and Allen Ginsberg, Glacier Peak Wilderness Area,
eight-day trek, September 1965. Photo: Allen Ginsberg.

Gary Snyder on a hill about a half-mile from his house in Nishinoyama-cho, Kyoto, Japan, summer of 1968. "I often walked up here to do zazen outdoors. A good view of the Kyoto Basin." Photo: Gary Snyder Collection.

Squaring the foundation, Kitkitdizze, summer of 1970. Photo: Jonathan Kuehn.

Masa and Kai, in the frame of the Kitkitdizze house, summer of 1970. Photo: Jonathan Kuehn.

Kitkitdizze house, summer of 1970. Photos: Jonathan Kuehn.

Gary Snyder and his mother, Lois Hennessy, at Kitkitdizze. Photo:
Gary Snyder Collection.

Gary Snyder's father, Harold Snyder, at his house in Petaluma, 1966.
Photo: Gary Snyder.

With sons Gen and Kai, Boulder, Colorado, 1983. Photo: Chris Felver.

Gary Snyder, Gen Snyder, Nanao Sakaki, June 1987, in front of Richard Nelson's place on Sitka Sound, Alaska. "We had been out near St. Lazaria Island with Dick in his Boston Whaler. Gen hooked this 70-lb. Halibut. It fed about thirty people from the Sitka Writers Conference." Photo: Richard Nelson.

Gary Snyder, Carole Koda, and her daughters, Kyung Jin and Mika, at Kitkitdizze, summer 1989. Photo: Gary Snyder Collection.

Jon Halper, Carole Koda, Gary Snyder, and David Padwa at Admiralty Island, Alaska, July 1989. Photo: Jon Halper.

Lunch on the Bedrock Mortar veranda, Gary Snyder reviewing a wilderness report, Allen Ginsberg's house, Kitkitdizze, May 30, 1989. Photo: Allen Ginsberg.

Poetics

Ursula K. Le Guin:
NAMING GARY

There are some poems
like a bear walking upstream
not worrying, walking
with its feet turned in
like bears do.
The stream leaps red with salmon
like the poems do.

There is a man
who takes his shoes off.
You look around and he is sitting
not worrying
with no shoes on.

A bear walking upstream
along a river is the river
and the salmon in the river
leaping upstream and is also
the fingerlings who will be slipping
quietly downstream
going to the villages
of the salmon
far out under ocean,
the First Salmon returning.

A man who knows where the villages are
and who are the important people,

the First People,
and how to talk to them,
is a man who knows
when to take his shoes off.
He leaves two kinds of tracks
and they are poems.
This man I call
Bear Walking the Watershed.

Allen Ginsberg:

MY MYTHIC THUMBNAIL
BIOGRAPHY OF GARY SNYDER

Grew up among Northwest lumberjacks, Indians, Wobblies & intellectuals, met W. C. Williams 1950 Reed College with friends Lew Welch & Philip Whalen. Meditated as early 1950s fire lookout Washington State, trail crew worker Yosemite National Park, graduate student Oriental languages U. Cal. Berkeley 1952–56. American literary cultural hero since his central participation in mid-'50s San Francisco open-form Poetry Renaissance and Beat Generation literary movement, Snyder's figure served as model for fictional protagonist Japhy Ryder in Kerouac's longhair-rucksack revolution breakthrough novel *The Dharma Bums*, 1958. Left for Japan 1956 to spend dozen years in monastic & householder study, writing, & zazen, later seasons in company of wife poet Joanne Kyger with whom made Dharma pilgrimage India. Snyder ripened as wilderness philosopher activist, integrating ecological planet karma with Native-American Poetry's indigenous household view. Built house in ponderosa-black oak parklike woods 3,000 feet high Western slope Sierras, working with wife Masa Uehara and sons Kai and Gen for two decades. Translated Stockholm to Beijing, Snyder notably furthered Ezra Pound's ideogrammatic lineage. Like Pound, key figure in the adaptation of Oriental Wisdom arts to the West, he translated Chinese & Japanese Classic gnomic texts, by-product of three decades' Zen practice. Traveled widely China to Alaska wilds; founded Ring of the Bone Zendo, named for late poet companion Lew Welch, on San Juan Ridge; joined by Carole Koda 1988; completing midlife tome on Poetics of Wilderness as of November 14, 1989.

—*N.Y.C.*

Michael McClure:

"PASTURES NEW"

Since the early fifties when Charles Olson published his "Against Wisdom As Such" in *Black Mountain Review* there's been very little wisdom literature written by those of us in the new thrust. But Gary has always written practical visionary poems that can be touchstones and stepping-stones for us. We can always go back to Gary's thought for a base and say, look, we can do this or that good thing, and we should know all the names of our flowers and birds and mountains. But one poem of Gary's, more than all the others, has stood out in my mind for the last few years. I've had the broadside of it on my wall and read it many times and return to it each time with even more and greater pleasure. Then one day I began to realize that the poem "High Quality Information" is wisdom literature—as much as is the *Tao Te Ching* or *The Cloud of Unknowing*. What I've done here is something like a gloss and something like a savoring of this poem:

High Quality Information

A life spent seeking it
Like a worm in the earth,
Like a hawk. Catching threads
Sketching bones
Guessing where the road goes.
Lao-tzu says
To forget what you knew is best.
That's what I want:
To get these sights down,
Clear, right to the place
Where they fade
Back into the mind of my times.
The same old circuitry
But some paths color-coded
Empty
And we're free to go.

A life spent seeking it   (I'll say! I've been watching Gary seeking that
    high-quality information for almost thirty-five years,
    seeing the lines deepen on the face and the gaze grow
    deeper, too, looking down past the surface of things. And
    the smile has grown more gentle.
Like a worm in the earth,   (—turning and lithely swimming
    through the damp gritty particles and the tasty sheddings
    and off-shimmers of near countless preceding lives.
Like a hawk.   (I remember how one day near Kitkitdizze we looked
    down from the gorge and saw an eagle fly slowly below us.
    We could almost see the cloudy mottle on the primaries.
Catching threads   (Woolgathering. As old Zen wise men went
    woolgathering with a wine jug, watching a spider drop
    down on its thread in the moonlight.
Sketching bones   (Goethe sketched bones too. There must be a hun-
    dred or a million bones beneath our feet at every step
    through the meadow in the forest.
Guessing where the road goes.   (While recalling that we come from
    nowhere and it's nowhere we go—with our children clap-
    ping their hands in the last clack of our heels.
Lao-tzu says   (He says the whole thing is an Uncarved Block. Some-
    times it's a block of pollywogs, or of deer in the yard.
To forget what you knew is best.   (—to make it not painful, to join
    the forgetting at the end of the road. Going to sleep by the
    fireplace, with muscles forgetting a day of chopping and
    carrying and typing.
That's what I want: (Gary, you speak for so many of us, for what
    you see is what we'd like to see too. I trust what you want.
To get these sights down,   (Gary, we'll get out of the greedy drunk-
    enness. It's an age of addiction to population and petro-
    leum, as you point out. But we see the high things because
    we are mammals.
Clear, right to the place
Where they fade   (This poem is so beautiful to me that, though I've
    read it many times, I love to feel it fade and shift its mean-
    ing into a dimming moire pattern. Then after a few more
    lines I go back and read and come at it again, and try to
    guess how to imagine *sunyatta*.

MICHAEL McCLURE   205

Back into the mind of my times.   (Our thoughts fade as we drive and
        as we write our poems, as our bodies rest on the plastic
        plush that was created, in part, by the wars of our times
        and partly by gentler acts that had no intention to pollute.

The same old circuitry   (All these years of the circuitry—and it is less
        than a sand grain in the earth that the worm moves through
        as he/she creates information affecting a future that spreads
        along the road to forgetting.

But some paths color-coded   (We were sitting in H. T. Odum's front
        room in Gainesville and he pointed out the color coding
        of the cardinals in the trees. But is there a color coding of
        an ecotone of the land where the road goes?

Empty   (No nothing. No more. Not even *nada.*

And we're free to go.   (Thank you, Gary. As John Milton said, "To-
        morrow to fresh Woods and Pastures new."

Philip Whalen:
LIBERAL SHEPHERDS

Although many of us are interested in trying to write in the same language that we speak, we discover that we need all the words that we can find in the Anglo-American canon as well as in slang, street talk, and scientific jargon. Many years ago, some friends and I had an argument about what one of them called "unmanageable" or awkwardly shaped or barbarous-sounding words. I suggested that we choose ten such words from the dictionary and let each of us write a poem employing these words. We were all young poets & were full of self-confidence & that wonderful thoughtless facility that typifies the young writer. Each of us came up with a poem & decided to try again. We made up a rule: Pick five words; make a five-line poem using all the words. Later on, we found it was better to use any prose book rather than the dictionary. Because of the five-line rule we began calling ourselves the Adelaide Crapsey-Oswald Spengler Memorial Society, in honor of the American inventor of the five-line *cinquain*. Miss Crapsey's invention was inspired by the Japanese *hokku*. For a season, whenever a few of us met with friends, we would introduce them into the society. When William Carlos Williams visited Reed College, he became an initiate. Of course, Mr. Gary Snyder was an early member.

Working as we then were, under the influence of Williams and Ezra Pound, we wanted simplicity, clarity, and precision of language. But if one of us needed the word "peduncle" it went into the text and stayed there. I took Mark Twain seriously: "The difference between the right word and the almost right word is the difference between lightning and the lightning-bug."

I've noticed with pleasure the reintroduction of the word "gross" into the spoken language. I've always thought of it as a "learned" word, remembering, for example, Aldous Huxley's use of it in *TIME MUST HAVE A STOP*. One character refers to another as "gross" with the sense "enormously fat." But hearing the word jarred loose a fragment of Shakespeare from memory, "something, something, shepherds give a grosser name." Only the other day I finally got to the neighborhood branch of the town library to find "long purples" in the *Shakespeare Concordance* so that I might find the complete line in its context:

> ". . . and long purples
> That liberal shepherds give a grosser name,"
> —*HAMLET*, IV vii 170

I had never learned that "grosser name," so I had been at liberty to imagine all kinds of things—lilac blossoms, cattails, all sorts of lengthy blooms. What was the right word? *The Riverside Shakespeare* (1974) note 169 on this line gives "*long purples*: wild orchids." I have seen similar plants in the forests of Washington and Oregon, but nobody had a name for them. The books said "Indian pipe," for example, but there were other kinds as well. I asked, but people didn't know or care.

I looked in Eric Partridge's *SHAKESPEARE'S BAWDY*. There is no entry under "long purples," but under *dead men's fingers* there's a quote from Lyte's *HERBAL* (1578): "the long purple is the Orchis, especially the variety 'Priest's Pintle.'"

Where I grew up, "pintle" is the usual word for "saddle horn." The pintle of a Western saddle is used to belay a lariat when one is roping cattle. The *OED* comes out flat: with "penis," and marks it "Now *dial.* or vulgar." (That word, "vulgar," I learned in grade school. It had an extremely pejorative meaning: "obscene; filthy; disgusting." Sometimes it meant using cuss words; other times it might mean using slang. When I studied Latin I found out it simply means "of the mob; of the people—unsuitable in polite society.")

The study and practice of Buddhism tends to clarify the boundaries of speech, what can and cannot be said. But even Buddhism sets up a paradox: Silence is best; contrariwise we must use words to teach Buddhism and to communicate with other people in the "real world." Zen people, who are very polite and very refined—at least as much so as the *OED* and *The Riverside Shakespeare*—simply say "Sit down and shut up!" and so I do.

20:IX:89

Anne Waldman:
VOYANT

I first read Gary Snyder in the early 1960s: *Myths & Texts*, Totem/ Corinth, published by the Wilentz brothers, who had the bookstore up the street (corner of Macdougal & Eighth).

I first met him at his New York University reading, introduced by Kenneth Koch. He was wonderful, of course. He had "presence," as we said in New York: wit, charm, assurance. Kenneth really liked his work.

There was a party at Kenneth's small apartment in the West Village afterwards. Drinks & canapés. A tight squeeze. Gary was attentive to the young of us. I remember him asking where New York's water came from. Or the electricity for that matter. Con Ed? I joked. I might have told him about taking LSD & seeing the wires pulsating through the walls of my apartment—& my sense of how the whole town was "wired" & how we were being negatively affected by this. He was expounding on the virtues of being able to put your hands on your power sources, at least being able to visualize them. There was also friendly poetry talk. This was 1967, '68.

• • •

This little suite of poems, *Voyant*, exists in appreciation of how I've felt empowered by Gary Snyder in his manifestation as poet, scholar-teacher, dharma-brother, & friend. His distinct & intelligent attentions to Gaia, to "terrible meditations / On the cells all water / frail bodies . . ." to "Poetry a riprap on the slick rock of metaphysics," to ordinary, magical, (& winning) common sense have been inspirations along the path. The twinkle in his eye is ancient. His beautiful & articulate poetry has been a companion for many years.

Voyant

for Gary Snyder

"The sun dries me as I dance"

—Gary Snyder

I draw breath & sing
Draw breath & sing
Breath makes heat in icy air
I know myself
(Draw breath & sing)
Earth-magnetized
Placed here as witness
Witness myself
Dig for me back to
Neolithic
Further back:
Chalcolithic
Upper Paleolithic
Way back before Abraham
Long before
you'd understand conception
follows hot love-making

Way back

Carve of me miniature statues:
Venus figures, Astarte plaques,
dzuli
Build the *tholoi,*
my shrine
where I shake
with the snake & lotus

•

"women your secrets aren't my secrets"

—G. S.

See me
      bow head
           touch base
                  Witness this mudra

        O men of little faith!

                   how bending

                      is like the bow

                          of an arrow

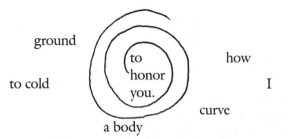

ground   to   how

                 honor
to cold   you.   I

                    curve
         a body

I'd go to hot hells if I could
Become cypher, burning hoop of fire

                 Jump in!

        I'll consume all desperate thoughts

             •

    my breath is warm
    arising as Sarasvati
    invents the alphabet
    I give you Sanskrit seed syllables
    I give you *pratitya samudpada,*
    the co-arising of everything & nothing
    I give you an alphabet
    straight from the belly
    OM MAMA RULU RULU HŪM BHYO HŪM

swelling to sing this to you
of Ekajati, creator of samsara & nirvana
(Draw breath & sing)
Ekajati with a hundred iron wolves as aids
Song of the wrathful wild protector
great Mother I give you
MAHĀ-AMṚTA-RAKTA-BALIṂ TE PŪJĀ HOḤ
push-pull, primordial rage
out an elder Vedic mouth

·

can't do without you

        Male Poet

                ·

breath of protozoa
sleep's breath
sharp investigator sees breath
    in shape of wrathful deities
breath across the arroyo, the gulf
breath decodes itself
breath decodes itself
poem at your feet, Gary

            ·

        dear Gary:

                deer come down from Sanitas Mtn.
            buck breathes against bedroom window
                    against a sickle moon
            crystals the pane
                    totem stag of my sight

            ·

Cars go nowhere today
stuck under bedlam-drift
all the townspeople laugh
17 below

I drag furs out of shaman chest
& bind myself in the animal-life
Tails wind around throat & waist
Underneath: grease arms & belly
    with musk oil
Mate with you tonight, fox
Grow hair if I could
I'd be red, red, red

                        •

Time doesn't exist
Nor does it "pass"
In abstract time, I go in reverse
from charnel-ground dakini
to dried-up-blood-between-legs-woman
to mother-births-precious-son
to Sumerian seductress rubbing her clit
    against a tree

Woulds't rather be Thel, unborn?

                        •

                No. Rather

Goddess Nidaba
(inventor of clay tablets
& art of writing)
I
continue
your
great
work,
type
the text
where I say
I do
this
I do that

I
do
this I
do
that
as witness
to any old
god in town
coming through me, to
get deciphered

                                        •

Gary tells me
the Diamond Vehicle
suits women
this time around
Finally, liberation!
All outrageous females
are skywalkers, he says
Of course (I can see them!
I can see them!)
adorning the 21st century

                                        •

Kālī-yūga
Already hungry ghosts dance
& batteries go dead on West Nicholl Street
Go for the long book
by candlelight
Roast meat over coals
(it's sweeter there)
"By this merit
may all obtain omniscience
May it defeat the enemy, wrongdoing,
from the stormy waves of birth,
old age, sickness & death
From the ocean of samsara
may I free all beings"

A child draws a Peace Center
on top of the photo
of Rocky Flats
Mother rejoice
The poet sees the end
& beginning
of days.

—Boulder, Colorado
Year of the Earth Snake

Alan Williamson:

SOME TENSES OF SNYDER

A Walk

Sunday the only day we don't work:
Mules farting around the meadow,
                  Murphy fishing,
The tent flaps in the warm
Early sun: I've eaten breakfast and I'll
              take a walk
To Benson Lake. Packed a lunch,
Goodbye. Hopping on creekbed boulders
Up the rock throat three miles
              Piute Creek—
In steep gorge glacier-slick rattlesnake country
Jump, land by a pool, trout skitter,
The clear sky. Deer tracks.
Bad place by a falls, boulders big as houses,
Lunch tied to belt,
I stemmed up a crack and almost fell
But rolled out safe on a ledge
              and ambled on.
Quail chicks freeze underfoot, color of stone
Then run cheep! away, hen quail fussing.
Craggy west end of Benson Lake—after edging
Past dark creek pools on a long white slope—
Lookt down in the ice-black lake
              lined with cliff
From far above: deep shimmering trout.
A lone duck in a gunsightpass
              steep side hill
Through slide-aspen and talus, to the east end,
Down to grass, wading a wide smooth stream
Into camp. At last.
           By the rusty three-year-
Ago left-behind cookstove
Of the old trail crew,
Stoppt and swam and ate my lunch.

—Gary Snyder

"A Walk" is a fairly typical early Snyder poem, quiet enough to have slipped past me three or four times before I saw into its inner life. I'd like to use it now as a way into Snyder's unique accomplishment as a poet of Zen and a poet of the American West. I found myself teaching it (for no better reason than that it appears in a common anthology) and, wondering how to show the students that it was more than a series of diary-jottings, I suggested we look at verb tenses. The bewildering, unconventional shifts we encountered led to a discussion of how we, in fact, experience time.

Some time, it would seem, is past tense even while we're living it. That may be because it is lived not for its own sake, but for the sake of something in the future:

Packed a lunch,

Goodbye.

Or it might be because we need to reassure ourselves we will survive it:

    I stemmed up a crack and almost fell
    But rolled out safe on a ledge
             and ambled on.

Here "I," the narrator, the storyteller, splits off in alarm from the person actually struggling up the rocks. "I" is not frequent in this poem; its only other occurrence coincides with another kind of detached time, the time of planning, spread out like a grid over past and future:

    I've eaten breakfast and I'll
      take a walk

As one learns more about Zen Buddhism, and Snyder's involvement with it, these nuances come to seem not only not accidental, but the very core of his subject. In Zen there is a great deal of talk about "the moment," not because longer stretches of time, and what can be accomplished in them, are unimportant, but because it is crucial not to be divided from one's own existence. In *Zen Mind, Beginner's Mind,* Shunryu Suzuki says,

You may say "I must do something this afternoon," but actually there is no "this afternoon." We do things one after the other. That is all. There is no such time as "this afternoon" or "one o'clock" or "two o'clock." At one o'clock you will eat your lunch. To eat lunch is itself one o'clock. You will be somewhere, but that place cannot be separated from one o'clock. . . . But when we become tired of our life we may say, "I shouldn't have come to this place. It may have been much better to have gone to some other place for lunch. . . ." In your mind you create an idea of place separate from an actual time.

There is a great deal of talk, too, about getting rid of the subject—not exactly because it doesn't exist, as in Deconstruction, but because conscious emphasis on it is almost always defense. An "I" whose energies are completely absorbed by an object or an action does not remember that he/she is an "I." In Suzuki's words again, "When you do something, you should burn yourself completely, like a good bon-fire, leaving no trace of yourself." How can poetry convey this laps-ing into pure attentiveness? Sometimes it comes dazedly, in the aftershock of risk and success:

> Jump, land by a pool, trout skitter,
> The clear sky.

Here we have something like a musical modulation between keys: the anxious self-addressed imperatives, the pure present, the absolute construction or verbless clause. Absolutes are common in this poem ("Deer tracks"; "deep shimmering trout"); they feel—as perhaps with all poets who use them—like little defiant rescues of pure mo-mentariness from the grid of generalized time that is built into gram-mar itself. Another way might be to use a present tense verb and interrupt it in the middle, to remind us that perception is quicker than even the simplest grammatical response:

> Then run cheep! away, hen quail fussing.

These are the extremes. Between them are many intermediate times, which escape the grammatical grid without claiming any spe-cial attunement. Present participles are a flowing activity; not wholly momentary, they do not separate out or calibrate, either. Ezra Pound's mannerism, "Lookt" and "Stoppt," is also attractive, as if the elided silent syllable pushed us over some edge into immediacy. These are the poem's ordinary recourses—along with the absolute construction—when it does not want to point us too strongly in either direction.

But what, beyond temporal modes, is the poem's subject? One way to approach it might be to look at what is never mentioned—the potential for fear, out among the rattlesnakes and "boulders big as houses," in the "universe of junk" of "Bubbs Creek Haircut," where there is almost no vegetation, and the one human trace was simply abandoned, years before. This fear, or metaphysical desolation, is not unfelt in the language of the poem, in "A lone duck in a gunsight-pass," or even the spare glitter of "steep side hill / Through slide-aspen and talus," the icy monochrome of "dark creek pools on a long white slope." Rather, I would argue, the desolation is continuously being disarmed, by the acts of minute attention in which subject becomes one with object and can no longer fear it. This is the real process, the real underlife of the poem, which allows it to arrive with strange dignity at the mild self-satisfaction of "Stoppt and swam and ate my lunch."

"How does one stand / To behold the sublime," Wallace Stevens asked. One of the problems for literature in the American West has always been how to deal with the sheer vastness, the pre-human alienness, of the landscape. Is it a place of liberation for the spirit, or an emptiness that will be filled by greed and ready-made religions, or else driven mad entirely? It is at once a moral and a stylistic question. John Muir attempted to import the language of Emersonian idealism, but it didn't stick, except in second-rate travel writing. Robinson Jeffers imagined the loneliness as a Calvinist God, demanding sacrifice and immolation; but beyond that God waited a calm maternal Nothing, "the matrix of all shining and quieter of shining." D. H. Lawrence valued the landscape precisely because it was so subversive of human purposes, and could madden—"The vast and unrelenting will of the swarming lower life, working for ever against man's attempt at a higher life" (*St. Mawr*, NY: Knopf, 1925, pp. 152–53).

Snyder's accomplishment has been to approach the whole subject without rhetoric, taking his cue not from Western writers, but from the terseness of Pound, the fact-oriented style of Williams, the calm, courtly descriptiveness of the classical Chinese masters. There is a self-annihilating love of the world in these styles, through which the Western sublime can simply be registered, losing none of its novelty or strangeness, but not causing excitation or terror. The "I" that is so mildly steadied at the end of Snyder's poem has had an experience of value, less confident than Muir's, far less darkened or troubled than Jeffers', derived from an interchange with the land. It is an experience, again, most nearly captured in the vocabulary of Zen: the "emptiness"—Suzuki calls it a "not rely(ing) on anything"—that becomes a "complete calmness."

It is an odd enough history, when one thinks about it—the coolness of Imagism and Objectivism, nourished on cities (New York, London, Paris), meeting a body of insight from the other side of the globe, and producing the first fully adequate realist poetry of the Wild West. But it is by such arcane chemistries—much more than by programs or schools—that the genuinely new in any art takes shape.

Gioia Timpanelli:
JUMPING OVER BEAR DROPPINGS

Once there was a little girl, about ten years old. She used to go pick berries every summer. Every summer she would go with her family and they would pick berries and dry them. Sometimes they would see bear droppings on the trail.

So begins Gary Snyder's retelling of *The Woman Who Married a Bear*, "based," he writes, "on a telling of Maria Johns (Tagish Athabaskan speaker of Tlingit descent, on July 16, 1948, as collected by Catherine McClellan) and a deep remembering." The second time I met Gary he told me this story, both of us sitting in stiff-backed chairs at a conference in New York City, but one could see the berries, and bears *did* appear. He tells the story gracefully and thoughtfully, having first done a good deal of musing and studying and reading and thinking and walking and living and reliving, so that now he can step aside and retell the story from this "deep remembering." And, after all, if there are struggles, which inevitably there will be, with the story or with his "Commentary," which follows the text, then he has only to go back to nature and listen with his keen ear and pay close attention to the ways things are done by both people and bears.

Picking berries takes patience. The bears draw over the shoots and delicately rake through the clusters with their claws. People make wooden rakes that look like bear-claws, and gather them to a basket held in the other hand. Some women are so fast! Picking with all the fingers of both hands, never bruising the berries. When the berries are ripe, people go out picking every day, and then dry or pickle them with sourdock for the winter. Eating them does no harm to the bush or seed. Maybe this story starts with berries.

Gary's "Commentary on *The Woman Who Married a Bear*" does begin with a litany of berries appropriate to place and therefore to the story: "Salmonberries, Crowberries, Nagoonberries, High Bush

Cranberries, Low Bush Cranberries, Thimbleberries . . ." and from a prodigious diversity of berries we come quickly to bears.

> From long ago the Brown Bears, the Grizzlies, (but we wouldn't speak of them directly by such blunt names) have come to the berry fields. They have been ranging and feeding since spring, ranging dozens or hundreds of miles, often alone. When they gather to the best slopes for berries, there may be many bears picking berries close together, so they manage not to wrangle.

Gary's "Commentary" brings us another story that fits *The Woman Who Married a Bear* back into its natural place. The original tellers and listeners all knew *that* story without having to mention it; in it humans share the center with trees and plants and animals and the slow, orderly cycles of nature: All share a communal life. Gary writes these new stories from observation and study and they remind me of the keen and memorable accounts found in the best natural history writing. (They are close to the poetic nature writings of Dorothy Wordsworth.)

> The salmonberries ripen early, and most of the others toward the end of summer. The berries' sheen, aroma, little spike of flavor, sweetness, handed down from long ago. Who is it for? . . .

In retelling the old story and writing the "Commentary," Gary has given us back the *whole* story. Both text and commentary are in the spirit of Chinese landscape scrolls called "Mountains and Rivers Without End," in which recognizable landscape is found side by side with mythological scenes. These new stories have the power of the poet to take the exact, the particular, and to suggest worlds we have somehow forgotten or purposely destroyed. Telling simple, chronological events has always been a way of telling stories; bears and berry fields have their own time and place.

Gary Snyder has been the champion of these traditional tales, of the oral tradition, of the story-maps, the *mappa mundi,* the earth plans told by people about the land and the animals, the ocean, the sky, the trees, the plants, stories told about themselves wherever they live on this earth. What concerns the oldest of these stories concerns him. They tell the details, show paradox, describe the complexities of the way of life lived in a particular place, surrounded by what we call "nature." (Does the whale sing "water"?—could be!) They are not about a dead past or a sentimental or unexplored past, but they are about the past/present/future all at once. When this spoken literature is told vividly, it comes to life again. If we have forgotten about salmon in the rivers, berries on the mountainside, the value of forests everywhere, the stories show us. They tell again and again the bare elements of a complete and soulful life, coming and continuing from the primitive, which, Gary reminds us, means truly "primary, first, essential."

> This is art, it is poetry, it is most profoundly political, this matter of acknowledging the persistence and ineluctable value of the primary, the vernacular, the local, the essential, the simple, the imperfect, the risky (accidents!), the familial, the potluck dinner, the cleanup, the wild weeds in the vacant lot. I have made this my art, my practice, my homestead.

Gary has found in the old stories and poems, and in the people who live them, a kinship that has been one of the inspirations of his own writing.

This story about Gary is based mostly on evenings shared presenting poems and stories. We have told old stories, new stories; stories from spoken and written texts; funny stories, trickster stories; ordinary stories with extraordinary things in them; extraordinary stories with ordinary things in them; walking stories, city stories, neighborhood stories. Gary has praised the old stories and they in turn praise *their* parents: place and the original beings; they praise consistently bear, coyote, cedar tree, mountains, streams, salmon, forests, wells, hearths, crossroads, rivers, oceans, clouds, deserts, and also—kit fox. (The kit fox who lives in the western deserts, grasslands, and tree-lined mountains of this continent is a small, slight fox with quite large ears. It is mostly nocturnal, has solitary habits, and is feisty when necessary. Usually it eats rodents, rabbits, insects—including scorpions—fruit, and berries.)

A few years ago, at a conference on animals, after hearing the Zen story of Ryokan and the thief, Gary told me this story:

> Once I was camping with a friend in the Panamint Desert, just one valley over from Death Valley, on a cool night in March, with the full moon out. We were already in our sleeping bags (I was sleeping on my stomach) and I had just placed a sack of chips above my head, when I hear this munching. I looked up and there

not eighteen inches away was a kit fox munching on those tortilla chips—and then, when I looked again—I saw the moon through that fox's big ears. That beautiful, illuminated, fuzzy creature!

Gary tells a good story, and if I've been just a fair to middling copier, you heard his voice in the story. When reciting, he is careful to pronounce each word; his voice is cadenced, melodic, intimate, and "storytelling." And like some storytellers who describe the story they are seeing (can you see this, can you feel that, can you smell the wet pine?), he brings words into exact and careful attention. He has the kind of voice that talks to each one listening, and it often has a good bit of mischief in it, a good amount of heh! heh! and joking, so that all of a sudden during a reading, when everyone has settled in, I've looked up to find Blue Jay has come to the party. In his writing, too, his speaking voice is always present, creating the "we" in storytelling. He's a good teller for other reasons as well: He says, "I was camping out in the Panamint Desert," and, correctly guessing I don't know where that is, he adds, "one valley over from Death Valley," giving me a familiar picture of the place so that by the time kit fox shows up, I'm there. The March night, the full moon, closing down on the day's work, putting the chips away, the time *after* you've said good night, between being awake and asleep . . . right on the edge of sleep . . . he reminds us of what we probably know already so that he has only to give the place before kit fox gives us the moon.

Yearning is a quality that carries us from the past to the future, more acutely alive in the present. It happens after one has glimpsed something truly desired, and when this happens, it opens a view never forgotten and, when found, never abandoned. There are many stories about following the heart's desire. Here is Gary's story of that moment from his childhood:

> I came here by a path, a line of people that somehow worked their way from the Atlantic seaboard westward over a hundred and fifty years. One Grandfather ended up in the Territory of Washington, and homesteaded in Kitsap County. My Mother's side were railroad people down in Texas, and before that they'd worked the silver mines in Leadville, Colorado. My Grandfather, being a homesteader, and my father a native of the State of Washington, put our family relatively early in the Northwest. Yet we weren't early enough. An elderly Salish gentleman came by our farm once

every few months in a Model T truck, selling smoked salmon. "Who is he?" "He's an Indian," my parents said–

Looking at all the different trees and plants that made up my second-growth Douglas fir forest plus cow-pasture childhood universe, I realized that my parents were short on a certain kind of knowledge. They could say, "That's a Doug fir, that's a cedar, that's bracken fern . . ." But I perceived a subtlety and complexity in those woods that went far beyond a few names.

As a child I spoke with the old Salishan man a few times over the years he made those stops—then, suddenly, he never came back. I sensed what he represented, what he knew, and what it meant to me: He knew better than anyone else I had ever met, *where I was* . . .

The old stories are just such maps that show *where we are*; these story maps begin for us individually in childhood. Gary writes:

> . . . as one explores outward from the safety of the cottage and the hearthstone one first begins on foot to discover a childhood landscape, to construct a mental map, to learn one's own personal mythology of lanes and pathways and little groves and thickets going wider and farther.

I asked Gary recently to tell me the first, very first memories he had of himself in nature, some pictures with no obvious story attached to them. This is what came to him during a mountain walk:

> When I was in first grade there was a mile walk to school on a dirt road that everyone took, but there was an alternative road through a forest. This trail came past our farm. I took that way, the forest trail, to school every day, alone, by myself. If others went that way, it was because I took them.

He continued,

> The second thing I thought to tell you is about a large cedar tree that was back of our house; it had arms, limbs that came down to the ground. I used to climb to the top all the time. I asked it questions and listened to the wind give answers; now, it *would* give you answers, but not in language. I drew a lot of comfort from this.

Well, stories begin at home, close to the bedding and the cooking equipment:

I would make a fire out in back and cook dinner. I made myself a cook kit of tin cans with wire handles.

We ask each other, "What did you do today? What happened?" And so by evening everyone is heard and considered and the day's events put into some modest form, a simple story. Hearing the stories is like taking a journey *and* staying at home, for through them we are constantly connecting, being carried out in wider and wider circles, until the stories can include vast regions. Here is Gary talking about his first mountain walks:

> . . . the first thing I ever did that totally blew me away was climb a snowpeak in the Pacific Northwest at the age of fifteen, Mount St. Helens, which got totally blown away later. I remember thinking in those days, "Ah! Japanese and European cities will come and go like foam on the waves, but the mountains will remain." Turns out Hiroshima has completely come back and reestablished itself and Mount St. Helens is partially gone. Everything is impermanent.

Today, after five hot autumn days, typical of the Northeast, I awoke to a chilling rain; this little cabin room is surrounded by a low cloud, the mountaintop behind is invisible, the valley below as well. Midmorning I got a call from friends just waking in Seattle. "It must be really cold there," they say. "No, actually it feels like Seattle," I say, "except as we talk I'm watching eighteen wild turkeys disappear in and out of this cloud we're in." In the Northwest of this continent there are days of fog and rain; and in Ireland mist, rain, and sun can all take turns on an hour's walk to town. Stories are so embedded in place that the creatures one meets in an Irish folktale will be different from the characters in a Sicilian folktale, where the bright sun shines most of the year, where the other world does not as easily come in and out of the story, but rather parades right there, bright and visible as a cabbage in a garden. Our Sicilian story-knots, that is, our troubles, appear right in the street, in the midst of our needs, where everyone sees us tripping over them. Once, in Ireland, looking out from Dun Aengus on the Aran Islands, a man pointed out to sea, to a spot where the light had just shown up a thin patch of foamed wave. "There's a fairy place," he said. I suppose literally and metaphorically one could go to fairy in that tumultuous sea. It seems we must work with what we have, and we surely begin with primary images of our place, which are always rich in details and diversity.

Whether the stories reflect a hunting and gathering society, as in Gary's *The Woman Who Married a Bear*, or the agricultural town society, as in Sicilian folktales, the storyteller and listener make distinction between acceptable behavior and aberrations, and everyone listening knows without being told what is *really* happening. Here is Gary continuing *The Woman Who Married a Bear*:

> . . . Girls had to be careful about bear droppings, they shouldn't walk over them. Men could walk over them, but young girls had to walk around them. But she loved to jump over the bear droppings, and kick them. She would disobey her mother. All the time she would see them and kick them and step over them. She kept seeing them all around her. She did this from childhood.

In the poetic "Commentary," Gary considers the story:

> Young girls like to run and jump and sing. Some of them like to poke fun, but it's not usually mean. Jump-rope, they jump and sing—hopscotch, they jump and sing. Still, a girl or a woman shouldn't jump over bear droppings, or any droppings really, and neither should men. It's fine to look at them and think about them. Perhaps she was being naughty but we also have to say that she was an exceptional little girl, who somehow felt drawn to the wild.

At twenty, Gary wrote an innovative and complex college thesis that was published twenty-eight years later in 1979 as *He Who Hunted Birds in His Father's Village: The Dimensions of a Haida Myth*. He wrote in the introduction:

> This essay was written some years ago when I was a green would-be scholar in Oregon. I set myself to the task of laying out the many levels of meaning a single myth could hold . . .

In Chapter IV, "Sources of the Myth," he writes,

> In this chapter we leave the realms of respectable cultural and comparative folklore. The purified and cautious students of Boas and the folklorists utilizing methods of the Finnish scholars and Stith Thompson consider any attempt to establish "basic causes" and "ultimate sources" risky business.
>
> The approach of this chapter cannot be justified in terms

of current critical method. Nonetheless, establishing multilevel significance in a myth requires that we search through scientifically unsound, and contradictory, outmoded, or suspicious theories. . . .

Well, he's jumping over bear droppings, so to speak, daring methods and forms, as a poet does. This innovative work Gary did as a student at Reed College, where he read anthropology texts, such as *The Woman Who Married a Bear,* and unexpurgated Coyote stories. "It gave me a new way of seeing animals, which seemed right." All is possible, even writing a story commentary that is poetry and prose, information and insight. All is possible when the *total* story is given back; perhaps the only difficulty will be in finding a language that can retell this old and new story together, that will reflect the integrity of the story: the story that we've inherited and the story of the way of life in which it is embedded, the story we need to hear again of the complex mosaic of all life (. . . the Brown Bears, the Grizzlies, (but we wouldn't speak of them directly by such blunt names)).

"Original Mind," writes Gary,

> speaks through the little myths and tales that tell us how to be in some specific ecosystem of the far-flung world—a foggy island, a chilly altiplano—as we sit us down around the fire.

Each year the world's riches diminish: the foggy island, the chilly altiplano, the rainforest, great mammals (what did Jonah learn in the belly of the whale?), the birds, the myths, the rich diversity of stories. For the last thirty years I have watched countless songbirds come back to this woodland forest and raise their young, sing their haunting thrush songs all summer, fly off in autumn to come back the next spring. From as many as ten nesting pairs, I've seen the numbers dramatically diminish until one year none came. Now one song in a half-mile of woods is a miracle.

For a long time, Gary Snyder has been both a vociferous speaker and a quiet and persistent worker of the old/new way of life that he writes and tells in his stories. He has the unusual capacity to remain cheerful in the moment (in the face of the earth's devastation), and to present a large and long, long view—a view that says things can change, and rather quickly, and maybe even for the better. The ability to hold the paradox is one of the gifts he brings.

In Gary's poem, "What Happened Here Before," he tells the story of the piece of land he lives on from minus 300 million years to now:

. . . now,

     we sit here near the diggings
     in the forest, by our fire, and watch
     the moon and planets and the shooting stars—

     my sons ask, who are we?
     drying apples picked from homestead trees
     drying berries, curing meat,
     shooting arrows at a bale of straw.
     military jets head northeast, roaring, every dawn

     my sons ask, who are they?

     WE SHALL SEE
     WHO KNOWS
     HOW TO BE

     Bluejay screeches from a pine.

This new/old story that Gary, among others, is telling may not look or sound exactly like the usual one with a beginning, a middle, and an end; we have our stories, the trees have theirs. It is the forest's story that needs to be heard. This story may not have our usual sense of time in it—but what is that, anyway? Navaho time, Tibetan time, Roman time, people say. They may soon say: Tongass Forest time, fish time, whale time, people-working-at-computers and people-picking-berries time. Gary is telling stories that reflect the way of life we now live, neither forgetting our grandparents nor our children, stories that tell us "where we are."

Describing Dorothy Wordsworth's writing, Virginia Woolf said, ". . . but the truth is sought, because to falsify the look of the stir of the breeze on the lake is to tamper with the spirit which inspires appearances." I suspect this is a good description of Gary's nature writings as well.

I have just been rereading J. M. Synge's *Aran Islands*, noting that it is often the person in the middle—that is, straddling two cultures or ways—who brings the enduring stories that connect them. Bless these messengers who know the beauty of permanence and the beauty of impermanence, who have reached the age of "obedient ears" (said Confucius of himself at sixty) and can hear "of a world above and a slippery tree or pole you can climb to get there; of worlds below and mudpeople dancing in the dark, of people and animals shifting shapes about, and of the need for compassion and patience and forbearance in winning aid from an ally like Mouse Woman . . ." Praise this messenger who knows that the surefoot and the long road and the messenger moving are one.

Clayton Eshleman:

IMAGINATION'S BODY AND
COMRADELY DISPLAY

In celebration of Gary Snyder's sixtieth birthday, I would like to briefly explore three themes: the poet as a *hagazussa* (fence rider, or boundary crosser), how my own apprenticeship to poetry was stimulated and focused by Snyder's friendship in Kyoto (1962–1964), and the circumstances and nature of a visionary experience there that engages the first two themes. While I was not Gary's buddy or peer, his presence pervaded not only my daily life but the most essential aspects of my poetic activity. I think it could be argued that in the case of a young, unformed poet and an older, considerably formed poet, the kind of relationship Snyder and I enjoyed is ultimately much more useful than living master-apprentice arrangements for the younger poet. We live in a period in which nearly every young person who wants to be a writer studies with someone. My direct apprenticeship, while in Kyoto as well as afterwards, was with César Vallejo's European poetry: i.e., with a text, not with the man.

For those of us who view the nature of reality as incomplete and still under construction, exploration is involved with seeking out "the other," personality transformation, and nest building—creating a place to *be*, in a poetry that is a fabrication of what one has rubbed against, picked up, swallowed, and so on, in the flux of one's adventures with what one is and, perhaps more importantly, with what one is not. D. H. Lawrence's proclamation, "Living, I want to depart to where I *am*," seems underwritten by Bashō's ". . . So—when was it— I, drawn like blown cloud, couldn't stop dreaming of roaming, roving the coast up and down . . ." which is the epigraph to Snyder's *The Back Country,* a book dedicated to another explorer of the boundaries of culture and wilderness: Kenneth Rexroth.

•

All twentieth-century artists of any merit dwell in one way or another on a periphery. Whether one sees this periphery as ontological (as a circle whose center is everywhere since it has no circumference) or sociopolitical (as a kind of floating outer edge of a power zone at whose epicenter is the American president and Congress), it involves the artist in an inside and an outside. For a moment, think of the active, traveling poet as a *hagazussa,* the witch who, in the Middle Ages, was said to sit on the *hag,* or fence, which was built behind the gardens and separated the village from the wilderness.[1] As the figure of the *hagazussa,* the poet could be said to participate in both of these worlds. She roams the forest, experiencing her wildness, or animal nature, within herself, under the visionary assumption that to be *consciously* tame one has had, at least once, to experience wildness. Or put another way: If I want to know what is inside, I have to have been outside. By extension: To know who I am, I have to have experienced what I am not.

We can now trace the origin of such a figure, in the form of the shaman, back to what appears to be the cradle of the mind: Upper Paleolithic decorated caves. Of course no one knows for sure what went on inside them in 17,000 B.C. when Lascaux was painted. But since many outer as well as inner cave entrances have been "signed" in such a way that they appear to have represented vulvas, or earth womb entrances, it is possible to argue that in such "rock wombs" the separation from the mother via dreams, initiations, possibly hallucinogens, was momentarily dissolved. That is, the primary dualities of life/death, subject/object, above/below, human/animal were obliterated. The individual "died" to be reborn, possibly as a shaman, or possibly as a fully functioning member of a tribal community at the mercy of *being* with very little sense of *having.* Such transformation of self, or "second birth," when it is for real, is not only a gigantically disruptive experience, but one which continues to "go off" throughout the life of the transformed, charging her or his utterance, as well as making, for most, life on the periphery highly unstable and often tragic.

In the case of certain Upper Paleolithic caves, even though we cannot literally read their information, we know that people actually went into their depths and left a record of their adventures with otherness as the first acts of what we today call art. By the Middle Ages, in Europe at least, this journey, while still quite physical, had become less a trek into an alien enclosure or total wilderness than a mental flight in which the fence rider (witch on a broom) soared off via ointments and/or hallucinogens to engage spiritual worlds that, depending on their own whims, mixed regeneration with degeneration. A "traveler" might climb a giant tree with runglike branches to reach first a copper city, then a silver and a golden one, or be held against a tree and sodomized by the Devil.

As the fence of civilization pushed further and further into the wilderness, such "ladders" to the other world nearly vanished. By the middle of the twentieth century we had, in effect, concentrated the abyss into such hell cores as Auschwitz and the atomic bomb, while the wilderness, or what was left of it, had become increasingly "denaturized" via technology and pollution. However, from the viewpoint of "the Great Subculture . . . that runs without break from Paleo-Siberian Shamanism and Magdalenian cave-painting; through megaliths and Mysteries, astronomers, ritualists, alchemists and Albigensians; gnostics and vagantes, right down to Golden Gate Park,"[2] the abyss or void (or in Buddhist terminology, *sunyata*) seems to be a multidimensional realm/nonrealm with Auschwitz at one extreme and Lascaux at the other.[3] Thus, in our time, the void has been constellated with a literal place of Hell and a literal although backdated place of Paradise.

Gary Snyder's assimilation of Far Eastern religion and culture is the most thorough of any post–World War II American artist. He is a kind of *hagazussa* who took the Far East as the goal of his flight and, instead of remaining there or becoming an Eastern guru here, has brought his flight information to bear on our culture and ecology via a resolutely American personality. In the late 1960s, he wrote "What You Should Know To Be A Poet," a deft, notational Poetic Curriculum proposing that poetic know-how is contingent upon cultural border crossing as well as visionary travel:

What You Should Know To Be A Poet

all you can about animals as persons.
the names of trees and flowers and weeds.
names of stars; and the movements of the planets
        and the moon.

your own six senses, with a watchful and elegant mind.

at least one kind of traditional magic:
divination, astrology, the *book of changes,* the tarot;

dreams.
the illusory demons and illusory shining gods;

kiss the ass of the devil and eat shit;
fuck his horny barbed cock,
fuck the hag,
and all the celestial angels
                    and maidens perfum'd and golden—

& then love the human: wives   husbands   and friends.

childrens' games, comic books, bubble-gum,
the weirdness of television and advertising.

work, long dry hours of dull work swallowed and accepted
and livd with and finally lovd.   exhaustion,
                    hunger, rest.

the wild freedom of the dance, *extasy*
silent solitary illumination, *enstasy*

real danger.   gambles.   and the edge of death.[4]

The crucial stanza is the one beginning "kiss the ass of the devil . . ."
and ending with "perfum'd and golden." The poet-to-be is counseled
not only to go to the library but, abruptly, to travel in demonic and
celestial realms, exploring desire, in order upon return to "then love
the human." The poem proposes that the poet is a figure of eclectic
but certain knowledge who, after flight, loves relationship, popular
culture, work, dance, meditation, "and the edge of death." The last
line evokes the shamanic sense in which one is only truly alive after
having proved a willingness to die symbolically in the leaving of this
world for another one. Commenting on "power vision," Snyder has
said: "It's a process of tearing yourself out of your personality and
culture and putting yourself back in it again."[5] And in an essay also
from the 1960s, "Why Tribe," Snyder wrote: "The Great Subculture
has recognized that for one to 'follow the grain' it is necessary to look
exhaustively into the negative and demonic potentials of the Un-

conscious, and by recognizing these powers—symbolically acting them out—one releases himself from these forces."[6]

•

Boundary crossing has a literal substratum upon which imaginative flight is poised, and one reason that Snyder's poetry and prose ring with authenticity is that he actually sat on the platforms of Daitoku-ji, learned Chinese and Japanese, and studied for years with a Zen roshi. Via Snyder's, Ginsberg's, and Cid Corman's poetry, a vision of Far Eastern sensibility has contributed to the undermining of the Protestant stronghold that until the late 1950s was virtually the only castle complex in the American landscape. It was my privilege, from 1961 to 1964, to spend considerable time with both Snyder and Corman in Kyoto.

I always saw Cid at a downtown coffee shop (The Muse), which he used as an "evening office," and while my visits were unscheduled, there was a certain formality present. The conversation was usually involved with poetry, translation (Cid was working on Paul Celan, Eugenio Montale, and Bashō during these years), editing (he was doing *origin,* second series), and literary news. I arrived with a set of things to talk about—it didn't feel right to try to just hang out with Corman. Unlike Cid, who only had a sleeping room, Gary and Joanne Kyger had a house, which was the site of many weekend parties, and Barbara Eshleman and I related to them on one level socially, as a couple. Contact with Snyder covered a lot that was not literature (he taught me how to ride a motorcycle, worked out in my judo dojo for a while, and so on), and thus he proposed more images of the life of a poet to me at that time than Corman did. I would probably have never ended up in Kyoto at all had Gary not proposed we move there when he and Joanne stayed with us in a Tokyo suburb in the winter of 1961 on their way to India. They offered us their house to use on our first Kyoto visit and invited Barbara to stay with them while I was finishing up my one-year stint with the University of Maryland Far Eastern Division in Korea, during the spring of 1962. They also found us a place to live, and pointed us toward jobs teaching English as a second language. They were comradely acquaintances during our two and a half years there. Kyoto in the early 1960s looked as if it might become a Far Eastern alternative to Paris—it didn't, but probably through Snyder more than anyone else, it became an accessible and amazingly reasonable cultural out-post for some half-dozen American writers during this period (one could rent half of a nineteenth-century Japanese house with a garden for $25 a month). Alan Watts, Allen Ginsberg, Philip Whalen, and Frank Samperi all visited while Cid, Gary, and I were there.

Snyder's greatest generosity consisted in his displaying himself ex-actly as he was, offering me an image of cheerful austerity to take with me in my wars with myself. It sounds simple enough to say this, but the impact of such a display is enormous. In *Maximus III,* when Charles Olson writes

> Enyalion
> is possibility, all men
> are the glories of Hera by possibility, Enyalion
> goes to war differently
> than his equites, different
> than they do, he goes to war with a picture

> far far out into Eternity[7]

he is asserting that Enyalion, in having "a picture," is armed in his border crossing, as his "equites" (horsemen, or knights) are not, and that by having a picture, or vision, he is able to range "far far out into Eternity." Ointments or hallucinogens by themselves (as thousands failed to discover in the late 1960s) are incapable of enabling the "traveler" to bring something back. Without a picture, or pattern into which to loose the experience, the potentially visionary dissolves within itself.

Snyder's display became a frame in which I was able to connect hard work, self-reliance, taking chances, goofing off, and wide read-ing; i.e., a continual crisscrossing of the nourishing emptiness of work with an appreciation of all that was not work. Walking to the market for whale steaks, sitting awash with memories on a deserted bell-shrine cross beam, going to hostess bars with students and not speaking English, finding myself in green spa water with Hiroshima survivors—all were part of the weave of a contextual loom, centrif-ugal in life, centripetal in art. At the same time, I was studying sec-tions from Snyder's long poem-in-progress, "Mountains and Rivers," as they appeared in *origin* magazine. In that major work, to be completed in the 1990s I imagine, events/things in space and time, set forth as equals, perform a grounded and kaleidoscopic inter-change. The "equals" (=) of "The Market" are underscored by a paragraph from a letter to Ginsberg (also to be found in *origin*):

> "6 hours to fly to New York or walk from a creek to a certain lake; things like Aden or Oman seen from afar; the falling-back-in-time of a striped lateen sail on the Red sea, what happened in certain towns, the kinds of cheap wines, gradual lowering of the north star as you travel south . . ."[8]

As Robert Duncan wrote, the 1960s was a time of all things coming into their comparisons.

It is important not to make all of this sound more coherent than it was, certainly in regard to me. I was *in* a dark woods more than I was *with* one. There was even a peculiar sense of wilderness in the foothills of Higashiyama (East Mountain) where we lived. One minute you were in a neighborhood, the next you were in a bamboo forest with rising and falling zigzagging footpaths, which might pass an isolated fenced house through whose gate slats amber interior light could be seen flickering. I used the neighborhood public bath, and on cold midwinter evenings clacked home over gravel in geta, red as a lobster, dazzled by a gibbous moon streaked by viridian clouds.

•

It seems that the image of Enyalion, as he who goes to war with a picture, and the image of the *hagazussa,* who perched on a periph-ery, traveling back and forth into the areas on both sides of her perch, are aspects of a larger, composite image. The discovery of a picture, or focus, may be *the* prerequisite for resourceful mental traveling. It is possible that it is the picture itself that is transformed during the flight, and that this moment of transformation is a crucial aspect of the nature of imagination itself. What the witch, or poet, envisions is often monstrous if for no other reason than that the act of making monstrous is the act of rendering something more amply, deeply, of showing to what extent a flexibility of mind can elaborate and di-mensionalize any material that is, in effect, fed into it. As animals we devour and excrete what our body does not use as fuel. As imagi-nations we also devour, but here a significant distinction takes place: Mental transformation can be total without a casting off of unused material. As usual, however, there is a price for anything that makes a claim on totality: Imaginative product is only alive to other alive imaginations. To a priest of the Inquisition, a witch's testimony only confirms his own prejudices. The wilder her story, the more it is, in his opinionated faith, a lie.

Without really choosing to, I became obsessed with a green, yellow, and red garden spider who had made a large web between a persimmon tree's branches and some bushes in the backyard of the Okumura house in which we rented two rooms. Throughout September 1962, I would drag a chair from the enclosed porch at the rear of the house, which I had turned into a small workroom, out by the persimmon, and "spider sit." I didn't seek out books on spiders, and during this period only made a couple of brief attempts to write "about" the spider. I kept noticing that her brightly colored abdomen was the size of a gonad, and at that point personalization stopped. At that point, my mind went blank and, sitting there, I seemed to draw an odd sort of nourishment from simply being by her. It didn't occur to me then that the wording of such a thought evokes infant and mother, but I think there was a reactivation of something that had been buried in me from the time I was very young until, in my search for some confirmation that writing poetry was to be my destiny, I found myself by this spider.

Such sensations of early attachment were made even more vivid when one morning I discovered the web badly torn—a disheveled mess—and the spider gone. A sensation of loss passed through me that as long as I stayed with it—simply with the sensation—seemed utterly acceptable, even noble. The moment I caught myself thinking: I feel this way about the disappearance of this spider, I felt more than embarrassment. I sensed that I had felt something that no one should feel, something "unnatural." Today, I can see how such "unnaturalness" can be understood as a movement toward the nonnatural or imaginative. That September morning, I had crossed via identification and loss into an area that I was not prepared to be in. To return to Enyalion: That morning I had been given a picture. My poetic problem was that when I returned to my workroom, to write, I was still in the grip of a "given," or Indiana frame of mind—meaning that I had not opened a via into the unconscious that the smiths of Indiana had, with my cooperation, of course, welded shut.

My need for poetic confirmation was backed by the fact that the poetries that had redirected my life in the late 1950s seemed to have in them, or in back of them, a passage into "the other side of nature," as Rilke put it, where a vision, totem, or profound insight occurred. It seemed that the novice's desire to be a poet had to be confirmed by an extraordinary gift from the poetic spirit itself, and that without such a confirmation there seemed to be something inauthentic about calling oneself a poet. In this sense, the *hagazussa*'s flight was less an ongoing nocturnal activity than a single rupture with daily reality. But it also did not seem to be something one could plan. I continued my daily schedule of reading mythology, poetry, and psychology, writing, and translating César Vallejo (three to four hours every afternoon), begging poetry for some sort of sign that I was not wasting my time.

The sign was delivered at the end of October in a twenty-four-hour period that in retrospect looks like an initiation planned by my unconscious. While most of the initiation was taking place, I was utterly unaware of it, and merely went along with the sequential outcome of what appeared to be a commonplace occurrence: While drinking sake with Barbara and Susumu Kamaike (Corman's Bashō co-translators) at a local sushi counter, a stranger to my right started up a conversation and invited me to come downtown to his bar and have more drinks. He did not invite Barbara or Kamaike. I turned to Barbara and asked: What do you think? She turned to Kamaike and asked: What do *you* think? Kamaike said: He looks ok. So, off we went.

We ended up in Uji, a tea-growing area thirty miles outside of Kyoto, waking up some friends of the guy who had a restaurant there, and drinking and eating until around 3 A.M. Somehow they all got me safely back to the Okumura house, and upon waking up the next morning, with a terrific hangover, I recalled a dream in which Gary Snyder, in a kind of steam shovel contraption, was lowered over a green felt-covered gambling table, where he astonished everyone present by picking up gold coins with his buns (some of the action of the dream had to do with Halloween: The night before, Barbara had given her junior high school English students an apple-bobbing party). I then spent most of the day trying to evade the day, feeling empty and degenerate. Not knowing what to do with myself, I motorcycled over to a bar dormitory to see if a male friend who managed a hostess bar was in. He was not, but the mama-san invited me in anyway, sat me down with tea and cookies before a TV set, and left the room. There was a teenage adventure movie on, in which a fat boy tried to climb a pole during a track meet and failed, to the glee of his peers. I suddenly thought of Robert Kelly (who weighed four hundred pounds in those days) and was moved to tears over what I took to be Kelly's difficulties as a man and as a writer. I found myself muttering "have compassion for Kelly" over and over, and when I left the dormitory I felt so sensitive it was as if my nerves were in the very surface of my skin.

Still not knowing what to do with myself, I cycled out to northwestern Kyoto to the Snyders' for an impromptu visit, and again found that the person I had come to visit was not home—but Joanne was, and again I was invited in for tea. We sat at the *kotatsu* for an hour or so, discussing Jung and some of his hard-to-grasp terms. I left near dusk and started home. Cycling down Junikendoori, a wide commercial avenue on which I had not been before, I began to hallucinate: The motorcycle became an ox, its handlebars ox horns; a lumberyard turned into a manger in which I saw wise men kneeling by the infant Jesus. It was as if my unconscious had abruptly smashed through its containing wall and was gushing onto everything I looked at. Given the fact that there were cars and buses in the street, the dangerousness of the situation kept me somewhat in contact with that aspect of reality; on the other hand, I felt weightless, buoyant, and encased in a sensual lusciousness, as if I were under water. Everything seemed insubstantial and in a constant flux of unpredictable transformation. I became aware that I was approaching a famous medieval landmark, Nijo Castle, which was big and square and had a moat. I was instructed to get off my motorcycle and circumambulate the castle, with the understanding that at some point in my walk the goal of the experience would be revealed. It was getting dark, and I wandered counterclockwise around the castle, amongst the tourists and floodlights. At the northwest corner I looked up and, maybe forty feet over my head, saw the same spider I had sat by in the backyard, clinging to its web with its back to me— but now it was bigger than I was, and bright red. It pulsed there, as if attached to the sky itself.

The spectacle was so overwhelming that I couldn't think, and the next morning when I awoke and tried to write down what had happened, my "regular" mind took over, and what I came up with seemed so inadequate to the experience itself that I put it in the drawer and tried to forget about it. But I knew a confirmation had taken place that I might never be able to adequately express. Perhaps it did not need to be expressed. Perhaps imagination's body had revealed itself to me for several moments, and would become an ally, enabling an interchange between inner and outer worlds. And if imagination did reveal itself as a lowly if transformed spider (the "natural" green and yellow markings having disappeared), then everything was material. And that meant that all the sensations and images that I had been considering nonpoetic (incomprehensible, embarrassing, too personal, too technical, downright disgusting, etc.) were grist for the mill. They might not equal poetry, but they were not to be shunned and repressed. Imagination's body is more than human.[9]

Gary Snyder's role in this poetic confirmation was indirect, but subtly pervasive. Thankfully, on the most important level, I was not his student, and was on my own. Had he directly promoted such an experience, I could never have really claimed it, as I do, as my own. But consider: I was in Kyoto because of his invitation and job information. He had taught me how to ride the motorcycle that brought me to Nijo Castle. I dreamed of him the night before the experience, and sought him out before it took place. He and Joanne found the Okumura house for us, behind which I discovered the spider. In other words, his comradely display had created a kind of stage, or dancing grounds, on which, if I was able, I might work out the rudiments or building blocks of an art. The picture had to be my own, as well as the flight. But, as I was slowly and painfully learning in those most precious Kyoto years, nothing realizes itself without a context. Some of Gary Snyder's grain swirls through my own.

—Ypsilanti
November 1989

NOTES

1. I am indebted to the first six chapters of Hans Peter Duerr's *Dreamtime* (Blackwell, 1985) for the material on the *hagazussa*.

2. Gary Snyder, *Earth House Hold* (New York: New Directions Publishing Corp., 1969) 115.

3. In Charles Olson's poem "La Préface," the words *Buchenwald* and *Alta-mira* are placed in the same line paratactically, with a bit of space between them; i.e., primordial creation and annihilation have come that close in our century. For an extended comment on the Olson poem and the killing centers, see "Go-lub the Axolotl" in my *Antiphonal Swing: Selected Prose 1962–1987* (New York: McPherson, 1989). Adorno is said to have stated that there can be no poetry after Auschwitz. Recently, in his magnificent poem *Khurbn,* Jerome Rothenberg has proposed that after Auschwitz there is only poetry.

4. Snyder, *Regarding Wave* (New York: New Directions Publishing Corp., 1970) 40–41. For a differing contextualization of this poem, see my *Novices: A Study of Poetic Apprenticeship* (Los Angeles: Mercer & Aitchison, 1989).

5. Snyder, *The Real Work* (New York: New Directions Publishing Corp., 1980) 4.

6. Snyder, *Earth House Hold,* 115.

7. *The Maximus Poems Volume Three* (New York: Grossman, 1975) 38.

8. *origin #2,* second series (1962): 63. In another letter to Ginsberg, part of which is reprinted on the same page in *origin #2,* Snyder writes: "Real love has a mean face & a sharp tongue & wisdom is a HORRIBLE MASK."

9. The spider vision has come up at other points in my writing. See "The House of Okumura VI" in *Coils,* "The Book of Coatlicue" in *El Corno Emplu-mado* 14, "Placements II" in *Antiphonal Swing,* and the 11th chapter in *Novices.* It was not, however, until rethinking the experience for this essay that I realized that I had inserted an offer of LSD by Snyder the following year into the actual time frame of the natural spider and the visionary spider. In doing so before, I had had to admit that not only might the description of LSD have played a role in the experience, but it was also possible that Joanne had put LSD into my tea right before the hallucinations. Now I am nearly sure that on no level did LSD have anything to do with the vision.

Jerome Rothenberg:
THE POET WAS ALWAYS FOREMOST

For me the poet was always foremost, & the legend of the poet secondary. The person is there is any case, but where I continue to see him best is as he emerges from his poems. It was Robert Kelly, I think, who first turned my attention to the work—around the time that LeRoi Jones's Totem Press was bringing out the edition of *Myths & Texts* with the Will Petersen calligraphic cover—& it was Robert Bly who made the contact. I had been seeing poems signed Gary Snyder for maybe a year or two before that & had by then formed a small sense of what he did. The Donald Allen anthology (published the same year) gave us some more of it, but otherwise, for me, there was no Snyder myth as yet. Only the poetry.

Its beginning & its end—among the stars—brought Dante to mind, or Thoreau in its claims to wilderness & a kind of ecstasy through wilderness; but mostly that here, in the territory he had chosen (of a poetry like Pound's, say, that drew from many times & places), there was a new space in which to work, with a link to the illustrious predecessors but opening old Whitman's democratic vistas in a way that most of those before him had failed to do. ("If Snyder hadn't been there," Richard Schechner said later, "we would have had to invent him.") It was a time, for poets, of rediscovery & extension, in which the modernist past (& all the premodernist pasts it laid claim to) were again there as resources to be used & to be addressed to a new &, so we thought, a very different generation. In this Gary had a *line*—both as verse & program—& it was that which we sighted & seized on in a reading of his work.

The time itself was still postwar—or what I've come increasingly to think of as postholocaust—even for those of us who were too young for it. I can't get at the heart of it even now, but something about that war, that point in history, had turned the great American modernists on their heads or, put another way, had infused the kind of work they left for us with what George Oppen pointed to as a new populism. With a new openness, too—or generosity with regard to who might be thought to belong. What Snyder gave us, then, was a kind of Wobbly modernism (even before the Zen): regional & specific, gritty, disciplined; true to his own voice, surely, but opening as well to larger worlds, as that sort of thing, that largeness, was happening also in Olson's work, say, or in Duncan's. It was a time, as I saw it, to reclaim & to expand—transform—the century's beginnings, & what he did, while it felt different from my own concerns then, seemed true & proven in the work. Alongside Duchamp's project ("to put art again at the service of mind") or Breton's ("the critical investigation of the notions of reality and unreality, of reason and unreason, of reflection and impulse, of knowing and fatally not knowing, of utility and uselessness"), it was soon possible to join & to relate Snyder's articulation of "the real work of modern man: to uncover the inner structure and actual boundaries of the mind."

The primary means for that uncovering is the actual work we do as poets—& *work* is a better, bigger word for it than *poem*—but it is or can be more than what that seems to say. To uncover or discover is to open to a search for sources—in the human past & in the greater world beyond the human. In this sense Snyder was then & was to become still more a leading figure. There is no poet I know with a surer sense of that possibility of staring our animal natures in the eye that he attributes to the shaman-poet—in any and all cultures, and & all times & places. It is no small thing that he does here: To open poetry again to the possibilities of a genuine engagement with nature & to know that to write of a tree is not a sin in our time, as Brecht would have had it, but an exploration of matters central to our survival in this world. So, in his poem, "The Humpbacked Flute Player," a landmark work for me, the poet is left in Canyon de Chelly, having invoked a world of Buddhist saints & American Indian ghost dancers, with no sense of guilt about the work itself, but letting the poem come to him, the old communion restored/redeemed, where

> up in the mountains that edge the Great Basin
>   it was whispered to me
>   by the oldest of trees.
>   by the oldest of beings,
>
>   the Oldest of Trees.
>
>   and all night long sung on

> by a vast throng
>> of Pinyon
>> Pine

It is survival that he celebrates here, & survival comes also into his sense of poetry overall, & with that a truly contemporary, truly meaningful approach to what I have elsewhere (& using the wrong word maybe) spoken of as an "ethnopoetics." It is part of Snyder's premise as a poet opening to larger worlds—that one moves from the regional (the bioregional at that) into a regard for other times & places. It was this, beyond the visions of those who preceded us, that he first knew how to make meaningful for our own time & place. For myself: Though I had come with others to the common store of ethnopoetics, it needed his impetus, his insight, to sense poetry not only as a work of mind in search of worlds & meanings, but as the "ecological survival tool" that he set out in his essay on "poetry & the primitive." In a letter that he wrote me when I was already deep into the work, he spoke of poetry in this sense as "a vehicle to ease us into the future." The bridging effect of that statement was tremendous—as if something vital, missing from our Great Collage, had there been set in place.

In retrospect I want to say at least that much in tribute.

—Encinitas, California
December 1989

James Laughlin:

NOTES ON GARY SNYDER

There is no one alive whom I admire more than Gary as a person— as a "soul," if you will, and an inspirer of other souls—but this is hard to get into words without becoming heavy or corny.

In the state of the world and our society today, Gary Snyder is surely the poet who gives us, both emotionally and intellectually, useful guidelines for what we can and must do.

As I see it, three influences or three traditions are fused together in Gary's work to give it its unique character and significance. These can be expressed variously, but I would put them thus: first, the meaning and utility that Zen Buddhism can have for us in the West; second, the importance of the concept of tribalism as derived from Gary's study of the American Indians and other primitive cultures; and third, ecology, not only as preservation, but as a way for us to have a rich and complete life in the environment of nature.

Gary's interest in Zen must have begun in the early fifties when he was doing graduate work in Chinese and Japanese at Berkeley. In the next decade, working his way as a seaman, he spent many years in Japan, where he formed an affiliation with a Zen monastery in Kyoto for intensive study. He applied Zen principles in a life devoted to "gardening and gathering shellfish." Diary entries in *Earth House Hold* record this formative period. Gary sees Zen not as an esoteric cult practice, but as teaching and discipline for a good life. He speaks of "careful attention to the immediate" and "being one with what you are doing." What he believes he puts into practice with those who come to the zendo that adjoins his house in the foothills of the Sierra. Zen interpenetrates his concepts of tribalism and ecology.

The power of Zen, Gary has said, is not like a political power, but is "the knowledge of the self, the power of no-power, a basic human possibility that can be uncovered anyplace, anytime. It's a process of tearing yourself out of your personality and your culture and putting yourself back in it again. . . . Through Zen we can understand the Buddhist concepts of oneness and uniqueness, our social or ritual nature and our personal perception."

By tribalism Gary does not primarily mean totem poles or shamanism, but simply people supporting each other and living in harmony with nature, including the animals. He once told me that when he died, he hoped it would be by being eaten by a bear so that he could reenter the food chain. In the past dozen years, he's spent several seasons in Alaska, in part to study bears; I've suggested that he take along a rifle.

Gary has written that he holds "the most archaic values on earth . . . the fertility of the soil, the magic of animals, the terrifying initiation and rebirth; the love and ecstasy of the dance, the common work of the tribe." He believes that "the real work of modern man is to uncover the inner structure and actual boundaries of the mind," and to that end, in his poetry, he seeks to reveal the "close correspondences between the external and internal landscape." In that sense the poet is a shaman.

Gary's ecology asks the basic question, "What are we going to do with this planet?" He goes beyond specifics such as deforestation and pollution to broader philosophical concepts. "My poems," he says, "call the society's attention to its ecological relationships in nature. It's a problem of love; not the humanistic love of the West—but a love that extends to animals, rocks, dirt, all of it. Without this love, we can end, even *without* war, with an uninhabitable place."

A few words about Gary's poetry. It is concrete, concise, and happily devoid of rhetoric and self-advertisement. It says what it means. Its characteristic procedure is to move from simple description to poetic and intellectual statements. A process and a meditation taking shape is often visible. Metrically, it is free verse in organic form, the content determining the line patterns, both aurally and visually. The language has its own terse tone. The sounds are those of Gary Snyder—nobody else.

Robert Sund:

YES, IT'S REALLY WORK!

In a letter to me in 1954 William Carlos Williams said that what was going on in America amounted to singing: ". . . the whole country thinks it has to sing, all the magazines and newspapers are full of it—with undistinguished results. If anything even mildly noteworthy comes of it everyone who can hold a pen thinks he is a poet."

Poets of the Western tradition, especially in recent times, damage themselves through artistic egotism. An identifiable pattern has been rampant in American twentieth-century work: special sensibilities; unique personalities straining for originality; isolated; miserable; skimming the lowest level of satisfactions.

But the exceptions exist now and then, and we celebrate them, as we celebrate Gary Snyder now, on the occasion of his sixtieth birthday in May 1990. Snyder's enduring fascination with the subtle art of poetry is one of his endearing qualities. It is good to see a man who prevails and does not abandon the work he has to do.

It's apparent that early along Snyder had some important insights. In "Hay For The Horses," for example, the old man remembers the day he first bucked hay:

> I thought, that day I started,
> I sure would hate to do this all my life.
> And dammit, that's just what
> I've gone and done.

Snyder knew where to look for what he needed, and to listen when he got there; whether to an old man in the Sierra, or—across the Pacific Ocean and back in time to the T'ang dynasty—to the monk-poet, Han-shan, whom he translated:

> Go tell families with silverware and cars
> What's the use of all that noise and money?

•

There are certain words that Snyder has livened up—lighted up—in the course of his life so far. *Work* is one of them. (I once construed a motto for myself: "Don't give me a job, I'm *working*.") Wendell Berry has spoken of this distinction also, remarking on the difference between "man hours" and true labor, where people work *among* and *with* others rather than *for* them.

I like a writer whose work links me with the work of other writers. Snyder passes on a lot in this regard. What distinguishes him from merely literary figures are his scholarly pursuits and disciplines, his mental clarity, his ability to synthesize, and his patience in the scrutiny of history and its particulars. His respect goes out into so many things in the world; returning to him, it further enhances and confirms his gift.

He has been determined. Some men are done in by their determination, maybe lose sight of everything between themselves and their envisioned goals; they get lost in predispositions, and *logos* becomes an overwhelming reference, like dense brush. Not many inspired poems can find a way through it. Among Snyder's intentions, the big one is to speak for life both near at hand and out at its farthest reaches, where perceptions gather, where voice becomes voice and enters into things; so light shoots out of the poem, as out of a turning prism, testifying to work done well.

Gary's first book, *Riprap,* comes from his days in the North Cascades and the Sierra mountains of California, when he worked on trails and sat in a fire lookout for a season or so, congenial in company and finding a way into his solitude, pursuing work and study side by side. If we follow the years of writing since then, we arrive at "Bedrock," a poem for Masa, his dancer wife, who accompanied him from Japan back to Turtle Island, to Kitkitdizze in the Sierra foothills of northern California. We observe a gradual widening out: from person, to family, to community. "The Bath" is one of his great celebrations, a fine meeting of audaciousness and restraint. We linger in the bathhouse—"*Is this our body?*"—and step naked into the cool night air, linked with the starry sky and one another.

Link is another word Snyder has enlivened. Links and loops and whorls, and nets of sound. Long loops that go back farther than we can see. A little flow of words together calls up elemental song, the pure and precise thing, like a fossil revealed when the hammer hits the rock and it breaks apart, bringing light to leaf or shell, and making us wonder again. The work of the poet and the geologist requires precise approach, respect, energy, enthusiasm, and the enjoyment of surprise. One has to hit the rock just right. The other has to find and strike that place in language and experience where it will break cleanly open to reveal what is inside.

•

I'd like to note this: *Snyder's poems have endings*. And I think his Zen study has contributed directly. The Tea Master, Okakura Kakuzo, traveling in America in 1906, noticed that Americans are good at beginning things, but not at ending them. (A vatic insight! Look at our country's nuclear waste, piling up for mankind in some undreamed-of future to deal with.) The Tea Ceremony always concludes with washing utensils and putting them away. The cleanup is not something that comes after the ceremony is over; it's as important as any point along the way. Not to be put off and tended to later. Washing cleans the slate; it is an ultimate respect. We can see how this works for poetry, too. The ending makes way for what may come, and leaves room for it to enter. The capacity to finish something is no slight thing!

•

Meditation, prayer, chanting, connect us with memory at the deepest level, where we reclaim what might well otherwise be lost. *This* work is *never finished* but only complemented by the freshest contributions a people and a culture can bring to it. In one of his poems based on a Mohawk Indian prayer—"Prayer For The Great Family"—there is the repeated line: *in our minds so be it*. A line such as this brings us near to the nature of the chant. It is probably correct to see the refrain line of the modern poem—Yeats and Roethke, for example— as a remnant of once-prevalent forms typically associated with chanting.

The old chanting and the new poetry are related. Individual voice is one blossom on the tree. A shared sound is emerging, as though from the land itself . . . slowly. We catch traces of it in the wind. Thoreau, in his "lost journal" (published for the first time in 1958), in an entry for October 4, 1840, wrote: "A true poem is not known by a felicitous expression, or by any thought it suggests, as much as by the fragrant atmosphere which surrounds it. . . ."

•

Regarding "influence": I know that among the poets here in the Ish River country, the best of them would gladly join in praise of Snyder's poetry, and of his other writings as well. But what has "flowed in" is not so easy to assess or simple to define. What it will be, in the cultural body, remains to be discovered gradually. What we have to thank Gary Snyder for lies not in the matters of details, but in the matter of sustaining principles. As Kenneth Rexroth said in his essay on Morris Graves, the function of the artist is to reveal "the place of value in a world of facts."

As poets, many of us feel we are all going alongside one another, like fish in the elements we know and depend on—making our way together. To each of us, a good poem is a confirmation along the way; we can only be grateful for it.

Yes, It's Really Work!
(for Gary Snyder)

Down through mud, through clay and rock,
the deeply dug well
gives up its cool, sweet water.

—Ish River
April 14, 1989

Wendell Berry:
A TRAIL MAKER

One thing that distinguishes Gary Snyder among his literary contemporaries is his willingness to address himself, in his life and in his work, to hard practical questions. He has not participated in the prevalent assumption that one may safely specialize in one's art and leave other matters to be managed by other specialists. Having never adopted that particular brand of modern "freedom," he has been free of a kind of modern nonsense.

Any awake readers who open a book of poems or essays by Mr. Snyder will find themselves in the common world of our day, face to face with the common problems of our day: a cannibalistic social order supported by a parasitic economy. Mr. Snyder has confronted those problems directly in his work, not as some kind of propagandist intent upon the survival of some minimal part, but rather as a human being in love with the idea of a decent human community surviving in harmony with its natural sources and surroundings.

The native settings of Mr. Snyder's intelligence, one might say, are the human "house hold" and the local habitat group. And his art seems to be driven by two passionate questions: How can we best live the domestic and communal life that specifies us as humans? And how can we secure the companionship and the varied helps of our fellow creatures? In this, he has been scrupulous not to be dualistic or exclusive. It is not for us to determine who our neighbors will be. His questions have been asked in and of his own place and neighborhood in the Sierra foothills, and he has practiced his answers.

I have always liked the epigraph or gloss that follows the title of Mr. Snyder's first book, *Riprap:*

> a cobble of stone laid on steep slick rock
> to make a trail for horses in the mountains.

And I like the title poem of that volume:

> Lay down these words
> Before your mind like rocks.
> . . . .

> each rock a word
> a creek-washed stone

The likening shines first this way and then that, like a knife blade held edgewise to the light, *both* terms working and necessary in the world. This is a trail both to be thought about and to be walked over. From his first book until now, Mr. Snyder has been cobbling together a riprap of words, images, poems, tales, arguments, facts, ideas, and actual rocks, laying down a trail over a steep slick place. Those below him on the slope will be grateful.

Tim McNulty:

THE WILDERNESS POETIC OF GARY SNYDER

The rich scent of early spring still lingers in the valley bottoms of the Elwha River, in the wilderness heart of the Olympic Mountains. Last night's rain has dusted the trees on the upper slopes with snow, and the early blooms of trillium and Calypso orchid wink out from the duff and damp needles of the forest floor. Each year at this time I find myself camped with a small crew in the upper valley of the Elwha, clearing the trail as the winter snowpack retreats to the higher slopes. "Spring opening" we call it, and the work is always varied: bucking out windthrow logs, repairing bridges, recutting drains, and rocking in sloughs or washouts. Though the weather is still a bit unsettled, it's always a beautiful time of year in the upper valley. Harlequins and mergansers are up from the saltwater, breeding amidst the snow-melt rapids, and elk are low in the forest, browsing the newly green-ing benches and bottoms before heading up to the high meadows.

This is the last night of an eight-day stay in the valley, and we've packed down to the old guard station at Elkhorn to shorten the twelve-mile hike out to the trail head in the morning. We've finished dinner and I've taken up my favorite seat against a post on the front porch to keep an eye on the meadow, with its shaggy old firs and sweet, spring-scented cottonwoods, and to feel the cool evening breezes begin to sift downvalley.

All evening deer have been browsing the new tufts of meadow grass, and rufous hummingbirds, just arrived from Mexico, are buzz-ing about the wild rose and salmonberry blooms. An osprey flaps by low over the river and returns a short while later with a trout clutched in its talons. In a small opening across the river, a bull elk has stopped to browse. He is soon joined by a younger bull, and the two animals linger in the falling light before passing on to unseen destinations downvalley.

This evening, atop the pages of my journal, I opened a well-thumbed copy of a book that has made the trip up this valley with me more than once, and turned to a poem called "Journeys."

It was more than twenty years ago, when I was a student at a large eastern university, that I first sampled the mists of a place that was to become home. They were distilled in the lines of a thin chapbook of poems I pulled from the dusty shelves of Gordon Cairney's Grolier Book Shop, off Harvard Square. Their author, Gary Snyder, was a young poet whose work I had just stumbled upon.

> Elwha, from its source. Threadwhite falls
> out of snow-tunnel mouths with
> cold mist-breath
> saddles of deep snow on the ridges—

It wasn't just the freshness of the images that startled me, or their clarity and precision, but a sense, as I read on, that here was a voice that evoked the rugged grace, the vast unencumbered presence of the North American wilderness in a reverent yet thoroughly unsentimental way.

I had been reading the work of older Western American poets: Robinson Jeffers, William Everson, and Kenneth Rexroth, among others. Each was a revelation in his handling of wilderness, landscape, and place as major themes in his work. It was among these poets, more than my contemporaries in New England, that I recognized that strain of natural order, individual freedom, and primacy of land that I had first discovered in the earlier writings of Thoreau and Whitman. Only here, those elements were rekindled in a new and expansive landscape. The wilderness Thoreau sought in the Maine woods still abounded in the mountains, deserts, and seacoasts of the American West in the first half of this century. In these poets, I'd found work that had been shaped and nourished by these wild and open landscapes. They had found in land itself a primary text— a quality all but lacking in the cultural forms of the day—and I drank it in the way a thirsty man drinks deeply of mountain snowmelt.

Wilderness was hardly a popular concern when *Riprap* first appeared in 1959. Conservationists had been trying unsuccessfully for more than a decade to get a wilderness bill passed in Congress, and road building and cutting of remote areas of our national forests was accelerating at a phenomenal pace. Though Jeffers and Rexroth had both used wilderness imagery in their poems, no poet had yet embraced wild nature as a suitable subject for modern poetry. Certainly no poet took it upon himself to be a spokesperson for wilderness. Yet in his first book, in poems such as "Mid-August at Sourdough Mountain Lookout," "Piute Creek," and "Above Pate Valley," Gary Snyder did just that. These poems and others conveyed a sense of wilderness not only as a subject worthy of serious artistic inquiry, but as a natural state of being, as vital and necessary to basic human consciousness as it is to the earth. This essential unity underlies these poems, and charges each image with resonance and intensity. "Wilderness" as place and "wildness" as universal state were seen as one.

These ideas were expanded in *Myths & Texts*, where the universality of wilderness experience was deepened through the perspective of Native American myth and shamanism. It was in *Myths & Texts* that Snyder framed the exploitation and destruction of the natural world within the context of Judeo-Christian civilization's historical treatment of native cultures, peasants, and workers throughout the world. The civilizations of ancient China, Japan, and India are also implicated in what is seen in these poems as an arrogant and systematic *pogrom* against both wild nature and its metaphoric counterpart in the human unconscious.

Into this context the poet invoked the healing vision of the shaman and the magical power of the poem as spoken word to transform. *Myths & Texts* is a remarkable book, presenting a comprehensive worldview of history and civilization, and offering the kind of spiritually integrated vision that could begin to resolve the cyclical destructiveness of history. That this was accomplished with clear, sharp, imagistic lines that at times evoked the purity of the Japanese haiku form was unprecedented.

> Thick frost on the pine bough
> Leaps from the tree
> > snapped by the diesel
>
> Drifts and glitters in the
> > horizontal sun.

Throughout Gary Snyder's poetry, there is a heightened, animated sense of the natural world. Each blade of grass, each tree and stone is infused with its own suchness. This deeply religious perspective informs many of the poems in *The Back Country,* but it attains its fullest expression in *Regarding Wave.* Poems like "Wave,"

"Song of the Taste," and "Kyoto Born in Spring Song" are lyric celebrations of the interdependence of all species and the energy path-
ways shared by every being. They are poems informed as much by
ecology as by aesthetics, yet to read these poems at their deepest levels is to partake of a sacramental relationship between the poet and
his world,

> Drinking clear water together . . .
>   speaking   new words,
>   the first time . . .

It is poetry in its oldest and fullest sense.

In *Turtle Island,* Gary's first complete book of North American
poems written after his return from Japan, this religious insight is
confronted with a rate of resource exploitation and ecological devastation previously unwitnessed in the Western United States. The
poems born of this are a marked departure from the imagistic lyrics
of his earlier work. They are sharper edged with a longer narrative
line, and the voice of the poet is implicit. These are political poems,
as concerned with the abrupt undoing of the natural world as with
the beauty and truth that world holds. In this sense, they are the
logical and responsible synthesis of Snyder's early work in *Riprap*
and *Myths & Texts,* and they carry a resonance and authority that
comes of long and passionate involvement.

   Turtle Island was an important and influential book for many in
my generation. It was a honed and well-crafted poetic statement, as
well as a catalyst and a call to action among poets. What I still find
amazing is that couched among these longer, narrative, and didactic
poems are carefully wrought lyrics that, to me, stand among Gary's
most insightful and accomplished poems. "For Nothing" and "For
the Children" are the first to come to mind—and that delightful
koan "Avocado."

I can't speak for poets in other regions of the country, but for those
of us writing and working in the Pacific Northwest, Gary's work has
been both an inspiring and tremendously liberating example. Rural
poets and their concerns have never been of overwhelming interest
to the urban/academic quarterlies and presses that dictate literary
tastes in most of the United States. But here in the Northwest, fol-

lowing largely along a trace pioneered by Gary's work, a community of poets and writers has dug in, paid close attention to what this place had to say, and produced a body of fine work that takes a first, important step toward reconciling the affairs of human culture with the long-range sustainability of the biosphere. In this land of densely timbered mountains, clear, salmon-rich rivers, and pristine coast-lines, poets like Robert Sund, Michael O'Connor, Jody Aliesan, Clifford Burke, Michael Daley, Sam Green, Judith Roche, Tom Jay, and others have gone a long way toward distilling the many voices of this place—what Robert Sund has dubbed the Ish River country—and speaking out on its behalf. It is an esthetic that has become such an integral part of my own work, I no longer think of it as separate. And I know that each of us, in his or her own way, owes a great debt to Gary Snyder, to his quiet, contemplative poems of Northwest landscape, and to his outspoken poems in defense of wildlands throughout the earth.

As the last light begins to slip away downriver, a black bear appears in the willows on the far bank, munching shoots and nosing about the rocks. Occasionally, when the wind shifts, he gazes over this way, eyes narrowed and nose high in the air: "Old man in the fur coat," "Honey-eater," "Ripper-up of the back screen door . . ." We share more than a river, or a world, and our kinship is as old as we are young. We were all people together one time. Maybe it's true, "In the next century / or the one beyond that," as Gary has written, we can live there again, if we make it.

—Elkhorn, Elwha River
Spring, 1989

Paul Hansen:
FOR COLD MOUNTAIN'S STREAM

Twenty-five years ago, when I was studying at the University of Washington, a fellow student mentioned that Gary Snyder, poet and San Francisco beatnik, had studied Chinese literature with one of the most vastly learned contemporary scholars of Chinese culture, Edward H. Schaefer. Not long after, I came across *Riprap and Cold Mountain Poems,* a celebration of radical—and radically ancient—life-styles and traditional scholarship. What a liberating experience to see that learning need not be stuffy, and that an unconventional life need not be a suicidal dead end.

Since then for me and, I have found, for most of those I work with and care for, Gary Snyder has been an indispensable guide in these interesting times of the late twentieth century—this has been true whether we have been primarily concerned with Oriental thought and literature, sanity in an increasingly tragic United States, or the Dharma itself.

More than a generation of seeking people have found what Gary Snyder says and does rings of truth and right livelihood. Simple to outline, these are rare and precious qualities. Although I am not well acquainted with Gary, I have experienced his personal courtesy and kindness. It is an honor to contribute to this commemorative volume.

•

Wei Yeh (Wei "The Wild," 960–1020), five of whose poems I offer in translation here, was born in Szechwan but spent his adult life in a rugged area east of the prefectural town of Shan-chou (approximately 11°E × 34° 30′N), Honan Province. Though he declined official appointments and chose to live as a recluse, Wei married and had at least one child. He maintained as well extensive relations with high state officials and both Taoist and Buddhist monks and hermits.

According to the *Ssz-k'u T'i-yao* editors, his poems were valued by contemporaries as equal to those of the famous Hangchou-West-Lake hermit Lin Pu (967–1028, better known by his imperially conferred posthumous name, Ho-ching). For hundreds of years now the poetry of the Five Dynasties and Early Northern Sung has been dismissed as a vestigial twitch of Late T'ang styles, and Wei's poems are hardly read at all today. If one agrees with Kojiro Yoshikawa that a major contribution of Sung poetry is its "transcendence of sorrow," then this neglect of Wei Yeh is an injustice. There is considerable humor in his work, and on the whole it is upbeat and vivid. It is my hope that he be more widely read in the future.

Describing My Feelings

Wei Yeh
Of the eastern suburb
Plans life to follow conditions.

Duties? Disinclined
To sweep the dirt floor.
Poorer yet,
Who resents Heaven?
Famous, I'm unpreoccupied
With wealth and honor;
Nothing to do,
I'm a minor immortal.

Unnoticed
The light flows swift:
This body
Nearly half a century.

**Late Autumn
Cherishing Thoughts of Master Jun**

Wind's pure, Moon white:
The season of red trees.
No cure
For walls of mountain
Between me and Master Jun.

I still love
The deep night,
The creek racing past the steps
To White Lotus Pond.

**Written
On the Wall
At the Recluse Yu T'ai-chung's**

You I like
Because like me,
You dwell by wood
And spring.

Washing an inkstone
Fish gulp the black;
Boiling teawater
Cranes avoid the smoke.
Idle, I sing praising
Our saintly dynasty,
And old, don't despise
The flowing years.

Anything
Besides talking poetry,
I take a sleepy look
At the couch.

Ode to Myself
At Forty

Though the idle mind
Remains unmoved,
I realize my memory
Is imperceptibly failing.

Shrinking from *go*,
It's hard to amuse guests;
When lute-playing comes up,
I call for my son.
Too lazy to work?
The farm tools believe it.
A scattered person?
My Taoist robes know.

In times ahead
How will I use
Brush and inkstone?
In the shade,
Revising old poems.

Written
In the Honorable Lin's Room
At the Cloister of Beginning Change
San-Men Gorge

All about waves strike;
The mountain seems to shake.
A monastery half-in-space
Caps the headmost peak.

The balcony doors and windows
Are mostly shut in the morning:
Monks, sitting or lying around,
Must hate to watch
The boats sink.

Robert M. Torrance:

GARY SNYDER AND THE WESTERN POETIC TRADITION

If we think of Snyder as a "Western" poet, it is Western America—
the Pacific Northwest, San Francisco, and the western slope of the
Sierra—that we are likely to have in mind: the West that connects,
as Snyder often reminds us, with East Asia along and across the Pacific Rim. In terms of worldwide poetic traditions and spiritual practices, on the other hand, it is with the East that most readers will
naturally link him, and for excellent reasons; his serious study of
Chinese and Japanese poetry and of Zen and other forms of Mahayana Buddhism (as well as of the ethnopoetic traditions that tran-
scend and broaden both the Eastern and Western inheritances) are
indisputably central to his poetry and his thought. Critical essays and
articles exploring the poetry and expounding the thought focus
most often, as we would expect, on such topics as Japanese Allusions,
or Images of China, in Snyder, or on Snyder and Taoism, The Influence of Zen Buddhism, or Buddhism and Energy: all pointing due
East.

Such an emphasis is understandable, indeed nearly inevitable,
since even the most casual reader, leafing for the first time through
Snyder's various collections of poems, interviews, and essays, would
almost certainly be struck, soon and often, by the predominance of
reference to things Eastern. This twenty-two-year-old summer lookout records in his journal (as printed in *Earth House Hold*) that he
has been reading the sutra of Hui Nêng and fretting with the thorny
Huang Po doctrine of Universal Mind. "First wrote a haiku and
painted a haiga for it," he notes one August day, "then repaired the
Om Mani Padme Hum prayer flag, . . . then shaved down a shake
and painted a zenga on it . . ." Here already we find the connection
between mountainous wilderness and Eastern art and thought that
Snyder had first experienced as a boy when he saw, with a shock of
recognition (as he describes it in his *East West* interview of 1977),
that the Chinese landscape paintings in the Seattle Art Museum de-
picted a geography "just like the Cascades": the Chinese painters' eye
for the *real,* as Snyder too saw it, was what distinguished them from

the meaningless Western landscapes in the next room, and drew him toward Eastern civilization and the mountains alike.

His study of the Chinese and Japanese languages and the Buddhist religious tradition, and his long journey to the Far East and his return, after passage through India, to the Far West that adjoins it, in a circle starting and ending with Douglas fir and ponderosa pine, followed from and enriched that seminal recognition, to which his poetry continues to give richly varied expression. The initially bewildering profusion of Chinese, Japanese, and Indian names scattered throughout poems concerned with rivers and mountains and their flora and fauna, with solitude and with family, with work and with love, are no mere arbitrary allusions but Snyder's means of meditating on the profoundly commonplace realities seen (or more often unseen) by the everyday eye, realities that we see more truly by seeing them for ourselves as Hui Nêng and Huang Po, Han-shan, and Seami—and Snyder—had seen them. Far from being random, these names, the more we read both of Snyder and of those whom Snyder has read, begin to *connect*, to take their place, piece by piece, in a tradition that is Eastern but—insofar as it does connect—also ours. They become, as Snyder writes in *Myths & Texts*, "not exotica but part of our whole planetary heritage," part of a tradition, however (as he remarked in "The Bioregional Ethic" interview of 1979), that "is *not* really there unless you make it so." Not he alone: you. And I.

The conviction that Snyder's literary tradition is essentially an Eastern one derives, of course, not only from critics' studies and readers' impressions but from Snyder's own words: "For me," he remarked in his "Craft Interview" of 1973, "it's the Chinese tradition and the tradition of Indian vernacular poetry, and also classical Sanskrit poetry of India, that I learned most from." Earlier poets in English practiced their art by translating or imitating Horace, Virgil, or Homer, and even Pound adapted Propertius and Sophocles as well as the Chinese; Snyder's translations are of Han-shan and Miyazawa Kenji. Moreover, his trenchant critiques of the ecological and human "destructiveness of Western civilization," and his sometimes categorical repudiation of a Western tradition that seemed to him "off the track" (as it did to others of a generation still sometimes popularly lumped together as "Beats"), reinforce the conviction that only in the poetic and spiritual traditions of the East did he find an alternative to one that could no longer be his.

Yet such a conclusion is obviously much too simple. To begin with, our casual reader, leafing back through all those volumes, will notice other names overlooked at first because they were *not* so strange. The young lookout on Crater Mountain and Sourdough was reading *Walden,* Jeffers, and Blake between sutras: "—study Chinese until eleven," he writes at one point, "—make lunch, go chop snow to melt for water, read Chaucer in the early afternoon." In Yosemite later, it was Milton he read by firelight and whose story, however "silly," he took to work with him "All of a summer's day," if not all of a summer. And though he may retrospectively have learned most from the Chinese and Indian poets, his acknowledged early influences include, not surprisingly, Whitman, Sandburg, Masters, Lawrence, Pound, Williams, Stevens, Yeats, and Eliot—who led him by way of *The Waste Land* to Jessie Weston's *From Ritual to Romance* and thence to Jane Harrison's *Prolegomena to the Study of Greek Religion* and the Welsh *Mabinogion.*

Nor did he leave these eminently Western sources of inspiration behind when he took ship for Japan; how, after all, could he? En route to the Orient through tropical seas, he cites Lawrence's *Aaron's Rod* in his journals (as printed in *Earth House Hold*), and we are surely startled to find him, as he observes ancient women in the smoky kitchens of Japanese temples, quoting not only Emerson's journals but the *Dunciad* of Alexander Pope. Explicit allusions to poets of the premodernist Western tradition appear from time to time in Snyder's poems, sometimes in striking contexts. Of a pine-cone pursued by squirrels in *Myths & Texts,* he writes, "What mad pursuit! What struggle to escape!" and Keats's great ode comes to mind again when he observes, painted on a cavern wall in India, "a man offering a girl wine, over and over, forever.—Like thou still unravished bride of quietness." Not only Buddhas and bodhisattvas but Artemis and Danae find a place in his verses, and in the wonderful "new poems" of the past forty years given shelter at last in *Left Out in the Rain,* we even find (among the sestinas and heroic couplets) Bacchus and Venus cavorting in a poem entitled—but can *this* be Snyder?!—"Versions of Anacreon." That off-the-track Western tradition, left out a long time in the cold and the rain, just won't pack up and leave. Though neglected, exposed, and seemingly abandoned, this ill-favored foster child of silence and slow time, as the poet might say, keeps trucking on.

Snyder thus completely eludes any simple identification with an Eastern *as opposed to* a Western tradition. Not only eludes, by making room for Western poetry and myth throughout much of his work, but explicitly rejects, by criticizing the excesses and failings of Eastern no less than of Western civilization. If the Western tradition is off the track, it has no monopoly; in his essay "Why Tribe" in *Earth House Hold,* Snyder remarks "that 'India' and 'China'—as societies—are as burdensome to human beings as any others; perhaps more so." In "Buddhism and the Coming Revolution," he censures institutional Buddhism for its readiness "to accept or ignore the inequalities and tyrannies of whatever political system it found itself under," and in the *East West* interview he remarks that the discovery that societies are human, not divine, and "that we actually have the capacity of making choices in regard to our social systems" came to Asia only in this century—and came from the West.

Given this open and critical eye, it is not surprising that Snyder's experience of Japan was by no means entirely of victorious Dharma Battles and Sudden Enlightenment (much less of cherry blossoms and chrysanthemums). While "Japan quibbles for words on what kind of whales they can kill," he writes in "Mother Earth: Her Whales" in *Turtle Island,*

> A once-great Buddhist nation
>   dribbles methyl mercury
>   like gonorrhea
>   in the sea.

and "Dullness in February: Japan," one of the "new poems" from the late fifties printed in *Left Out in the Rain*, evokes

> Brutal sergeants, vicious aesthetes,
>   the meeting
> Of the worst of East and West.
> Silly priests in temples
> Far too fine for now.
> Discipline for what end? . . .

and concludes

> Perhaps some flame remains.
>   I hope
> Again some day
> To hit the night road in America
> Hitchhiking through dark towns
> Rucksack on my back,
> To the home of a
> Poverty-stricken witty
> Drunkard friend.

Silliness was not confined to Milton or Christianity, after all, nor did Han-shan's *Cold Mountain* offer the mind and imagination their only prospect of rambling free from trouble.

Far from exalting the East at the expense of the West, Snyder's work repeatedly and deliberately transcends and invalidates any easy distinctions between them. Our decreasingly casual reader, looking back at all those names that first attracted attention, will remark how often the Eastern and the Western, the strange and the familiar, are juxtaposed or conjoined: Yakamochi and Thoreau; Plato, Aquinas, Buddha; Ahab, Cybele, Seami; the Duke of Chou and John Muir; Bodhidharma, Lenin, Crazy Horse, Confucius . . . In a poetic world where Artemis rubs shoulders with Kali and the Pleiades share the night sky with Han River, the conjunction of names in itself compels the reader to break down any facile dichotomy between East and West, and to seek the commonalities that unite them in a Great Subculture stemming from the heretical movements of an earlier day, and ultimately from the shamanistic culture that is our most truly planetary inheritance. The common ground of the hierarchical civilizations lies underfoot; here there is no distinction of East from West, and the Buddha, Crazy Horse, and Thoreau share the same space, which is ours.

Snyder elsewhere employs more complex and subtle means than juxtaposition, such as punning and allusion, to overcome the false and distorting dualities of East and West. Of all Western divinities it is perhaps the great goddess and huntress Artemis, who turned Actaeon to a stag for glimpsing her nakedness, that most insistently recurs in his lines: When we read, in *Myths & Texts*, that "Actaeon saw Dhyana in the Spring," the poet's riddling koan can be understood only through the identification of that primordial goddess, the luminous Diana, with the sudden enlightenment through meditation that is dhyana, ch'an, or Zen. Fierce Shiva the Destroyer is invoked to inform the races "That Chaos is the Pattern under Structure" (a lesson Dionysus or Apollo, destroyers of Pentheus and the crazed Cassandra, could have taught equally well), but is invoked, of all places, in an artfully crafted sestina (from *Left Out in the Rain*), thereby uniting East and West with a vengeance. Here as elsewhere the Eastern names themselves frequently lead us in unexpected ways not away from, but back to, the West (for Far West and Far East, we remember again, are nearly adjoined). Even when Snyder marvels "what sense the old boys made—Confucius, Lao-tzu, Tu Fu, Sesshu and the rest," the rest will perhaps include, for readers attuned to the rhythms of modern poetry in English, not only other ancient Eastern sages but the eminently Western, and much more recent, poet whose reflection on the European Old Masters in "Musée des Beaux Arts" finds a responsive echo here amid the dullness of February in Japan.

Echoes of Western poets even in ostensibly "Eastern" poems are not infrequent in Snyder; all that reading in Whitman, Jeffers, and Williams, Yeats and Eliot, even Chaucer, Milton, and Keats, was not a legacy he could ever leave (or wish to leave) entirely behind him. But although his occasional use of strict stanzaic patterns like the sestina is of course highly exceptional and even self-ironizing, it is inevitably his language and poetic form that above all mark Snyder, for all his extensive debt to the East, as a poet of the Western tradition. The language, however bestrewn in places with Eastern vocables, very much remains American English, and we need not subscribe to Whorf's extreme form of linguistic relativism to concede the obvious yet deeply significant fact that the very grammar and syntax of our language continually and inescapably shape the way we conceive and picture our world. Less trivially, the language of Snyder's poetry belongs to a colloquial tradition that persistently undercuts any sharp distinction between poetry and everyday speech, and this is a distinctively Western, and a particularly English and American, tradition.

Snyder was attracted, as a translator, to the rough and fresh "T'ang colloquial" of Han-shan, but colloquial speech, insofar as it can be distinguished, is a rare exception in the refined and densely allusive language of classical Chinese (to say nothing of Japanese) poetry. In China, Japan, and India alike, for all their differences, the split between literary and spoken languages was for the most part far more rigorously observed, before the mid- to late-nineteenth century, than it has been in any Western country for most of the time since Latin gave way to the European vernaculars in the late Middle Ages and Renaissance; only under the impact of the West did Asian vernaculars extensively reinvigorate or displace the time-honored but ossified conventions of literary languages unspoken for centuries. In his use of colloquial speech Snyder, like other American poets of his generation, is in a tradition that looks back, even before the poetic revolutions of the twentieth century, to Whitman, to Wordsworth, to Shakespeare, and to the often rough and always fresh Chaucer ("Thy drasty ryming is nat worth a toord!")—but hardly at all, in this crucial regard, to the classical Indian, Chinese, or Japanese poetic traditions.

If his use of colloquial speech allies Snyder far more closely with traditional Western than with traditional Asian (or indeed traditional shamanistic!) poetic diction, the affiliation is even more strongly marked in the preference he shows, along with so many other poets of his place and time, for loosely structured and flexibly varied poetic forms responsive to the rhythms of speech. The contrast with classical Japanese poetry could not be more strongly marked. For more than a thousand years, between the *Man'yôshû* and the Meiji Restoration, almost no poem written in Japanese exceeded the thirty-one-syllable boundaries of the traditional *waka* or *tanka,* and the principal formal innovation was the introduction of the still shorter, seventeen-syllable *haiku;* both these stringent forms were invariably regular, moreover, in alternating lines of five and seven syllables. (In contrast, Snyder's "Hitch Haiku" in *The Back Country* range, at a rough count, from eleven to twenty-six syllables with no regular alternation: these are very Western "haiku" indeed!)

Chinese prosody was far more varied and permitted poems of much greater length, but its classical forms dictated not only a standard number of syllables (characters) in each verse but often a strict and generally invariant pattern of both tones and rhymes. Thus even the relatively "colloquial" Han-shan's poems generally "employ the conventional five-character line," Burton Watson writes in the introduction to his translation of *Cold Mountain,* "and consist usually of eight lines. The even-numbered lines rhyme, the same rhyme being used throughout a single poem. Some are in the rather free 'old poetry' style; others in the more exacting *lü-shih* or 'regulated verse' form, with its elaborate verbal and tonal parallelism." Paradoxically, it is not Snyder's more typical free verse poems, but his occasional experiments with fixed Western forms like the sestina, that most closely approximate, in a different idiom, the intricate artifice characteristic of classical Chinese poetry. Once again it is on the Western tradition that Snyder principally draws, great though his debt to the East may otherwise be, for his flexible poetic forms: not only (and obviously) on the modern American tradition stemming from Pound and Williams, and from Whitman before them, but more broadly on the long English poetic tradition in which blank verse (sometimes, as in Shakespeare, intermingled with prose) and loosely defined forms of the ode provided models, even before the innovations of modern free verse, of metrical and prosodic variability far more readily adapted to the rhythms of colloquial speech than almost anything in Chinese, Japanese, or Indian poetry before these were transformed, in modern times, by the influence of the West.

One of Snyder's finest poems, "Axe Handles," provides a paradigm of the ways in which his essentially Western poetic tradition mediates the wisdom of the East. In verses of tightly controlled but variable length and stress, the poet recalls the time when he fashioned a hatchet handle for his son Kai from a broken-off axe handle, taking his pattern from the handle of the hatchet with which he was cutting. A phrase first learned from Ezra Pound, "When making an axe handle the pattern is not far off," rings in his ears, and recalls a similar passage from Lu Ji's fourth-century A.D. "Essay on Literature," *Wên Fu*, taught to Snyder years before by his own teacher Shih-hsiang Chen:

> And I see: Pound was an axe,
> Chen was an axe, I am an axe
> And my son a handle, soon
> To be shaping again, model
> And tool, craft of culture,
> How we go on.

The Chinese proverb whose connection with lived experience the poet here discovers characteristically first came to him (like his interest in Chinese poetry itself) through the mediation of a Western poet; it no less characteristically finds expression in a poem whose rhythms, too, are those of a twentieth-century Western poetic idiom midwived, in significant measure, by the very same Ezra Pound. That is "how we go on," also known as tradition.

Pound's example suggests, indeed, that one way in which Snyder belongs to the modern Western poetic tradition is in the very assimilation of Eastern thought and poetry that he has carried still further than other poets of our century who have likewise responded to their attraction. Once upon a time, in Byron or Hugo, Orientalism was a mine of colorful exotica, normally of Near Eastern extraction—while for Tennyson the cycles of Cathay rolled monotonously by as England industriously opened the future. But for Eliot, in our own century, the peace that passeth understanding could find expression in Sanskrit, and for Yeats the ancient glittering eyes of Chinese travelers carved in lapis lazuli could express a gaiety transfiguring the dread of his time. Pound's absorption of the Confucian classics, and Snyder's more rigorous and demanding study of Buddhism, enrich and continue this opening to the East that is characteristic of the modern Western tradition. Or rather, the opening of tradition once again transcends and unites East and West. For the assimilation of Eastern influences by such Western poets as Eliot and Yeats, or indeed Pound and Snyder, is dwarfed in scale by the massive impact of the West on Chinese and Japanese poetry (to say nothing of fiction) in our century; when Snyder, for example, translates a modern Japanese poet, Miyazawa Kenji, he is transmitting into English a "new style" of poem that would have been inconceivable before Japanese poetic tradition had itself been radically transformed by its new openness to the West. The planetary heritage is one that makes specifically Eastern or Western influences difficult, if not altogether impossible—in either case, in the end, irrelevant—to isolate or distinguish.

But if assimilation of Eastern influence places Snyder not only or mainly in a modern Western, but in an increasingly worldwide poetic tradition responsive to "primitive" song and story no less than to "civilized" thought and culture (be they of East or West, North or South), in a longer historical perspective this very openness can perhaps lay claim, despite the lingering arrogance of recent imperialisms, to being characteristically Western. The contrast with China is of course particularly striking. With the momentous exception of Indian Buddhism, until modern times the Middle Kingdom barely acknowledged the existence of other cultural traditions worthy of notice, and apart from Buddhist sutras, translations from other languages were virtually unknown. The ancient Greeks, it is true, likewise tended to view cultures other than their own as "barbaric," but as part of a larger Mediterranean civilization the Greeks recognized and reluctantly admired traditions, like those of Egypt and Babylon, which they knew to be older, and sometimes suspected might even be wiser, than their own. Can we imagine, on the other hand, the representative of *any* civilization saying in the *Analects,* as Plato makes an Egyptian priest condescendingly say to Solon of Athens in the *Timaeus,* "Confucius, Confucius, you Chinese are all children"? The ancients whom Confucius revered, as he himself would be revered for millennia to come, were already assumed to have been inevitably (for what alternative was there?) Chinese.

It is with the Greeks, indeed, that a Western tradition of openness to the East begins—very warily, to be sure—that will culminate, despite many detours and repudiations ("better fifty years of Europe . . ."), in our own age. Not only Babylonian astronomy and Egyptian spirituality but the Phrygian and Thracian ecstatic religions that took shape in Cybele, Dionysus, and Orpheus, the stimulus of Persian Zoroastrianism to pre-Socratic and later to Gnostic thought, and the idealization of Indian Brahmins as "gymnosophists" of magical powers were among many Eastern influences contributing over the centuries—especially after the conquests of Alexander—to the continuous transformation of Greek civilization, much as more recent influxes of Eastern religions, Zen Masters, and poets are contributing to the transformation of our own. (Even classic literary works, like Homer's *Iliad* or the *Histories* of Herodotus, that depict the encounter between West and East in terms of a conflict in which the Greeks are victorious display an astonishingly sympathetic fascination for the defeated Trojan and Persian peoples.) Still more striking was the transformation of Roman culture by the conquest of Greece—"Captive Greece," Horace wrote, "took its fierce captor captive"—and of other cultures still farther East; in the myth celebrated by Virgil, Rome owed her very origin to Trojans exiled from their homeland in Asia Minor.

But it was neither captive Greece nor captive Troy, but captive Judaea that most thoroughly transformed the culture of its Western captors, both Greek and Roman, when the new Christian religion eventually prevailed over its Eastern rivals, the worships of Mithras and Isis. For centuries to come, European culture would periodically renew itself by new openings to the East, most notably through receptivity, after the first Crusades, to the Arabic philosophical commentaries and translations of Aristotle that revolutionized medieval thought. Even in the colonialist nineteenth century, at a time when Manchu China, to say nothing of Tokugawa Japan, was striving to prevent all forms of contagion by any culture alien to its own, European scholars took up the serious study of Indian, Chinese, and Japanese languages and literatures, which the Jesuit missionaries had begun. And while scholars undertook the vast project of translating the classics of the East and ethnographers recorded myths and rites from the Arctic to Tierra del Fuego, poets from Goethe to Edward Fitzgerald were engaging with Hafiz and Omar Khayyám much as their predecessors had engaged with Homer and Virgil, and as their successors, Pound and Snyder among them, would engage with the *Shih Ching* and Li Po, Han-shan and Miyazawa, Black Elk and many whose names are unknown, thereby continually widening the confines of a once but no longer merely Western tradition.

The very fragmentation and diversity of its languages and literatures has no doubt contributed to making Western civilization, both in ancient times and since the Crusades, generally more receptive to outside influences than Islamic, Brahmin, or Chinese civilizations have been through much of their history (with some very important exceptions) before the modern age; for all its recurrent classicisms and lingering parochialism, the Western tradition has been too multiple and too protean to remain closed or stagnant for long. And from the beginning, when the first Western ethnopoet, Ionian Homer of the islands or coastland of Asia Minor, where Near East adjoins Near West, sang of the war between Achaeans and Danaans on the plain around windy Troy, the East above all has been an unfailing source of fascination, both as antagonist and as mentor, to its self-consciously fractious yet admiring young rival to the West. None who responds to the allure of that Other has remained immune or unchanged on returning: so Helen of Sparta, in our first poet's story, returns from her ten-year Eastern sojourn to her red-haired warrior husband, but returns with new and magical powers as Helen (henceforth and forever) of Troy. It is in this sense, most of all, that Gary Snyder, through incessant assimilation and transformation of Eastern poetry and thought in his circuitous journey from Pacific Northwest to Kyoto to San Juan Ridge, belongs profoundly and fully—to the very extent that he can never belong exclusively—to a Western poetic tradition that looks back far beyond Ezra Pound to primordial Homer.

How we go on . . .

Jack Hicks:
THE POET IN THE UNIVERSITY

The poet sits in an eye of May morning, wildflower incense lazing from his office. Two certificates hang on the walls: one noting completion of a summer reading program with the Seattle Public Library (1946), the other proclaiming his 1988 induction into the American Academy of Arts and Letters. The room is quiet, off a culvert of pleading telephones, reams of spent memoranda, sullen students hunkering for late professors. But for the incense and a small Buddhist shrine, at the center of which is an astonishing photograph of the Yamabushi deity Fudo Myo-o, tattooed in rich color from neck to buttocks on the back of a friend, the office is exceptional only in sparsity and restraint.

In a dark blue suit, Gary Snyder looks like any other English professor, until you get to the *feet*. The shoes are White's boots, hammer-toed at ten years old, with a burnish in the black of the leather. Fine tools, well attended, and Snyder proudly pronounces them "the dress boot of preference, the elite among Pacific Northwest workingmen's gear." They set him off from the academic pack.

White's dress workboots, then, and the hidden Sanskrit tattoo on his left calf: emblems of pasts flourishing in this nine-floor ferroconcrete stack of offices, a structure of which poet Karl Shapiro (a retired University of California at Davis faculty member) once wrote,

> "all the bad Bauhaus comes to a head
> In this gray slab, domino, this plinth
> . . . rearing like a fort, with slits of eyes
> Suspicious in the aggregate."

It seems ironic that Snyder has had an office here since joining the English Department/Creative Writing Program—near the top of this scholarly warehouse, food chain, information system.

He has taught at UC Davis spring quarters since 1986, but his ties with Davis reach back more than two decades. In February 1966, Snyder, Allen Ginsberg, and Richard Baker—returning from inspecting a 100-acre site near Nevada City, which they later purchased for $45,000—stopped in for a reading Ginsberg had scheduled earlier. Six years later, in 1972, Snyder first read his poetry at Davis. He was brought through the efforts of grad student Chris Wagstaff who, in turn, introduced him to University Library staff Donald Kunitz, Nelson Piper, and Noel Peattie. These three had begun an impressive archive of contemporary literature, and they talked enthusiastically with the poet of mutual interests. Thus Gary Snyder's first connections with UC Davis were through friends, students, and bibliophiles.

Financial need drives most poets into the grove of academe, but as a highly sought campus visitor, Snyder had no real need of continuing academic links. By 1970, he was one of eight or ten serious American poets who could live decently on readings and royalties. Those funds, family and reinhabitation at Kitkitdizze, and a wariness of the American academy—all kept him from a regular university role.

He limited himself to one- to three-day campus visits in fall (mid-October to early December) and spring (April to June), on tour for weeks at a stretch, stacking three to four readings per week. It looks fine on the page, but the toll on writers who take this road is great. With this in mind, when I wrote in March 1975 to detail an upcoming reading at Davis, I asked his interest in spending a quarter as writer-in-residence. Again, a graduate student was instrumental. Scholar/poet Lee Bartlett (now at the University of New Mexico) was working closely with Snyder, and had already probed his interest. I made the inquiry more formal.

A cautious response: "As for the possibility of teaching at Davis, it is true . . . I am interested, but it would have to be a year or more in the future as I am deeply involved in writing and other projects that would make teaching difficult at this time."

Having come across him in airports on two or three occasions, I knew the demands of the reading circuit on his time and energy. It was clear what he offered us, and I was determined to convey the fruits of teaching at UC Davis: a history of cordial relations between writers and scholars unusual in the academy (Will Baker, Sandra Gilbert, Michael Hoffman, Diane Johnson, and Karl Shapiro worked in both sectors); a growing Creative Writing program; a good library with a strong Special Collections. We would pay him well and offer small classes of bright students, and we were two hours from his home.

Senior faculty were enthusiastic but unbelieving, but the pieces were falling into place. One day before his reading, a distinguished colleague summoned me to office. I was the Contemporary American Lit man, the designated assistant professor go-between for the priests and the infidels, and I had a charge. To wit, to go to the pre-reading restaurant—specialists in great haunches of "slow elk"—to certify they offered vegetarian fare, for the poet could be no carnivore. Further, to assure a rainbow of *fresh* fruit juices could be had, to slake his trochilidic thirst.

I stroked my beard; I clarified, delicately. Ah yes, very well. Go *now*. An arched full professor eyebrow hinted that my tenure—not too distant—rode on the mount of my catering skill.

The eatery manager greeted me as if I were an imam or Hasidic rabbi. We took a private corner, the walls papered with old photos of great beasts in yoke: steers, draft horses, coffles of oxen. We haggled, the menu—a disputed territory—between us. We could go ovo-lacto, but not full-tilt vegan; the house offered the mango-papaya nectar, free. We nodded, we stood up, we shook on it. A done deal.

We ten sat the next evening at a long table in a private room, an unsteady mixture of sacred and profane. When the poet appeared, in tasteful hides and owl amulets, he was shown the head chair, seated. On the wall behind his head was a poster for a hand meat grinder, circa 1920, an ebullient pink piggy stepping into the silvery maw. The beast reappeared as a chain of little laughing sausages at the bottom. We were a curious, mildly stiff group, but the poet's manner put us at ease. As his first formal gesture, he by-passed the nectar and ordered a double Jack Daniels, rocks. My superior gazed off into the middle distance.

After a half-hour of curious chat, we ordered. Snyder chose a large steak, charred and rare. "Oh sure, I eat meat," he responded to the inevitable question. "I get my protein wherever I can." I smiled, and my senior colleague sniffed in displeasure, as if a noxious wind had been broken at our side. So much for the ethereal creature some had expected.

The reading went beautifully. Over breakfast the next morning, Bartlett and I talked with Snyder of his teaching here in detail. He listened, asked questions, drew the nature of his proposed gig and university life into focus.

The Davis connection grew in 1978, when Nelson Piper, Don Kunitz, and associates drove up to Kitkitdizze to discuss the library's housing Snyder's papers. By now, a weave of blood and friendship had grown between the Ridge and Davis. Snyder was comfortable here, and he was concerned with the state of his personal papers: with the space they demanded, the weathering they'd already undergone, but mainly with the threat of summer fires that often wasted the foothills. Storing them with trained archivists seemed an attractive solution.

Piper and Snyder agreed that the University would be a temporary repository, with the papers open by permission to serious scholars. At the end of the meeting—to the surprise of the librarians—the poet suggested they begin *now,* before the imminent fire season. So the university car was unceremoniously crammed with fifteen to twenty black plastic garbage bags and cardboard boxes—the first installment of writings accumulated over thirty years.

The relationship was made permanent in 1983 when UC Davis acquired the letters, raw manuscripts, and occasional papers. At this writing, the Snyder Collection is used often by international scholars, is almost fully cataloged, and includes 100,000-plus items (in seventy archival boxes).

In early 1985, Snyder's friend and neighbor Scott McLean (a Davis colleague) mentioned the poet was interested in pursuing our offer, maybe on a regular basis. As director of the Creative Writing program, I took the matter to English Chair Michael Hoffman, a novelist and advocate of the CW program. He elicited strong commitment from Dean Leon Mayhew, an ally of the arts at Davis, and we invited Snyder to give a reading and talk things over. Two weeks after the reading, Hoffman and I went up to Kitkitdizze to talk some more.

We arrived near the end of an intensive, week-long *sesshin* at the Ring of Bone Zendo, conducted by Roshi Robert Aitken. We were both decently traveled and liked the call of the unfamiliar, but neither of us was ready for the radiant passage of that afternoon. As Hoffman recalls:

I know you'd been up there several times, but I only knew his work. He would be a *major* presence in any university, but while I liked him, I knew him very little. For all I knew, he lived in a tent, on chamomile tea and bean sprouts. He was very gracious, showed us around, showed us his new Honda generator and photovoltaic panels—power sources. We talked about everything except the job. We had tea, a little lunch he'd made, beer. I felt he was gauging me. A heavy subtext: "Can I do business with this guy, this university?" In short, we did business Japanese-style, never even mentioning business. Then he invited us to sit in on Roshi Aitken's *teisho*. That seemed to be the second stage of whatever ritual we were in, and what a stage it was.

Seated in our versions of the lotus, we felt alien inside the small zendo, as if we had stepped from Sproul Hall (Davis's English Department headquarters) into a moon colony of gray-swathed Zen adepts, all busy at a work we could not recognize. The room was suffused with the aromas of incense and Ponderosa pine, and the chanting, stick clapping, and bell ringing were unsettling. We did okay in Paris or Tokyo or Moscow, but we were lost on the San Juan Ridge.

Gradually, a resonance gathered up through the Doug fir floor. Roshi Aitken commented wryly on "Nansen Kills a Cat," the knotty fourteenth koan of the *Mumonkan,* both bemused at and respectful of the very different struggles of flock and the laity. Uneasiness yielded to restful attention. When he finished, we exited slowly, loathe to leave what we had entered anxiously. I felt like a well-sounded gong, peaceful in the afterclap.

The three of us retired to a picnic table between the pond and the main house, and within an hour, negotiations were completed. Snyder seemed mildly surprised at the salary a major poet could command, and I think he realized—for the first time—the full implications for his time, stability, and artistic concentration. We had agreed on an annual spring quarter at Davis, at the highest level of full professor, with perks, starting in 1986.

His academic salary freed him from the reading circuit, which proved not merely grinding, but limiting in ways unsuspected. "In a very real sense, my intellectual life—my reading and thinking—was shaped by my public speaking topics. I sensed that I had begun to serve functions that once served me. The change was to become more private, then, less the public figure and more the thinker and writer. I actually said to myself, 'I think I'll stop playing around about being a writer and get serious.'" Strange words for an author of twelve books.

Snyder jokes at the irony of Snyder and Allen Ginsberg (at Brooklyn College) in buildings they once entered and exited quickly. "I wanted to see how it was on the other side," he needles. "You guys all looked alike to me on the road. From the air, America was a labyrinth of colleges joined by clouds. I was met at each place by the same assistant professor, and we always ate the same lunch. He wore a tan corduroy jacket like that one." He points at me. "And his attitude was a curious mixture of arrogance and deference."

Too, Snyder wanted to broaden the contexts of his thought and writing. With time to voyage more freely on his own, he has traveled to cityscapes like New York and Beijing, and often to the last American wilderness, Alaska. Recent poetry finds the wild alive in the urban ("Walking the New York Bedrock" and "The Persimmons"), and the sophistication in the "primitive," as in "The Sweat."

If his recent poetry is energized by the shuttle between the two—especially the work resumed on *Mountains and Rivers Without End*—he seeks the same for his prose. "I wanted a broader spectrum of information and commentary via the university—I was narrowing too much within West Coast environmentalism and ecopoetics. For example, with influence from my colleagues and students, I've worked into poststructural Marxist theory (semiotics and deconstruction) and feminist thought. Those areas provide the juice nowadays, and while the critique made sense to me at nineteen—when I read Engels' *The Origins of the Family, Private Property and the State*—more recent turns are very fruitful, really challenging. Especially ecofeminism."

The university values the presence of a figure like Gary Snyder, trades on his international reputation. But he did not come to be a silent gem in our tiara. He is strongly critical of the academy's social role. His own Reed College was "deepening, challenging . . . like a Kendo *dojo,* where you practice sword fighting with bamboo poles. With an umpire (professor), so nobody gets killed. When I got out, I was ready for 'the real world,' where they sometimes use real swords. I convey this ideal image to my students."

But Reed is rare, and the poet sees "a deep paradox" between the calling of the writer/humanist and the service of the university. "A love/hate relationship. We get comfort, a great library, good colleagues and students, and money and time to write. But we tend to ignore our part in the political and corporate interests of the state. The poet in the university buys into the cultural elite too easily, working up the money/power/prestige ladder."

He works within our walls, but remains radically skeptical, writing recently, "Large institutions like universities are so much a part of history and society that I am under no illusion they can be, *per se*, transformed. They are, however, very porous and contain much. They are an excellent habitat and harbour things within themselves (like the canon of American Literature harbours Thoreau and Whitman) that could—under the right conditions—germinate and start some new directions."

Scholarly interpenetration—the shuttle between teaching and writing—is an academic ideal, and the concept organizes Snyder's varied undertakings at his Davis "harbour." Some noted writers rent their names high to colleges, as an ex-football player peddles his face to a beer company. With just as much commitment. One notable met his yearly winter workshop at an Eastern school twice, then retired to his place in the Caribbean, to a palmy address to which his students might send poems, if necessary. Snyder works the job here. He is diligent with his courses: this time around, a graduate poetry workshop and an advanced seminar on the literature of wilderness. The work is evident in the carefully organized "self-published" anthologies used for each, and in the stream of visitors played through classes and colloquia (and back through his and our writing).

With university support, he has developed several "habitats for germination." Notably, the "Places On Earth" speakers series has brought Wendell Berry, Allen Ginsberg, Louise Erdrich, Maxine Hong Kingston, Peter Matthiessen, Barry Lopez, Ursula Le Guin, and others—writers who share a penchant (and a talent) for conjuring place as a powerful, informing presence in literature. What began as a mainly "literary" series has diversified (as have the audiences), and the dialogue has intensified. A 1989 colloquium with David Rains Wallace, for example, found his *Bulow Hummock* a plain for struggle between scientists and humanists. And Marc Reisner (*Cad-*

illac Desert) came under dual siege from aesthetes ("It's not really literature") and water scientists ("Too many anecdotes and narratives").

Snyder gravitates to writers at the interstices, those who challenge his (and our) habitual modes of thought. This is a valuable and unsettling contribution, and he fully relishes it, often standing aside to watch occasional riptides (or dead water). Nor is he immune, as we have all found in the searching scrutinies paid his work by feminists and radical theorists. Such exercise invigorates, and occasionally frustrates—for both students and faculty—for it runs against the custom of prepackaged learning dished out in uniform three-hour seminars and research papers read aloud.

"The Writers' Theater," a forum to revive the oral/folk roots of narrative, poetry, and song, is a similar, smaller undertaking; long range, the most important work Gary Snyder has set in motion has been in exploring an interdisciplinary program in Nature and Culture. There are few such academic programs in the United States, and it seeks to find and nourish deep affinities between scientists, humanists, and writers.

Cutting across traditional disciplines, such a program, Snyder roughs out, would "enable us as students and teachers to cross-fertilize what we can know from, say, period literary studies, environmental history, philosophy, and wildlife biology, to get an angle on (for example) the extinction of the Anatolian lion, the Roman arena, the lion skin of Heracles, the lions children dream about (and large and powerful toys), African game ranching, Lion as king-of-the-jungle, and campaigns to stop hunts of mountain lions in California in 1988."

A faculty group led by David Robertson, Scott McLean, and Robert Torrance has moved quickly. The May 1989 meetings drew parties from thirteen disciplines, from Native American studies to microbiology. A UC Davis task force of scientists and humanists is currently exploring models for a full-fledged interdisciplinary undergrad degree program.

The importance to Snyder is clear: "I have a feeling that doing work like this Nature and Culture program is really what I came to Davis for. I had ideas from the beginning of making connections with those doing related work in many fields, departments, information systems."

·

Sproul Hall and the university are information systems, a notion to which Snyder warms as he packs up for his noon poetry workshop. "Actually, an *eco-information chain*. At the bottom, undergrads and grad students—the primary grasses—are doing basic photosynthesis. Their work sprouts up in seminar papers and dissertations, and they are both nourished and gobbled by the herbivores. Junior faculty. Just as the bison kicked up the soil, scattered seed, shit on them, really helped create the great grass ranges.

"Herbivores concentrate the data, and this is food for the hyperspecialized omnivores and carnivores—the senior faculty above. They harvest information, compress it into scholarly journals and books. All over campus, in tall buildings like this, you have these narrow food chains/information systems ruled by the great mammals within their English or Plant Genetic kingdoms.

"At the top? I hate to say it, but in the Davis eco-information chain, poets and writers are up here, grazing all the high-energy foods produced in each building. She/he finds images, stories, Great Myths—syntheses the specialist can't or won't produce.

"Who eats the poet? Really the worms, that's all. When there are no predators over you in the food chain, nothing feeds off you until you die. The lion rules, but the worms, jackals, vultures always eat the last meal. They recycle the energy and it all starts over."

Delighted with the prospect, he leaves for class.

The last words on the poet in the university are rightly from students, for they brought him here and continue as his primary clients. Spare them the perils of being named at too tender an age. One young man talks of the wilderness literature seminar: "At times, discussion is awfully 'range-y,' and you wish he'd stop and summarize, make transitions and connections. But a little later, I make them myself and they stay with me. And there are *eruptions,* people almost shouting—atypical of academic seminars. Like the day a legal director for Earth First! came in and said we were all bullshit intellectuals—learning wilderness by doing little watercolors of flowers. That was great.

"Sometimes" (he lowers his voice) "I wonder if there are University Thought Police out there, and if they'd let him do what he is doing if they knew. The implications of all this seem inimical to the university as it exists."

A second student, a talented woman with a stinging verbal gift, is a fiction writer in her first poetry workshop. She is not awed. "I made up my mind to take a course with Gary Snyder before I left, and to be honest, I expected a closet sexist and a nature fascist. The feminist rap on him was he heard only men, and if you weren't a backpacker, or if you came to class with a Diet Pepsi, forget it. That simply hasn't been true.

"He opens things up around here. Sometimes, poets get, 'Oh, wow! Let's all celebrate the sensitive way you celebrated the marvel of those chrysanthemum petals.' But there's been none of that preciousness in workshop.

"Good visitors drop in and discussions take off. After Greg Keeler, we decided there are two kinds of political poetry: *Suckers*—rare—seduce you to the point. *Whackers* assault you with the message. Carolyn Forché is a notorious whacker. As Elvis Costello says, 'Let's all light matches in an American stadium and make Mr. Pinochet quake.' I cited *Turtle Island* as a blatant whacker, and Gary defended it strongly. But first he listened.

"The man has a *following*, but he certainly doesn't cultivate it. He has a sense of humor, a failing for terrible jokes. And I like the way he uses quiet directive questions to skewer nonthinkers busy trying to kiss ass.

"So I was expecting Wilderness Boot Camp For Guys, but no. It's stimulating, and you're free to disagree. He always speaks for the truth of the moment, and I'm a fantasizer, a habitual liar on the page. So we clash. But I think he respects me and my work, thinks it's good I'm on the planet. And I'm glad he's here, too."

NOTE

All cited material originates in letters from and conversations and interviews with Gary Snyder between February 17, 1975, and May 25, 1989. I am indebted to Michael Hoffman, Donald Kunitz, David Robertson, and Scott McLean for suggestions in reconstructing the poet's history at Davis. The graduate students quoted will remain anonymous, as per our interview agreements on May 27 and June 1, 1989. Full citations, transcripts, and/or tapes may be made available to interested scholars with serious projects. Last, the reference to Karl Shapiro's poem is from "The Humanities Building," collected in *Adult Bookstore* (New York: Random House, 1976).

James Koller:
"WE SHOULD GO BACK"

we should go back
we don't

—Gary Snyder
from *Myths & Texts*

One knows, moving, that one will meet others who also have things of their own to do. When such meetings occur, one is reminded that one's own life wants to be consistent, in and of itself. It makes things easier; it isn't important to understand or even know what another thinks, except as those thoughts directly relate to what you find yourselves doing together.

There are styles to meetings of equals. The style of frontier meetings has always been most to my own liking. Such meetings are mostly brief and usually hospitable. Knowledge of place and the comings and goings of comrades is exchanged. When hungers are recognized, they are often celebrated—even those who prefer their own to others' company, on occasion, need to "chew things over," to close the gaps in what they think they know, and often do it with a brash openness that is appropriate to the suddenness of some lives and deaths.

Gary Snyder has been able to appreciate my sense of such meetings. "Well, if it ain't Old Wolftit!" he once shouted, greeting me in a crowded room.

Our talk has nearly always centered on the physical matters at hand. He borrowed and still has one of my digging bars. There were few trots into any "theory" behind any "practice"—we seemed to understand immediately what we had in common, and left our differences for others to discuss. One of the only times we spoke of poetry, I told him how when my first wife left me, she quoted back to me one of the lines from *Myths & Texts* I'd read to her. Gary responded that few had understood what he was doing in that book.

Those who know they understand where and how they belong, however out of place they know they are for those around them, do function in that time and place—grow there as seeds blown in might, to a singular maturity and certain death, fill the space they find themselves in, in their own way. And leave their seeds.

—*2 Sept 89*

Drummond Hadley:

GARY SNYDER

A ghost now who wears the masks of
all the ages crooked as a cucumber.

There he goes in a wooden horse-drawn wagon
with Wendell and Drum across the Kentucky River countryside.

Blue mountains and rivers with no end go passing by
one white cloud on the way.

I am a Chinese bride, he calls, singing,
being carried off to my wedding day.

I am a ruthless outlaw, taken,
bound now for a scaffold to be hanged.

I am a condor chick, wet bald head
peeping, breaking from this egg.

Masks of all the ages, you mountains and rivers with no end,
an old friend comes to you now singing along his way.

Frank Jones:

EXCELSISSIMUS

After the apex, what?
Why, of course, one peak
after another.

Dharma

Robert Aitken:

THE TOKU OF GARY SNYDER

A monk said to Chao-chou, "I have long heard about the great stone bridge of Chao-chou, but now I've come and found just a simple log bridge."

Chao-chou said, "You only see the simple log bridge, and you don't see the stone bridge."

The monk asked, "What is the stone bridge?"

Chao-chou said, "Horses cross, donkeys cross."

Chao-chou is the long-lived Ch'an (Zen) Master who is best known for his response to a monk's question about the Buddha-nature of a dog. "Doesn't have any," he answered—in Chinese *Wu*, in Japanese *Mu*. He taught in the town of Chao-chou, and so became known by its name. The great stone bridge, built more than two hundred years before his time, still stands—an archaeological wonder of modern China. It was also a marvel in his day, and Chao-chou himself was equally famous.

So the monk was playing with names here, expressing his disappointment at Chao-chou's manner and appearance. But Chao-chou was unruffled. Instead of drawing himself up in defense, he temporized gently, giving the monk some scope in which to turn around. "You only see the simple log bridge, and you don't see the stone bridge."

And so the monk rose to the occasion and grasped his chance: "What is the stone bridge?" This was the kind of question that allowed Chao-chou to shine. "Horses cross, donkeys cross." These final words, in context, form the point of the case, but here I should like simply to highlight Chao-chou's integrity.

If Chao-chou had been taken in by the monk, and had tried to stand on his dignity, the whole conversation would have been so ordinary and conventional that his other seemingly wise words and deeds would have been called into question. He was, however, standing on his own two feet as a teacher. He was in touch with the perennial fact that he finally displayed to the monk and to us all, and he could not be thrown off by the relative superficiality of some-body's criticism.

All this is by way of showing (yet again) the importance of de-votion to purpose. This importance is understood very well in Asia. The criminal who converts all circumstances to enlarging the scope of his crime is pursued and prosecuted, but he is also admired for his single-mindedness. Today in Japan, the businessman who comes to the end of his life after creating an empire of profit is respected, though whatever suffering he might have created is also acknowl-edged. It is the sage like Chao-chou, however, devoted to the task of teaching all beings, who is honored without reservation.

This honor is really an acknowledgement of power, not the power of control, but the power of a life of wisdom and compassion, that by its very presence is persuasive. It is the leadership recognized in traditional societies, not dependent on manipulation and connec-tions, but resting firmly on human nobility that is evident to all.

This power is called *te* in Chinese, *toku* in Japanese. It is the *te* of the *Tao Te Ching,* which Arthur Waley translates, *The Way and Its Power*. It is the *toku* of the founders of Japanese institutions who are revered and quoted long after they are gone. The great criminal will be locked away and the great business magnate will soon be forgot-ten, but the one who has cultivated the virtues will live on in a par-ticular appeal to the inherent nobility that is latent in us all.

It is a particular appeal because it comes from a unique human being. Buddhist metaphysics identifies this particularity as the Nir-māṇakāya, the infinitely varied creativity among individuals that is exemplified in the Buddha Shākyamuni. He was a teacher for the ages, but he was also a singular person. His words and deeds arose from a unique vessel, just as our own do. The sage is one who cul-tivates his or her own nobility, using the teaching that has been handed down as guidance, but evolving and maturing from the pri-vate compound of affinities that was seeded at conception.

Each of us has incipient toku, incipient nobility. Most of us ma-ture with a blend of noble and weaker motivations, and probably even the Buddha and the Christ had occasional wayward thoughts. Nobility is like a navigational beam that keeps one on course through zigs and zags, acknowledging that nobody is perfect, least of all the one who practices perfection.

Well, this is an essay to honor Gary Snyder, and this lengthy preamble is intended to introduce Gary's toku, his devotion to his purpose of wisdom and compassion, and the authority and acknowledgement it has brought. His purpose and his toku grew out of his Zen Buddhist experiences, but they are also from his practice of poetry, his intimate feeling for nature, his training as an anthropologist, and his heritage of old-left, working-class antecedents. These elements, including Zen Buddhism, are all of a piece with his native talent, but my assignment as one with whom he studied Zen for ten years is to search out how Zen Buddhism in particular has informed his work. The work itself is taken up in other parts of this book. This is an essay about motive.

I met Gary in 1957 when he was studying and working at Daitoku-ji ("Great Power Temple") in Kyoto, but that occasion was only a how-do-you-do. We corresponded intermittently, and I kept up with his poetry as it appeared in journals. During the great efflorescence of the 1960s he began writing in the *Journal for the Protection of All Beings* and other underground papers, and in 1968 I commented in our newsletter, *The Diamond Sangha:*

> Gary Snyder has been writing lately under such titles as "Buddhism and the Coming Revolution" and "Buddhism and Anarchism." Appearing in the underground press, these articles have received wide attention for their application of Buddhism to the current upheaval in the United States and abroad. . . .
>
> The way of the West, as Mr. Snyder says, has been social revolution—the Way of the East has been individual insight into Shunyatā [the void]. Each needs the other. We must stand upon the morality of our undefiled insight, and bring the world about.

Well, I don't write like that any more, and neither does he. However, he is still firm in his vision. Recently he wrote to me,

> Two years or so ago I commented during the question session after a talk you gave in Ring of Bone Zendo that "The failure of Socialism is the tragedy of the twentieth century." I was quoting some European thinker. I do not take that to mean that it is a tragedy that Socialism did not work out (though in a way it is) but that it is a human tragedy, in the sense that so many of the brightest and best of Europe, America, and Asia gave their lives to the dream of it, especially in the early decades of the century, and it proved to be so cruel an illusion. The anarchist position that I took for so many years was in a sense a matter of holding to the pos-

sibility of a third way, neither capitalist nor state socialist. I still do, though I rarely use the term anarchism any more because it immediately evokes the idea of "anarchy," which is not what anarchism was ever intended to mean in terms of political philosphy—and yet it is impossible to get away from that association. . . .

If the moral leadership [of world powers] is completely going back to the democratic capitalist camp, then I hope capitalist thinkers will finally get serious about their global responsibilities. The U.S.A. and Japan in particular must make an effort to discover some mode of economic self-discipline and self-restraint in the matter of how capital always seeks growth and profits, lest the world and its ecology be totally consumed by the profit economy. . . .

I am thinking that perhaps the Marxist-Socialist camp was doomed all along to return to some sort of market capitalism, because its own materialist ideology set it up for ultimately going along with whatever economic system is successful and productive in gross terms. In that sense market-capitalism works. A kind of simple materialism is at the root of this behavior on both sides.

The Buddhadharma [the Teachings of the Buddha and his successors] does indeed have a role to play in helping the people of the world shake off the tangles of simple-minded materialism.

In 1969, when Gary published *Earth House Hold,* he had recently returned from many years of Zen Buddhist study in Japan. His Zen teacher, Oda Sessō Roshi, had died only two years earlier. It was this teacher who advised him, and I quote here from "Four Changes" in *Turtle Island:*

> —become one with the knot itself,
>   til it dissolves away.
> —sweep the garden.
> —any size.

The knot is the primary koan, or theme, of Zen practice, and its dissolution is the experience of seeing into the true nature of things: evanescent, interdependent, and creative. It was with this experience that Gary returned to the United States. Speaking to me recently about his teacher's advice, Gary remarked that he understood Oda Roshi to mean that the garden can be quite large in scale, and that engagement is important.

On my first visit to San Juan Ridge some fifteen years ago, he spoke of "community as dōjō," and this expression is vintage Snyder and vintage Buddhist, though it might need unpacking for the general reader. *Dōjō* is the place or spot of the Tao, and is today the name usually given to the gym where people work out in martial arts. However, it has the most antique origins, and is translated from the Sanskrit word *bodhimanda,* the term for the spot under the Bodhi tree where the Buddha was enlightened. In the Zen Buddhist context, it is the meditation hall—the room where the Zen Buddhist does what is conventionally considered to be the essential Zen work. "Community as dōjō" extends *the real work* to the boundless garden of Oda Roshi's vision, and in fact in that early conversation Gary cited Oda Roshi's words by way of commenting on his understanding of community.

Community is *sangha,* another key Buddhist term, traditionally the kinship of the Buddhist clergy, but metaphysically the kinship of all beings. Oda Roshi's advice and Gary's response are altogether in keeping with the Mahayana Buddhist outlook and with Zen Buddhist experience, but they are not the usual view of Japanese Zen teachers, who for political and cultural reasons tend to keep the Dharma, the law of the universe, rather strictly confined within monastery walls.

Looking back at *Earth House Hold,* it is worthwhile to pause at *House Hold*—not written *household,* with its meanings of home and family, but in two words, with an echo of very old implications: "Earth Holding," or "Earth Treasure"—the very meaning of Jizō (Kṣitigarbha), the Earth Store, or Earth Treasury Bodhisattva.

The bodhisattva is the "Enlightening Being" who vows to work together with everyone and everything toward universal understanding. In folk Buddhism, the bodhisattva is rather like a Christian saint, to whom one can supplicate. For Mahayana teachers such as those in Zen, however, the bodhisattva is you and I, when we are committed to the world's work.

Jizō is one of the two or three most important bodhisattvas in the Mahayana Buddhist pantheon. He is everywhere in Japan, even in these modern industrial times, holding his own in stone images at crossroads, even at busy city intersections. He is the archetypal personage who brings liberation from anguish for beings in the world, even for beings in hell. And that liberation is realization of those three irreducible aspects of reality that becomes clearer with Zen practice: the insubstantial nature of life, the interdependence of all beings, and the precious uniqueness of each being and each species, genus, and culture. It is the three-part truth that is treasured in the world, in the earth. It is the treasure of all beings: people, animals, plants, and inanimate objects.

Gary is the first to make fun of such grandiose language, though their implications fuel his life. As he wrote in *Earth House Hold:*

> You be Bosatsu,
> I'll be the taxi-driver
> Driving you home.

"Bosatsu" is the Japanese pronunciation of Bodhisattva. As Gary explains with a quote from the *Diamond Sutra:* "If a Bodhisattva retains the thought of an ego, a person, a being, or a soul, he is no more a Bodhisattva."

Gary is there nonetheless. "Technical Notes and Queries to Fellow Dharma Revolutionaries" is the subtitle of *Earth House Hold,* and the book is his collection of *upāya,* skillful means for turning the Wheel of the Dharma, one of a great many such upāya in his opus, in his teaching, and in his community organization. The juxtaposition of "Dharma" and "Revolutionaries" springs from Oda Roshi's cogent advice, and also from Gary's own position as a scion of the old left for whom it is clear that the revolutionary is a person of virtue.

I think it is likely that Gary's experience of growing up in an atmosphere of Depression-era leftist thought tended to separate him from his peers and to give him a perspective that most of the rest of us, coming from more conventional families, could not enjoy. He was ready for Zen Buddhism as a sound teaching that (among other things) exposes our acquisitive society for what it is, what it does, and how it must correct itself.

At the outset of his study he was skeptical, but he eventually adapted to, and enjoyed, traditional Zen temple life. Then when Oda Roshi died, it seemed clear that he should return to the United States to take the wheel for people and other beings in the West. "I'll be the taxi-driver / driving you home"—to our true home that we are in danger of losing sight of, and indeed of losing altogether. Down to earth and its treasures, Gary exposes in his particular, creative way the ephemeral nature of life, the mutual interdependence of all of its elements, and its precious quality. Yet his Buddhism is only metaphysical after the fact, just as his anthropology is not locked in academia, his working-class background is not bound to the routine of construction and driving trucks, and his poetry is perennial while its language is often from the world of labor.

Through the centuries, Buddhism has been in the process of moving out of the monastery and into the world, away from the clerical, the monks and nuns, and into the home. Gary Snyder's work is an important part of this process. He makes Buddhism accessible to Western readers, though he mentions it by name only occasionally. He also makes Buddhism accessible to itself. The *Diamond Sutra* makes clear that there is no term, no archetype, no doctrine, that does not self-destruct. Gary shows how this functions: With no buzz words and no buzz attitudes, perennial common sense is informed by the teachings of Shākyamuni and his successors, and that is the Buddhism that its founder intended.

I think Gary probably appreciates Bashō's verse:

> Journeying through the world,
> to and fro, to and fro,
> cultivating a small field.

But his field has many dominions, as this book shows. It also shows that he, like the rest of us, has faced a process of decisions that occasions have presented—in his case setting graduate school aside, seeing a bit of the world while working on freighters, studying Zen in Japan, marrying and fathering children, returning to the United States, settling at San Juan Ridge, establishing and leading the Ring of Bone Zendo, and so on, to his most recent decision to take up teaching as a tenured professor. My sense is that, from the outset of his self-taught zazen in the lumber camps of Oregon, he has been guided by the same motive that guided Chao-chou in his conversation with his new monk: to use every opportunity to turn the Wheel with and for all beings.

The fulcrum of this work for Gary is the Ring of Bone Zendo and the larger San Juan Ridge community, near North San Juan and Nevada City, California. Here in the Sierra foothills, Gary and his wife of that time, Masa, with the help of friends, built a substantial home in 1970. This early group has remained largely intact, for its members have purchased land nearby, and take part in an organically developed community. The Ring of Bone Zendo, built entirely with community labor in 1982, has a regular schedule of meditation meetings, public talks, and retreats, and is a spiritual and social center for people living on San Juan Ridge, but it is by no means a traditional temple surrounded by believers. Diverse multicentered activities—annual May Day and Halloween festivals, arts and music programs, community organization for the protection of the environment and its animals, and old-fashioned neighborliness that provides child care, emergency transportation, and support of the needy—make this a Zen center unique in North America in its application of the Buddha Way and the perennial way to local conditions and mores.

One of the Ring of Bone members remarked to me, "There is not a program here, not even, quite literally, a hammer or shovel, that does not have Gary's seal on it." Probably Gary would feel that is saying entirely too much, but it is true enough to be significant. With the Zendo and the Ridge as his home, he has also reached out to fellow poets, to fellow environmentalists, and to traditional peoples with whom he feels close affinity, working the soil of poetry, the essay, classroom and zendo presentations, and community organization with a lifelong purpose that simply became clarified with his Zen practice: to engage in showing in every way possible, using the tools he has sharpened and his talent for swinging them, how we are all of us here together only briefly, how we should take care of one another while we can, and how we can enjoy our heritage. This is the toku of Gary Snyder, and I am very grateful.

Ryo Imamura:

FOUR DECADES WITH GARY SNYDER

Back in the early 1950s, when I was still a young boy of seven, there appeared at my father's Buddhist temple in Berkeley a young graduate student named Gary Snyder, slim but strong in physique, a quick smile in his eyes, and an unmistakable omniscient presence about him. He impressed me immediately with his humorous stories and wondrous insights, as much as a young boy of seven can be impressed.

Gary talked with great passion about his love for the mountains, waters, and trees, the interdependency of all life, the defilements of the earth through petrochemical usage, the wanton destruction of forests, and the warming-over of the earth—decades before the popular issue of the "greenhouse effect" surfaced.

It was about the time of Gary's arrival that many other Caucasian and Japanese Buddhists began to meet for classes and discussions on a regular basis at the Buddhist Study Center, the educational wing of my father's temple. Looking back at this period, many of the scholars, poets, philosophers, and artists involved at that time would become well known as pioneers of American Buddhism in later years. They included, among many others, Alan Watts, Alex Wayman, Phil Whalen, Jack Kerouac, Robert Jackson, Will Petersen, Claude Dalenberg, Richard Gard, Glen Grosjean, Taitetsu Unno, and Leslie Kawamura. They were often joined by eminent Japanese scholars such as Hajime Nakamura, Lama Tokan Tada, Shoson Miyamoto, Yoshifumi Uyeda, and Ryugyo Fujimoto.

I remember the incident that made me a fan of Gary's for the rest of my life. My parents had invited him over for dinner soon after he had returned from a study trip to Japan. Usually our guests brought cakes and other sweet delights as gifts for my three sisters and me. When Gary arrived, we crowded around him to find out what wonderful confection he had brought us. To our dismay, we saw only a bag of ordinary apples. After dinner, Gary excused himself and locked himself in the kitchen for about ten minutes as we wondered what he might be doing in there. He emerged with several paper plates filled with apple wedges. He then informed us that each plate contained a different kind of apple. We were to taste a wedge from each plate and guess the kind of apple, which was written under each plate. Not only was the activity fun and educational, but it also reminded me to try to remain open and nonjudgmental. And I couldn't help but be impressed by the effort that Gary must have expended to bring us a gift that was both meaningful and healthy.

My father was also taken by the unique qualities of this young man. He felt that Gary made the teachings of the Buddha take on a new life and meaning. It wasn't that Gary talked all that much about Buddha per se. It had more to do with his sensitivity to the environment and his intuitive understanding of compassion that quietly but powerfully affected those about him. As I recall, my father began giving talks on environmental concerns soon after Gary's arrival. I often wondered how Gary so influenced my father, because my father was a very quiet and private man, and they hardly ever talked directly with each other. Somehow, through osmosis, my father was able to absorb the clear perspectives of this young man.

Thinking back to that period calls to mind a rather humorous memory that still brings tears of laughter to my eyes. My father used to make frequent trips to Japan after World War II to visit the family temple in Fukui. On one of his trips, he visited Gary, who was studying in a Zen monastery near Kyoto. When my father returned from Japan, he related to our astonishment that he had taken a motorcycle ride with Gary around Kyoto. My staid and quiet father riding around on a motorcycle was something none of us could even imagine. I am sure no one else could have convinced my father to get on a motorcycle. Even back then, Gary's free spirit invited everyone to be liberated.

Through my teen and young adult years, my contact with Gary was quite limited, although I would occasionally hear of his latest accomplishments from my parents, who maintained their close ties with him. They would give me his poetry and articles about him, perhaps wishing that I would grow up to be like him and possess his vision and commitment to all that was good and right in the world. Certainly I admired him from a distance, but, even more importantly, his presence caused me to feel extremely inadequate in my limited role as a Buddhist priest. In my world of ancient tradition and long family lineages, it was both wonderful and unsettling that someone like Gary, without formal Buddhist title or rank, could become so vitally essential to the future well-being of the Buddhist world.

Gradually, in my own limited way, I became involved in questioning the assumptions that provide the foundation for our blind and destructive ways and my own role in them. Considering his almost lifelong presence in my life, I am sure that Gary was a great influence in the evolution of my partial awakening to things-as-they-are.

In 1983 Gary and I, along with Joanna Macy, were elected to the Board of Directors of the Buddhist Peace Fellowship, to join co-founders Robert Aitken and Nelson Foster. Jenny Hoang, Fred Epsteiner, and Catherine Parker joined the board the following year. For two years we struggled to keep the infant organization afloat. Despite the many pressures, our meetings were always loving and productive. Gary often served as the calm center, which kept our shaky boat from capsizing in the stormy sea.

I was especially impressed with Gary's steadfastness, clarity of purpose, commitment, and generosity. It still amazes me that this famous man volunteered to serve as the treasurer, and was an exceptional one at that, while I played the more titular role of chairperson for one of the years. He spent many a day balancing the books, dealing with the banks, and making financial reports. And when there was not enough money in the coffers, he gave a benefit reading in Los Angeles, which immediately put us back in the black. What a treasurer! Needless to say, it was a great joy and pleasure to work with Gary on the Buddhist Peace Fellowship Board for those two years.

My father passed away in 1986. I recall the unbounded joy he expressed when Gary visited him in his last days—like a long-lost son returning home. My mother continues to regard Gary most highly, with special affection and respect. My three sisters think of him as their brotherly teacher. Visiting his home in Nevada City is considered by my family to be like a holy pilgrimage, in that one cannot help but return home more complete and human than when one left.

I continue to hold dear my friendship with Gary. Just like my father, I, representing another generation, am embraced by his inexhaustible compassion and wisdom. In his own free way, Gary has become timeless.

David Padwa:

WHAT'S THE SANSKRIT WORD FOR COYOTE?

Around Columbia University in the early 1950s I knew Carl Solomon, Gregory Corso, and Allen Ginsberg, and I had met Kerouac a few times. When the subsequent literary surge out of California began I paid attention as Gary's name and vigorous poems came floating East on numerous occasions. I had a vague impression of some hulking lumberjack who stirred coffee with his thumb. The notion of a "dharma bum" was particularly pleasing to me.

During the fifties I had begun to find my intellectual home in Buddhism. I didn't have a teacher but was not uncomfortable with the path of an autodidact. A vectoring of many forces led me on, which finally crystallized when I grasped that this was a "religion" based on a philosophy of emptiness, impermanence, and a quality called "suchness." I couldn't believe my luck. Around that time I had a large book of Buddhist sculptures. Most of the sublime faces showed a tantalizing hint of a smile. Why does the Buddha smile? I resolved to meditate on this and passed many hours with a photo of the Korean Miroku (Maitreya) now at Horyuji in Nara in Japan. Somehow, it all came together for me just about then. In the thirty-odd years that have since passed, any discoveries and insights revealed by my explorations into the nature of Buddhist dharma have inevitably seemed deeply familiar. "Of course," I say to myself, "of course."

In 1967, after a second passage through India, I planned to stay in Japan on my way back to the States. My friend, the inimitable, irreverent, and ever-joyful Alan Watts, whose free-wheeling words on Buddhism had served as useful handholds in earlier years, was also there that September. (Alan talks about Gary that autumn in his autobiography, *In My Own Way*. Talking with Alan over sake, I scribbled his words on a scrap of paper: "The basic questions: [thoughtful pause after each one] Where did it come from? Are we going to make it? Where are we going to put it? Who is going to clean up afterwards? Is it serious?").

Alan had sent a message to Kathmandu suggesting that I meet him in Kyoto. This worked out fine, and within a few days of my arrival he had introduced me to Ogata Roshi's informal *sangharama* for transients at Chotoku-in (Shokoku-ji). I was given a six-mat tatami room in the same hall where Sesshu the painter had lived in the fifteenth century. Ogata spoke English and in the 1930s had been at the University of Chicago, my alma mater. We got along rather well. Nothing very deep or rigorous, but lots in the way of friendly talk over breakfast after morning zazen, and some pleasant experiences of Buddhist "kidding around" (the *Hahayana*). Sometimes we pay too little attention to the kind of good-natured teaching that precisely conveys "the unbearable lightness of being," and I have always been partial to this style. A week or so later Alan said, "You've got to meet Gary Snyder," and introduced us. He was two years older than I was. We quickly found commonalities: friends, places, books, shipping out to sea, worldviews. This was no unlettered lumberjack, but an intellectual. And unlike most intellectuals I have known, he wasn't stupid.

I think I recall the first time we talked, just the two of us. We strolled through a temple ground somewhere in the city. We were talking about the difference between the illusory and the imaginary. While I no longer remember who said what, or even very much about the details of our conversation, I retain to this moment an impression of the clarity of Gary's thought, the masculine confidence of his views, and the relatively egoless vigor with which he expressed himself. I had a strong sense of Chaucer's "gladly would he learn and gladly teach," no trace of a man trying to score points. Anyway, we got on.

He and Masa had recently married, and they lived in a small house rather near the edge of town. The early evolution of Gary's significant Buddhist library was clearly evident. The house was a friendly social point and on more than a few occasions I slept over on the tatamis rather than make the trip back to Chotoku-in. Through Gary I met Philip Whalen, Julie Wellings, the Benedictine Dom Aelred Graham (who also wrote about that autumn in *Zen Catholicism*), Irmgard Schloegel, Edouard Roditi, Cid Corman, Bob Strickland, the Chief Monk of Daitoku-ji, and various others. (In later years I met a variety of Buddhist scholars through Gary: Philip Yampolsky, Burton Watson, and Alex Wayman.) I remember Phil Whalen's birthday party at the Snyders'. Every Buddhist noisemaker a sentient being might want (wooden fishes, bells, gongs, clogs, drums, shakuhachis, all in assorted sizes) was employed to make up a dharma percussion and conch band.

One day he said, "Let's go for a hike." At six in the morning he put on a badger-skin apron turned back-assward and we headed up into the hills, which began at the doorstep. That was the first time I followed his strong, rhythmic, sure-footed steps up some hill. I am taken with his love for strenuous physical values. We spent most of the day going up and up, with the briefest lunch break, on faint trails through magnificent forests of cryptomeria pine. The views were all from scroll paintings, in eighty shades of grey green. We topped out on the highest ridge. None of us was talkative. Time to go down. "Let's bushwhack," he said, and we were off cross-country down incredibly steep, rough, and complicated watercourses. This was the first time I heard about the Yamabushi sect, and Gary's informative lecture was given on the move as we struggled down the hillsides through a thick and blind undergrowth that went on forever. One couldn't see Gary, but we followed his thrashing and listened to him drone on about Buddhist forest cults. It was an amazing performance. Hours later we emerged at a tiny mountain village where the wife of the local Zen priest tagged Gary's Japanese language skills and invited us to meet her husband. He decided to give us tea. The rustic simplicity was a perfect setting. Napkins and bowls were laid out. Water boiled. He opened the tea caddy and, with amused surprise, saw that it was empty. Oh well. He poured from an old pot and used his tea whisk on what was only hot water. We all sipped appreciatively, pretending. The tea ceremony should lead the guests to reality. At dusk we took a bus back to Kyoto. In retrospect, it was the kind of day Gary has been giving me for years.

A week or so later, while Julie Wellings was sweeping acorns in the monastery's courtyard, Ruth Fuller Sasaki, abbess of Ryosen-an, Daitoku-ji, who was largely responsible for Gary's coming to Japan, died. I never knew her, but I went with Gary to a private memorial alongside her remains. We sat with her for a long time and Gary chanted the Hannya-Shingyo.

Eating at the Snyders' always involved cooking over a hanging firepot and reciting the English translation of a Buddhist grace over food. Gary's English renderings of Buddhist ritual texts (gathas, prayers, memorials, vows, blessings, and so on) have always seemed especially impressive. His small collection called *The Wooden Fish* is a masterpiece that should be reprinted. His version of the Four Vows never reifies and stays fresh at each utterance.

After I had been a few months in Japan, the weather grew very cold. My room at Chotoku-in was unheated and this contributed to my feeling that it was time to move on. Gary's last words to me as I parted Kyoto stayed with me for a long time (still with me, actually): "Let's do something together," he said. The threshold year of 1968 culture lay ahead.

When the Snyders started their family and came back to California from Japan, they moved temporarily near Mill Valley, to Roger Sommers' collection of houses on top of the ridge overlooking the canyons where Green Gulch Farm and Muir Woods are located. (Alan Watts later died up there and Gary wrote a revealing poetic tribute to him.) The place was conveniently near San Francisco but beyond the earshot of urban noise. Margot St. James was up there; also Elsa Gidlow, and Alan and Jano Watts. I was an occasional visitor. I saw immediately that Gary wasn't affiliating with any of the various Buddhist *sanghas* in America, yet somehow was feeling friendly about all of them.

Gary and I briefly worked on an idea to do a film script based on the transmission from the first to the second patriarch, that is, from Bodhidharma to Hui-ko. The event was moved to the seventeenth century and the characters were to be American Indians. We decided to visit Anasazi sites in the Southwest to pick up vibrations from the landscape, and arranged to meet in Santa Fe (which was a fateful occurrence for me as it led to my moving there from New York and strongly shaped the rest of my life). We rented a car and headed up to the Four Corners area. Nanao Sakaki was with us, as were Simon Ortiz and one or two other friends. We saw Chaco Canyon, Shiprock, Monument Valley, and Canyon de Chelly. (I know of at least four poems that came out of that trip: about four-corner hopscotch, the redneck bar in Farmington, New Mexico, the Black Mesa strip mine, and the Anasazi.) We went down to see Antelope ruin in Canyon del Muerto. It was unbelievably quiet. In the afternoon we sat in some shade. Gary went off some few hundred yards, unrolled his portable altar, and sat in erect spine, motionless, for a long time. Later, still at the same spot, he opened a notebook and wrote for a while. (I saw him do the identical thing seventeen years later in the Brooks Range in Alaska.) Nanao's wonderful planet-loving heterodox Buddhism was a formative source of strength and innovation for Gary. Simon, profoundly schooled at Acoma Pueblo, illustrated something extremely deep about ancient ways. I was responsible for the view from Manhattan. It was a marvelous trip. Nothing was left untouched.

At about this time Gary decided that "home" was going to be up in the Sierra foothills, where he owned a piece of land on San Juan Ridge, between the middle and south forks of the Yuba River, with Allen Ginsberg and Dick Baker. I remember going up there with him to fell and later to strip logs for the wonderful Japanese-style house that would be built. He called the place "Kitkitdizze" after the Maidu Indian word for the woody shrub that is the principal ground cover there. He was clearly in the process of reinventing Turtle Island.

More important, his great contribution to the evolution of an American Buddhist *sangha* was beginning. No priests were required. This was for householders, manual laborers, skeptical intellectuals, families with children, professionals, dropouts of every description, American Indians, scientists, scholars, bums, and lucky folks who had never heard the word. The practice was ecumenically traditional: sit, study, adapt, directly penetrate toward one's true nature. The first zendo was the meadow, and the deer on the ridge became acquainted with Buddhists and came close. This was the early 1970s.

Gary persuaded me to share some undeveloped land next door, and it gave me chances to visit over the years. There was always work. Social capital was being created every day. I remember when the fruit trees were planted. I remember when their first fruits were eaten. I was there when the well was drilled and remember a Maidu-Buddhist ritual confection to mark that event. There were always maypoles to be set up, visitors to look after, wine to drink, motors to fix, children to cosset, boards to paint, baths to take, books to discuss, fences to repair, meditations to sit, chickens to feed, Buddhist philosophy to discuss, firebreaks to cut, tall tales to tell, underbrush to clear, and rituals to invent.

Gary contributed something large to the cultural forces that started to sweep through America from the time he returned in 1968. I believe that he was personally developed to the point where he himself was not greatly acted upon by what was happening at that time (I say this respectfully), but somehow he laid a wrap on events and managed to torque them over a few degrees—and small angles project out to subtend vast arcs. His essay on Buddhism and "the coming revolution" illustrates what I mean. The revolution never came, but the dharma was being absorbed. "But permanent revolution is like permanent surgery," I said to him. "Ouch," he said. I asked him why Japan as a nation, the recipient of Zen teaching, was such a sad industrial sleepwalker. "They got the message," he said, "but they never opened the envelope." American Buddhists seemed to be interested in opening the envelope, in Gary's view. Notwithstanding the poignant knowledge that we were living in "a dharma-ending age," there was something young and fresh about being born as an American *sangha*.

We discussed whether a Western *sangha* needed an updated *vinaya*. He wrote me the following:

> Seems to me it poses yet-unresolved problems (sectarian & other)—(egos)—high-visibility—self-consciousness—and yet may be necessary. I've been reading *Vinaya Texts* translations (5 vols!) and much is tedious and legalistic. Mustn't lose sight of "All Beings" sense of *sangha*—"the inner laws of things," the *vinaya*. We have to make/be a people (diné, natives, in touch, in place) before we can begin to be a spiritual *sangha* (the historical *sangha* can exist by virtue of its closeness, trust, support by, peasantries and peoples—(like guerrillas —"fish in water")—*one* level is to build that, people to "support" the *sangha* (—new religions can always draw support from disoriented urban classes—but then they are saprophytes and have little long range strength (like Mithra-ism)—Am not really making objection but sharing thoughts. Like, I am concerned that the Buddhist groups in US have "right occupation" behind them—Could one crossbreed Vinaya Council with medicine/pow-wow circle idea and focus on *gharba-dhatu* "how to live in our place" as well as *vajra-dhatu*— "how to realize mind" perspectives?

That was toward the end of 1972, and it shows the consistent link between places and mind, between locus and logos, that is so prominent in Gary's writing. The little place of San Juan Ridge. The middle place of Planet Earth. The big place of this Universe.

Gary is a prodigious correspondent. In an age when epistolary skills are dead it is always a special pleasure to open the mailbox and find an envelope bearing his unmistakable italic. My own letters were fewer, but I would frequently send him clippings that I thought he ought to see and, years later, when he broke down and had a phone put in, I would call from time to time. Over these years I'd guess that I've had more than a hundred letters from him. Some were five-line notes, others went on for pages; about a third were typed and the rest were by hand. Frequently there was a poem or a small enclosure. I'm not a collector and feel like a vandal confessing to the fact that I don't have more than a few (which seem to have survived by accident). There's one provenanced "on the Okhotsk Sea, Hokkaido" when he made a trip to that northern island, dated July 17, 40072. It includes this three-liner:

> Riding the
> slender boat of *Mu*
> knifing through.

That says it, doesn't it?

In 1972 the United Nations convened an international conference on the environment in Stockholm, Sweden. A number of us thought it might be useful (or fun) to produce an "alternative" conference at the same place and time. It produced only a depressing mixture of Swedish self-righteousness, Third-World industrial lust, hippie idiocy, mindless leftism, and shameless egotism. Many peaceniks and incipient "Greens" were present, as were Melissa Savage, Jack Loeffler, David Brower, Stewart Brand, Wavy Gravy, Paul Ehrlich, Margaret Mead, Barry Commoner, and twenty-odd Indians from various parts of the Americas (the Hopis had deer-skin IDs as their *only* travel documents, no problems). Also Gary, reading poems and wondering where the Buddhist dharma of right action and right views was going to fit into all of this emerging eco-politics. I think it was around then that Gary convinced himself that it would have to start and finish with right meditation.

Back at Kitkitdizze the zendo moved from the meadow to an awning, passed through the Snyders' living room, and went upscale when it located in the barn. No place for silk brocades; this was a rough, backcountry circle of friends. Ring of Bone Zendo it was called (after the marvelous poem by Lew Welch). Bob Greensfelder, Will Staple, Chuck Dockham, and Masa (especially) provided granite support for the *sangha* of San Juan Ridge. Calendars and notes were sent regularly to active and associate members. The *sesshins* took on evocative names ("Seeds-to-Snow," "Great Cold," "Snow-to-Flowers"). A connection to the Hawaiian Diamond Sangha was stitched together. Aitken Roshi and others came to visit or teach.

Although the particular circumstances of its origins gave it a Zen lineage, that particular connection linking back to the historical Buddha was almost incidental. The Ring of Bone community never developed the stink of sectarianism, and the study and practice of dharma was genuinely ecumenical. There was room enough in the big garage for all the vehicles. In time, a handsome dedicated year-round zendo and community hall was built (entirely by the volunteer efforts of hundreds), with a connecting kitchen and teachers' residence. It is impossible to say whether or not this place will survive just a few years or last for many centuries.

I never knew anyone who could live as richly, as elegantly, on so little money. To visit Kitkitdizze was to attend the home palace of a forest king. Nothing of real worth was lacking; there was a bottomless inventory of high-level objects and activities that most of us could not imagine. (My boys will never forget the recurve bow and quiver of arrows with sponge rubber tips that let them mock-hunt the deer browsing about in the cooler seasons—the arrows thumped them on the side, and they looked up without bolting, with their patient soft eyes saying, "Haven't you outgrown this dumb game yet?") This oxymoronic picture of spartan luxury has a simple explanation. We sat on the ground watching the moon. "The fact is, Gary," I said, "this is really an extreme form of elitism." He replied with a thin smile: "Shhh!"

Over the years Gary's livelihood was achieved from his writings, and not less through his readings. On hundreds of platforms he blended the familiar themes of dharma, ecology, and poetics in an artful mix of reciting poems, talking essays, trying out ideas, answering questions, and sharing thoughts. Gary has been to more college campuses than any secretary of education could contemplate. He's probably introduced the small seeds of Buddhist thought to more places than anyone else in America. Although he was no stranger to the prominent gilt-edged powerhouses of the university world, he was never particularly taken with the precious, self-absorbed, and received pretensions commonly found there. Instead, he seemed studiously to prefer smaller, more innocent, "backcountry" institutions, which could remind him of the braver intellectual openness of undergraduate days at Reed College. Finally, almost inevitably, he became a professor at the University of California at Davis.

One of these days mainstream Western academic philosophy is going to discover the Buddhist void, *sunyata*. In the last forty years, linguistic philosophers, existentialists, semioticians, the new anthropologists, and all the deconstructionists have gotten very close. But still no cigar. The dread engendered in the European mind by the concept of emptiness as a manifestation of despair, of satanic nihilism, a *black* vortex where "everything is permitted," spinning out personae like Aleister Crowley, Charles Manson, and Adolph Hitler, is very strong in our society. But one day, when they run out of the recourse of every conceivable evasion, our philosophers will have to sit down in a quiet place and observe mind directly.

The understanding and experience of voidness as bright transparency, as pure openness, as suchness, as "amazing grace," whose essential and ineluctable countersign is compassion, still remains ahead for most of our intellectuals. But it is inevitable. And when it happens, as it may soon, there will be an overcompensated and exaggerated rush to restudy Nietzsche, *abhidharma*, Stcherbatsky's "Logic," Sanskrit terminology, koans, and so on. "The full catastrophe," as the classics say. Later, when the dust settles, people will want some clues to using dharma in contemporary daily Western life. To whom or what will they turn? Where will they find earthen clues grounded in the humane secular skepticisms of scientific linguistics, ecology, storytelling, paleo-history at the dawn of human sapience and sentience, "wilderness," the relations between women and bears, mind self-observed, physical labor, and endless mountains and rivers? Where else but in the compressions of Buddhist poetry! These are, in fact, the new *vinaya* texts.

Most religions are beds of superstition aspiring to ethics and spirituality, and many Buddhists follow a superstitious practice. Yet Buddhism, as taught by its founder, is unique in its reliance on direct observation and examination, rather than magical faith, in striving for high goals. Gary strikes me as an exemplar of the possibility of determined religious practice stripped of mumbo-jumbo. There's nothing grim about it, either. This is the kind of *dharma* we need in our time.

Well, old-fart age is approaching, though the Sage of the Sakyas stayed young into his eighties. To sum up: Gary's no-nonsense Buddhist style is the important contribution: free of superstition, and playing the mindful heuristics of poetic ritual. He is my slightly older brother. I don't mean to make him more than he is. He isn't. And after all, there's a lot of Coyote in him and it's not a good idea to speak too well of Coyote.

Dale Pendell:

A RAVEN IN THE DOJO:
GARY SNYDER AND THE DHARMA

✱✱✱✱✱ ✱✱✱✱✱

When I think of Gary, I think of his grin. A wonderfully devilish grin. I think I will start with that. . . .

✱✱✱✱✱

A lot of our best conversations were when we were squatting, in what's been called Asian-style—just squatting on the flats of our feet following the innuendos of an idea: Gary's eyes getting narrower and narrower as his grin, contra-wise, grew wider and more devilish.

✱✱✱✱✱

Gary's ability to fit small pieces together into big, coherent pictures is stunning. Interconnections. Art of reading signs, and the signs interlinking history, biology, politics, poetry, and Buddhism. Wilderness of paths and pathless.

A facility with ideas that impressed and delighted again and again, kind of like watching Hesse's *glasperlenspiel* in real time.

✱✱✱✱✱

I went along with Gary on one of his reading trips to Sierra College. We parked in the parking lot, and as we were walking toward the classrooms, we passed a red Porsche. Gary cast an eye over it and mentioned how someone invested a great deal of work and money to have that machine. Well, we were all living without electricity, pumping our water, hoping that our cars wouldn't collapse the next time we drove down the Fire Access Rd., so a Porsche was the same thing as a Lamborghini or a Ferrari, and in the same class as any Chevrolet newer than ten years old, so I forgot about it.

Eventually we got to a class and Gary started talking. He said, "What is it that motivates us? Why do we do things?" And so on. Why do some people become corporate executives and others, well, I can't really remember, biologists or artists, but the answer was that it was because of a feeling—to be in contact with a power. And then he talked about that car. How for some people, it was driving a red sports car that gave them the feeling of being alive and in contact with the other power.

And from that he built a whole delivery connecting eco-politics to everyday life, connecting the Pleistocene up through the Paleolithic to the exponential equations of fossil fuel consumption.

*****

Gary has been one of the outstanding missionaries (Gary would loathe that word) of Zen Buddhism in the United States. A lot of it was his alter ego, Japhy Ryder, but that doesn't diminish the accomplishment. It was natural for people to look to Gary as a Zen teacher.

*****

On San Juan Ridge, hereafter to be called the Ridge, where Gary and Masa dug in at Kitkitdizze, zazen and study groups were a part of the life that Gary shared with his neighbors. Small group sits evenings or early mornings, bundled figures in the meadow tucked in around the manzanita, hordes of demonic mosquito-demons surrounding each. Study groups groping up through the three bodies—the nirmanakaya, the sambhogakaya, and the dharmakaya. On and off. Like so many of our practices, but mostly on. And Gary and Masa maintaining a regular sitting practice themselves through the times when there was no group sitting.

*****

Many acts of kindness. Gary is one of the more generous men that I've known. Generous with his hospitality, and generous with his time and resources. And professionally generous: Many times I've seen Gary mention or credit an unknown colleague or comrade in a paper or at a reading when such mention was demanded neither by law nor by decorum.

*****

Teaching really means example. Study groups, theory, history; all that is important, but the nitty-gritty is the way the individual teacher moves. One time, in the time before Aitken Roshi came to Ring of Bone, I asked Gary for formal koan instruction. He declined, saying that, technically, he wasn't qualified. I have always held that response as a mark of Gary's great personal integrity. And as the years have passed, my appreciation of the gesture has increased.

*****

Gary's style tended toward samurai, and not everyone was comfortable with it. That no-nonsense, no frills, no mushy-mushy style from Japanese Rinzai. But let's not confuse style and substance. What I appreciated was when Gary would hold back, let someone else try something, even bungle it, when he could have done it right anytime. That kind of teaching. Keeping quiet in a discussion. Not that Gary didn't always get his way. . . .

Well, almost always.

*****

We sat together one night a week, and had group discussions, usually at Gary's house around the fire pit, different ones of us leading, crouching lower and lower to the floor if the fire was smoky. And sitting Rohatsu. Working *sesshin*-style. Coming over each evening, sitting, sleeping over and sitting again in the morning. The last morning we always hiked up to Bald Mountain, usually cold, sometimes frozen, a line of ragged men and women threading their way through the darkness to chant and circumambulate the stone circle shrine as the sun rose, conches blowing, birds starting, fingers stiff.

*****

And one year, can't remember which, there were enough of us, the sitting was regular enough, that we began doing other *sesshins*. Experimented. Gary had built a barn, so we dubbed it the "barndo" and had some sleep-over *sesshins* there.

*****

Style. Gary's unsuccessful effort to keep socks out of the barndo. Bob Greensfelder wondering about the acceptability of down jackets (they rustle). Then came the Great Cold, frozen air drafting through every crack in the walls and doors, ice forming in the teacups, ahhh, Gary still barefoot. . . .

With all the layers of clothing, we'd really lay into the kyosaku, the cracks reverberating through the dawn. "The best kyosaku is a Louisville slugger planed down." I think Steve Nemirow said that.

*****

There was a feeling expressed by some folks on the Ridge that the Zen thing was for "Gary and his boys," and that to do it one had to be "tough." As one of the boys, I think this was untrue and unfair.

On the other hand, though, there *was* something, what was it, the stocking/barefoot thing? Some hint or feeling that "dharma combat" might, ultimately, be decided by pugilism. . . .

Sigh.

*****

So gradually zazen became more regular. Gary had a vision, and he gave the vision a name. "Ring of Bone." Named for the poem by Lew Welch and expressed at an anniversary of his disappearance. We were having *zazenkai* and *sesshins* in the barndo, sleeping over, sitting all weekend. We were preparing ourselves, and when at a business meeting Gary casually brought up the subject of teachers, there was a lot of interest. We talked for a while, different ones of us suggesting this teacher or that: Would Sasaki come up from L.A.? Would . . . who else? Can't remember. Then Gary told us about Robert Aitken, that he'd been corresponding with him.

*****

With Aitken Roshi's arrival the changes were immediate and profound. A new kind of intensity and presence, a lightness. Gentle, unathletic, scholarly, Aitken introduced a participatory alternative to oligarchy that was quite un-Japanese.

Aitken was quite different from Gary in temperament. Both men are intellectuals, both poets, but not in the same ways. Aitken's art goes into his *teisho*. There is something fuguelike about some of Aitken's teishos. Gary has this expansiveness, pulling seemingly disparate details into grand unified fields.

*****

So I wondered about Gary, how he would take it, a real full-blown roshi at the center of what he had patiently sat by, sat with, watered, labored for, encouraged in countless ways that most people never even saw. I wondered how it would be for him.

I got my answer. At our first *sesshin,* and all of us beginners with Aitken's style, discipline was a bit lax. I was an officer (jisha, I think), as was Gary, and so I was staying at Gary's and Masa's house. We were using a tent as the hojo, and the most level surface, and not so very level, was so close to the barn that the people in the *dokusan* line could hear little bits and pieces of conversation in the tent from time to time. One time Gary had been in line in front of me, and had gone in. I remember hearing some kind of rush, or sudden movement, from inside the tent. Later, in the house, Gary had this dazed smile. Shaking his head, he said, "Man, he's good!"

And through the next years after that Gary was tireless. He was a Zen student again. And announced himself as such. I had the feeling that there was no admission to advanced standing, that he was thrown in right at the beginning, and he grabbed both oars.

The big difference in the sangha was that now Gary was getting a lot more help. And with that we built a Zendo.

*****

Let's skip the ego thing, but consider the status of "persona invest-ment." What is it? A mask larger than life so that those in the back can see. A costume, dramatic force. Or a cage for the heart? Which drama is which, which is commitment, the role or the unmasking?

*****

Teachers. The best teachers. . . . Not to disparage scholars. Scholars are fine and sufficient in themselves, and can teach what they know. But once in a while there are a rare few of the other kind, those who know that there are stakes on the table and that the clock is still run-ning. They invite/cajole, challenge, or humiliate. That something is going on and that like it or not you are a part of it. . . . Gary was that kind of teacher. (Karl Ray and Norman O. Brown were two others.)

*****

Commitment. A patient urgency—that poetics is wedded to history, when "history" means future history. Commitment as bedrock, so teleology is just one possible result.

*****

Gary's intellectual integrity is inseparable from his engagement: political, poetic, and spiritual. I don't see how any such web can be seamless, but Gary's way is pretty smooth. If there are conflicts between them, which one is primary? Don't think I could say.

*****

Example. The best teachers teach by example. Teaching by example is the essence of commitment. Not you or I or any of us but the work at hand, that there is such.

*****

How do you know if a potential teacher is of the "persona investment" type? It's easy, actually. Bait them. Some are like old dogs: No matter where you poke them they hardly roll. Those are the lovable teachers. Mellow, old Tokusan with his bowls.

Hah! Then there are those who are like cats, pretty touchy in some spots.

A standing joke on the Ridge was that if you joked about Gary's smoky house, Gary would get as smoky as his fire pit.

My advice: Always bait your teachers. Do you really want them if they can't take abuse? Heh, heh. (This goes double for therapists, along with their fees.)

*****

My own spiritual teachers have split 50/50 on the ego side: some pretty fond of their images, others like saints. The former kind work better informally, I think.

Well, I take that back. What do I know?

*****

What I know is that if Gary could shoot better in the dark he'd never have written that "True Night" poem.

*****

Sometimes we want our teachers to be more than human—and then we get disappointed. Isn't it enough to have been through that with parents?

An eager hand waves from the back of the class: "No, I want my teachers to be more than human. I want them to be Buddhas."

Shall we explain to him the phrase "mere formality"? Who will step forward and explain this to him? And who will step forward to affirm? Or to deny?

✳✳✳✳✳

My own teachers, 50/50, cats and dogs, I found the reconciliation I was looking for at the Boston Museum of Fine Arts. Two anonymous paintings hang in the Asian collection: one of Manjusri, and beside it another of Samantabhadra. Ming dynasty. Pre-Columbian.

Manjusri has this imperturbable calmness—this serenity—not a disengaged blissful serenity, but an enfolding, spacious clarity. A clarity with a yielding quality: If you push it, there's nothing there— while if it pushes you, you gasp for breath.

Ahh, then Samantabhadra, the painting that had called to me from across the room. Devil, through and through. Brow furrowing down, eyes narrowed to shining slits, and that grin!

✳✳✳✳✳

This must be Raven, who stole the fire—and lived to tell about it. Little here that's "saintly." Why isn't he in Tantrism?

The eyes glint with the penetrating insight—"yeah, right"—denial with double affirmative.

✳✳✳✳✳

Science and analysis share the quality of penetration: "The thesis is disproved, as is its antithesis."

And Zen is spiritual science, with the experiential representing the empirical. Replication demanded. An environment not unfriendly to skeptics, I should say. And Gary is a skeptical humanist. For all of his embracing of things ritual and magic, he's not a Believer (in what I guess I can still call the "Aquarian" sense of the word). The crystal is hidden in the shaman's cheek.

✳✳✳✳✳

Eyes slitted, shining with a private joke—private joke open to all. Samantabhadra: a reaching out quality. The eyes invite us in—into something crazy and sharp, and with an unpredictable quality. Something that makes us laugh.

*****

Hello. Whose grin is that? Who is shouting "kwatz!" Walls crumble. You are home.

*****

Teaching, Teacher, teach what. Gary's main teaching is not how to write a good poem; that can't be taught. Nor Zen, in the sense of "having the eye"—that can't be taught either. His teaching comes from what he has done with his life, by his example. The salient points are commitment, and generosity. It's for us to pass the teaching on.

*****

Raven, Samantabhadra, Coyote on his haunches at the edge of the camp, eyes expectant, patient, and aglint.

Jacquie Bellon:

Bellon

Having pictured myself making love with a
Datura flower I conjure your words: "With
joyful interpenetration for all" and know you've
been there, your nose in pollen your tongue in nectar.

Carole Koda:

FIRST WINTER

Gary is clicking away at his computer keyboard. He still types on it as if it were his old manual typewriter—the rhythms are clear and loud and companionable. He laughs at something he's just written, looks up briefly from his computer screen, and says, "I've been wasting my life." "Why?" I ask. "I could have been a writer all these years!" He's delighted. Dressed in jeans and long underwear, layers of shirt/sweater/jacket, lavender bandana, and fleece-lined leather hat, he looks like some kind of recurrent dream that I have about a cowboy. And he imagines the ten years of research notes, filed articles, letters, midstride inspirations, friends and neighbors' stories, as errant little dogies he's bringing into the corral for a momentary reunion in his new book of essays. He was thinking that they'd ranged a lot farther out and is constantly surprised and relieved at how sweetly they coax in, how fresh they look.

We've been sharing this barn workspace for about six months. It was built for horses, but soon became a zendo, and later a boys' bedroom and dance studio. Now it's filled with saddles, our combined libraries, and mountaineering equipment and a couple of computers. It's cold here in the winter. We sometimes type with fingerless gloves and can't quite keep the blood returning to our brains without long underwear.

I am sitting close by the Ashley woodstove looking at my knees. "What are you working on?" he asks. "A little remembrance of Gary Snyder for his birthday. Got any ideas?" Most of Gary's friends are looking back at years of long association. I am remembering two years—millennia of minutes, most of which are still playing vividly through this body. He grins and says, "Why don't you write about how Gary Snyder became a writer?"

Gary's been working on this book for several years. Last year he began preparing me for the focused writing period he's in right now. He described a grouchy, distant, impatient, and uncommunicative artist totally absorbed in the manuscript. Although I might feel like leaving him, I should please be patient because eventually it would be finished and we could step out, celebrate in a prolonged kind of way. From a distance it sounded manageable; but after I dug myself up from valley soils and let all my fine root hairs hang out up here in the foothills, I began to feel uneasy. "What is it about writers and domestic life?" I muttered through my filter mask as I crawled around under the house—jacking up joists, pounding in pier blocks, trying to level and strengthen the floor. I thought about the tenacious resentments and unfortunate habits of mind and body that can come out of Big Production time and applied the obvious metaphor of the moment. No harm in shoring up the basics here—making explicit what lovers want to assume they know about respect, trust, private demons, and recreational imperatives. We took the time to do that: a step toward bringing family making and book making into the same territory.

Now, beginning with Gary having to completely reorganize his library (moved from the house) and office (moved from Allen's cottage down the hill), he is three months or more into this project. He has scanned his three-by-five card file (representing years of notes), devoted a week to learning new tricks on his Macintosh, reacquainted himself with the rolling file that holds all the notes for this book, and completed three new chapters. There are days when Gary is working at nothing but the manuscript—early morning til late night, with very short breaks for meals and coffee. Everything happens with great intensity on those days: a plunge into someone else's book to check facts or new theories, several hours of writing or editing. Sometimes he is eager to talk through a new set of ideas, other times he looks a little shocky and doesn't try much more than polite exchanges at the dinner table, maybe a new blues line.

I grew up on a rice farm in the central valley of California. My parents ran the farm and mill together in a warehouse office about fifty yards away from our house, same distance as it is to the barn. When my father was engaged in a project—like building the flour mill—he went out early, came home for meals, and worked at his drafting table past our bedtime. Sometimes to relax on weekends he and my mom dressed up like Japanese-American Westerners—boots, bolo ties, circle skirts, and dancing slippers—and went out to potluck and square dance. So the rhythm of the richly concentrated workday is literally familiar to me—except that now I see it from the perspective of the grown woman, the partner, the mother.

There is a constant pull in Gary's life between time needed for writing and the numerous daily requests for his presence or performance at an event, encouragement of someone else's project, critical review of same, letter of recommendation. (This, in addition to a large and loved circle of personal correspondents.) Many worthy efforts—only a small fraction of which he can consider. Sometimes we go through the built-up piles of mail together, Gary catching me up with his life by telling stories of how he met this person or connected with that group. I am impressed that after so many years, he still doesn't decline requests lightly, having developed a genuine comradely spirit for other writers and environmental activists.

Some days he never gets to his desk because of town errands, too many home chores, arrival of friends from far away, a day to ski or walk, leaving home for a series of lectures, readings, meetings. But most days are a steady mix of a few good hours of writing or research and some choices from the Basket of Things to Do that is our life here: chopping wood, fixing the many broken or cranky machines and encouraging the others, driving car pool, zazen, chatting with neighbors, sorting through about five pounds of mail a day, cooking and cleaning, getting loose with the kids, talking on the phone to all sorts of known and unknown folk, keeping all the university work up to date. (Every two or three days Gary has long telephone chats with his mother. "Gary," she says, "don't write essays . . . nobody's ever going to remember you for that. Write love poems.")

As long as there are large chunks of time for writing, these are not distractions, but sharpening stones—as are the day's exchanges and silences, brief or prolonged, that weave between us in the barn or the house or on the trail. Now I begin to understand the economy of my childhood household, see for myself that a deeply felt partnership can liberate the energies to move creatively in solitude or together with family and friends. Children are not hindrances in this context, but the unruly sparks that keep us working madly while they dream.

Through all this, the irritable, solipsistic, high-strung artist has emerged only occasionally—like the sound of a wind-stressed limb falling in the woods. A quick little snap, and it's all over. No trace. So the lingering memories of this time may be the small daily details: Gary's waking routine of pouring two cups of coffee from the thermosful he made the night before, moving slowly to conserve heat between flannel sheets. Talk of the night's dreams or the history of the Byzantine Empire (especially Theodora's penchants) or the car pool schedule or winter habits of crickets. That morning ritual complete, he dresses fast and sometimes rouses the girls singing. To the one who claims she hates cheerful morning songs, he sings, "Sleep creep stay in bed now . . ." Then off to start the fire in the barn.

Thankfully, we are Unruly Sparks, too: our earthwise bodies keep us from burning too many computer commands into our brains. When the work has gone to thuds and caffeine, we head out for an hour or two on paths that Gary, friends, and family have opened over the years—many of which are gradually becoming obscured by overgrowth of chaparral. Sometimes we have to stoop over and shrink through the manzanita and ceanothus branches; other times we go down to hands and knees, following the maxim we relearned this summer: You can go anywhere if you're willing to crawl. Recently, feeling cold and midwinterish at our desks, we walked to a little subvalley very near the house . . . and suddenly were in a spring climate, surrounded by large flocks of robins and woodpeckers. The sensual little blurp sounds of the robins warmed the air, a surprising contrast to our north slope, which still holds snow above the ice-skinned pond.

Coming back home, Gary walked fast downhill through the forest—his pace so steady that it looked slow. It reminded me of our backpacking trip this summer, which included a climb of one of my favorite northern Yosemite landmarks, Tower Peak. Ascending the mountain, we moved up together over the smooth granite slabs, then into a gully of slightly more difficult "hands and feet" climbing. At the summit we relaxed into the sleepy calm that comes with a little altitude, tired bodies, and sun: pilot biscuits and salami, loose talk, speculation on the landforms around us and the smoke below, nap. We descended the chute carefully to avoid disabling each other with rock missiles, but when we reached the more open slopes I noticed that I was starting to run.

All these years I thought that Jack Kerouac had been exaggerating in his description of Gary descending Matterhorn Peak (or at the very least, that the quick descent style had to do with the slidy scree gully they came down). To my complete amazement and delight Gary strode out over the the slabs, gaining momentum for the broken jumble of granite blocks below. When he met them he began to leap from one boulder to the next, sometimes dropping five or six feet to come to rest on a thin ridge of rock, sinking down and re-balancing to catch his breath and go on. He liked making a quick pinball move that required planting both feet against a vertical slab as he jumped down a steep little drop, slowing himself just enough that way to keep his balance when he landed below. The deep warm ruby light of his earring played through glints of quartz and feldspar, teasing me to stay close for pure kinesthetic pleasure. He would stop to rest, laugh, and say something nonchalant, like "I couldn't do this in my forties because I was too worried about my knees."

Something is coming together—a confidence and joy with prose, a multilayered balance of going out and staying in, a feel for when to leap and when to nap. So now he thinks he'll be a writer, thinks he's getting the hang of it. I'm thinking that he's only a writer as inevitably as he is a pump repairman, a father trying to find his way through and with his children, a rambunctious and tender lover, an afficionado of local politics, a thoughtful student and teacher of the dharma, a predator of books, a man filled with curiosity and confidence about the world as it is, an inspired stir-fry cook who clears and cleans the counter before he sets to work.

—*Kitkitdizze*
14 February 1989

Gary Snyder:

OFF THE TRAIL

for Carole

We are free to find our own way
Over rocks—through the trees—
Where there are no trails. The ridge and the forest
Present themselves to our eyes and feet
Which decide for themselves
In their old learned wisdom of doing
Where the wild will take us. We have
Been here before. It's more intimate somehow
Than walking the paths that lay out some route
That you stick to,
All paths are possible, many will work,
Being blocked is its own kind of pleasure,
Getting through is a joy, the side-trips
And detours show down logs and flowers,
The deer paths straight up, the squirrel tracks
Across, the outcroppings lead us on over.
Resting on treetrunks,
Stepping out on the bedrock, angling and eyeing
Both making choices—now parting our ways—
And later rejoin; I'm right, you're right,
We come out together. *Mattake,* "Pine Mushroom,"
Heaves at the base of a stump. The dense matted floor
Of Red Fir needles and twigs. This is wild!
We laugh, wild for sure,
Because no place is more than another,
All places total,
And our ankles, knees, shoulders &
Haunches know right where they are.
Recall how the *Dao De*
Jing puts it: the trail's not the way.
No path will get you there, we're off the trail,

You and I, and we chose it! Our trips out of doors
Through the years have been practice
For this ramble together,
Deep in the mountains
Side by side,
Over rocks, through the trees.

Culture and Politics

Dan Ellsberg:
THE FIRST TWO TIMES WE MET

I must have read *The Dharma Bums* as soon as the paperback came out in October 1959, because it was in my mind when I found myself in Japan in January of 1960. It was mainly because the Ryoanji rock garden was described briefly in that book that I decided to take a day off from my work in Tokyo to go visit it in Kyoto.

Like, I suppose, everyone else who read Kerouac's novel, I wished, after reading it, that my life had brought me next to his character Japhy Ryder at some point, or to someone like him. It didn't seem likely that there was anyone else much like him, though it was obvious that Kerouac was describing a real person. I had even read his name in some review, though I couldn't have recalled it.

I wasn't in Japan that winter as a dharma bum. My paycheck came from the Rand Corporation, which got most of its money for research on national security from the U.S. Air Force. At the moment I was on loan to a project run by the Office of Naval Research, advising the Commander-in-Chief, Pacific (CINCPAC) on problems of the command and control of nuclear weapons.

A particular task I had set myself was to find out the ways that individuals who were in a position to launch nuclear weapons, directly or by sending out orders, might be able to start a nuclear war on their own. There were quite a few such ways and people, I was discovering. The next question was how to change the system so that this couldn't happen.

It seemed to me a very urgent problem, almost entirely secret from the public (both things, despite my efforts, are still true). In pursuing it, I had been talking to atomic control officers all over the Pacific, at alert strips in Okinawa and Korea, in command posts of the Seventh Fleet at sea in Taiwan, in underground headquarters in Hawaii, and, now, in Japan.

I was working conscientiously, obsessively, as is my nature, with no time-out for sightseeing. The one daytime exception, up until then, had been my pilgrimage, one Saturday, to the Zen monastery in Kyoto.

After looking at the rocks in the raked sand at Ryoanji I walked back a couple of miles to my hotel in the early evening. Most of the way, I found, was lined with very small hostess bars, each one with a different, perfectly crafted national decor: a tiny German bierstube next to a French bistro next to an English pub, each one with just four or five bar stools inside with gorgeous hostesses on one or two of them.

It was like nothing in America at the end of the fifties. What this district of Kyoto held out to an adult male (an oxymoron, especially in that era) was as exotic to my eyes as the Ryoanji garden where my walk had started. It was a pleasure just to open the doors as I passed and look in, which was all I felt I had time to do, if I were to see them all.

Then I opened the door on a room like a beer hall that was quite large and not fancy, unlike all the others. A lot of people, nearly all Japanese, were sitting at tables drinking beer or eating. The only unusual thing here was the waitresses, a dozen or so ordinary-looking Japanese women wearing nothing at all but transparent shortie nightgowns. I decided to go in.

I sat at a table by myself and looked around. At a booth at the side of the room two bearded Americans in jeans were sitting with some Japanese, drinking beer. When they saw me looking at the menu, which was in Japanese, one of them, a huge man with a big beard, came over to ask if he could help me. He gave my order to a waitress in good Japanese, and suggested that I join his friends.

They made space for me on a bench, ordered more beer, and introduced themselves. The two Americans both seemed about my age (I was almost twenty-nine). The one who had brought me over, Bob Strickland, was making a living teaching English in Kyoto; in the States he had been, among other things, a member of the motorcycle gang Hell's Angels.

The other, looking much smaller next to Bob and with a short, neatly trimmed beard, spoke very quietly, and I didn't get his name over the noise in the room. Later I picked up that he was taking a weekend off from a monastery where he was studying Zen. I asked him his name again and he put out his hand and said, "Gary Snyder."

It sounded slightly familiar. I asked him where I might have heard it. He asked, "Do you read poetry?" I said I did, and thought for a moment, and the name I had forgotten came, improbably, back to me. I looked hard at him and said, "You're Japhy Ryder." He nodded. I said, "You're the reason I'm in Kyoto."

He looked exactly as he was supposed to. In fact, marvelously, he turned out to *be* very much as Kerouac had described him.

We drank beer and talked for a long time that evening, mostly listening to Strickland's tales of Hell's Angels and his equally hair-raising experiences afterwards as a repossessor of property for non-payment of loans (a "Repo Man").

The next morning Bob called my hotel and said that Gary had invited us to spend the day with him at his place outside town. I rode on the back of his motorcycle, out past rice fields, to a Japanese cottage where Gary lived when he wasn't at the monastery.

There was a new motorcycle in the small yard in front, bought, Gary told me, with earnings from a recent tour in the merchant marine. Inside, the house, with bamboo walls and tatami mats, was immaculate. There were no chairs. One room, a sort of library where Gary worked, kneeling or sitting cross-legged before a low reading table, made a strong impression on me. It had books lining three walls: one wall of books in English—largely archaeology, anthropology, and poetry—another wall of books in Japanese, the third, Chinese.

We sat or stretched out on the tatami mats and talked all day and into the night. A couple of times Gary cooked us Japanese meals. There was a young Japanese student, evidently a disciple of Gary's, visiting from Tokyo. He told me that Gary was very well known among Tokyo students as a pacifist, as well as a poet.

In this company I was a pretty exotic figure myself, to put it politely. They didn't get many chances to meet a live, walking representative of the military-industrial complex, and I looked like the real thing.

I had been a Marine company commander just a few years before, and I still had close-cropped hair, cordovan shoes, and my green nylon Marine raincoat, with an expensive camera and a Rolex watch from a Navy PX. I was an employee of the Rand Corporation, on Defense Department contract working for CINCPAC.

They were surprised—Gary told me later—to be getting on with me so well, considering what I did for a living; that is, considering who I worked for. Strictly speaking, they didn't know what I did, since I couldn't tell them. I didn't tell secrets to the public in those days, and there were (and still are) few secrets more closely held than the details of nuclear operations that bear on the risks of nuclear war by accident, false alarm, or unauthorized action.

Instead, we argued about pacifism. I wanted to see if Gary could convince me of the compelling nature of absolute pacifism (no one ever has, totally, though I am still listening, from a position that gets ever closer), and he came as near as anyone.

I recognized a very subtle arguer; but it so happened that I knew the dialectics of this issue unusually well from many debates with a pacifist friend at Harvard, Everett Mendelsohn, and I found that I knew counters to Gary's line of argument that he was evidently unused to hearing.

Several times he went suddenly silent after I had made an unfamiliar point. His young Japanese disciple was very struck by this; at one point when Gary was off making tea, he told me admiringly, "I've never seen anyone *stop* him like that before."

I took what satisfaction I could from that, because I had already sized up my host that day as—something I was not used to feeling— a better man than I was. His life was more together. I was as smart as he was, but he was wise.

That was an unsettling thing to find in someone who was almost exactly the same age; he was less than a year older, but he seemed to me very much my senior. I could easily imagine taking him, like the Japanese student and apparently many others, as a teacher.

We had some things in common, more than he may have realized then. I had, then as now, a passionate obsession with preventing nuclear weapons from being used by anyone ever again that he probably would have respected if he had known it.

But he matched the intensity and the taste for adventure that we shared with a composure, a capacity for sudden calm, a deepness of vision that I lacked. And to an extraordinary degree, he was in charge of his own life.

I had never met anyone like him. I felt, more than envy, glad that I had had a chance to discover him, to find this particular model of the way that a life could be lived.

After many tales—"There are a lot of funny stories to be told," he commented late that night after my account, rarely shared, of the surreal circumstances of my loss of virginity in Laramie, Wyoming—he gave us blankets and we went to sleep on the tatami. The next morning he said good-bye warmly and threw us out, saying he had to work.

I went back to Tokyo to my own work, to the investigation of inadvertent nuclear war that I hadn't discussed in Kyoto. It was on that trip that I had discovered, among other things, that President Eisenhower had delegated the authority to use nuclear weapons in a crisis to commanders like CINCPAC in case communications with Washington were out (as happened, on the average, part of every day).

I also learned that month that the Navy, without the knowledge of civilian authorities in Japan or, possibly, in the United States, was storing nuclear weapons in the tidal waters of Japan, on the Marine base of Iwakuni, in violation of the U.S.–Japan Mutual Security Treaty, which had been signed that year (despite mass demonstrations against it).

Gary and his friends in Tokyo would have been quite interested. God knows, I didn't dream of telling them. It might have had a better effect than what I did do. That included telling Kennedy's Secretary of Defense, Robert McNamara, and his National Security Advisor, McGeorge Bundy, the next year.

Otherwise, I kept the secrets, even when McNamara and Bundy chose, rather than to upset the military, not to do anything with the information: which was easier for them to decide so long as Congress, the public, and our allies were kept in the dark—by me, among others. Thus the delegation of nuclear authority persisted, and the nuclear weapons ship stayed moored in Japanese waters.

So it went in my work in the sixties. I uncovered flaws in secret government operations, informed my bosses—up to the secretary of defense, sometimes the president—and gave recommendations; then I collaborated in keeping it all secret from the public and Congress. It was a process that made me feel useful, but—because of the last step—had no useful consequence.

When I went to Vietnam in mid-decade, it was more of the same. The difference was that the shortcomings I was finding in secret policies were killing people every day, and threatening to kill a lot more. In the terms of Gary's path, it was not Right Livelihood.

I didn't hear that from Gary; I didn't see him or hear from him again in the sixties. Still, my memory of him that weekend stayed with me in the back of my mind as a kind of touchstone: an image of an alternative way of living. But doing it his way—deciding on my own to speak truth to the world—still lay some years off for me.

Three more people, among others, helped me reach that point. The first one, Patricia, I married, though not all at once. She came to be with me in Saigon, twice, and the second time we were engaged. But she gave me a hard time about my association with the war.

She took me to see refugee camps around Saigon—where people lived in a swamp of mud and sewage, fleeing the American bombing in the countryside—and managed to convey the feeling that I shared responsibility for all of this, although she knew that I had opposed the bombing, bureaucratically, both in the North and the South from the beginning.

"How *can* you be part of this?" she cried at me in fury one fatal night, when a Canadian just back from North Vietnam described the effects of the bombing in the North.

"You know that I'm *against* the bombing," I remember answering, writhing under her attack; "I'm trying to *stop* it . . . you talk as if I'm partly to blame for everything."

She was right, of course, as I realized much later; but at the time I wasn't able to see that, and it felt unfair. Finally I couldn't take it anymore; I broke the engagement in the summer of '66, and we didn't see each other again for three years, the first of which I remained in Vietnam.

I came back in mid-'67 determined to see the war ended but still not clear there were better ways to do that than to work from inside, counseling presidential advisers and candidates in secret. Among other things, I worked, with others, on a Top Secret history and analysis of U.S. decision making in Vietnam, initially for Secretary of Defense McNamara.

Then I met two other bodhisattvas: in 1968, an Indian woman named Janaki Tschannerl and, in August 1969, a young American, Randy Kehler, on his way to prison for noncooperation with the draft. Their way was Gandhian, not Zen Buddhist, but they were both a lot like Gary in their way of being and in the impression they made on me.

Between them—and the books that Janaki led me to, by Martin

Luther King Jr., Barbara Deming, Gandhi—they converted me, not to the absolute pacifism they shared with Gary, but to Gandhian nonviolent action, *satyagraha*: in particular, truthfulness, Gandhi's "truth force."

By the end of September 1969, I had decided not to let a security classification on truths the public needed to know keep me any longer from conveying them. My friend Tony Russo—who had been fired from Rand earlier when he started writing truthful reports about torture and the use of herbicides in Vietnam—had a woman friend with a Xerox machine.

With their help, I started copying the seven thousand Top Secret pages of the McNamara study in hopes that they would be released in the Senate or elsewhere that fall. I expected that soon after that, I would have to go to prison for the rest of my life.

In early November, Patricia arrived to visit me—we had gotten back in touch that summer, after three years—just as I had decided to go to Washington to offer the first batch of documents to the Senate Foreign Relations Committee. I invited her to come with me—without telling her why I was really going—and we've been together since that day.

A month later—just twenty years ago, as I write this—I proposed to her again. She didn't accept right away, but before she finally did I told her what I was doing and what I faced, and she soon became what she has been ever since, my partner, as well as my lover and closest friend.

In the language of my trial: She is my unindicted co-conspirator. (Years later, when we were being booked together for an antinuclear arrest, she remarked that she had never been fingerprinted before; I finally figured out why she had never been indicted for copying and distributing the Pentagon Papers, which had her prints all over them.) We married in August of 1970, just before we were to move from California to the East Coast.

But the Pentagon Papers—as the McNamara study came to be known after I gave a copy to *The New York Times* in the spring of 1971—didn't come out right away. Senator Fulbright, to whom I gave the documents between November 1969 and the following spring, finally backed off in mid-'70 from his assurances that he would hold hearings and release the study in defiance of the administration.

In September of 1970 Patricia and I were staying in Big Sur for a few days before flying to Boston. I had a copy of the Pentagon Papers, still unreleased, in our bags in the trunk of our rented car.

I didn't know how or when I would get them out, hence when I would go to prison. There were just a few people I especially wanted to see again before that happened. Randy Kehler was one; I managed to visit him in La Tuna Prison before the Papers came out and to tell him what I was planning. Janaki was another. And, it came to me, Gary Snyder.

When I heard from someone in Big Sur that he was living in Marin, north of San Francisco, I felt like reporting in to him. Patricia, a nature mystic and a meditator, was as eager to see him as I was.

He was said not to have a phone, but we had an address and directions. We drove to Sausalito, located the compound—where Alan Watts had lived—on top of a hill . . . and found the place deserted. Finally someone appeared and told us that Gary had moved away: to Nevada City, wherever that was. Nevada? All they could tell us was a P.O. box on "Allegheny Star Route."

We had detoured a long way for nothing. We were driving, disconsolately, down a narrow road from the hilltop when we had to pull over to let a tall truck pass. On an impulse I called out to the driver—the cab towered above us so I couldn't see his face—if by any chance he knew where Nevada City was.

A voice called down, "Who you looking for?" I said, "Gary Snyder." Without any pause, or comment, an arm extended down from the cab holding a piece of paper. I took it, and found myself looking at a hand-drawn map, in ink, showing detailed directions from the hill we were on to a location in the Sierra foothills with an X marked "Gary Snyder's house."

It was eerie. I heard the voice say, "Just got back from there." The arm went back in the cab and the truck pulled away. We stared at the map, looked at each other . . . evidently we were meant to go to Nevada City.

Eventually we found ourselves at the end of a forest road, close to the X on the map. We got out, followed the sound of voices down a path through the trees, and came to a clearing where people were eating lunch at a rough table, next to the foundations of a house.

Gary was sitting at the table. He came toward us as we left the car;

he looked unfriendly. They didn't like visitors, he said. They'd been getting too many.

I introduced myself hastily, reminding him of our meeting ten years earlier; I realized that there was no great reason he would remember it. But he said that he remembered it very well; he was glad to see me again. He had liked me a lot, he told me later, though he didn't agree with me and didn't like what I was working for.

As we talked about the war over lunch, it got through to him that some changes had occurred, and the warmth he was already showing grew more intimate. Meanwhile, *he* was just about exactly the way I remembered him; I was still just as taken with him.

By the time we had to leave, I wanted to give him some indication of what I was doing now. I told him I was involved in an action that had to do with putting out information about the war, about secret decision-making and lies. It might be big, I said. But it would probably mean that I would be put away for quite a while. (My indictment, the next year, posed a maximum sentence of 115 years.) I thought he would be interested to see the information when it came out; he agreed.

I didn't show him any papers from the trunk, so as not to implicate him; but I hinted that he was implicated anyway, in the process of my awakening. I wanted to thank him.

We weren't eager to leave the forest, but we had to get to the airport. He urged us to come back and visit him when his house was finished. We did, years later, after the trial.

Paul Winter:

IT WAS THE WHALES THAT BROUGHT ME TO GARY SNYDER

"Is it all lost? Was it ever real? A world where men and women, trees, grasses, animals, the wind—were at ease with each other's song?"

(from Gary Snyder's Preface to *Turtle, Bear, and Wolf*, by Peter Blue Cloud)

A Pacific wind was calling me in the late seventies, and the voice that emerged from it was Gary's. The whales had drawn me in 1975 to British Columbia, where my group and I played a benefit concert for Greenpeace, and I went out into the ocean on the Greenpeace boat and saw whales for the first time. There was something going on among all these whale-folks that I found enormously stimulating, some sense of community with the land and the sea, and the spirit of that came back east with me to Connecticut and began to infuse our music.

The next year, in November 1976, the growing North American "whale network" convened in Sacramento, where Governor Jerry Brown had declared "Whale Day" and was hosting a weekend symposium called "California Celebrates the Whale." There I heard Gary for the first time, as he offered to the crowd of three thousand his poem "Mother Earth, Her Whales." Gary's voice and poetry spoke directly to me, ringing of life experience, in contrast to most of the poetry I'd encountered in college classrooms. Here was someone singing from the heart of life.

Gary's became a new voice in my musical pantheon, and I looked forward to hearing him again. Seven months later, in June of 1977, I had the opportunity at the annual Lindisfarne Conference held in an old Episcopal church in New York. Lindisfarne's founder, William Irwin Thompson, suggested that my Consort and I play music along with Gary's reading at the conference. So the five of us sat down with Gary about an hour before the presentation, read together through Xeroxed copies of the poems, and simply assigned different instruments to improvise antiphonal responses to each stanza. The performance went beautifully: The words and music seemed to enhance one another, and the playing had that quality of "beginner's mind" that a rehearsal might have spoiled. Luckily, we recorded it, and the album of that performance should finally be released in 1991, entitled *Turtle Island*.

That initiation forged a bond, and Gary and I began corresponding about the possibility of future performances. The next summer my album *Common Ground* came out in celebration of the community among different cultures and creatures. In planning the West Coast tour of that music, I invited Gary to join us, and in March of 1979 we traveled up the California coast with a real seventies entourage, including Tai-Chi dancer Al Huang, a timber wolf, Gary, and the Consort. That tour gave me my first chance to travel and spend some time with Gary.

The Consort, alone, played the final date of the tour in Sacramento, on the spring equinox, and the next day Rusty Schweikert, the former astronaut who was then working in Governor Brown's administration, took me over to the capitol to visit the governor. After chatting awhile about music, the environment, and the record business, I mentioned in passing that I should be leaving since I was going to drive up to Nevada City to visit Gary, and Governor Brown said: "Why don't we *all* go up to visit Gary." So four of us—Rusty, Jerry Brown, Jacques Barzaghi, and I—drove the two hours up into the Sierra Nevada, and arrived at Gary's just after sundown.

Gary was at that time serving on the California Arts Commission, and the governor valued him highly as an adviser. As Gary had no phone then, whenever Jerry needed to ask Gary about something, he'd send a state trooper up the mountain to deliver the message. I loved hearing about that—the Statesman consulting with the Poet. That's the way government ought to be run.

Gary's beautiful hand-hewn homestead has a central fire pit in the floor, similar to that in a tipi, and we sat around the fire until late into the night, discussing grand subjects and world issues. (Jerry was then gearing up to run for president.) The next morning, as we resumed discussion around the breakfast table, Governor Brown called to us as he was brushing his teeth in the kitchen sink: "Well, what about the Russians?" And Gary responded: "That's easy. Just send over five thousand poets and have them send five thousand poets over here." It was prophetic. Just a few years later that's what began to happen. I thought of Gary's remark often during the summer of 1985 when the Consort and I toured the United States with Russian poet Yevgeny Yevtushenko.

I stayed on a few days at Kitkitdizze after the others returned to Sacramento, and that experience at Gary and Masa's had a profound impact on me. I was encouraged to find there on the West Coast the same thriving model of living "the Good Life" that I had experienced earlier at Helen and Scott Nearing's saltwater farm in Maine. Here was further affirmation of the rich and complete vision of living close to the earth that I had been exploring since 1965. Gary was a man living *with* the earth, having a deep experience of himself in nature, in meditation, in family, and in community, and yet he still spoke to a larger audience. His song resonated throughout the Western world. Gary and Masa's example, as had Helen and Scott's, helped me overcome the feeling of being "out of the mainstream." They showed me that I *was* in the stream, I just had to embrace the larger river.

It has always seemed to me that Gary's speaking and writing voice reflects the music of his life-style, the art of living that he seems to have mastered. What touches me is that Gary *is* music—grace, kindness—a clarion song. I had come to know Gary first as a voice, then as a person. I heard him speak and sing his poetry before I ever read him in print. And I so resonated with the music of his voice, and with his friendship, that everything I've read by him since seems like music to me: Something in me glows again, rekindling my optimism and enthusiasm. The same clear song, the same kindness, the melodious laughing twinkly-eyed lightness, the thoughts rooted in earth-experience—it all comes through in Gary's writing and his being. It speaks of a life remarkably integrated with the earth.

I think of Gary as part of the American lineage that extends from Thoreau through Charles Ives to Scott Nearing and Pete Seeger—voices from the "quiet corner" of our culture, all artists who went to live with the land, built their own homesteads, and made their lives their song. These remarkable people, I think, have been alike in urging us not to get caught up in the praising of remarkable people, but rather to discover and sing the ways in which each of us is remarkable.

THE WHALES AND THE WOLVES

It's been twenty years since the astronauts first saw the whole earth from space, and during this time two creatures symbolic of the new awakening have come into the forefront of our consciousness: the whale and the wolf.

Prior to the 1970 album *Songs of the Humpback Whale,* most people probably still believed that a whale would swallow you if you were unfortunate enough to get near it in the ocean. All we knew was the Jonah story, and the fearsome beast in *Moby Dick.* Now, a short two decades later, whale *watching* is a bigger business than whale *killing.* A similar turnaround has happened with wolves, in the popular consciousness, thanks to John Harris, who in the late sixties began taking two timber wolves, named Jethro and Clem, to schools and communities around the United States. Over the fifteen years of his tireless campaign, hundreds of thousands of schoolchildren learned from these presentations that wolves are not a threat to humans; that this long-maligned "monster" of the forest is not at all our enemy, but rather a creature of nobility and intelligence.

Back in "the old days" of the early seventies, when many of us were getting our feet wet with the whales, the rallying cry used to be "save the whales." Now a friend wants to put together an album of all the songs people have written about whales and title it *Saved by the Whales.* There is, in this shift, I think, some evidence of our growing up. The whales and wolves have come into our lives, and brought many of us humans together. We are learning to revere these creatures as elders, as we evolve from stewards to students. It's as if the "Great Director," seeing Her drama in trouble, has sent in these teachers, in the nick of time, to show us how to act, on this earthstage. And there, behind the scenes, is Gary, always offering encouragement, quietly cheering us on, smiling "yes" to our efforts and our dreams, reminding us, with a chuckle, "It's a Grand Show, isn't it?"

Richard Nelson:

AN ELDER OF THE TRIBE

Clear air over California; smooth and free at thirty thousand feet. We'd left the clouds of Washington and Oregon behind. Faces pressed against the windows, Gary and I were like a couple of kids flying for the first time. By a stroke of luck the jet was only half full. A few passengers glanced up as we scuffled between rows of seats, first to the left side of the plane, then to the right. Gary pointed across the dark ridges of the Coast Range to a distant lagoon split from the Pacific by a finger of sand: "Humboldt Bay . . . the towns are Eureka and Arcata. The big headland is Cape Mendocino."

After a few minutes of gazing we crossed to the left side again. Gary identified a mass of high, clouded peaks as the northern Sierra. Off to the east, blue mountains and valleys faded away in tiers. "That's basin and range country," he explained. "The farthest ones are in Nevada."

Incredulous, I asked: "You mean, from here we can see across the whole breadth of California?"

"One side to the other," he affirmed.

During those moments, the land seemed to shrink before my eyes. I realized that the California in my mind was grossly magnified compared to the real California beneath the jet. Because my traveling companion knew the geography of his chosen place, I understood for the first time how small the planet truly is.

As we continued southward, Gary named towns, rivers, and peaks, and picked out subtle changes in the vegetation. A soft, contented smile never left his face. Then he pointed ahead: "Up that way is Grass Valley and San Juan Ridge." My eyes wandered through the maze of Sierra Nevada foothills. Deep within this territory, Gary Snyder had not only made a home but also shaped a *definition* of home for a new generation of inhabitants.

Gary and I had spent the previous days at a gathering of Alaskan environmentalists, where he generously gave the weight of his presence to the fight against wanton clearcutting of the Tongass National Forest. He had listened to the discussions, offered perspectives gained from similar battles in California, mingled freely during social hours, then feasted an enthusiastic audience with his words and poems. At the end, "Smokey the Bear Sutra" brought everyone to their feet. During those moments of celebration, in a room packed with like-minded people, it was easy to indulge dreams of crushing victory over the U.S. Forest Service and the timber corporations.

Nearing San Francisco, we switched to the right side of the plane again, for a view of Bodega Bay and the seaward reach of Point Reyes. As Gary gestured toward familiar places and explained what they meant to him, I remembered a similar experience years before, when I had been traveling to a remote village in northern Alaska. Sitting beside me in the cramped single-engine Cessna was a Koyukon Indian elder named Joe Stevens. The sprawl of forest and muskeg beneath us was part of his trapline—the country where he was born and the homeland of his ancestors. He named lakes and streams, indicated the routes of winter trails, and pointed out favorite hunting and trapping areas.

As I now looked at Gary Snyder's face, I thought of Joe, and of his wife Sarah, and of other Alaskan Native elders I had known over the years. Despite his vastly different background, Gary seemed very much like them. In the Native American communities where I have lived, elders are accorded high status and respect. This is not just a longevity bonus; in societies based on oral tradition the older people are treasured as the sources of knowledge, wisdom, and experience.

Above all, the elders possess an incredibly detailed, refined, and sophisticated body of information about the surrounding environment—weather and sky, lakes and rivers, valleys and mountains, forests and tundra, fish, birds, and mammals. This knowledge is based on a deep respect for accuracy, and it is carried in rich vocabularies that describe and conceptualize every aspect of the natural world. Some of the elders' knowledge has come down through the generations before them, and some is based on their own lifetime observations.

I remember an Inupiaq Eskimo hunter named Sakiak, a man whose recorded knowledge of animal behavior would fill a stack of volumes. After seventy-odd years of studying the world around him, he remained as observant and curious as ever. For example, when the men hunted bowhead whales each spring, he still clocked how long each passing whale stayed underwater and counted how many times it blew before diving again. As a result, he had an uncanny ability to predict where each whale would reappear and how long it would stay on the surface. Sakiak was no longer quick and supple, no longer expert with a rifle, but the younger men often asked him to join their hunts for caribou, seal, walrus, or whale, so they could listen to his advice and learn through his instruction. He was a living encyclopedia of the natural environment, a man whose mind represented several thousand years of cumulative, intimate experience in the arctic world.

Such curiosity and attentiveness toward the surroundings is an essential source of the elders' knowledge, ultimately the basis of their livelihood and their sense of connectedness to nature. I saw a similar attitude in Gary a few years ago, as we hiked through an open muskeg near my home. In several places, he noticed broken sea urchin shells perched atop mossy, knee-high tussocks. "How did they get here?" he wondered. Although I'd walked the same trail dozens of times, I hadn't thought about the unusual placement of these shells. And I could only guess that, for some unfathomable reason, otter or mink had carried them here from the distant shore. Then, months later, I saw a raven flying over the trees, headed toward that same muskeg . . . with an urchin in his beak. And suddenly I knew the answer: He would eat the morsel while perched on one of those hillocks, away from shoreside competitors and well situated to spot approaching danger. I immediately wrote to Gary and told him the story. By watching and questioning and listening, the elder learns.

Of course, much of Gary Snyder's knowledge about the natural world has come through his wide explorations in the scientific and historical literature. I once saw Gary present an all-day seminar on the mythical connections between humans and animals. Drawing from scant notes and a prodigious memory, he ranged through an incredible breadth of ideas about animals, from medieval Europe to ancient China, from aboriginal Australia to contemporary America. I was amazed by the span of his knowledge, which differed in content but compared favorably in depth and insight to that of elders like Sakiak.

During their lifetimes, Native Alaskan elders witness many changes in the environment: winters becoming warmer, rivers altering course, lakes filling in, plant communities undergoing succession, animal populations experiencing regular cycles or being affected by human use. From this comes a practical understanding of natural dynamics—an indigenous tradition of ecology and wild-life management that provides the foundation for a sustainable, long-term inhabitation of the home terrain. For example, Koyukon Indian trappers told me, with considerable pride, how they limited their yearly catch of fur species to assure that animal populations re-mained healthy. They also emphasized the importance of teaching this self-regulation to their children and grandchildren, who would eventually follow the same trails.

In his writings and teachings, Gary Snyder draws from an ecolog-ical wisdom similar to that of Native American elders, though it de-rives from a wider range of sources, including the literature of Western science, ethnographic accounts of traditional cultures, and personal experiences with land and people. Native elders focus their teachings on a single, closely defined place in which the landscape, plants, animals, and humans form a tightly bound, physically inter-dependent community. Gary Snyder's work recognizes and cele-brates these same local relationships, and then generalizes them to all of humanity living in the single community of earth. I believe that elders from many cultures are now making a similar expansion from the local to the global perspective.

Physical connections within the living community are one dimen-sion of this perspective, and spiritual connections are another. Among Alaskan Native people, elders are the keepers of Distant Time stories, which explain the origins and transfigurations of the world in an ancient, dreamlike society of animals and humans. As Sarah Stevens explained, Distant Time stories have the same power and significance for Koyukon people as Genesis has for orthodox Christians. Contained in these accounts are elaborate codes of moral behavior, essentially the same as biblical commandments but cen-tered on ways of living in right relationship to nature. Guided by such ethical codes, Native Americans inhabited this continent for fif-teen thousand to thirty thousand years, and the land remained so pristine that European settlers called it a "wilderness," as if no one had ever been here.

Distant Time stories and the moral codes they contain are in great peril today. Most have never been recorded, so they are preserved only in the memories of tradition-bearers. What new generation of elders will pass them along? Gary Snyder has provided an example, not only in his written work but also in his role as a father. His youngest son, Gen, remembers Gary telling him Native American stories—not as curiosities, not as simple entertainment, but as a way to understand and interact with the world. Gary has found guidance for living responsibly with the environment not only from accounts of the Distant Time in many different cultures, but also from his own Zen practice, from his studies of Buddhist thought, from the insights of Western science, from philosophers and poets, singers and mystics, Bohemians and backwoodsmen.

This respect for wisdom emerging through any and all sources may be characteristic of elders in most cultures. For example, my principal teacher among the Koyukon was a woman strongly devoted to the teachings of her grandfather, but also much influenced by Christian beliefs and Western education. When she told Distant Time stories, she often compared them to episodes in the Bible and asserted that each reinforced the truth of the other. Her favorite examples were two accounts of an ancient worldwide flood, survived by pairs of animals who repopulated the land after the waters subsided. In the missionary's story the animals were taken onto Noah's ark, and in her grandfather's story the Great Raven put them aboard a raft. With regard to moral lessons, she found the two traditions in fundamental agreement: "I don't see why we should choose just one, because both of them show us right ways to live."

This same openness to learning from all sources is a quality I have often seen in Gary Snyder. For example, at the environmental meeting in Alaska I saw him in conversations with a whole range of people, not just the recognized "experts" or "authorities" on various subjects. He was fully engaged with each person, listening intently, sometimes finding a quiet place afterward to write in his ubiquitous notebook. I especially remember him talking with a logger who also happened to be a conservationist, a man who looked as if he'd left his chain saw and cork boots just outside the door. The two of them sat together for a long while, sometimes laughing and sometimes serious, and what I noticed most was the undivided, respectful attention Gary gave to him.

Once again, I was reminded of my own elder-teachers: Joe Stevens, Sarah Stevens, Grandpa William, and others I'd met over the years. Each was widely recognized as an authority and tradition-bearer. Each had achieved knowledge equal to that of a highly trained scientist or academic in my own culture. And each was a listener, attentive to the thoughts and experiences of other people, regardless of how different their backgrounds might be.

Sarah Stevens often emphasized the importance of showing respect—toward her own people, toward people from other cultures, and toward the whole surrounding community of nature. In her world, there are no lesser humans, no lower beings. All are infused with power, sacredness, and knowledge. Elders, like Sarah, also demonstrate their respect through acts of kindness, sharing, and helpfulness toward others, values which are strongly emphasized in Inupiaq and Athabaskan Indian cultures. Whatever comes to a person is a gift—whether it be food, friendship, or knowledge—and in return a person should pass something along to others. My initial contact with Gary Snyder was such a gift, a letter he wrote concerning our shared anthropological interests, suggesting we might get together to discuss them. It was the first of many kindnesses that have followed over the years, including lessons on history and philosophy, shared experiences in wild places, and practical advice about the business of writing. Gary's generosity has always reminded me of the village elders, especially their concern for showing younger people how to live from the land and how to deal with the growing complexity of their world.

By saying these things, I do not wish to praise the Native elders beyond what they really are. Also, because their traditions emphasize equality, most elders are shy or wary of conspicuous admiration. An Inupiaq proverb warns: "Don't let your head rise too far above the others." Of course, each elder has qualities that are both exceptional and commonplace, and each suffers the same flaws or frailties that plague the rest of us. Gary Snyder would probably appreciate having this said of him—that he is an ordinary man, gifted in his own ways but otherwise much like everyone else. I doubt that he would want more than admiration for the things he does kindly or well, and acceptance or patience for the rest.

When I consider what knowing Gary Snyder and studying his work has meant to me, he stands comfortably with the Athabaskan Indian and Inupiaq elders who have been my friends and teachers. Like them, he is a leader, one who contributes importantly to shaping thought and behavior in his society as a whole. Like them, he is a teacher, one who passes along knowledge he has acquired and works to shape useful perspectives on the world—nature, culture, and community. On a more personal level, Gary Snyder and the Native elders have strongly influenced the way I have chosen to live, in a small rural community, as close as possible to the surrounding wildness, hunting and fishing for a major part of my family's sustenance, and devoted to staying where I am. They have also influenced my character and interests, my beliefs, and my entire sense of person. And they have given vital guidance in my own search for a responsible, ethically based relationship with the environment.

Native Alaskan elders have given their people a set of values to choose from and a living example to emulate; Gary Snyder has done something similar for his own people. He has reinforced the wisdom found within Native American cultures, enriched it with perspectives from other worldwide traditions, and brought it into the context of contemporary Western society. He has also built a broad philosophical foundation for the more specific and grounded examples that traditional cultures provide. To my mind, Gary Snyder is a rarity in this modern world: an elder of the tribe. The highest respect I can show him is to mention his name along with those of Sakiak, Sarah Stevens, Grandpa William, and Joe Stevens.

I do it with gratitude and admiration. And I do it with a sense of hope, that the wisdom of today's elders, passed down through countless generations before them, might guide us all toward a more harmonious and sustainable way of life on earth.

As Gary writes in *The Old Ways:*

> We're just starting, in the last ten years here, to begin to make songs that will speak for plants, mountains, animals and children. When you see your first deer of the day you sing your salute to the deer, or your first red-wing blackbird—I saw one this morning! Such poetries will be created by us as we reinhabit this land with people who know they belong to it; for whom "primitive" is not a word that means past, but *primary,* and *future.* . . . These poesies to come will help us learn to be people of knowledge in this universe and community with the other people—nonhuman included—brothers and sisters.

After an easy landing at the San Francisco airport, Gary and I took the freeway east. As we crossed the broad Sacramento River estuary, he spoke of vast salmon runs, now almost vanished. Then came the level expanses of the Central Valley, and talk of pronghorns, skies

darkened with millions of waterfowl, dense settlements of the Yokuts
. . . all lost in the past. The road steepened, narrowed from four lanes
to two, twisted along sidehills and valleys, finally dwindled to a gravel
track through dense forest. Near midnight we turned into the driveway at Kitkitdizze: tall ponderosa pine, brittle grass in the clearing,
five or six deer beside the house. Their eyes shined brightly in the
headlights.

"Lots of them around the place at night," Gary said. They danced
away, only half afraid, as we stepped from the car. We went to the
barn where I would sleep; then I watched him follow a moonlit path
back toward the house. How familiar it all must be, I thought, like
touching a loved one's hand.

Home.

Lee Swenson:

SWIMMING IN A SEA OF FRIENDS

When new friends (or sometimes even old ones) ask what I do, I answer, "I swim in a sea of friends!" Certainly, Gary Snyder has been a most significant friend in that great sea.

What I want to do in this brief tribute to the value of friendship is to paint a bit of the picture of how Gary and I make a living or how we make do as modernized hunter-gatherers; how, though we might seem to be "independent" individuals doing our own thing—in fact, we feel deeply embedded in a place, northern California, and in a wide circle of friends and living ideas. A place to wander from . . . and ideas and friends to wander with.

Perhaps our greatest common delight is in the creation of the history of the present—storytelling that draws from the distant past right up to the present time, from the Paleolithic to contemporary northern California. As storytelling becomes industrialized by modern psychology and sociology, we feel the need to sustain the community-building art of storytelling. We create our story through an informed spontaneity that calls on our rich past and acknowledges our standing on the shoulders of our elders.

One way into this hammock of affection—with strings, knots, and holes—is to think back on how Berkeley and the San Francisco Bay Area as "history" presented itself to us—Gary and me—as young men in the 1950s.

Just two hundred years earlier the first European had walked over the South San Francisco hills to see the "densely" populated bay land. One of the most imposing features of the Berkeley shoreline was the enormous shell mound—thirty feet high, one hundred yards long, or the size of a football field. For more than seven thousand years, the local natives threw cleaned shells over their shoulders, slowly building up this gigantic monument to the abundance of the San Francisco Bay. By the 1940s the shell mound had been bulldozed away, replaced by the huge Williams Paint Factory, with its global neon symbol: Williams paint flowing down over half the world.

The diaries of the first Spanish shipmates to sail into the beautiful bay—then twice as big as it is now—glow with accounts of the abundance of fish, animal, bird, and human life. "O Los Dios, every ten miles another language, a different tribe." Natural life was overflowing with millions of birds; Berkeley's eleven creeks were spawning grounds for dense fish runs. It was a deeply manicured treasure. Annual burning after seed cropping kept open the underbrush for the deer to browse among the acorn-bearing oaks and for bay laurels to yield leaves of seasoning.

Berkeley was an abundant overlap of circles of sustenance, from subsistence hunting and gathering in the seasonal cycles, from miner's lettuce to salmon spawning in the creeks; when one source of food dried up, the gatherers could move on to another, always able to fall back on the staple acorn mush.

These diverse, cyclical, overlapping circles of support offered a culturally defined year of harvesting, nurturing, cropping, and tending. From this enormous abundance, the Ohlones in Berkeley lived lightly, never counting on any one source to support them and always keeping many overlapping circles of sustenance alive and possible.

Also part of the web of history that Gary and I walked through in 1950s Berkeley were the living remnants of the Arts and Crafts movement where many houses were built by (most notably) Bernard Maybeck and Julia Morgan. Morgan alone built more than eight hundred homes with her craftsman-centered atelier/workshop.

The Arts and Crafts movement exerted a deep influence on Morgan. Begun by John Ruskin and William Morris as a reaction against the blight of industrialization in England, it quickly spread to America and soon made its way to the West Coast. The emphasis was on recapturing a simpler way of life, lived in harmony with nature. A building's materials were to come, if possible, from its own environment; simplicity and utility were the goals. Details were to be based on local traditions and natural sources, not pattern books. Architects associated with the movement worked with craftsmen, sculptors, and painters in a return to the collaborative ideals of the Middle Ages. They did not copy past styles but worked out "free" versions of them. No meaningless ornamentation was permitted, and unpainted, unadorned materials were preferred, with construction elements left visible to reveal the highly skilled workmanship.[1]

Another key historical figure was Jaime de Angulo, the legendary novelist and brilliant linguist of Native Californian languages, who died in Berkeley in 1950. Two interesting items from the *de Angulo Reader* chronology follow:

> 1935—De Angulo's home in Berkeley, built on land provided to him by the architect Bernard Maybeck, becomes the center of the local Bohemia. On any given weekend, or weekday for that matter, the house might be filled with visiting anthropologists, such as Malinowski or Sapir, de Angulo's Indian friends from the North, wandering jazz musicians from over in Oakland, and assorted poets and artists from all about the area.
>
> 1949—Jaime de Angulo reads "Indian Tales" to an "astonished audience" over the local public broadcasting radio station, KPFA. "Indian Tales" becomes the most popular program in KPFA history, and is aired in the mornings twice a week.[2]

All of this and a lot more was in the air of the Bay Area. Not that one thinks "Arts and Crafts movement" or "Bohemia" as one bicycles past a Maybeck house or as Gary and I lecture together in the historic Julia Morgan Theater. Rather, there was and is a flourishing Bohemian culture that one could, even if mostly unconsciously, mine for ways to create our lives together. While a graduate student in Chinese Studies at UC Berkeley in the mid-1950s, Gary moved into and fixed up a back cottage that cost fifteen dollars a month. By living on the floor, Japanese-style, he was able to live simply but comfortably in the small space on sixty dollars a month. Then, and now, Berkeley is a great bicycle town. Gary could pedal over to the Richmond–San Rafael Ferry, have twenty-five-cent hash browns, eggs, and coffee in the ferry's steamy cafe, get off, and bike around Mount Tamalpais to visit Alan Watts, or go by the Berkeley–San Francisco Ferry to see Allen Ginsberg or the City Lights Bookstore (founded in 1953).

This is one of the key ways Gary has kept "independent" for so many years. He has learned how to keep his overhead down, how to "hunt and gather" for some weeks of the year, and how to live lightly. Keeping the tools simple, neat, and in repair has given him time to think, write, and wander—a "liberating austerity" based on sustaining friendship and having time for one's "own" life work. Ivan Illich ends his introduction to his key political book, *Tools for Conviviality*, by referring to Thomas Aquinas, who defined "'austerity' as a virtue which does not exclude all enjoyments, but only those which are distracting from or destructive of personal relatedness. For Thomas, austerity is a complementary part of a more embracing virtue, which he calls friendship or joyfulness. It is the fruit of an apprehension that things or tools could destroy rather than enhance *eutrapelia* (or graceful playfulness) in personal relations."[3]

An alert, lively mind lives on many levels and fills in many of the niches of human curiosity. How do we speak? Who and what do we learn from? What do we eat, and who eats us? The map of Gary's mind is rich and diverse, ranging from eleventh-century Chinese poetry to free-form modern verse, from tree harvesting in Ancient Greece to the U.S. Forest Service's management that directly impacts the daily life of Kitkitdizze and the North San Juan Ridge.

It is all these "fields," these overlapping circles of human sustenance, composted over years of digging, turning, folding in, that give Gary many "crops" to harvest. This cross-fertilizing dump-heap gardening with lots of margins and wild spaces left unmanaged leads to a rich diet and gifts to give away. For Gary sees language and culture as wild systems.

So the undergraduate anthropological work at Reed College led to a prose thesis that fed poetry. Over the years, more was folded in: Chinese studies, natural and cultural history, Buddhism, Zen training, and Japanese poetry—with the last three "fields" coming after ten years in Japan. Right before Gary left for Japan in 1956 there was the now-famous North Beach reading by Snyder, Allen Ginsberg, and Jack Kerouac. Gary read firewatch, dharma bum, bear-shit-in-the-trail poems, fed by the word droppings of Robinson Jeffers and Jaime de Angulo.

When Gary and Masa returned from Suwanose Island, Japan, in the late 1960s, they joined in the search with Suzuki Roshi and the San Francisco Zen Center for a rural retreat monastery setting. One gem they found was Tassajara Hot Springs; another was a beautiful, spring-fed, Douglas fir and black oak Sierra foothills piece of one hundred acres. Gary purchased it with friends Dick Baker (Suzuki Roshi's successor at the San Francisco Zen Center) and Allen Ginsberg. Gary and Masa called in friends to build a California-Japanese farm pole house; the poles were stripped and the wood was milled from trees felled from their land. No paved roads and no electricity (and no phone for the first fifteen years). Land taxes on an "unfinished" house were fifty dollars per year, and outbuildings added on over the years—first the sauna, which saw a huge flow of Sunday friends sweating and scrubbing each other's backs.

This was the great earth-mover phase of reinhabitation of North San Juan Ridge. Building local culture, in ways the harder work, followed this "easier" spring box of water systems, garden-building phase—the house-holder stage. Local "hunting-gathering" followed, from firewood to deer to communal labor that was supplemented with other gathering trips by Gary: poetry readings, conference lectures, consulting on Native affairs in Alaska. These were the cash crops.

What I'm trying to portray here is both Gary's uniqueness and his "commonness." He has cultivated many friendships—and interests—"fields" that he can gracefully play in, all the time keeping a huge but very responsive correspondence (quick, typed postcards using little wasted motion). He's an efficient "businessman" who can eye the crowd in the hall, figure the take, and see a fair share all around. Benefit readings fit in with cash crops: I remember once when Gary promised to do a fund-raising reading for a Zen center near Lake Wobegon—a year and a half from then! His Zen friends protested, "But we need the money now." Gary replied wisely, "You'll need the money then, too."

Generosity reaps into the great flow of readings. More than thirty years of making poetry—in a good year Gary creates ten to fifteen usable poems—have resulted in a real gold mine for us, and for him.

At the core of this is a disciplined mindfulness—not overworking any one area or city (San Francisco can bear three to four readings a year, often with diverse subjects and poet-philosopher friends, whereas a reading every two or three years in Santa Fe fills the hall), bringing into town all the hill folk, providing income and work for local organizers in a money-scarce region. Reciprocity. All the time giving finely honed talks—prepared work always on the fresh, lean edge of dialogue.

Getting good road kills is another fine hunter-gatherer skill of Gary's. Whenever Gary talks-meets-eats with others, his mental and little loose-leaf notebooks come along. A good road kill—the ripe fruit plucked—bang, directly into the next poem-lecture-reading!

All this description is part of a long, ongoing conversation among a worldwide circle of friends, including Ivan Illich with his lifelong work on the history of the creation of scarcity and the social construction of needs. Illich himself draws deeply on the work of another Viennese historian of ideas, Karl Polanyi, whose classic, *The Great Transformation: The Political and Economic Origins of Our Time*, portrays the transformation of the marketplace from the edge of society into the center.[4]

In February of 1984 Gary and I shared a wonderful evening of dialogue, called "Anarchism, Buddhism and Political Economy," with a lively gang of some four hundred folk and friends packed into a recycled military building at Fort Mason in San Francisco. The exchange went back and forth, from reflections on Paul Goodman, Illich, and Polanyi to Gary's years of community experience on North San Juan Ridge to my years as director of the Institute for the Study of Nonviolence and the Farallones Institute.

From this evening emerged the Recovery of the Commons Project, which has been the core of my life work for these past years. The idea isn't to try to reproduce the golden age of hunter-gatherers or medieval guilds, but rather to use Goodman's idea of taking the free space in our lives and pushing it out till it makes up most of our social life. Thus the ever-active work/play of creating our own commons.

As Gary's introduction to the Recovery of the Commons Bundle #1 said:

The Commons is this universe we live in, these cells, these bodies and minds we all share. Historically the commons is the hinterlands, the space between villages, shared forests and meadows, wild land and open space outside the village deer-fence.

The commons is the hunting territory, the wild plant and herb-gathering valley, the mountainside for firewood, the pasture. The commons is not just common property, it is the next order of organization of the community, the neighborhood of other beings. The air, the water, the tropical rainforests, the starry night sky, old growth Douglas fir stands, birdsongs, are the commons.

Original nature, original mind, basic joy and basic pain. Birth at home and death with friends (or with the boots on)—is the commons. A free vernacular language, jokes and riddles, parties and dances, religion or no religion—are the commons. The bounty of nature, the sun and the green, the genes. Cabbage and eggplant.

The commons are our common sense. Common, commune, communion. Recover the Commons.[5]

Vernacular people and places have their own particular and unique history of the commons, of its destruction by the superheated penetration of the marketplace economy, and of the multiple forms of ongoing resistance to this invasion. In seeking to push the economy back to the edge—to keep the core of daily life in friendship and reciprocity, doesn't mean we ignore the economy or our need for cash. Rather it is seeking the balance between nonharmfulness to others (and to ourselves in refusing demeaning or dehumanized work) and living highly and well. Over the many years that I have known and worked with Gary, I am continually amazed and delighted by his deep curiosity, his disciplined care of place, tools, ideas, and friendships, and his generosity of time and energy to benefit others.

Nurturing, cropping, weeding—all these "fields" to gather from—from dharma bum friends to animals as teachers to Zen as the pain in the legs, Gary keeps himself—and us—alive and well. He knows, as his fellow landholder, Dick Baker, said, "Trying to make reality repeatable is what the Buddhists call suffering." So Gary keeps on moving in the mind. There is as much to learn from his daily life as from his written work.

—*June '89*

NOTES

1. Sara Holmes Boutelle, *Julia Morgan, Architect* (New York: Abbeville Press, 1988), 9.

2. Bob Callahan, ed., *A Jaime de Angulo Reader* (Berkeley: Turtle Island Press, 1979), 251.

3. Ivan Illich, *Tools for Conviviality* (New York: Harper & Row, 1973), xxv.

4. Karl Polanyi, *The Great Transformation: The Political and Economic Origins of Our Time* (Boston: Beacon Press, 1957).

5. Gary Snyder and Lee Swenson, *Recovery of the Commons Bundle #1* (Self-published Xerox, 1984).

Charlene Spretnak:
DINNERTIME

"I had long been familiar with Gary Snyder's poetry, but a few years ago I also began reading in the collections of his essays and interviews. As I got into them, I thought to myself, 'Hmmmm . . . this is pretty interesting stuff—but these ideas and ways of thinking are in the air these days so perhaps they're not *so* original.' Then I'd come to the end of the essay and see that it was dated nineteen-*fifty*-nine! Gradually I came to realize that some of the most insightful ideas about nature and culture and spirituality, about how we live and how we might think about living, are indeed 'in the air these days' because Gary Snyder helped to put them there."

With those words I introduced Gary in November 1986 at the Viriditas Lecture in Berkeley, sponsored by Friends of Creation Spirituality. (*Viriditas,* "greening power," is a word coined by the twelfth-century mystic Hildegard of Bingen. She taught that a deep understanding of the relatedness of all life was the source of being "green and juicy," the optimal spiritual state.)

Before the lecture my husband and I had gone out to dinner with Gary and Masa at a Chinese vegetarian restaurant. For some reason our conversation turned to cultural ways of dealing with death. Masa, and Gary even more so, described the system of family tombs in the hillsides of Okinawa and elaborated on the effects of such continuity and the presence of the dead. It felt right to be taking food and talking death. All so elemental—like Tibetan monks using half-skulls for their eating bowls, staring straight into reality. On the other hand, I became aware through peripheral vision of nearby diners staring straight at us with icy disapproval. I understood. It was bad form to push tantric practice onto others who have only *mu shu* on their minds. Thankfully, the conversation died down. We ate wholeheartedly and rushed off to the lecture.

Some one thousand people had filled the sanctuary of a large Congregational church, a simple but elegant room with high walls of pale yellow and with a deep blue carpet. I had ordered a large spray of flowers to stand in front of the lectern, an autumnal arrangement that was the florist's rendition of "good, wild, sacred." Gary himself wore a navy blazer, gray slacks, and a silk scarf. He looked both dignified and artistic.

Within the context of that rather formal setting, Gary proceeded to relate various thoughts about wilderness, wildness, and wisdom. About halfway through the talk, while speaking of ecological interconnectedness, he looked up from his notes and said to the audience, "Your ass is someone else's dinner." For a split second it seemed that every molecule in the sanctuary froze. Then there was laughter and lots of broad smiles, including Gary's. I for one hoped the brass in the sponsoring organization were laughing as well (they were), for I had promised them a class-act lecture series. More than that, I enjoyed Gary's demonstration that even public speakers should get to have a little fun now and then.

A year and a half later, during a ten-day *vipassana* meditation retreat, I was lying on my sleeping bag during the lunch break looking up at the translucent beige roof of my tent. Just to the left of the ridge was a tiny insect about the size of a dot. Suddenly from the right side of the roof came a fast-moving larger insect, although only twice the size of the "dot." It scurried across the roof, gobbled up the smaller creature without missing a step in its rapid pace, and disappeared over the far edge. Instantly these words arose in my mind: *Your ass is someone else's dinner.*

It is impossible to think of Gary's saying that without seeing that twinkle in his eyes, the light he lets shine so often, transforming his face into . . . what? A playful Ch'an master? A Celtic nature sprite, the persistence of his maternal Scots-Irish genes? It's the combination that intrigues. Like the evolutionary delight of his eyes and his mouth at wry language play, his writings are melded from primary sources: a boyhood in the country; long periods in the mountains; a sense of the pragmatic and mythic import of native cultures; the Buddhist knowledge of mind; his political development from Marxism, anarchism, "and beyond," as he says, to his rich sense of bioregionalism and his recognition of the potential of Green politics; and his understanding that the Earth is alive and sacred. It is people who aspire to whole wisdom—and its cultural expression—who help our species grope a way out of fragmentation, ecocide, and species suicide.

Gary is also a good fighter. I have deeply appreciated his support and encouragement at those times when I have stood up to bullies. After I had moved into dangerous territory, his wise words propped up my courage and renewed my determination.

I find even more admirable Gary's openness and intellectual curiosity. When I first heard him, some years before the Viriditas Lecture, it was clear from his presentation that he'd read *and appreciated* some rather obscure feminist work on the Goddess, the body, nature, and culture. That response is far more rare than one might expect—and, indeed, I think the full capacity for valuing the radical female voice arose within Gary only at midlife. Some of his early poems ring with the tone of a rip-roarin' mountaineer grabbing pleasure where he dares. The women in the early works are often presented as slightly alien creatures who are perceived to be in an adversarial relationship, at some level, to the poet. He takes the challenge but keeps his distance as a defense; better than being someone's dinner. Later, much later, the poet is a mountain man with roots sent deeply, slowly into Mother Earth. He reveres femaleness in all species. He approaches it as a pilgrim. Now his bodymind is filled with the nourishment of the mythic female. The poet is transformed. He is not afraid.

Dave Foreman:

GARY SNYDER: TRIBAL FOUNDER

One of the significant failings of our society is that it does not provide positive role models for young people. "What is a Man?" "What is a Woman?" "Who sets the standard for me as an adult?" "Where is an example of how I should conduct myself?" One only has to glance at the periodic public opinion polls of "the most admired men and women" in America to see how poorly we are addressing this need.

It's been my good fortune to have encountered four individuals in the generation before mine to serve as my examples of what a twentieth-century American is supposed to be.

The first exemplar whom I encountered was Celia Hunter. During the time I worked for The Wilderness Society (mid- to late-seventies), she was the president of the Governing Council and then executive director of TWS. An army pilot ferrying planes across the Atlantic in World War II, the first woman bush pilot in Alaska, founder of Camp Denali, and distinguished Alaskan conservationist, she is, despite being little known to the public at large, one of the towering figures of our era. Not only did she teach me about feminism (and a redneck horseshoer from New Mexico had a lot to learn!), she taught me more about personal leadership and basic human integrity than anyone else I've known.

After I left mainstream conservation to help start Earth First! in 1980, Edward Abbey and I became friends. Abbey was not a hands-on conservationist (he was admittedly naive about the internal machinery of governmental process), but he was, I believe, the leading spokesperson of our time for wilderness. Only Henry David Thoreau, John Muir, Aldo Leopold, and Rachel Carson have reached people with the message of the wilderness to a comparable extent. Abbey was also a Mudhead Kachina, the trickster, Coyote; pissing on what was "politically correct," continually challenging us to look deep into our dogmas, to eternally seek truth. Moreover, he did more than anyone has to create a warrior mystique for Earth defenders, forming the archetype of George Washington Hayduke, the mythology of The Monkey Wrench Gang. Were environmentalists wimps? A bunch of effete, Volvo-driving suburbanite wusses? Not on your life.

About the same time I became friends with Abbey, I came to know David Brower. Brower, the "Archdruid," had been a shadowy, almost mythical figure during my mainstream conservation days, someone belonging to history with giants like Bob Marshall, John Muir, Howard Zahnhiser, Aldo Leopold. . . . In recent years, one of my greatest pleasures has been to share the stage with Brower on numerous occasions before a variety of audiences. Thirty-five years older than I, Brower can drink me under the table night after night, inspire college students with vision and excellence after my voice has failed, and constantly maintain a good heart toward the foolish and the venal that transcends my misanthropic soul. Brower never tires, never loses vision, never despairs, and never sells out.

In Celia Hunter, I found the Wise Woman, the leader every tribe needs. In Ed Abbey, I found the Desert Prophet, the man who reminds us constantly of the real world, and who keeps us from falling into trite dogma. In David Brower, I found the charismatic War Chief leading younger warriors into the fray. These are the demigods of my pantheon, the elders of my tribe.

But there is a fourth elder, too. Someone who simply shows me how to live. A practical man, interested in tools, in day-to-day living, but who is also a poet, a visionary, and a warrior.

There are strong reasons why I shouldn't see Gary Snyder as one of my role models. He and I have had a long-standing but friendly debate over monkeywrenching—the destruction of machines and property in order to protect wild nature. Gary is, of course, a Buddhist, and I have little patience for things Japanese, Eastern, or religious (I was greatly impressed when I discovered he wasn't a vegetarian!).

In part, it is those disagreements that have made me respect Gary. Even when I haven't agreed with his position, it is clear that Gary has fully thought it out, has chewed it over. He gives new meaning to deliberateness, to thoughtfulness.

But most importantly to me, Gary Snyder isn't merely fighting the current destruction. He is exploring the new-old ways that will enable the future children of Turtle Island to create a sustainable, respectful culture that can live in harmony with the land community for a thousand years—Future Primitives. He is forming substance out of chaos, wisdom out of madness, tribalism out of individualistic anarchy; teaching us, without pedagoguery, simply how to live and how to live simply.

Gary Snyder. A thousand years hence, many of the new tribes of Turtle Island will have a folk hero like him—the legendary half-god, half-man who created the tribe after the collapse of the previous stage of the world.

George Sessions:
GARY SNYDER: POST-MODERN MAN

Gary Snyder has already taken his place alongside Henry David Thoreau, John Muir, Robinson Jeffers, and Arne Naess as one of the great spiritual/environmental leaders and teachers of the nineteenth and twentieth centuries. The environmental philosopher Max Oelschlaeger claims that "Snyder is the first truly post-modern man." Snyder has managed to embody and live this ideal to a very high degree: an inspiration for us all.

Snyder's life and writings span the countercultural protests of the 1950s beatniks and the 1960s hippies, as well as the ecocentric/bioregional/deep ecological movements of the 1970s and 1980s. Through all of the confusion, turmoil, and nihilism of the post–World War II period, Snyder has steadfastly worked toward the fusion, in theory and practice, of the most positive cultural developments of the latter half of the twentieth century: (1) the introduction of Eastern religious thought and spiritual/psychological techniques to the Western world, (2) the reevaluation and understanding of primal cultures and the "old ways" of living on the planet, and (3) the rise of the science of ecology and an ecological understanding of humanity's place in Nature.

Like most of the fifties generation, my first introduction to Gary Snyder was through the writings of Jack Kerouac. As a Central Valley California boy studying philosophy at Fresno State, I came across the appealing character of Japhy Ryder (Gary Snyder), the elflike mountain climber and student of Zen Buddhism in Kerouac's 1958 novel, *The Dharma Bums*. Fresno's version of "on the road" consisted of "dragging the main" (*American Graffiti*–style). By the early fifties, I escaped some of the influence of the American teenage culture by embracing the mystique of mountaineering and the cult of John Muir and Dave Brower.

One of my first climbs was Matterhorn Peak in the northern High Sierra with the Bay Area Sierra Club Rock Climbing Section in 1953, when I had just turned fifteen. Thereafter, I was doing roped climbs in Yosemite, Kings Canyon, and elsewhere almost every weekend.

Part of the story line in *The Dharma Bums* involves Kerouac and Snyder climbing Matterhorn Peak (Kerouac didn't reach the top), which, of course, piqued my interest in Snyder. On October 25, 1959, several climbing friends and I made an early ascent of the north arête of Matterhorn Peak. We found this entry in the summit register:

> October 23, 1955
> Gary Snyder
> Clear and cold
> "Even the mountains shall become Buddhas"

I first saw Gary at Humboldt State University in 1968 when he was reading poetry to a packed auditorium of enthusiastic students. The ecological/environmental excitement on campuses that led to Earth Day 1970 was reaching its peak. I remember the local bookstore owner eagerly looking forward to the arrival of Gary's new book, *Earth House Hold*. My graduate studies in linguistic philosophy and philosophy of science at Chicago were mostly ecologically irrelevant, and so the return to California and the year of teaching at Humboldt was an environmental eye-opener. The *Sierra Club Bulletins* in the closing years of the Brower era (1967–1968) carried articles by Paul Ehrlich on overpopulation, and Lynn White's indictment of Judeo-Christian anthropocentrism and the environment. Ehrlich's *The Population Bomb* was published in 1968 and was used in classes on campus. I borrowed a copy of Raymond Dasmann's textbook, *Environmental Conservation,* from a natural resources student who lived across the street, and thereby came in contact with the concepts of ecosystems, food chains, thermodynamics, and energy transfers in biological systems. This is radical stuff, I thought. Why hadn't I been taught this in school before?

I next saw Gary reading poetry at an Earth Day conference at the State Resources Building in Sacramento in 1970, and again at the Conference on the Rights of Nonhuman Nature at Claremont, California, in 1974. We began corresponding off and on. I was working on a bibliography of deep ecology in 1979 when Gary and Masa invited me to stay with them for several days. After those many years of reading the poetry and essays, it was a somewhat magical and overwhelming experience to meet Masa and the boys, Kai and Gen, and to be in the midst of all the places Gary had written about: the deer fields, manzanita, oak, and kitkitdizze, the Japanese farmhouse, the pond, the bath house, and the vegetable garden. Gary introduced me to the literature of Diamond's anthropology, bioregionalism, reinhabitation, and Third World ecodevelopment, which I incorporated into the bibliography. It was reassuring and inspiring to see these ideas actually being lived with such down-to-earth practicality and grace on the North San Juan Ridge. Since then, there have been many trips to the Snyders', which included visits with Robert Aitken, Nanao Sakaki, and Dave and Nancy Foreman, and the dedication of the new Ring of Bone Zendo. These stand out as especially warm memories of stimulating conversation around the little fire pit in the living room, of walks in the forest and to vistas above the Yuba River. Gary and Masa have remained good supportive friends over the years.

Gary Snyder and Arne Naess are the two most influential worldwide exponents of what Naess called, in 1972, the long-range deep ecology movement: Snyder the essayist and poet, Naess the technical philosopher. Both have spent a great deal of time in wilderness and wild places and both are mountaineers. Gary has essentially filled in the concrete detail of spiritual bioregional living and political activity that is implicit in Naess' more abstract philosophical articulations. Aside from Snyder's poetry and essays, a good place to obtain an overview of the subtlety, richness, and depth of his thinking is in the collection of interviews from 1964–1979 (*Gary Snyder: The Real Work,* edited by Scott McLean, 1980). Two of Snyder's more philosophical essays, which span much of his thinking, are "Four Changes" and "Good, Wild, Sacred."

Snyder's "Four Changes," Lynn White's "Historical Roots of Our Ecologic Crisis," and Paul Shepard's "Ecology and Man" are, in my estimation, the three classical deep ecological/ecocentric essays of the 1960s. "Four Changes" was written in 1969 and first published, along with Snyder's "Smokey the Bear Sutra," in *The Environmental Handbook* (edited by Garrett DeBell, 1970), and later revised in Snyder's *Turtle Island* (1974). David Brower had just left the Sierra Club and started Friends of the Earth in 1969; he managed to have the *Environmental Handbook* published in one month to be available for Earth Day in April 1970. A perusal of the *Handbook* provides a feel for the environmental concerns of the 1960s: several articles by Ehrlich on overpopulation, Lynn White's paper, the two (anonymous) pieces by Snyder, and articles on the death of the ocean; pesticides;

air and water pollution; wilderness; energy misuse, automobiles, and overconsumption; economics and education; and ecotactics.

Snyder's vision in "Four Changes" was far in advance of other ecological thought of its time, and still is, for that matter. This little essay demonstrates that he had worked out a coherent, sophisticated, spiritual, ecocentric position, both in its theoretical and practical aspects, before 1970. The four changes were described under the headings of (a) population, (b) pollution, (c) consumption, and (d) transformation. The ecocentrism, or ecological egalitarianism, was expressed in the claims that "all living beings are my brothers and sisters," and that "the unknown evolutionary destinies of other life forms are to be respected." He proposed that, as of 1969, "the goal would be half of the present world population, or less."

He argued for voluntary simplicity in order "to live lightly on the earth, to be aware and alive, to be free of egotism, to be in contact with plants and animals . . ." Snyder claimed that "most of the production and consumption of modern societies is not necessary or conducive to spiritual and cultural growth . . . [one must] be a good member of the great community of living creatures . . . Economics must be seen as a small sub-branch of ecology."

Snyder's deep ecological/social vision is most emphatic in the transformation section:

> We have it within our deepest powers not only to change our "selves" but to change our culture. If man is to remain on earth he must transform the five-millennia-long urbanizing civilization tradition into a new ecologically-sensitive harmony-oriented wild-minded scientific-spiritual culture. "Wildness is the state of complete awareness. That's why we need it." . . . Nothing short of total transformation will do much good. What we envision is a planet on which the human population lives harmoniously and dynamically by employing various sophisticated and unobtrusive technologies in a world environment which is "left natural."

Gary has always had a great respect, and even fascination, for ecologically appropriate technology and tools, and this comes out in his proposals for a bioregional balance of agriculture, ecological restoration, and wilderness:

> A technology of communication, education, and quiet transportation, land-use being sensitive to the properties of each region.

Allowing, thus, the Bison to return to much of the high plains. Careful but intensive agriculture in the great alluvial valleys; deserts left wild for those who would live there by skill. Computer technicians who run the plant part of the year and walk along with the Elk in their migrations during the rest.

He also counts himself a feminist and agrees with Naess that human population must be reduced not only to protect wildness and biodiversity, but for human cultural diversity as well:

> Women totally free and equal . . . A healthy and spare population of all races, much less in number than today . . . cultural and individual pluralism, unified by a type of world tribal council.

In short, this is an amazing document, far ahead of its time in the late sixties, but one containing a worldview and proposals that people might now be ready to take seriously at this late stage of environmental holocaust as we head into the perilous decade of the nineties.

But always there is an ultimate respect for the wilderness, for our own "deepest natural inner-self wilderness areas," and for the deserts, forests, oceans, and mountains and their nonhuman inhabitants. In a very insightful essay ("Gary Snyder's Descent to Turtle Island," *Western American Literature*, 1980), Edwin Folsom claims that:

> Snyder's major accomplishment is a rediscovery and reaffirmation of wilderness . . . Snyder announces the opening of the frontier again and attempts to push it eastward, to reverse America's historical process, to urge the wilderness to grow back into civilization, to release the stored energy from layers below us.

Gary has probably identified most closely with the traditional American Indians and other tribal peoples of the world and with working out contemporary versions of these "old ways": the bioregional and reinhabitory approach. In his 1982 Schumacher Lecture, "Good, Wild, Sacred," he refers to the Nisenan or Southern Maidu, the Kalahari Bushmen, and the Utes of the Great Basin and draws upon examples from the Australian aborigines and the ancient Ainu of Japan. The challenge for modern people, says Snyder, is to arrive at a "condition where wild, sacred, and good will be one and the same, again."

In 1976, fellow poet William Everson claimed that "Snyder has for two dozen years been hewing out the guidelines along which the greening of America must proceed, and his work has not been in vain." Let us hope that America and the rest of the world are now ready for the spiritual/ecological transformation.

R. Edward Grumbine:
A WILD FOX BARKING

I

I first encountered Gary Snyder in 1970 through *Earth House Hold* and a dog-eared broadside version of "Four Changes." I was seventeen and headed for college and what was to be my life's work as a teacher of conservation biology, natural history, and wilderness studies. What struck me in those writings still resonates today: the spirit of Turtle Island, the depth of the wilderness within, and the interpenetration of people and place, culture and nature.

Today wild beings and places exist in the face of great peril. Twenty-five percent of the world's species may become extinct within twenty years. We are adding 90 million humans each year to an already overcrowded planet. Global temperatures are predicted to rise three to eight degrees Fahrenheit in the coming decades due to the burning of fossil fuels and the cutting of tropical forests. Human disruption of nature is now severe enough for biologists to notice the negative effects of isolating ecosystems into island-like chunks. The world of late twentieth-century industrial civilization is losing its biological integrity.

From the standpoint of the struggle to preserve wilderness and biological diversity, Snyder's work has been both prophetic and profound. When queried in the early 1970s about what he feared most, he replied, "that the diversity and richness of the gene pool will be destroyed." Today, there is little doubt among most members of the scientific community that the rapid loss of biodiversity is the most dangerous problem facing humanity. The bulk of Gary's work, whether poetic, bioregional, or Buddhist, has spoken for the well-being of the planet, and is a great teaching. Returning to *Earth House Hold* and "Four Changes" twenty years later provided me with lessons in ecological humility and wisdom. Here is a brief sketch.

II

"Four Changes" calls for action in four areas of human behavior: population, pollution, consumption, and transformation. These categories match well with three of the major dilemmas of protecting biological diversity: population growth, resource depletion, and basic incongruities between biology and politics. As a conservation biologist, I would follow Snyder and give population reduction top priority. But to focus on biological diversity I would incorporate pollution into consumption and look closely at vital needs. Finally, recognizing that entrenched values do not change overnight, I would press for Gary's formulation of ecological housekeeping.

Population

Snyder foresaw human population overshoot before the 1970s' Earth Day and Paul Ehrlich's *The Population Bomb* brought the problem to society at large. But Snyder is more than a neo-Malthusian. For him, the proper question is not how many, but *who* are the neighbors? The tribe of *Earth House Hold* is made up of humans "in affectionate company with the sky, winds, clouds, trees, waters, animals, and grasses." Gary's presentation of all beings-in-relationship, the myriad facets of the ecological-self, is his greatest insight. It is *this* backcountry, *this* bear, *this* breath. His vision is radical, neat, and true.

And still not widely shared by others. It is the rare demographer, politician, or citizen who shows concern for the fate of nonhuman populations as *Homo sapiens* expands its numbers and niche. Secretary of State James Baker sums up the politician's view: "No U.S. political leader who wants to remain in office will endorse a slow-growth platform." Even environmentalists have refrained from pushing for any kind of sensible population policy. Instead, they embrace "sustainable development," a new pragmatic approach whereby we can grow forever with "technology mitigating unavoidable impacts."

Snyder's recommendations, made in the 1960s, still apply today: "Far less population and lots more national parks." However, after twenty more years of exponential growth, it will be difficult to avoid a global population of six billion to seven billion humans without an effort unprecedented in history.

Consumption

> Forest equals crop
> Scenery equals recreation
> Public equals money
> The shopkeeper's view of nature.
> (*Earth House Hold*)

When I reread the "Lookout's Journals" in *Earth House Hold*, it becomes obvious that the U.S. Forest Service has not changed much in thirty-seven years. But clearcut logging has dramatically accelerated and today species like the northern spotted owl and the grizzly bear are threatened with extinction. The timber cut has more than doubled in much of the western Cascades since Snyder scanned for smokes in the early fifties. The greater North Cascades ecosystem has been bisected by a paved highway, and many of its valleys have been roaded and logged.

Some progress in habitat protection has been made. What was once national forest when Snyder worked in the Skagit River watershed is now a national park surrounded by Forest Service lands. But visitors to the park clamor for more scenic pullouts, new visitor centers, and car campgrounds, and the Park Service may accommodate them.

The trend is unmistakable. Development fragments wild habitat into discontinuous patches. Conservation biologists identify this process as habitat insularization. The Park Service labels it "recreation amenity development." The Forest Service calls it "multiple-use-sustained-yield."

What is the true nature of consumption?

"9 August 1953. Sourdough Mountain. North Cascades: Discipline of following desires, always doing what you want to do, is hardest."

This is a consumption koan.

What Snyder is pointing us toward is the distinction between wants (desires) and vital needs. In desiring to "liquidate" the remaining ancient forests of the Cascades, the timber industry denies the needs of northern spotted owls and a host of other old-growth-dependent species. Those who would save the diversity of ancient forests only for human recreation are blind to the lives of nonhuman beings. The California red-backed vole and the northern flying squirrel have no "need" for us as they follow their desires, yet we are entrusted with their survival.

"True affluence is not needing anything."

Transformation

At the summit of Glacier Peak, wild Cascades, mid-1960s: "You mean there's a Senator for all this?"

There has never been a senator who spoke for the vital needs of mountains, canyons, and rivers. Now, as species are disappearing, we realize that the boundaries of our best-protected lands, the wilderness areas and national parks, are insufficient to serve the needs of large, wide-ranging mammals: bear, elk, cougar, wolf, wolverine, and others. The winter range of mule deer is not included in Yosemite National Park. Much of the water that is required by the native denizens of the Everglades comes from outside the park. Yellowstone, largest U.S. reserve outside of Alaska, does not protect the habitat of the grizzly bear. A Park Service research scientist sums it up: "Fifty-five percent of U.S. national parks provide little protection beyond the life of individuals or a few dwindling generations that presently constitute the population."

The problem is that politicians, not biologists, designate national parks. Look at Yellowstone. Its legal boundaries, straight and square, have nothing to do with the ecological requirements of its wild inhabitants.

The single most pressing transformation is one where people would begin to place biology before politics, "housekeeping on earth" beyond "the housekeeping of various social orders." Earth House Hold.

Until we practice good housekeeping, natural ecosystems will continue to drift toward a zoo-like state and biodiversity will be at risk. The insidious danger is that our technocratic worldview will demand that we become more efficient producers and consumers and manage the planet ever more closely through highly refined data bases. Scientists have yet to follow Snyder and move beyond a narrow objectivity to discover the magic of "the very Eye that looks."

III

It all begins in paying attention.

We were attending a weekend workshop in the hills outside of

Ojai, California. Late autumn, strong Santa Ana winds, chaparral country, a gossamer haze on the ridges. The majority of the group was from Los Angeles, with little outdoor experience. Gary talked all Saturday and Sunday morning in the meditation hall, a sort of informal *mondō*.

After lunch, we gathered in the field outside the zendo and headed out on a trail through mixed chaparral and oak-woodland to greet autumn. We discussed why fire is so much a presence in California ecosystems and looked for adaptations to frequent burning (root crowns, burls, allelopathic leaf litter). Plants we identified: chamise, two species of manzanita, coast live oak, poison oak, ceanothus, holly-leaved cherry, and more. Scrub jays followed us through their territory. Then I found, trailside, three slender coyote turds. The scat contained obvious hair and seeds, undigested sign. People crowded around.

"What do you think these seeds are?" Gary asked.

"Fruits of *Prunus ilicifolia*, the holly-leaved cherry, passed through; about the only fruit to eat this time of year," I replied. I had found them in years past in chaparral near my home up north.

I could see Coyote Old Man come that much more alive to these disaffected city dwellers.

Later, someone found a wood rat's nest in a thicket of manzanita. People were amazed that the rats lived year-round in such unkempt quarters.

"We've been able to carbon-date some wood rat nests back about fourteen thousand years' continuous habitation," I offered.

Quality nest sites are uncommon and probably serve to limit wood rat population size. There are only so many homes for juveniles to disperse to, and a site is never unoccupied for long.

"I didn't know that," said Gary. "I'll have to remember that, take a look at the wood rats where I live. What would it take for us to live in our house for fourteen thousand years continuous dwelling?" he asked the group.

The folks from L.A. thought about the lives of wood rats. Maybe they remembered the L.A. River, now channelized and buried underground. A little flash of biology and the politics becomes less real. The real work sinks in.

The best teachers are always ready to learn.

Peter Berg:

BEATING THE DRUM WITH GARY

I

As an internal exile in the U.S. of the mid-fifties, I read beat poetry with great excitement and maybe even greater relief. Excitement over the direct, hip-inflected language and rebellion that it expressed. Relief that the dozen or so of us who represented the entire underground at the McCarthyite University of Florida, where the scrawled posters that were put up clandestinely at night read "Integrate in '58," weren't alone. Beat writings were as much a summons as they were literature. We felt that we could connect with those kindred spirits even if they were thousands of miles away. While still a teenager I set out to literally do that, leaving college first to hitchhike to Chicago and other parts of "real" America and finally to arrive in San Francisco like a pilgrim, solitarily stalking North Beach and breathing the City Lights Bookstore and Co-existence Bagel Shop air of liberation. A defiant culture was tangible on the street and it seemed a complete world of progressive consciousness, from philosophy and politics to music and painting. It even bore the promise of some mysterious soul-level power that could eventually subvert and transform the Eisenhowerhead American Empire.

But admittedly that would take some time, and since I was an unemployed dropout it made peculiar sense in that brief period between wars to get rid of the draft specter by going into the Army. There was a small possibility of being sent to Europe. Instead, the following tedious months were spent in various Southern states, behind a desk with a nameplate to which I added Lao-tzu's advice, "There is great wisdom in the void. Be silent, be absolutely empty." It became an opportunity to read all the books on Indian, Chinese, and Japanese poetry, prose, and plays that were skimpily available then, and to memorize parts of the *Tao Te Ching,* some poems of Li Po, and haiku by Bashō. At discharge time I had actually gotten to Paris (only for a month but proudly with forged orders and ripped most of the time on hashish) and caught up with contemporary

Asian-influenced writing in everything from Donald Allen's *The New American Poetry* anthology to Diane diPrima's mimeographed magazine, *Floating Bear*. After we finally met years later, I surprised Gary Snyder by remembering some lines from his early "T-2 Tanker Blues."

In the early sixties any vagueness about the preceding generation's spirit of dissent was swept away by the emergence of a clearly rebellious descendent movement. It had two main streams: society-changing through political activism, and mind-changing through meditation, art, and drugs. They overlapped more often than not—pot-smoking peace demonstrators, Gandhian acolytes in civil rights marches—although both contained elements who considered the other wing to be a direct contradiction. By the mid-sixties these were known respectively as "politically responsible" New Leftists and "mind-blown" hippies.

One profound moment of torch passing from underground beatdom to the new two-edged counterculture occurred at a benefit in 1965 for the San Francisco Mime Troupe. In fine political protest fashion, the Troupe had just been busted for performing a free show in the park without the required permit, which it had refused to obtain. Thousands of supporters magically materialized and wound around the skid row block where the Troupe's studio was located, waiting to hear Allen Ginsberg read, Frank Zappa's Mothers of Invention play, and others perform on stage together for the first time that night. Mime Troupe Director R. G. Davis greeted fellow New Left activists and thinkers while Business Manager Bill Graham marveled at the crowd and became inspired to promote his own shows at the Fillmore Auditorium.

The unexpected outpouring for this benefit stirred another kind of response among many of the Mime Troupe performers and writers. Earlier I had developed the concept of guerrilla theater as a way to perform pieces in the midst of political demonstrations such as the Free Speech Movement's occupation of UC Berkeley's Sproul Plaza. The benefit crowd revealed that there was an even greater audience for no-stage, participative theater among the rising wave of seemingly nonpolitical defectors from mainstream society. In 1966 a dozen of us left the Troupe to found the Diggers and begin life-acting a "free frame of reference"—free food, free clinic, free crash pads, free store, free events in Golden Gate Park, and even an actual twelve-by-twelve-foot bright orange picture frame placed in front of some of our doings—for the multitudes who were coming to the Haight-Ashbury district to declare themselves in one way or another for peace.

We saw ourselves as theatrical provocateurs of the psychedelic streets, challenging dropouts with visions of a creatively and sexually liberated, cooperative, and ecologically conscious social order to replace the one that was fighting the Vietnam War. One of our open-doors events at the Straight Theater featured a nude dance by Jane Lapiner's ensemble, a cargo net for climbing, Steve Miller's band, tree fronds for waving, film loops of natural events including seeds sprouting and volcanoes exploding, and a political speech parody by filmmaker Bruce Conner. I had a poster of Lyndon Johnson hugging Ho Chi Minh made for the event and titled the whole thing "The End of the War."

The Diggers were attempting to deal with "politically responsible" and "mind-blown" directions at the same time, but friction between the two still occurred in a kind of running debate about whether people were trying to escape society's problems or confront them. One incident in particular pointed up the kind of differences that continued to remain. *The Oracle* newspaper, a militantly Aquarian Age bastion that tended strongly toward LSD-inspired artwork and mysticism, had received Snyder's poem "A Curse on the Men in Washington, Pentagon." A heavy internal debate about publishing it ensued because some of the editors projected an appeal for actual violence into these lines:

> As I kill the white man, the 'American' in me . . .
> This magic I work, this loving I give
> That my children will flourish
> And yours won't live.

The Diggers were delighted that a leading Zen Buddhist figure had placed himself in such definite opposition to the war and rushed to print it as a street handout through the Communications Company. Later it appeared as the first piece of writing in the collected *Digger Papers*.

The Haight began building toward a major event as more people arrived and media of every variety descended. It came in early 1967 as the Human Be-In, a celebration that drew thousands of revealers and revelers to Golden Gate Park. The Diggers expected it to be a great success because our own free events in the park drew huge crowds with only a day's notice on Haight Street. But we were disturbed by the lack of political content reflected in the lineup of speakers listed for this signal "gathering of the tribes." Advance posters for the Be-In were sending a one-sidedly blow-your-mind message.

Claude Hayward, a staffer for *Ramparts* magazine who later quit to help found the Communications Company, sensed that there was a potential story as well as some diplomatic benefit in bringing Be-In figures and Diggers together for a discussion. He arranged for Emmett Grogan and me to meet with Gary Snyder and Allen Ginsberg to hear each other out. I suspected that Allen was somewhat media-struck during this period and basically out of touch with developments in the Haight, while Snyder had only recently returned from a long stay in Japan and could well be out of touch with the whole U.S. scene. Emmett and I enumerated the divergent attitudes and directions of Aquarian Agers, hip merchants, and Diggers, and asked that the two prominently featured poets use their influence to get anti-war and black speakers or speak themselves on those subjects. Ginsberg was very interested in what the Diggers were doing and remained mostly silent while soaking up the Haight news. Snyder identified himself as "an old Wobbly" and seemed defensive about being seen as only having spiritual interests. He was curious about the anarchist philosophical background of the Diggers (one reference of our name was to seventeenth-century English precursors of anarchism). I responded with probably more heat and volume than was necessary that the current Diggers should be seen as successors to the moribund Wobblies and bearers of the grand anarchist tradition begun with the Paris Commune. Forcing the issue that prompted our meeting, I added that Love Generation otherworldliness would undo whatever hope for actively transforming society might exist among the mob who would come to the Be-In. Then Snyder began asking me a series of rapid-fire questions that showed both the value of his Zen training and the depth of his own concerns.

"Why do you want to transform society?"

"Because too many people are oppressed."

"Why do you care about that?"

"Because it stifles their freedom and creativity."

"Why does that matter?"

"Because people can create a more equitable society and stop destroying the planet."

"Why are those things important?"

"Because humanity can do better for itself."

"Why do you care about humanity?"

"Out of love for people."

With that he stopped asking questions of the kind he might well have quizzed himself with and said, "Why didn't you say that in the first place? You don't have to open a can of worms and come out with a string of negatives to believe in something beneficial. And you're not immune to this love stuff yourself, are you?" It was an impressive and convincing performance. We established a relationship as comrades then that has continued to now, and I began to appreciate him as a working ally and clever strategist. The Diggers decided to serve free food rather than boycott the Be-In. It proved to be an astounding panoramic display of the influences bursting into popular consciousness at that time (including declarations against war and racism) wrapped in the glow of pot and Owsley's donated acid.

Later in that same conversation Gary said something that I quoted in the essay "Trip Without a Ticket" that was written to announce the Digger vision of the Free Store: "First you gotta pin down what's wrong with the West. Distrust of human nature, which means distrust of Nature. Distrust of wildness in oneself literally means distrust of Wilderness." To give some idea of the significance of sentiments like these to the counterculture at that time, Paul Krassner, who edited *The Realist* and later published the *Digger Papers*, said "Trip Without a Ticket" was the first place he ever saw the word *ecology*.

The Haight continued to attract more and more people, reaching its greatest number during the summer of 1968. Then a decline began that was at least in part a result of deliberate city government intervention. San Francisco's police, health, and administrative authorities declared war on the unmanageable little neighborhood that had become a worldwide symbol of cultural rebellion. Three-man police patrols walked through every half-hour, and paddy wagons made frequent surprise sidewalk ID checks. New one-way routing of automobile traffic turned once-languid Haight Street into a mini-freeway.

Installation of glaring chemical vapor streetlights heightened the effect of an occupation zone. People who had been shut out of shared apartments and crash pads by the health department huddled blanket-draped in doorways of hip businesses that had begun to fold.

The Diggers decided to retaliate by spreading Haightness through the entire city, beginning with an occupation of City Hall steps every day at noon for a period starting with the vernal equinox and ending on the summer solstice of 1969. Calling this effort "Free City," we read poems and manifestoes, performed songs and street theater, got busted for wearing masks and American flag shirts, distributed food, and even offered free shampoos in the Civic Center fountain. When the summer solstice arrived there was a final farewell series of Digger-style free concerts in five parks scattered from Hunter's Point to North Beach's Washington Square with the theme "San Francisco Enters Into Eternity."

By then a full-scale retreat from rapidly deteriorating Haight Street was under way, and some veterans of the amazing cultural liberation and subsequent siege that had happened there joined groups of new settlers who had earlier headed to the land to pursue Earth-based values. Some former street radicals and artists had begun pioneering Black Bear Ranch in the remote Siskiyou Mountains as an egalitarian commune with Digger support. The last Digger street communications were titled "Planetedge Papers" and contained naturalist Sterling Bunnell's thoughts about humans as part of the planet's life.

II

While living at Black Bear and seeking signs of the next direction our seemingly vast but vulnerable social upheaval would take, I decided to visit some of the other new communities that were coming together in northern California. Richard Werthimer, a progressive lawyer who had once volunteered to get me and other Mime Troupers off after an arrest for performing a guerrilla theater show with giant puppets in the middle of Haight Street, had told me he was a land partner of sorts with Snyder, Ginsberg, and others on a place near the Yuba River in the Sierra Nevada foothills and that an alternative community was developing there. When Judy Goldhaft and I arrived, we found a very hectic house-building scene in progress, but Gary and Masa were cordial and offered an overnight camping spot near some kitkitdizze, the low-growing, sweet-creosote-scented shrub that Snyder named his place after. We were invited to attend the next day's sunrise chanting and talk that Gary offered the team of Zen students who were helping with the house.

In the morning we walked to a naturally sepulchral spot where the glinting orange yellow sun was shooting perfectly straight and thick first rays between tall ponderosa pines. A few semicircular rows of young students were chanting along with Gary while his infant son, Kai, crawled toward a small brass bell set on the ground in front of the group and tried to ring it. Snyder put Kai on his lap and proceeded with the day's teaching about early Zen practitioners on the West Coast. Previously he had invited me to ask about anything that was unfamiliar, but I was surprised when he turned toward me, sitting away from the group, and asked if I would pose a question that might prove useful to everyone.

It was a strong personal moment because spiritual practices, whether public rituals or solitary meditation, are anathema to me. I've read enough Buddhist writings to know basic precepts, but I've never considered myself a follower. Whatever I asked would have to be honest to the role of an inveterate outsider and yet show respect for the interests of the group.

I decided to confront what had always been a particularly hard-to-accept facet of both Buddhism and Japanese culture that is illustrated by the conclusion of the play *Chushingura*. Banned for centuries in Japan because of its potential to arouse public unrest, the story had been revived and made into an extremely popular epic film on the scale of *Gone With the Wind*. It concerns a virtuous nobleman who is falsely accused of misconduct and, failing to convince the emperor of his innocence, commits suicide to preserve his honor and keep the family holdings intact. His enemies greedily seize the property anyway, and his dedicated retainers plot to go underground, working at various menial jobs until a time comes to avenge their lord's death. When the moment arrives years later, they reassemble and heroically overcome the main villain's guards and kill him. But their victory breaks the severe prohibition against commoners killing an aristocrat, no matter how evil he may be. With no other honorable recourse open to them, they commit mass suicide.

I asked why they didn't keep fighting so that the revolutionary content of their act could be understood and shared by other victims of that corrupt social order. Or was it really revolutionary at all? Killing themselves didn't directly communicate a need for change; instead it acquiesced to the status quo. Was suicide more honorable than revolution in Buddhism? If so, was that part of Snyder's Zen teaching?

It wasn't the most delicate case to bring up in that formal situation, but Gary made a fast and powerfully declarative response. He told of being branded a political conservative by Japanese contemporaries when they learned he was studying Zen. It was Zen priests who prayed with young kamakazi pilots before their suicidal missions. Zen was seen as a kind of palliative for the upper classes who didn't sufficiently resist bushido-minded military expansionists before and during World War II. It was completely out of favor with post-war intellectuals in Japan.

Snyder urged the class to learn from this example not to allow North American Zen to be used by the power structure and become debased through institutional approval. The best way to do this would be to ally with Nature rather than with the state. North American Zen should be paired with awareness of Native American veneration for life-affirming Mother Earth instead of attempting to transplant Eastern attitudes. A great transformative change was beginning in Western civilization, and Zen should be taken up as one appropriate spiritual path for living on Turtle Island. Then he thanked me warmly for the question and dismissed the student-workers.

III

In an attempt to discover whatever common threads might be running through other land-based situations, I joined a caravan of former Diggers, including Peter Coyote, that set out from the Bay Area in summer 1971 in half a dozen trucks converted into house-campers. We aimed for San Juan Ridge to make Snyder's place the first stop on what eventually became a coast-to-coast circuit ride around North America.

Gary guided us to some Bureau of Land Management land that had a small spring to camp by for a few days while we talked about future political directions and visited the Ridge community. As a symbol of our intentions and a gesture of thanks, caravaner Paul Shippee offered to build a spring box to keep the water clean and establish a site for groups of travelers like ours. Snyder provided a thick well-aged board to saw into appropriate lengths and some zinc-coated nails to put them together. We were all determined to make something that would endure for at least one hundred years.

Snyder and I talked over the apparent conflict in what each of us was doing. Although he was making a local stand and concentrating on community and regional issues and I was setting out to view as many places as possible, there was an intimate connection between our approaches. I would learn if there was real potential for a widespread land-based ecology movement. He would discover whether the Ridge community could strengthen and mobilize behind its own ecological concerns. We would share experiences when we met again.

That winter I had gotten as far as Nova Scotia and visited with the expatriate American poet Allen Van Newkirk, who had edited a hybrid natural sciences and literary broadside-style magazine named *The Holocene Gazette and Country Traveler*. We spent several snowed-in days sharing our underground political histories and current mutual interest in the broad connections between society and ecology. I had become acutely aware through slow traveling across the continent that ecological disasters were much more widespread than most people imagined. General unconsciousness of the need to protect natural systems extended from spraying Agent Orange on hardwood forests, to kill and replace them with fast-growing pines for pulpwood, to dumping mining tailings where they leached out poisons into drinking water. Each region possessed its own set of problems based on the characteristics and resources of the place, but political jurisdictions often followed arbitrarily drawn straight lines that didn't match natural borders, so that long-range solutions couldn't be put into effect.

Allen was interested in researching, classifying, and preserving all of the natural features within a given geographic area. The ecologist Raymond Dasmann, working at the International Union for the Conservation of Nature and Natural Resources, was developing information of this kind for native plants and animals in what he termed "biotic provinces." Allen felt that more characteristics such as climate and landforms could be included; he liked the term "bioregions." He planned to start an Institute for Bioregional Research to begin finding out what they were and where their borders lay.

Both of us felt that the environmental movement as it had proceeded until then was completely inadequate to deal with the underlying problems that industrial society created for the biosphere. Cleaning up after larger and larger disasters wasn't going to keep them from happening in the first place. The only way to succeed at preventing them was to restructure the way people satisfied basic material needs and related to the natural systems upon which their own survival ultimately depended. Allen was disaffected from looking for popular political solutions and preferred to develop concepts and information that could be used on an academic and agency level. I disagreed with that approach and wanted a new cultural and political formulation that would put ecological concerns at the center of society. The upcoming 1972 United Nations Conference on the Environment in Stockholm appeared to be the handiest world-scale opportunity to sound out our concerns, and we agreed to meet there with other nongovernmental sorts who were being attracted for similar reasons to this first-time event.

The presence of thousands of activists and demonstrators who somehow managed to transport themselves to Stockholm proved that ecology wasn't just a North Atlantic cause. Included in the wide range of uninvited attendees who I dubbed "the planetariat" were Japanese minamata disease (mercury poisoning) victims, Vietnamese Buddhist monks, Eritrean rebels, Sames (Laplanders) from the Arctic Circle, Native Americans, and Swedish anarchists with black and green flags. For most of them no real answers to the issues they represented came out of the official gathering. Instead, the conference crystalized the frustration people were feeling about the inability of any established institutions to deal with planetary problems. Snyder blasted it as an exercise where "robot nations . . . argue how to parcel out our Mother Earth." And if the U.N. couldn't provide an effective forum, what body could? I came back determined to find a method for constructing a human-species-on-the-planet-together politics from the ground up.

The first step was to complete the trucking trip and return to establish a home-region base in northern California. Stops along the route showed what a large and diverse number of new settler groups there were in rural areas from Vermont to the Smoky Mountains and from the Ozarks to Huerfano Valley, Colorado. Whether their major interest was in organic farming, alternative energy, natural healing, shared living, or dwelling closer to wilderness, they shared a common commitment to the places where they lived that went far beyond conventional governmental consciousness.

The next step was to create a medium that could help form a network among these groups and others like them anywhere in the world. It would have to be mailed but should avoid the top-down editorial policy and standard format of a commercial magazine. I decided to make what Snyder later named a "bundle," an envelope containing separately printed pieces that reflected a common theme but could stand on their own as a map, a poster, a calendar, a photograph, or even a piece of cloth to sew onto something else.

In Sweden I had learned about the reindeer-herding Sames who seemed to be European Indians and represented a link between indigenous people on both sides of the Atlantic. When I saw a drawing of one of their shamans playing a hoop drum painted with natural symbols and singing about the connections between them as a moving reindeer bone pointed them out, I decided to make it the publication's logo. The drum's symbols were like the pieces in the envelope. The order they were read in and the interpretation each person gave them were similar to the shaman's song. It made perfect sense to call it *Planet Drum*.

Raymond Dasmann replied to a request for articles about his biotic provinces research and his idea that large areas of wilderness be preserved as a Fourth World by suggesting that we meet to talk over the whole range of eco-political possibilities. It was the beginning of a collaboration that shaped the future direction of Planet Drum Foundation. Ray had expert information about ecologically defined geographic areas and knew firsthand how far destruction of the planet had progressed. He had worked with enough state, national, and international agencies to know their limits and distrust their capability to come to grips with ultimate ecological realities. When I proposed that new land-based and other groups could identify with and restore their local areas in ways that were more thorough-going and socially transformative than were possible through established governments, he was enthusiastic about the prospect and wanted to help. Dasmann had studied northern California for years and felt that the unique habitats that were there warranted declaring it a separate life-place. I was using the term "reinhabitation" to describe the process of becoming aware and responsive to areas rather than merely residing in them. The State of California Office of Appropriate Technology had asked me to give a talk that I titled "Reinhabiting the Northern California Bioregion." *Seriatim* magazine published this and Ray then sent it to *The Ecologist* in England for reprinting, but they declined because it was so unlike their usual material. Ray offered to edit and rewrite some sections and submitted that version as a coauthored essay that was finally accepted. "Reinhabiting California" has since become a main source for defining bioregions in both human and natural terms with reinhabitation as the appropriate way to live in them.

IV

It turned out that the mid-seventies were an extremely fertile time for spreading these ideas. A core of ex-Diggers including David Simpson, Luna Moth, and many others had remained connected together as a large, mutually supportive family and helped produce the first *Planet Drum* bundles. Linn House and Jerry Gorsline assembled one titled "North Pacific Rim Alive" that established a place-located theme and pattern for the many bioregional publications that have appeared from other places since. Their coauthored essay "Future Primitive" is an inspired invocation of a shift in civilization values, and House's "Totem Salmon" clearly states the importance of another species to human inhabitation around the North Pacific. Snyder consulted on some aspects of the bundle and contributed part of his journal from Hokkaido coupled with a scientific discussion of native plant zones that are related to that island.

Judy Goldhaft oversaw the creation of The Reinhabitory Theater, which toured northern California with modern renditions of local Native American and new settler stories interspersed with descriptions of Shasta Bioregion's natural history. Performed by a combination of former Mime Troupe and Firehouse Theater players and produced everywhere from theaters to Grange halls and open pastures, the show was both humorous and ecologically radical and it helped focus local community attention on bioregional concerns.

Governor Jerry Brown's surprisingly open administration was under way and Snyder was appointed by him to head the Arts Council. Gathering up some socially and ecologically conscious artists (including other aficionados of bioregional ideas) to serve with him, Gary established districts for awarding grants that deliberately corresponded to northern and southern bioregions. I had wanted to create a Planet Drum bundle for northern California and felt it would have to be book-size to do justice to the range of subjects that should be covered. During a visit to San Francisco, Masa and Gary attempted to convince me that the Council should be approached to fund the book project. Gary brushed away my reluctance to deal with the government by pointing out that "When a head of state goes so far as to request a hermit poet to come down from the mountain, then the poet is obligated to try to do his best." His inference was that the poet was now asking for my best. The result was *Reinhabiting a Separate Country: A Bioregional Anthology of Northern California*, with original contributions from indigenous elders such as Bessie Tripp and Charlie Thom, and from writers, artists, and natural scientists including Ernest Callenbach, Robert Curry, Ray Dasmann, Jim Dodge, Rasa Gustaitis, Jerry Martien (Dr. Loon), and many others who declared a definite culture for and commitment to the region.

Gary also pushed bioregional consciousness into public view by helping to arrange a weekend-long San Juan Ridge conference at the local Oak Tree School. His essay "Re-inhabitation" in *The Old Ways* was transcribed from a spontaneous address given there.

Snyder attempted to expose as many Brown administration officials as possible, including the governor himself, to these ideas. At one highly convivial Ridge celebration he offered a meadow at Kitkitdizze for a performance of The Reinhabitory Theater and invited Brown, some of his appointees, including Rusty Schweickert, and a large representation of the local community to attend. The latter yipped and cheered during the show and afterward mingled barefoot, in deerskin vests, hair braided with feathers, with the sportshirt- and slacks-clad administrators. Brown had already been naturalized in a naked sweat bath when Gary made a point of asking me to give him the Frisco Bay Mussel Group's "Watershed Guide" poster and "Living Here" booklet that had been created to express opposition to the Peripheral Canal. This scheme to divert a significant portion of the Sacramento River around the Delta and therefore away from San Francisco Bay so that it could be used by southern California agriculture and Los Angeles had originally been supported by established environmental organizations such as the Sierra

Club and Friends of the Earth before the Mussel Group started its campaign, but they were subsequently influenced to oppose it.

Brown continued to lukewarmly approve the idea.

Snyder led the two of us away from the crowd and left us in a grove of fir trees. The governor listened to my explanation of why the northern California bioregion needed to be protected from exploitation of its resources and made the observation that no one could or should stop the flow of people into California, so there would continue to be a need to export northern water southward.

I suggested that a number of things could be done to both slow down migration into the state and reduce internal population growth, but he shrugged these off as actions that were likely to create more opposition than positive results.

He then stated that continued population growth was related to continued economic growth. With a misplaced attempt at irony he added that it was in northern California's best interest to keep the biggest number of new people in the already-dense southern part of the state, so it was worth giving up the water to keep them there.

I observed that continued colonization might eventually lead to northern California's secession.

Brown didn't comment on the likelihood or practicality of this outcome as I thought he might. He said, "Who would want to be governor of a smaller state when California is now the tenth largest political entity in the world?"

I left this conversation feeling that it was hopeless to try to move the governor further in the direction of bioregional appreciation, but it is to his credit that, for whatever reason, he later reversed his position on the Canal and came out against it.

V

During the conservative political retrenchment that emerged during the late seventies and grew through the eighties, bioregionalism endured without official support and made important gains on the grass roots level. In 1979 Planet Drum convened "Listening to the Earth: The Bioregional Basis of Community Consciousness," a four-day conference in San Francisco that drew around a thousand people to hear discussions ranging from "Technological Influences on American Culture" to "Our Place in the Water Cycle." Speakers including Morris Berman, Murray Bookchin, Stephanie Mills, and Roderick Nash offered a preview of eco-philosophical positions that later became important rallying points. Snyder appeared with Bookchin on a panel entitled "A New Context for Growth and Development" that pointed up a growing schism between social and deep ecology approaches. Gary took a long view of the human species when he observed, "It would not be shameful to say 'go back,' nor would it necessarily be utopian or romantic since utopia is a word that implies a future-projected, ideal society, and the past happens to be real and not ideal. So talking about the past is by definition not utopia." Murray proved the accuracy of fellow panelist Ernest Callenbach's comment that social ecology was more informed by politics than biology when he responded, "I'm a utopian . . . I want to go back so that I can go forward again," and argued for those who are "aspiring for power over their lives" and have "acute ecological consciousness, and a social consciousness, and a moral consciousness, (and) also an intense political consciousness."

Planet Drum's review *Raise the Stakes* was begun shortly afterward to promote the formation of bioregional groups and to network among them. By 1989 *RTS* was able to list nearly two hundred of these groups, publications, and contact people for areas stretching from Hudson Estuary in New York to Kansas Area Watershed and from the Gulf of Maine to Ish River Bioregion straddling the U.S.-Canadian border on the Pacific coast.

Snyder has a been a contributor of poems and commentaries to *RTS* since the first issue and helps the movement grow by speaking about bioregionalism and referring people to Planet Drum on his travels from Alaska to Sweden. He told an Australian interviewer, "I work with a group called Planet Drum and it is one of the centers of the emerging planetary ecological movement." The formidable personal underground that has grown up around his work continues to be a source for bioregional organizers and activities. Gary sometimes sends their names himself and asks that they be contacted.

For me the most unique and somehow dependable aspect of our comradeship over more than twenty years is the overlap and fit of ideas about what is important at a particular time and what to do about it. Recently I've been tilting in reviews and letters with thinkers who put forth the point of view that Nature should be further dominated and fixed by humans, even to the extent of governing the overall process of biological evolution. It's a much more important issue to me than the squabble over deep versus social ecology, because it invites the possibility that wildness will no longer be considered an operative reality and Nature will be seen as thoroughly domesticated. That would leave the unpredictable human brain as the dominant force in the biosphere, or so the deluded proponents of this line of reasoning believe. I sent Gary copies of what I had written and learned in reply that he had begun a book based on "the practice of the wild." He sent some early chapters for comment and I was able to read the remarkable and valuable list of contrasts he sees between "civilized" and "wild" in terms of individuals and societies. Once more he got there just in time.

He keeps helping to hear the music and beat the drum.

Dell Hymes:
A COYOTE WHO CAN SING

Trying to find focus for a piece about Gary, I realize I may be on the wrong side of the country. Gary found a way to sustain a living on the West Coast; I never did. Looking west out this window, I can imagine that the horizon is the Washington side of the Columbia, slanting upward somewhere across from Oregon near The Dalles. Driving that way in the early light, if you kept going, you might come to people fishing. And if you do go straight past a certain store, rather than follow the curve of the road, you in fact come to a stream that could be coming down a mountain canyon in the Cascades. But being at the Blue Ridge is not the same as being in the part of the country where we met, and where our imaginations were first at home.

Let me say a little about early days and our relationship, then offer something that expresses a connection between then and now.

Gary and I met at Reed College at the end of the 1940s. A collage of memories has lost the vividness it kept for years, but certain names, places, tunes still flash to mind when much else has been forgotten: Alexander Leitswiçz; Robin ("Why is the world all going in twos?" she said, coming out of the dormitory one day); 1414 SE Lambert Street; Stanley's houseboat; Lew's singing ("I think I'll never miss, I think I'll never miss, In-di-an-á-po-lis," he brought back from a trip to a dentist there during a visit to us in Bloomington—and "Omaha, Omaha, Omaha's a simple city").

In 1950 and 1951 I and Gary were successively the first (the only?) graduates from Reed with degrees jointly in anthropology and literature. The combination seems familiar now. Then it was odd, a tribute to an accommodating college. I went on to Indiana University in Bloomington, for no very clear reason other than that I was interested in Indians, and it offered folklore and linguistics along with anthropology. The summer of 1951 I returned to the Northwest to try to use a wire recorder and learn something about Wasco at Warm Springs Reservation. Gary was also working there, in the woods (see "A Berry Feast"). I remember pinecone fights at the place on Schoolie Flat where other Reed folks stayed, and finding kittens abandoned at the edge of the Deschutes, below the bridge across it at the eastern edge of the reservation. Gary took one, I another. He called his Io Zagreus; I called mine Sapir.

There has been sometimes a bit of tension in my relationship with Gary. For a short time, he took a path on which I stayed (Sapir), then he left it behind to take a path (Io Zagreus) a part of me would envy.

But in the fall of 1951 he also came to Bloomington to study anthropology and linguistics, and we shared an apartment above a little Chinese restaurant on Kirkwood Avenue. Lew came down from Chicago to visit after the meetings of the American Anthropological Association in Chicago that fall. We all rode back in a car with the philosopher of anthropology, David Bidney, who confirmed for Lew the word he wanted in a poem for a stand of trees, *menorah*. A few women came and went, and I learned to make "loggers' special," and put it in a poem years later about one of the women and an anthropological conference. I tried to learn to use horsemeat for spaghetti, the way Gary did, and once after he had left I offered it to Rene Girard and his wife. They were models of pleasant politeness. But the most vivid memory of that place is the night of a party, when the proprietor of the restaurant below ascended the stairs in anger at the noise, and he and Gary had it out in Chinese—he in Cantonese, Gary in Mandarin, I think.

And there was one academic parable. The chair of the anthropology department at Indiana was intrigued by the arrival of a poet, and made Gary his assistant in his course on American Indian languages. The course was considered advanced but the chair channeled into it willy-nilly a second tier of students who had no previous background. As assistant, Gary was to help the students without background keep up (that is, he was to tutor them in phonetics). He himself had not had that background, and worked hard to keep ahead of the others. Grades came, and his was B +. The chair explained that Gary had indeed done well, so well that he had decided not to grade him with the second tier after all, but with the advanced students. Hence, B +.

That didn't encourage sticking it out in graduate school. This is not to suggest that the incident of a grade explains his departure. Indeed, Indiana was a reasonable place for someone with Gary's interest in American Indian traditions. It had an unusual conjuncture of faculty interest. The anthropology department had been started and was chaired by a specialist in Indian languages, C. F. Voegelin, who edited there the only journal in the field, *International Journal of American Linguistics;* anthropological interest was strong in the fledgling graduate program in linguistics; there was a folklore program, headed by the dean of American folklore, Stith Thompson, who had been a dean at Indiana, and whose *Tales of the American Indians* remained a basic source. Literary criticism was prominent as well, at least in the summer, when Indiana for a while inherited what had been the Kenyon School of Letters. But financial support was slim, and Gary had need at the time for dental work. Teeth can concentrate the mind. Indiana was not much of a place to pursue an interest in China and Japan. Its intellectual opportunities were mostly signposts along well-paved roads, but there was word of stirrings in the Bay Area of a new kind. Altogether, a small town in southern Indiana could not compare with the Pacific Coast. In midyear (early 1952) Gary was off to San Francisco to study Chinese and Japanese intensively and to become the poet and person this volume honors.

There were regular letters for a while, and copies of his books, occasional meetings, occasional misses. I looked for him in Kyoto in 1968, and did meet Masa, but he had not been able to get back from an island. When he was settled on Alleghany Star Route, I was able to send him his set of the seven volumes of the *Thompson Motif-Index of Oral Literature* that had moved about with me since Bloomington. (I should have sent the ten volumes of the *Oxford Universal Dictionary on Historical Principles,* bought at Camerons' in Portland for $6.50 and inscribed in green ink—"Garyth and/Alysoun/Snyder/ Sept MCML"—and will if he wants it.) We visited him at Kitkitdizze one day, and looked up to see Allen Ginsberg walking over for advice on the building of his own place. A later summer, Gary and his family, Bill Stafford and his wife, I and mine, were collected together for lunch one improbable day on a plateau overlooking Warm Springs, all at the family ranch of the poet and student of Indian literature Jerry Ramsey.

II

The world of starting out seems far away. Something more than memory keeps connection alive now that the years of finishing up are near. Anthropology stayed a part of Gary; poetry, sometimes to my surprise, stayed with me. A return of interest in the poetic character and translation of American Indian texts made us part of an emerging network of people concerned with "ethnopoetics." One notable event was a two-day meeting in New York organized by the anthropologist and late-flowering poet Stanley Diamond. In the midst of an emerging enthusiasm for poetry as a mode of anthropology, I remember disagreement as to who could count as poets, what as poetry.

No disagreement, only camaraderie a few months later at the annual meeting of the American Anthropological Association, that year in Washington, D.C., the first that Gary had attended since Chicago 1951. Several of us read (Stan had decided by then that I might qualify as a poet), and I will always be glad of the chance to introduce Gary, and of his generosity in introducing me. I had in fact something of a paper, an argument, illustrated with poems of my own. And since presidents of the AAA no longer gave presidential addresses (I was president that year), I counted the paper and the poems as my unofficial address.

But now, to write just about and for Gary.

Two things stand out. The first is that Gary, more than any other, perhaps, has made being a poet count in the United States in the way that it counts in Russia. In Russia the role is there for those who can claim it. In the United States these days, it is not. It takes a truly remarkable person to create it, to make the work of writing poetry make a difference to what many understand about their place in the world, and indeed, to what some do with their lives. Perhaps it is not an accident of origin that the few others who come to mind are of the West (notably, Robinson Jeffers), or, when not of the West, of a commitment to a life on the land (Wendell Berry, Robert Bly).

The second thing is Gary's second book, *Myths & Texts*. I had the copy he had just sent me while alone a few weeks in the summer of 1960, in Berkeley, where my family and I were moving for what might have been the rest of our lives.[1] Alone in the house, reading the book, the words from Pacific Coast Indian texts leaped out at me, seemed blazoned on the page, echoed in a chanted voice. I rushed about, tracking them down in the collections we both had read (except that I remember "We wash our hair in urine in this town" and now can't find it).

The notes that resulted, I think and hope, are with other papers of mine in the Library of the American Philosophical Society—not a bad place, since that library is a great repository of materials in the languages of American Indians. But whether or not the pages ever reappear as a bit of philology to satisfy a curiosity, what Gary did with them in his poems is permanently important. The skill and accuracy with which he placed the Indian lines in his important long poem helps make their traditions part of the literature, the continuing imagination, of the continent in which they arose.

And Gary's use of the lines fits the way in which the myths are part of the lives in which they arose, in which they were sustained and recreated. One part of the year, winter, was for telling the myths in full, a sort of world renewal rite, recalling in winter the summer travels of transformers when the present world was made, ending so often with invocation of summer weather, or a berry or a bird that would be part of summer. For winter was when the lived world shrunk, the spirits and dangers of the peripheries of the world came close, people hunkered down in underground lodges, food grew scarce, none fresh to be obtained until spring, and the next season of the round of the world returned. Outside that sacred winter season, myths could not be enacted, performed—rattlesnakes might come. But myths could be quoted. Seeing a coyote cross the road, a Wasco might say, *"Wálu gnúXt"* (I'm hungry), something Coyote says in myths. That would be for the pleasure of it. But mention of a story might have moral application. Cibecue Apache place names commonly identify a story, and one can simply name a place and have that name recall a moral relevant to someone present.[2]

It is part of Gary's accomplishment to have broken with the sentimental and stereotypical. The quotations allow Indian voices to speak for themselves. Of course the frame, the integration, is his, just as Native American authors today draw on traditions, their own and others, in new works. It is understandable that some should argue that only Native Americans should write about Native Americans, use Native American traditions. Gary has been explicitly attacked on this score. A flip answer is, okay, we won't use anything Indian, don't you use anything that isn't. A serious answer is that a world in which traditions are exclusive property—Chinese literature exclusively the property of the Chinese, French of the French, Greek of the Greeks, all others stay out, would be a world of cultures as fortresses, of compartments at a time when human beings need to unite. And understanding is a dialectic. Outsiders miss what insiders intuitively grasp; insiders miss what they take for granted, or cannot observe. Either perspective alone is inevitably partial, inevitably biased. And one sad consequence of history is that a good part of Native American tradition (and ancient tradition elsewhere) is now accessible only through scholarship. The understandings that informed it at its origin and as it flourished are recoverable only through study of what remains, texts—a time-consuming study that few care for and few have opportunity to pursue. Those of us who work in scholarly ways to "liberate" the poetic form of narratives from the arbitrary paragraphs in which they have been entombed are attempting to restore them to descendants, who can take pride in the ancestral heritage, and to give them currency to others, who can learn respect. Sometimes one can indeed bring to life submerged voices, those of women.[3]

III

An essential way to be true to the traditions, then, is to enable elements of them to enter world literature, become active, echo within its aural montage, tapestry, as elements of Western precedent and tradition do. That Gary found a way to do this is a remarkable, insufficiently noted achievement.

And it fits the situation of many Indian people he and I have known. Much survived the initial onslaught of disease and dislocation, and even sustained efforts to suppress "savage" languages and traditions, as long as the languages were spoken at home, the children were there to hear them, and the way of life was close to home. Still, the twentieth century has seen steady erosion, especially where numbers have been few. In later life an old man at Warm Springs might remember of a myth a graphic vignette. Here is something a Wasco, Hiram Smith, told me the summer of 1951, when Gary and I were both first at Warm Springs. Let's call these three lines "Bat and Eagle."[4]

> Ats'íqula kwápt gakdúgwi itxúdlit iqaínuL báma
> *Bat then took tobacco smoke*
> Kwapt Ich'ínun akdíluxwa ishiaǵchba
> *Then she put it in Eagle's nose*

Daxka dáuda ángi iyaGwámniL gáliXuX
It was with this he kept his heart (kept alive).[5]

In the myths and texts that Gary has read there is sometimes a captured father, hung in an enemy's lodge to die. Someone small enough not to be easily seen, and able to be high, does something to preserve him. Here it is to give tobacco, a spiritual substance. His sons, or brother, sometimes disguised as women of the house, rescue him at last. This image alone would let us know the story was told among the Wasco.[6]

A few lines may sometimes be all there is, the whole story: why Robin mourns in spring and what he says, what Butterball Duck and his wife sing about each other. I think what Mr. Smith told me about "Grasshopper" the summer of 1954 (a summer Gary and my wife and I passed each other on the Mount Hood road) is such a whole.

Wilx gachígalq
The earth burned
Bila bila bila bila gaqLlchmaqwaX
They heard someone whooping, 'Bila bila bila bila'
Qúshdiaxa Ich'ílaq
It was the Grasshopper
Kwapt galik 'áLXiwélx ik'ánanámshtaq
Then he climbed up a weed
Qidáuba palalai Ich'ilaquksh kwadau ìtsnL'áXL'aXuks dáuyaba
                              wígwa wílxba
*   That's why there are plenty of jumping and flying*
*   grasshoppers on earth today*

Mr. Smith explained:

> "'Bila bila bila bila' is a sort of whoop
>   like that of a man getting on a bucking horse
>   who think's he's going to ride it.
> "Here it means
>   that Grasshopper is running away from the fire
>   and knows he's going to make it."

You may have noticed that the number of lines in "Bat and Eagle" is three, and in "Grasshopper" five, and that even the number of phrases in the explanation is five; that's not an accident. Wascos organize stories that way. And it is more than counting out, or a way of remembering. Each sequence comes to a point. If it has three parts, the first is a setting or onset of action, the second an onset or ongoing, the third an outcome. If it has five parts, the third is a pivot, an outcome to the two that precede, an onset to the two that follow. All this serves the principle of style that Kenneth Burke long ago called the arousal and satisfying of expectation. It works at every level of a story. Even quite long myths have an architecture built up that way. Sequences of lines become part of sequences of stanzas, stanzas part of scenes and acts. Finding this out, finding out how a story works in this regard, is more than finding an external framework. It can be a way of discovering meanings that might otherwise be missed. Poetic form and the teller's point go hand in hand. Poetic form is a guide to understanding.

I believe Gary would agree, and I would like to share a short myth for which this has proven true just this past month. The core of the discovered form is appropriate to Gary; so is the image of Coyote.

The figure of Coyote is so attractive to many of us today that we may overlook the limitations that Indian people often placed on him and other tricksters (such as Mink among the Lushootseed Salish of Washington State). Often there are situations in myths in which someone has a song Coyote cannot learn, or Coyote gets a song he cannot keep, or has others sing only so he can pretend to doctor a girl. There is just one Oregon myth I know in which Coyote truly cures. Its discovered form shows that he does so in six steps, three of separation, three of integration. That dialectic, sorting out what is genuine, then making it a living whole, seems true to Gary. So does the image of a trickster who can truly revitalize, out of ashes renew life.

A word about the myth. Almost everything we know about the myths of the Clackamas, who lived near Oregon City, Oregon, comes from one woman, Victoria Howard. In 1929 Clackamas was thought to be extinct. A linguist from the University of Washington, Melville Jacobs, a man who devoted himself to recording the traditions of Northwest peoples in their own languages, discovered that Howard was fluent in Clackamas, and worked with her in what proved to be the last months of her life. Her mother's father had been a Molale, and she heard this story from him. He did not remember the plot of the story, how the resuscitation came about.

What he did remember was the mighty act, and Coyote finding it
within his power. That is what we now can know too.

Shaman Coyote doctored[7]

[Preamble]

My mother's father made a myth.
He would say,
  "I think Coyote lived there.
  "Some friend of his got burned,
    completely,   5
      he became just coals."

[I] [Friend burned to coals]

Probably his friend and he lived there.
Now I do not know what got to them,
  it killed them.
Coyote was *not* set afire,   10
  just his friend was set afire,
    all of him turned to coals,
    just coals.

[II][i][Separation]
(A)

Pretty soon Coyote came to.
Now he saw his friend is all burned up.   15
He thought,
  "I suppose I am a shaman.
  "Let me try to doctor him."

(B)

He gathered up the coals,
  and collected the ashes, the bones.   20
I suppose he made things for his heart,
  his lung,
    his liver.
These things now he covered over.

(C)

He sat.   25
He painted his face,

one side of his face he made black,
    one side he made it grey

Now he sang,   (D)
    he said,   30
        "*Kohlen! Trennen Sie!* [Coals! Separate!]
        "*Kohlen! Trennen Sie!* [Coals! Separate!]
Five times.

He rested.   (E)
He uncovered them,   35
    he looked at them:
        the bones are something a little different.
                             [ii][Separation 2]
He covered the ashes and coals.
Now again he sang,
        "*Kohlen! Trennen Sie!* [Coals! Separate!]   40
    "Ha ha ha ha ha ha ha."
Five times.
He rested.
He uncovered them:
Now the ashes and coals *are* different.   45
                           [iii][Separation 3]
He thought,
    "Good indeed, I suppose I *am* a shaman."
        He covered them.
Now again he doctored.
He sang again five times.   50
He rested,
    he uncovered them.
        "Dear me!"
Now the bones are different,
    the ashes and coals are different.   55
                      [III][i][Integration]
Now he was glad.
    he covered them.
Now again he doctored them,
    he sang.

The fifth time he rested.   60
He uncovered them:
    "Dear me!"
Now the bones are joined,
        his entire body.

                                          [ii][Integration 2]
He thought,   65
    "*Now!* Now I shall make him get up."
He covered it.
Now again he sang,
        he doctored.
The fifth time he uncovered it.   70
    "Dear me!"
Now the person's body is whole.

                                          [iii][Integration 3]
Again he covered him.
        He sang five times.
            He rested.   75
                He uncovered him.
                    Now he had revived that person.

                                                    [Close]
I do not recall,
        perhaps that was a woman,
            perhaps a man.

                                                             80
Now I recall only that much of it.

NOTES

    1. At that time he also had me invited to contribute to *Rhinozeros* (1961) a
pair of spontaneous parodies, as it turned out, put also into German by the ed-
itor, Rolf-Gunter Dienst, in the company of Gary himself, Phil Whalen, Mike
McClure, David Meltzer, Ed Dorn, Anselm Hollo, Robert Kelly, Larry Eigner,
Ginsberg, Orlovsky, Corso, and others; and to Tom Raworth's journal,
Outburst.

    2. There is more about when one quotes myths, and when one can perform
them, at the end of my paper "Two types of linguistic relativity," in William
Bright, ed., *Sociolinguistics* (The Hague: Mouton, 1966). What the Apache do
is sensitively explained by Keith Basso in his paper "Stalking with stories:

Names, places and moral narratives among the Western Apache," in Edward Bruner, ed., *Text, Play and Story: The Construction and Reconstruction of Self and Society* (Washington, D.C.: American Ethnological Society, 1984).

3. One Clackamas Chinook tragedy of mother-daughter confrontation has now been included in a feminist anthology, along with two texts with a rediscovered pattern of ironic exchange about whites: Victoria Howard, "Seal and her younger brother lived there," in Marian Arkin and Barbara Sholar, eds., *Longman Anthology of WORLD Literature by WOMEN 1875–1975* (White Plains, New York: Longman, Inc.), 106–9.

4. Wasco has some sounds that English does not. x is like the "ch" in German *Ich*, X like the "ch" in German *Ach*; G and q are g and k made further back in the mouth, at about the same place as X; ' is a catch of the vocal chords like that in the middle of "oh-oh," L is the sound of Welsh "Ll" in "Lloyd" (rather like "th" in "thin" but with the tongue pressing one side of the mouth); an acute accent with e underneath it has a sound like the e in "butter" or "towel."

5. The Wasco words say "that this (the tobacco) (emphatic) his-heart (that is, life) it-was, became." Mr. Smith said in English, "She kept him alive."

6. A version of the myth told in the related Clackamas dialect indicates that smoke nourished the father because he had a fire spirit-power (Melville Jacobs, "Fire and his son's son," *Clackamas Chinook Texts, Part 1, International Journal of American Linguistics* 24 [2] [April 1958]; and *Clackamas Chinook Texts, Part II*, Bloomington: Indiana University Press, p. 125). But the father is not Eagle; Eagle, prominent in Wasco, does not figure in any Clackamas myth known to us. And in the Clackamas version, when the two sons approach the enemy place, they encounter grizzlies. Mr. Smith told that part of the myth as a scene in which one son uses power that flashes from his eye to wither the mouths of each of five named fish, messengers sent by the chief who holds their father. Their mouths today reflect the number of fingers each had inserted in its mouth (one, two, three, four, or five). (That part entertained two Wasco ladies at Warm Springs, Adeline Morrison and Viola Kalama, some years ago, so much so that Mrs. Kalama last summer asked again for a copy of it.) The noted folklorist Jeremiah Curtin recorded a version of the story in English at Warm Springs in 1885, one that has interesting details as to the gambling that leads to the father's death, his gradual dismemberment, and his eventual restoration ("Eagle, A Klamath man, goes to the Columbia River to gamble," in "Wasco Tales and Myths," published in Edward Sapir, *Wishram Texts* (Leyden: Publications of the American Ethnological Society 2, 1909). This version has only a father's head on a pole, lacking the poignant image of a father barely alive, fed by smoke by small creatures. It has messengers whose faces are burned, but none are identified; there is no indication of a consequence for the burning, and that it happens to five is simply stated; there is no dramatization of each in turn. What Mr. Smith recalled, then, is distinct: a realization in the Indian language itself, seventy years

later, the language then nearly gone; a recalling of images of specific persons in sharply etched scenes.

7. The text and original translation are in Jacobs, *Clackamas Chinook Texts, Part II*, pp. 433–4. I have revised the translation, worked out the organization of the lines, and supplied headings. Coyote sings the first song in Molale. German seems a way of getting an analogous effect. Probably there was a second song, maybe "Bones! Join up!"

Stanley Diamond:
PRIMITIVE AFTERWORD

Dear Gary,

We have known each other for a quarter of a century—not very long in the life of a clan, a redwood sapling, the memory of bears, but an achievement among the time-bound creatures of our brutally signifying society. And since we have written to each other over the years, I thought it would be a good idea to continue our correspondance, putting what I intend to be my final reflection on the primitive in a letter to you in your honor.

Over the years we have both been under attack for our complementary critiques of contemporary civilization, and our efforts to enter into the spirit of primitive, kinship, tribal, communal, sacred peoples. All poets worth their salt have felt a particular affinity with the Crow, the Eskimo, the Ibo, the Jivaro, with all aboriginal identities. It has been noted time and again that primitive people speak poetry; poetry is the language of their everyday life, of their visions, of their rituals, of their created realities. And any poet worth his salt knows that in our society this poetry has become the suppressed common language of humanity, as the bureaucratic mythology of sheer signification, and denotation, takes over. Plato was too modest; he wrote not only for a thousand years, but through the present, into our future.

We have been called "romantic," as a kind of epithet. The word itself is appropriate but, as you know, it is consistently misused almost as a reflex by the pragmatic, hard-headed critics who could just as well be writing about the universal and progressive movement of the Chase Manhattan Bank to #1 Karl Marx Square, Moscow.

Since memory is shriveling everywhere, as data banks increase, I suppose I should take a fling at defining "romantic" in its traditional resonance and basic anthropological significance. Rousseau, and the German romantic historians, were probably the "originators" of the romantic movement, which ran its course from the late eighteenth century to the mid-nineteenth. Rousseau's percept of pity—sensing, and responding to, the inwardness of the other—was integral to the focus of many writers of the romantic period on (oral) poetry, folk music, and local customs, and thus to their growing distrust of the mechanical certainties and complex constraints of industrial civilization. They rejected the formulation of merely abstract "truths." In Germany the romantic movement, in part influenced by the French, in part innovative, paid close attention to history, and insisted that no historian could neglect the actual experience of people in everyday life in a given time and place. Empathy was the key concept here also; imagining oneself in the other person's place became a common denominator for historical inquiry from that time on.

What is amusing about this is that anthropology itself emerges from the romantic movement—"participant observation" (behaving like, hence "knowing" the other), the dominant field method, would be fully understood by Herder and was, in fact, recommended by Rousseau. Moreover, the romantic consciousness was opposed to all forms of elitism, whether aristocratic, or classical, or meritocratic, or ethnic. Individuals were to be respected as such, revolutions were eventually to be fought in the name of so-called ordinary people and, as a minor development, anthropology emerged focusing on the oppressed, the tribal, the peasantry, and the poor. Of course, the imperialist opportunism of the academic discipline typically obscured, and continues to obscure, its romantic, transformative genesis.

So the disparaging use of "romantic" is a kind of self-devouring, a genuflection to the moribund temper of contemporary industrial civilization. Nonetheless, every poet worth her salt knows that the weakness in the romantic tradition was not, and could not be, expressed by academic opponents. What was lacking was the perception of transcendence.

It is perhaps worth noting, in a rather different vein, that the medieval church had condemned romantic love (illegitimate passion)— and its resultant iconization of the beloved—as a Christian heresy, a deflection from the love of God. But these points are not made by our critics, who consistently confuse the romantic with the merely sentimental, or the idyllic, or the absurdly visionary, even the dishonest, and so on.

The opposition to the use of the term "primitive," which epitomizes our (at least my) critics' attitudes, was originally generated by the fear of anthropologists concerning what was conceived to be the derogatory implications of the word for the people so designated.

The actual meaning of the term is "primary," but it was assumed that primitive meant inferior, immature, undeveloped. In the second generation following Boas, himself a romantic in the spacious sense of the term, in reality a romantic scientist, such anthropologists were haunted by their own ethnocentrism, and their inadvertent admission of it by the psychological loading of a perfectly innocent term. An aspect of this particular objection was the refusal to acknowledge radical cultural/historical differences with stateless peoples through the whole period prior to the development of civilization, and of course thereafter. That is, human nature was, after all, human nature; hence the focus on culture, as normatively defined and/or as the basis of distinctively human, continuously creative, reciprocating/symbolic behavior declined. Invariably, or so it seems, the scholars who waged this semantic war were politically conservative, and well entrenched behind the conventional defenses of their discipline.

But more recently, something approaching an assault has been regenerated against the uses and meanings of the term as a fundamental concept. This is more interesting, because it is more complex, and even more revealing. The argument runs as follows:

Primitive people no longer exist; they have long since been incorporated—beginning at least in the fifteenth century—into the imperial civilization of the West, both directly and indirectly. Hence to speak of them in the ethnological present is to distort history unconscionably, disregard the monolithic character of the modern world and, some would add, do the people under consideration no good, because their existences are being both misrepresented and reified. However, I should note parenthetically that none of these systems theorists has worked extensively, if at all, with tribal, kin-organized, or primitive peoples, and thus they limit themselves to universals, and/or the expression of progressivist determinations. Despite the arguments from history, there is a peculiar lack of historical perspective.

The basic focus on primitive peoples in the history of anthropology has many dimensions. The most obvious is, of course, the imperial encounter wherein anthropologists have played an ambiguous role. On the one hand, they have frequently served the imperial metropole, as, for example, in England, the Soviet Union, France, and the United States; on the other hand, many anthropologists have attempted to learn from their experiences, and have returned, as Rousseau admonished, more critically aware of the flaws, more than flaws, the lack of human grounding of their own civilization. It is for this reason that primitive societies have most often been defined, comparatively, by absences or omissions such as "no developed division of labor," "no formal educational structures," and so on; anthropologists have lacked a disciplinary language and the cultural experience to define their positive attributes. Here, as Evans-Pritchard pointed out, the poet, or the poetics of anthropology, becomes necessary.

Significant, also, is the way in which these distinctions have been contextualized in anthropology, reflecting the more general, both conscious and unconscious, obsession of Western civilization with the multifarious, often projective notions of the primitive. Even the most accomplished British social anthropologists, who ordinarily have little truck with culture (reminiscent of the new anticultural wave in American anthropology) in their bread-and-butter academic work, are quite capable of collaborating in a book edited by Evans-Pritchard, *The Institutions of Primitive Society,* which adds up to a critique of Western civilization along the full range of sociocultural phenomena. Here they sound surprisingly like Boas and the generation that followed him, among them Radin, Lowie, Jules Henry, Gene Weltfish, and others. One concludes that inherent in the anthropological undertaking is this restlessness and dissatisfaction concerning the character of civilized existence.

I cannot separate anthropology from the situations of anthropologists, at least as most of them have existed throughout the history of the discipline. For the realized notion of the primitive is normative; it leads to a denial of the possibility of aggressively knowing the other as an object, that is, of scientifically knowing the other—in Auden's usage, of controlling the other.

The knowledge of any particular primitive society arises from the conscious and unwitting questions asked by the ethnologist. So the notion of there being an absolute truth of primitive existence out there is a Cartesian illusion and, sometimes, a competitive, "positivistic" falsehood. One cannot become a Crow, or an Anaguta—that would demand the experience of a lifetime. But one can turn the questions asked of the Crow or Anaguta back upon the agent, and that, of course, is the great strength of critical anthropology: to know ourselves against the ground of the other, relearning something of the necessities of a human existence while at the same time struggling against the imperialization of the people from whom we have learned; and to demand that they have the right to choose their own paths through our contemporary chaos.

Such an anthropology is also the source of what Ernst Bloch called, in a different context, revolutionary hope. It was certainly the basis for Marx's perspective on socialism—indeed, for the whole socialist movement in its necessarily utopian telos, whether acknowledged or not. As Engels put it to the German Social Democrats in 1891, disturbed as they were by the notion of a dictatorship of the proletariat: "Look at the Paris Commune, the Paris Commune, that's what Marx and I meant by the dictatorship of the proletariat."

There are, after all, only two ways of looking at transformative history: either through the excavation of the past as a dialectical process (utopian), or as an intensified projection of the present (dystopic), from William Morris to Zamiatin. The difference between these two views can be politically defined: Conservatives and fatalists of all varieties scant the dialectical potential of the political process, ranging through structuralism, mechanical materialism, and idealism (vide, for example, Spengler), through the new varieties of world-systematizers, deny the possibilities of transformational change, not infrequently assuming a permanently negative definition of human nature, and/or a metaphysically based ahistorical evolutionary determinism.

Yet, the strong focus on matters primitive in the arts, in literature, and among critical anthropologists retains its force. Indeed, it would hardly be possible to be a socialist in the absence of that historical grounding; or, I would go further, to have faith in a human future.

Moreover, the overall division between primitive and civilized has served as the governing paradigm for modern social science in general. The principles involved in the constitution of these paradigms have been either positivist/progressivist, or dialectical/dialogical/critical. That is, speaking ideationally, a dialectical thinker within the academy may be interesting but remains bounded by the prevailing thrust of social inquiry. Who, then, are the architects, and what is the terminology of this grand division that has so haunted the West, whether positivist or dialectical?: Durkheim (sacred-secular), Weber (bureaucratic-traditional), Kroeber (folk-sophisticate), Redfield (moral-legal-technical), L. H. Morgan (kin-civil), Tonnies (community-society), Maine (kin-territorial–contractual), Radin (primitive-civilized), Marx and Engels (primitive-civilized), and so on.

Of course, some of these scholars have omitted the middle term, namely the state formative process, in which the local community maintained its identity albeit tempered by the very effort to sustain itself against the predatory thrust of the emerging central power. Still others, such as Benedict, Linton, and Sapir, have emphasized that the proper focus of anthropology is the local group, the community, the place where people live. But in the megalopolitan West, it is increasingly difficult to discover where people live, since they are working, and perhaps trying to live, in industrial, business, government, or educational collectives of one form or another, mistaking the *Gesellschaft* for a *Gemeinschaft* or at least hoping to convert the former into the latter as a desperate expression of their needs. All dystopias have been based on this latter process. Big Brother is after all not so far from Uncle Sam or the motherland or the fatherland.

Hence, there is one dynamic that has been largely neglected in defining the primitive. It is one thing to assume that specific societies have been irrevocably changed and their cultures rendered moribund. But it is quite another to claim that the process of primitive formation and reformation no longer exists. For even in the face of imperial control, a dialectical response is evident almost everywhere. Every sodality, voluntary grouping, fraternal effort at mutual aid, every organization that implicitly or otherwise protests the exploitation built into class-split, labor-fragmented, state societies, is a renewal of the initial communal challenge that primitive organization held for the bureaucratic state as states developed. And I must add finally that the multiple pathologies and addictions of this society, which hardly need be mentioned here, serve as displacements for the grief and frustrations of untold numbers of people as culture is reduced to the mechanics of production and reproduction, approaching, as Kroeber strangely understood, the dead repetitiveness of merely social acts. Still, one senses in its supposed absence the striving for a renaissance of a communal, yet individuated, existence, a primitive existence, a poetic existence.

Such visions and needs will continue to transform the lives of individuals, and eventually, if we are to survive, of society.

Your work has illuminated these matters, Gary of the wilderness.

Thomas Buckley:

FIXING THE WORLD

Julian Lang, a Karuk Indian from northwestern California, told me about the *pikyaavis,* the "world-making" or "world-fixing" at Katimin, on the Klamath River. He said, "As Indians, we don't have many responsibilities, but one of them is to fix the world." Julian is a noted ceremonial singer, and he talked from a singer's point of view about *pikyaavis* and other dances that the Karuks and the neighboring Yuroks and Hupas put up to fix the world. As part of the Karuk ritual, men go out and shoot arrows at a target tree. By doing this the men wake up the spirit in the tree and get its attention so that they can talk with it. Julian compared dance singing to this:

> You're singing an old song, you're singing so hard because you know it's an old song and it's older than anybody living right now and what you're singing is something that means you can connect people with that oldest time, the oldest thing that you know or that you come to know and that you believe in. So then you're drawing them back to a point. So if there are doctors amongst them then maybe that will spark that power, and they could be some kinds of singers themselves. Sometimes you see little kids that are sitting there just in awe at what's going on around the dance-making, all the [regalia] laid out, and they're looking at it. And you look at them and you can see—hey! This little kid may grow up to be somebody. And just having it out there. . . . The whole idea of displaying that stuff is to spark people inside . . . if that power is in there sleeping inside them. . . . In the ceremony you're waking up those people, that power inside the people, so when that wakes up and it looks at that stuff and it sees all that kinship, pretty soon it wants to go into that stuff again and it wants to participate in that stuff, and it turns the people back into Indians.

Indirectly, I first came to the Klamath River country and the Native peoples there because of Gary Snyder's writing. His poems and essays serve time and again to wake us up, to call us back into the fullness of our humanity. In my own case I have come to see the world in ways that are now inextricably bound up with reading Gary's work for all of my adult life.

In 1960 I was eighteen and so green I didn't know that my current hero, Japhy Ryder, in Kerouac's *The Dharma Bums,* was a real guy named Gary Snyder. I was in Cambridge, Massachusetts, and I'd found The Grolier Book Shop in Harvard Square. In the glass door there was a hand-lettered sign that said "NO TEXTBOOKS." The walls of the small room were lined shoulder high with shelves of poetry, novels, and criticism, some of it already musty and seemingly passé—James Branch Cabell, John Galsworthy, Edna St. Vincent Millay, Christopher Morley. Yet what I remember far more clearly is the big table that stood in the middle of the shop, stacked with obscure little magazines and wild-looking new books by poets I'd never yet heard of. I remember Philip Whalen, Diane diPrima, books from The Pocket Poets Series, and a little yellow book of translations from the Chinese. And there was, one winter afternoon, a small blue volume bound in the Japanese manner that I liked just because of its cover: It was Gary's *Riprap.* Opening it randomly I read about bucking hay, a poem that I knew to be true by my own summers' experience on eastern dairy farms. And I read about forgetting about reading, and yearned for it:

> I cannot remember things I once read
> A few friends, but they are in cities.
> Drinking cold snow-water from a tin cup
> Looking down for miles
> Through high still air.[1]

Clear as a bell, familiar as coming home; I'd found a friend and a guide, a sensibility: Japhy Ryder himself.

I sat away whole winters in The Grolier, with the owner, Gordon Cairnie, a fine old gentleman, on his saggy brown leather couch, talking, listening to the radio, finding some warmth in cold New England. That was where I first heard that John F. Kennedy had been shot, rushing in off the street with the rumor, Gordon turning on the radio, aghast. I didn't last much longer in Cambridge after that. I went West, headed for the high, still air, the clarity I'd found in the small blue book of poems, like no others I'd seen.

•   •   •

It is not easy to fix the world, to fully inhabit the ancient place, "Earth House Hold," as Gary Snyder calls it; to do what he calls "the real work."

On the last day of the Jump Dance at Pecwan, on the Klamath River in September of 1988, the temperature stays above 100 degress Fahrenheit for the seventh day in a row. Even the spectators who are attached to the two feasting camps fast that day, not just the dancers and dance-makers and medicine men. Only children eat breakfast, though the rest have coffee, and the adults drink no water, just a bit of thin acorn soup to wet the mouth and throat. Maybe a hundred people are there. In the hours before sunset the heat hangs in the river canyon and presses down on the dancers in the house-pit, trapping the woodsmoke laden with the heavy scent of burning angelica root together with the fire's heat. When two girls come into the pit to dance for the Sregon side they are dressed in heavy shell-hung deerskin skirts and wear tens of dentalia necklaces, maybe thirty pounds of dance stuff each. They stand patiently at the ends of the line of singers and dancers in the heat and smoke until one crumples to the dirt floor with a great clatter, in a dead faint. And then everyone has to know what the singers and dancers have known all week: Fixing the world is not easy. It is something that you *do*.

In the Klamath River canyon at Pecwan the choppers from the Campaign Against Marijuana Planting (CAMP) shatter the afternoon sky. On the forested sidehills automatic weapons' fire adds punctuation. Occasional cars pass by slowly on the narrow road. In the dance-house pit the singing goes on, the two lead singers' ineffably sad songs overlapping and weaving each other, bound together by the slow chorus.

Outsiders have come to the river to grow high-grade marijuana. They hired local people to work for them and also brought in motorcycle gangs as mercenaries to guard the herb patches, and the bikers set up methedrine labs and people used that stuff until they called Weitchpec "the little town that never sleeps," and there were murders. The helicopters came and people practiced with assault rifles in the hills: trying to fix the world in every which way.

On the last day of the Pecwan Jump Dance I sit with some dancers by the river in the shade of a camper. An osprey rises high over the riffle, then dives in a flash of buff feathers and spray and the silver of a writhing fish as it rises again.

"It's hard to be an Indian," says Julian Lang. Gary writes,

> rattlesnake nose-pits
> sense heat
>   "See" the heart in a
>   mouse
>   beating;
>   strike for the meat.[2]

—the "original vow."

• • •

I traveled the length of Nebraska at least thirty times, measured it out by foot, bus, car, truck, thumb, and airplane. In 1969 my first wife and I came back east in a beat-up Microbus, a broadside of Gary's "Smokey the Bear Sutra" ("may be reproduced free forever") taped inside a back window. We stopped for a burger somewhere in Wyoming and came out of the joint to find a tall, leathery, middle-aged man in blue jeans by the bus, hands on hips, reading. Done, he turned around to greet us with a gap-toothed smile. "Wa'll," he said, "That just about says it all, don't it?"

Back and forth, northeast, northwest. At the mouth of the Klamath River one summer in the late seventies, I was with a Yurok elder, Dewey George, who was advising the folks there on the south side regarding a Brush Dance that was coming up. Earlier I'd made a little money and picked up a four-wheel-drive International Harvester Travelall, and it was parked on the river bar. Some young Indian guys came walking by, joking. One of them looked at the chrome logo on my truck, looked at me, said to his buddy "Oh yeah—he travels *aaallll* around," and they walked off, laughing.

Gary's books had been like cairns along the trail, telling me I was still on course or, at least, if I was lost I was in good company. Now they were telling me something a little different, or I was hearing them differently, or maybe it was just age. Anyway, ten years ago, I stayed east on a family place, on Cape Cod, in Massachusetts. I'd happened to find a job near there and there I was, next to Bean Pond. The place measures 3.7 acres, and it's enough, overgrown with cedar scrub and poison ivy when I got back. I walked behind a Gravely tractor cutting brush, picked up the wing feather of a yellow shafted flicker by the shop, thought across the ten thousand things as found

there: water lilies, bladderwort, mullein, sweet pepperbush, shad-
bush, winterberry, broom crowberry. "Too green," said Georgia
O'Keeffe, and turned back for Texas. "Too far," I thought, finally, and
stayed home. The land itelf, mostly sand, moves on, no more than
fifteen thousand years since the last ice left it here. The lot map
doesn't come anywhere close to mentioning the grasses the Gravely
cuts. Like the man in the first poem that I read in *Riprap,* thirty years
ago,

> "I first bucked hay when I was seventeen."

In upstate New York, reading Kerouac and dreaming of California . . .

> "I thought, that day I started,
> I sure would hate to do this all my life.
> And dammit, that's just what
> I've gone and done."[3]

And how lonely it would have been, doing it without Gary Snyder's
impeccable, diamond-bright, and compassionate company.

NOTES

1. Gary Snyder, "Mid-August at Sourdough Mountain Lookout," in *Riprap,*
Ashland: Origin Press, 1959.

2. Gary Snyder, "Original Vow," in *Left Out in the Rain,* San Francisco:
North Point Press, 1986.

3. Gary Snyder, "Hay for the Horses," in *Riprap,* Ashland: Origin Press,
1959.

The author thanks John Balaban and Louisa Solano for their help on the present
essay.

Ron Scollon:

SNYDER'S CULTURE

It is hard to say when I first met Gary Snyder. For some years I told the story that the first time I ran across Gary Snyder we didn't exactly meet. The way the story went, I was in the Blue Moon in Seattle having a few beers with a philosopher friend who'd been at Michigan when I was there, before I dropped out: Morrey Starsky. I'd just come back from a trip to Japan in which I'd spent all my money and not learned very much. Some people in a booth across the aisle were becoming more noticeable as the evening went on and finally one of them stood up. He had been urged by the others to give an impromptu reading of a few poems by Theodore Roethke. Roethke had just died.

I asked my friend who this was reading the poems. Starsky told me it was a guy who sometimes worked the merchant marine and who came around sometimes, a poet named Gary Snyder. And so my first image of Gary was of him honoring another poet. In my mind I had first seen and heard him through the poems of Roethke, and for many years after that I read Roethke and heard what I thought of as Gary's voice in my mind's ear. It was only later that I came to know Gary in the voice of his own poems and even later before I came to know his voice in the *ceilidh*, that old Celtic tradition of staying up late with tea or whiskey and telling stories and singing songs until no one can think of any new ones.

Unfortunately, like many stories, while this could have been true, it wasn't. At the time I was in the Blue Moon Gary was in Japan and there is no telling now who that poet was I heard reading back then.

The resistance of this story to modification by the truth lies in the fact that there are many ways of knowing Gary Snyder and his work. A couple of summers ago we sat around at Kathleen Lake in Canada's Kluane National Park in the highest corner of Canada's Yukon: Gary and his son Gen, their long-time friend and poet Nanao Sakaki, Dick Dauenhauer—at the time Poet Laureate of Alaska—my wife Suzie, and our kids Rachel and Tommy. Those nights are long in summer and as the sun worked its way around just under the northern horizon we worked our way through a certain amount of spirits and many, many of the old camp songs. Gary, like the rest of us, was a kid once and his mind got loaded up with some of the same corny songs the rest of us had learned.

All the way from the high seriousness of his public work to the low fun of kid-songs lies the contribution of Gary Snyder to twentieth-century culture. *Culture.* There's a word to look at more closely, because one of the most important aspects of Gary's work— and by work I mean to include not just the poems and the essays and the interviews that have been published and the readings of his own writing and that of others; I also mean to include the talk from small conversations to colossal *ceilidhs* lasting for days—one of the most important aspects of Gary's work has been to get us all to think again about the idea of culture.

Culture. The people who read poems are certainly cultured. For some time that's been a kind of hallmark of the cultured person in the society based historically in Northern Europe—China and the rest of Asia, too. Gary's contribution there has been considerable, with more than half a dozen books of poems in print, one with a Pulitzer Prize.

Yet much of Gary's work has set that idea of culture into a frame. The poems themselves treat topics at a long remove from the book-lined study and the graduate library: getting the wood in, fixing the old Willys, merchant-marine labor, picking mushrooms, logging, mountain climbing, wilderness exploration. Much of the substance of Gary's poems is found in the daily work of keeping our society and our earth going, maybe even restoring some health here and there where we can.

So the cultivation built into this idea of culture isn't the mono-culture of the refined aesthetic and linguistic judgment; it's the cultivation of the ordinary life most of us live, or if we don't live it ourselves, it's the life of those whose work allows the others to get out of doing it. Gary has said that we live in a culture bent on trying to get out of doing our work.

Gary's poems are an interesting example of day-to-day culture that walks right into the study to remind us that the work is still going on outside. But notice: He took off his boots at the door and washed his hands and face. He reminds us of the work but still respects the quiet of contemplation. Work is one way, study is another. The point is not to lie to yourself about what you're doing or about what those inside or outside are doing either. This is "the real work"—doing what you're doing honestly, not being elsewhere in your mind all the time.

Culture. Anthropologists have used the word, too. For them the word is almost an opposite to the idea of high culture. Culture is what everybody has; it's how you talk about the distinctiveness of a people. American culture these days in the anthropological sense has almost no room for high culture. American culture is fast food, thirty channels of TV, *USA Today,* gun violence, and all the rest. But more often the anthropologists' word *culture* is used for the others they've tried to understand. For Gary those have been the indigenous peoples of the world, starting with the Haida and other North American cultures of the Pacific Coast of Turtle Island. Gary's idea here is simple, direct, and very effective: If you want to know the life of the land in a place (and you should), learn it from the people who have lived there long enough to know it, to name it, to sing about it, to eat its plants, berries, animals, and fish; people who have been there long enough to know and worship its sacred places and to mourn for their loss.

Culture in this meaning isn't a monocultural rarification of possibilities for a place; it is not specialization; it isn't cutting out all the weeds and putting up a fence, scaring off the birds and small animals and putting a lot of junk on the soil so you can get one isolated species to grow there. Culture in this sense is paying attention to what grows up when you don't do anything, eating what comes when you don't interfere; it's making yourself ready for the wildness of a place.

So Gary in his work has led the way in reminding us that our earth, our Gaia, has a life—no, *is* a life—and the junk we're doing to her is not only lethal, it's very expensive. Real culture lies in getting back in tune, in learning what the earth and her people have been for all those years before we started up trying to change her so we can figure out how to slip a little more gracefully back into harmony.

These ideas are all around in his work, the poems, the interviews, the essays. He talks about these things when he reads, when he chats, when he climbs (in between little lectures on Restoration Drama when a 45-degree descent seems precipitous). You also don't get far into a chat with Gary without running into Asian culture. An early training in Classical Chinese as well as his Zen training have formed the context for the development of much of Snyder's thinking over the years.

I have had the interesting experience this past year of introducing Chinese graduate students of Western literature to Gary's poetry. It wasn't long before we ran across the *Cold Mountain* translations. In Taiwan this early T'ang dynasty poet, Han-shan, is not as widely known or read as I had thought, especially among students of Western literature, and it has been fun to watch these students of literature meet one of their own poets through the translations of Snyder.

Culture. What is it after all? A few years ago some of us in Alaska, with Gary Holthaus of the Alaska Humanities Forum as a prime instigator, started trying to get a fix on what the humanities might be these days. We asked Gary to help us give some thought to the question. Although it is hard to say just where we ought to draw lines, it seems pretty clear that in the West the humanities are all tied up with literacy. In the crudest formulation of the problem you could say that the National Endowment for the Arts funds people doing things (art), and the National Endowment for the Humanities funds people writing about them (humanities). But in Alaska many of our most thoughtful humanists are bearers of ancient Alaska Native traditions, traditions that until recently have not used writing. On the other end of the question a lot of people are asking whether the massive increase in electronic communication, especially television, might not signal the end of the humanities as we've known them.

We convened a series of meetings in which Gary figured in as one of the main discussants, and what we found him saying set a frame around our more ordinary concepts of the humanities and culture. It went something like this:

Consider that mankind has been about the same since the Neolithic right down until just recently. In other words, if you go out into the mountains to live for a while, your experience there (barring notice of your Gore-Tex and freeze-dried foods) is pretty much like most humans have known for twenty thousand or more years. And that common experience is primarily oral, not literate. We talk to each other, tell each other stories; we look around and read the signs of the clouds and winds or of the rocks and the overburden of earth; we watch for animals, tracks, and scat to learn who has been there before us or who might be around ready to pay a visit right then. Our main human interpretive activity has been this reading of signs and trying to make sense of our reading. That's been culture for most people who have ever lived and still is for many people now living. If we take that as the basic idea of culture, it's easier to see how things fit in, from Socrates to semiology, from the *Shih Ching* to television soaps. The stretch running in the West from Homer down to now is one—and just one—local, ethnic, maybe even brief manifestation of the human love for signs and their interpretation, and you can enjoy that fun whether you are writing critical papers or swapping stories around the evening fire after a hard day's hunt or climb; you can enjoy the fun whether you have the credentials earned in hard academic study or the credentials earned in a life of careful labor or hunting. None of us has an inside line on it, but some get better at it than others because they nurture their knowledge and take care of their tools.

So the culture and literacy of Gary Snyder is learning to read the signs around us, but not just any signs; his idea of culture is learning to pick out the voice of the Earth herself from among the chaos of signs. It's also learning how to speak to others living with us now and to those who come after us about our life on Earth now with its many illnesses. Snyder's idea of culture is turning toward healing this Earth's life as we continue trying to understand who and what we are.

—Providence College
Shalu, Taiwan
March 1989

Suzie Scollon:
GENUINE CULTURE

People have been bouncing around the Pacific Rim far longer than we give them credit for. Gary Snyder was the first one I heard about who went west from the Northeastern Pacific Rim to learn something and returned not only to tell about it but to put it into practice. Lloyd Reynolds, professor of art at Reed College, was one of the few faculty members who ever mentioned Asia. In his art history course he devoted as much time to East Asian as to European art. I had gone to college to get away from my Chinese family and the rest of the upwardly mobile Oriental community in Honolulu. So I was surprised but intrigued to hear Professor Reynolds talking about Right View, Right Practice, nirvana, the uncarved block, Sung Dynasty landscapes, ch'i. He also talked about Blake and the third eye, Zen in the art of archery, and the danger of overconceptualization. I still have the reading list he gave us.

From time to time he would talk about Gary Snyder, who had returned to the States after studying Zen in Japan and settled in the Sierra Nevada with his wife, Masa, and his son Kai. *Kai* meant "open," he said. He would bring this up often in connection with the single vision of people who perpetuated the war in Vietnam. Snyder thus became associated in my mind with the antithesis of warmongering tunnel vision.

The war made it difficult to concentrate on academic studies. Unwittingly under the influence of *The Dharma Bums,* which I only read many years later, I hitched up and down the coast and drove from coast to coast. Gary Snyder was a campus legend. As a new student, I wasn't on campus for two hours before being told by a guy with beautiful shoulder-length hair at the old coffee shop that Snyder had written half his senior thesis there. Finally, looking at the published version the other day, I find it's about a "swan maiden" tale like the one I ran into last year in Taiwan and the one my Korean students tell. They also tell about Tangun, their first ancestor, son of a heavenly prince and a bear who, by enduring many days confined in a cave with nothing to eat but garlic and chilies, became human.

When I first met Gary he was giving a reading in Fairbanks, talking about circumpolar bear legends. It was thirty below, and he read a poem with the lines,

> We could live on this Earth
> without clothes or tools!

"It seemed like a good idea in California," he explained. After a discourse on the deforestation of China, he asked, "When were you at Reed?"

"In the mid-sixties."

"Oh, that was the low point in the history of the college."

I hadn't thought about it that way, but it's true that the guys at that time were more concerned about avoiding the draft than anything. "No wonder Miss Kelly said we were resistant to learning. And there were a lot of drugs. But it wasn't all negative. People were reading your poetry and getting together to practice zazen. And dropping out to homestead in Canada." They were like mycelia, feeding on the detritus of the old culture underground, before mushrooming into communities more in tune with the Earth. After leaving Reed, I had been trying to make up for lost time by studying Chinese and Athabaskan linguistics.

As I traveled around the continent with very little money, cooking rice and lentils by Primus or campfire, I was playing out a trend started by Snyder and others decades before. It was a tradition passed on largely by word of mouth. When I drove up the Alaska Highway to meet Ron twenty years ago, I had a copy of *Earth House Hold* in my pack. I must admit I never opened it the whole trip.

Snyder's contribution to culture was only beginning to be felt, vaguely, by a generation dissatisfied by the postwar rush for prosperity—and a generation suspicious of the old culture found in books. I suspect Snyder's influence was spread as much by readings and talk as by print.

Culture. We had been using Sapir's article "Culture, Genuine and Spurious" to teach introductory courses in linguistics. I had been introduced to Sapir, Whorf, Hymes, and ethnobotany by David French, but it wasn't until I got to know Athabaskans that I had given any thought to genuine culture. And Athabaskan students didn't seem to have any trouble with the concept. In hunting and gathering cultures, all actions are integrated into a meaningful, harmonious whole. There is no waste, no pollution.

Gary Snyder has reminded us of the old meaning of cultivation of the soil, of plant and animal communities, as well as of development of the mental and physical abilities necessary for the maintenance of all of these in harmony with each other. We have become accustomed to thinking of culture in terms of human culture, whether "high" or "pop," especially what can be transmitted by high-tech recording. While Snyder is conversant with culture in this sense, what really interests him is not bits of culture that can be cataloged and acquired so much as mind-sets and worldviews that can help us heal the Earth.

He has had his antennae out for six decades, sensing the Earth and stars, the wisdom of the Muse, the lore of ethnobotanists, the mind pollution of schools and the media. Though the destruction of the Brazilian rainforest he wrote about in *Turtle Island* is now the subject of magazine cover stories, his prescription is not readily understood and is considered hard to swallow, especially by members of American minorities and developing countries that have been striving for a generation or more to overcome what they consider to be superstition and to enjoy the benefits of industrialization.

Genuine or real culture cultivates the health of the Earth in harmony with the minds and bodies of individuals, families, and communities. Real values in this culture are the health of the biosphere as well as of man. Work is valued for what it contributes to the health of the spirit, mind, body—of individual, family, sangha, nature, Earth.

Snyder's contribution to culture is his ability to distinguish between genuine and spurious, his insistence on Right View and Right Practice. His cultivation comes not only from the libraries, which he has called his grandparents, but from work at all levels of society in contact with soil, trees, rocks, machinery, people, ideas; with Nature original and unadulterated. He is not so much an anthropologist studying culture objectively as an agent of cultural evolution, a yogin putting into practice the collected wisdom of primitive and civilized people in the last forty thousand years, actively trying to overcome the narrow anthropocentric view of culture to include nonhuman life. He is interested in Turtle Island and other indigenous cultures as well as European and Asian civilization, not for the purpose of typology but as compost for a new civilization.

Ron and I were ourselves trying to salvage what we could of the five-hundred-year landfill operation, starting with Gutenberg's invention of the printing press. We had collected what we could of what was in print that would help us think about the world we lived in. In our living room we had assembled Snyder's books, books from Reynolds' reading list, collections of Alaska Native texts, books about language, philosophy, the media. We called the place The Gutenberg Dump.

I remember sitting by our woodstove at the Dump one night after Gary had done a reading sponsored by the Alaska Humanities Forum. It was a strange feeling. Our conversation ranged over linguistics, ecology, and I don't know what else. Gary was making notes about Sapir, using Chinese characters. He seemed to be some kind of embodiment of Lloyd Reynolds and my grandfather. I had never seen anybody using both alphabetic and Chinese calligraphy at the same time. He was salvaging from two ancient literate traditions, trying to understand the difference between wild and civilized language.

Gary was talking about getting higher up the information chain. The job of the poet is to take the work of information hunters such as linguists and anthropologists and digest it for human consumption. This is putting it too narrowly, of course. Though human beings must feed on the information, their processing of it affects the whole planet. And our waste is not all compostable or even combustible.

By working and traveling by foot, talking with people, Gary tries to expand his mind to approach the size of the Neanderthal's brain. Using himself as an informant, he lets mind weeds from all continents take root in the living organic matter of his late Neolithic-postindustrial mind. Living close to nature, he sifts through the contents of the old civilizations, seeing what takes root in the humus of the ground where he stands, what can be transplanted to the different regions he frequents.

He is interested in language not as a linguist describing the ecology of language, but in seeing what happens if you treat language as a wild, open, fluctuating system. What happens if you listen to the Earth instead of English language tapes, which he describes as "sewers and highways"? How can we change the language we speak in ways that will bring order into our chaotic world? Rather than debate about whether language influences culture, he tries to see how much language we can dispense with. He thinks that as linguists we tend to overemphasize the importance of language.

Like Nanao, he is one of the primitives of a new civilization, and now that he is coming of age he may be considered one of the elders.

Wes Jackson:
EVERLASTING LIFE

We can take part of the credit here in Kansas for Gary Snyder, for in a way he is a child of the prairies of central Kansas. His great grandmother is buried thirty miles west of here near the ghost town of Carneiro near the old emigrant wagon road by a big stone that once had a child's hand engraved on it. But that's just to establish a connection.

In 1971, some California friends said I would like Gary Snyder's poetry. I had not read any of it. I liked more than his poetry; I liked his essays, too. Like countless others, I felt an immediate kinship with Gary, partly because I had long held a strong interest in the upper Paleolithic and he did, too. Some of my friends (and more of my enemies) said I was too preoccupied with the idea of what it meant to be hard-wired for countless Paleolithic predispositions. By discovering Gary Snyder, I had one more in my corner willing to speculate on what life must have been like following the retreat of the ice and what that means to us moderns.

Gary's writings have given me and countless others the courage to seriously think about the life of the gatherers and hunters and the nature of their landscapes before agriculture. An extension of this interest contributed to my thinking of an agriculture in which nature is the measure. We have included that thinking into a philosophy here at The Land Institute, a philosophy which is now the foundation for all of our research. We look to the unplowed native prairie as an analogy when we design our experiments each January.

The poets in my life seem to have honed my thinking even more than agriculturists and naturalists, even though I don't read as much poetry as I do, say, scientific papers, but Gary Snyder and his work (along with Wendell Berry) hover around here every day guiding my thoughts and actions.

There is a law, I think, a law which implies that our "values dictate genotype." I know there are Chicago Board of Trade genes in our major crops now, ensembles of genes that would not exist were there no Chicago Board of Trade. There are also computer genes and fossil fuel wellhead genes—nucleotide units arranged to accommodate human desire and needs. It pleases me to realize that, in the plant species with which we work, one day we will begin to accumulate "Gary Snyder genes," ensembles of genes that would not exist if Gary Snyder, his writings, and his conversations had never existed. It is pleasant to contemplate a future in which every spring, as perennial roots push forth a new growth, we will witness the resurrection of Gary Snyder in every plant body, and if that's sustainable, it will be an everlasting life. Think of that: the resurrection of the body and of the life everlasting. To Gary Snyder, and Buddhists everywhere—you're welcome.

NOTES ON THE CONTRIBUTORS

ROBERT AITKEN is master (roshi) at the Koko An Zendo of the Diamond Sangha, a Zen Buddhist society which has headquarters in Honolulu. Born in 1917, Aitken is an authorized successor of Yamada Koun Roshi and the San-bokyodan lineage of Zen Buddhism, and maintains a full schedule of teaching and writing. He is the author of five books: *A Zen Wave: Bashō's Haiku and Zen* (Weatherhill), *The Dragon Who Never Sleeps: Verses for Zen Buddhist Practice* (Larkspur Press), *Taking the Path of Zen*, *The Mind of Clover: Essays on Zen Buddhist Ethics*, and *The Gateless Barrier: The Wu-men Kuan* (North Point Press).

JEREMY ANDERSON was born in Seattle in 1934, graduated from Yale University and received a master's degree and doctorate from the University of Washington. Married to Janet (Bogle) Anderson, he had three sons and taught geography for many years at Eastern Washington University in Cheney. An avid mountaineer, he died after a fall while climbing alone near Mount Rainier in October 1987.

CAROL BAKER graduated from Reed College. Her career has included being a police dispatch operator, a children's TV scriptwriter, an exotic dancer, a counselor, and a mother. She currently teaches aerobics and works in a Portland, Oregon, bookstore that specializes in murder mysteries.

WILL BAKER writes novels and non-fiction books. A regular contributor to the *Whole Earth Review*, he has taught English for the past 20 years at the University of California, Davis. His most recent novel is titled *Track of the Giant*.

JACQUIE BELLON was born in Saigon in 1941, and graduated from the Chouinart Art Institute, Los Angeles, in 1963. She has lived on San Juan Ridge since July, 1969, when she moved there with her six-week-old son (Aaron) and then-husband, Steve Sanfield. An artist, she has a home that overlooks the South Yuba Canyon.

PETER BERG, a founder of the concept of bioregions and the bioregional movement, serves as director of the Planet Drum Foundation and is contributing editor of its publication *Raise the Stakes* (P.O. Box 31251, San Francisco 94131). A regular contributor to numerous publications, including *CoEvolution Quarterly/Whole Earth Review*, *Creation*, *Not Man Apart*, and *Resurgence* (UK), he has edited *Reinhabiting a Separate Country: A Bioregional Anthology of Northern California* (1978) and coauthored *A Green City Program for San Francisco Bay Area Cities and Towns* (1989).

WENDELL BERRY, poet, novelist, essayist, and farmer, lives in Henry County, Kentucky. His latest books are *Remembering* (a novel) and *What Are People For?* (essays), both published by North Point Press. He teaches at the University of Kentucky.

BRUCE BOYD graduated from the University of California, Berkeley, and has lived on San Juan Ridge for 20 years. A practicing country architect and builder, he lives with his wife, Holly Tornheim, and their daughter, Eva.

THOMAS BUCKLEY is a cultural anthropologist teaching at the University of Massachusetts, Boston. A long-time student of Asian civilizations and of the native cultures of North America, he has done fieldwork in native northwestern California since the early 1970s. His essays have appeared in *Parabola*, *The Windbell*, *News from Native California* and elsewhere, most prominently in professional journals. His recent work includes *Blood Magic: The Anthropology of Menstruation*, with Alma Gottlieb (University of California Press, 1988).

CLIFFORD BURKE grew up along the confluence of the Tolt and Snoqualmie Rivers in Washington. After attending college in Bellingham, he moved in 1963 to San Francisco, where he was apprenticed in printing to Adrian Wilson. Widely known for his work directing Cranium Press, Burke returned with his wife and two daughters to the Skagit delta area in 1978. Claire Van Vliet's Janus Press published his poem *A Landscape with Cows In It* in 1988 and *Type from the Desktop* was published in 1990 by Ventana.

MICHAEL CORR was born in Seattle in 1940. He graduated from Antioch College and the University of Washington, where he earned a Ph.D. in medical phyto-geography in 1985. A poet as well as a wood-carver and printmaker, Corr illustrated *The Fudo Trilogy*, *Turtle Island*, and several broadsides of Gary Snyder's poems. He currently lives in Japan.

PETER COYOTE came from nowhere and is working his way back.

JERRY CRANDALL is a native Oregonian, born in Portland in 1930. He earned degrees in English literature from the University of Oregon and, since 1964, has taught at West Valley College in Saratoga, California, where he has gained a reputation as a Shakespearean. "Although I work in California, my spirit has never left Oregon or the Northwest."

DOC DACHTLER was born in North Dakota in 1944, and moved to Davis, California, in 1957, where he graduated from the University of California in philosophy. He moved to the Sierra Nevada mountains in 1967 and has been a schoolteacher, school janitor, orchardist, Nevada County Planning Commissioner (1977–1980), and writer. Two books of Dachtler's poems, *Drawknife* and *Waiting for Chains at Pearl's*, and two tapes of his songs and verses, *Too Funky For You* and *Buffalo Freeway*, have been released. He presently works in residential and commercial construction, with a special interest in historical restoration.

ROBERT DAVIDSON was born in 1946 in Alaska and raised at Old Massett in the

Haida Gwaii/Queen Charlotte Islands. Since 1965 he has lived and worked in and near Vancouver, British Columbia. In 1969 he and his brother Reg Davidson carved and raised the first totem pole in this century in their home village of Massett. Davidson, his wife, and two children return frequently to the Queen Charlottes: "The fishing is an annual event in our lives and it really slows me down to the natural cycles of life, such as the tides and the return of the salmon, and it makes me realize how fragile our whole existence is. Also, in the cultural realm, every time we have a potlatch it is a way of expressing Haida knowledge and there are always new people speaking and taking the responsibility for carrying it forward into the future."

STANLEY DIAMOND is Distinguished Professor of Anthropology and Poet in the University at the New School for Social Research in New York. His fieldwork has been extensive and includes work with the Seneca, the Iroquois, an Arab village, a collective settlement in Israel, and tribes living on the high plateau of north central Nigeria. He is the founder and editor of *Dialectical Anthropology* and his books include *In Search of the Primitive: A Critique of Civilization*.

JIM DODGE is the author of three novels (*Fup*; *Not Fade Away*; *Stone Junction*) and three chapbooks of poems. He lives in northern California.

DAN ELLSBERG graduated summa cum laude and received a Ph.D. in economics from Harvard, writing both his undergraduate and doctoral theses on "Decision-making Under Uncertainty." In 1958 he joined the Rand Corporation as an analyst of the Pentagon's defense and nuclear war strategies. He was one of the authors of the Pentagon Papers, the top-secret study of America's twenty-three-year involvement in Vietnam. After releasing the Papers to the public in 1971, Ellsberg was indicted on twelve counts of espionage, theft, and conspiracy, for which he faced a possible 115 years in prison. The case was dismissed in 1973 because of the government's misconduct. Since then, Ellsberg has been a peace activist—lecturing, writing, doing research, and participating in acts of nonviolent civil disobedience, which have brought him several dozen arrests. He lives in California.

CLAYTON ESHLEMAN, former editor of *Caterpillar*, teaches at Eastern Michigan University, where he currently edits *Sulfur*. His recent publications include *Conductors of the Pit: Major Works by Rimbaud, Vallejo, Césaire, Artaud, and Holan* (Paragon House, 1988), *Antiphonal Swing: Selected Prose 1962–1987* (McPherson & Co., 1989), *Hotel Cro-Magnon* (Black Sparrow Press, 1989), and *Novices: A Study of Poetic Apprenticeship* (Arundel House, 1989).

DAVE FOREMAN was born in New Mexico in 1946 and is a former professional horseshoer and mule packer. During the 1970s he worked for the Wilderness Society as their Southwest Regional Representative and later as their lobbying coordinator in Washington, D.C., leaving in 1980 to cofound a more militant preservation group—Earth First! From 1981 to 1988 he was editor and publisher of the *Earth First! Journal* and is the coeditor of *Ecodefense: A Field Guide to Monkeywrenching* and coauthor of *The Big Outside. Confessions of an Eco-Brute* will be published by Crown in the winter of 1991. In a case that drew national attention, Foreman was arrested in May 1989 by the FBI on charges of conspiracy to damage power lines. The case has not yet gone to trial. He and his wife live in Arizona.

DAVID H. FRENCH is Professor of Anthropology, Emeritus, at Reed College. He was born in Bend, Oregon, in 1918, and studied at Reed (1935–1938), Pomona (B.A., 1939), Claremont (M.A., 1940), and Columbia (Ph.D., 1949). The transfer to Pomona occurred because Reed was apparently not going to offer anthropology courses during his senior year. He has been engaged in broad fields of activity, including social and cultural anthropology, ethnobiology, and linguistics, and has taught generations of students at Reed (1947–1988) and held visiting professorships at Columbia and Harvard. After decades of work with Northwest Indians, French received a Certificate of Appreciation from the Confederated Tribes of Warm Springs, Oregon, in 1989. The American Anthropological Association also awarded him a Distinguished Service Award in 1988. He continues to reside in Portland, where his retirement activities focus on research and writing.

ALLEN GINSBERG was born in 1926 in Paterson, New Jersey. His most recent publications include *Collected Poems: 1947–1980*, *White Shroud*, and *Annotated Howl*. His newest album is *The Lion For Real*, on Island Records. A book of photographs spanning more than thirty years of friendships is forthcoming from TwelveTrees Press in California. Currently Distinguished Professor of English at Brooklyn College, Ginsberg continues to teach every summer at the Naropa Institute's Department of Writing and Poetics in Boulder, Colorado.

BOB GIORGIO was born in 1933, and attended the Pratt Institute of Art, The Cooper Union (Certificate in Design, 1960), and the San Francisco Art Institute (B.F.A., 1961). He has made experimental films, botanical prints, photographs, and paintings, and also produced a series of blockprint broadsides and a handmade limited-edition book, *True Night*, with Gary Snyder's poem. (A few copies are still available from the artist at Sweetland Road, N. San Juan, CA 95960.) He has lived in Nevada County, California, since 1969.

R. EDWARD GRUMBINE was born in 1953 in southcentral Alaska, grew up in Maryland, and been a wide-ranging student of wild ecosystems. He has been director of the Sierra Institute, the wilderness studies field program of the University of California, Santa Cruz, since 1982. A graduate of Antioch College and the University of Montana, Grumbine's studies have focused on plants, community ecology, and the relationship between wilderness and human consciousness. He is currently working on a doctorate in translating conservation biology into sustainable management practice for national parks and forests.

DRUMMOND HADLEY was born in Missouri in 1938 and received a B.A. and

M.A. from the University of Arizona in Tucson. He studied with the Black Mountain Poets in 1963 at Vancouver, B.C., and at Berkeley in 1964. Following graduation from college, Hadley worked as a cowboy on ranches in Arizona, New Mexico, and Old Mexico. He now ranches near the Mexican border with his wife on a commercial cattle ranch which he has owned and operated since 1972. He is the author of three books of poetry: *The Webbing*, *Strands of Rawhide*, and *The Spirit by the Deep Well Tank*.

JON HALPER was born in 1952 and has lived in the Pacific Northwest since his late teens. He has worked as a tree planter and forest fire fighter and done fieldwork in anthropology. A graduate of The Evergreen State College and the University of Washington School of Medicine, he lives in Seattle and works as a physician.

PAUL HANSEN was born in 1940 and raised in California. He pursued doctoral studies in Chinese at the University of Washington and has lived in the La Conner/Skagit area for the last twenty years where he paints, writes poems, and translates from the Chinese. His books include *Before Ten Thousand Peaks* (Copper Canyon Press) and *The Nine Monks* (Brooding Heron Press).

JACK HICKS is associate professor of English at the University of California, Davis, and director of the Creative Writing Program. He has authored two books, both critical studies of contemporary American fiction, *Cutting Edges* and *In the Singer's Temple*, and numerous articles, many as a popular journalist. He is currently working on *Black Water: A Season in Moscow*, based on experiences in Moscow as a Fulbright Professor.

DELL HYMES was born in Portland, Oregon, in 1927, and went to Reed College (1944–45, 1947–50, with two years in the army between). He pursued graduate studies at Indiana, earning a doctorate in linguistics, and has had longstanding involvement with North American Indian peoples' languages and traditions, with special interest in the Chinookan cultures. Hymes has taught at Harvard (1955–60), Berkeley (1960–65), Pennsylvania (1965–87), and is currently at the University of Virginia. He is the editor of *Reinventing Anthropology* (1969) and author of numerous papers: "Now [I] am mostly concerned with 'ethnopoetics,' discovering patterns and meaning in oral literature."

RYO IMAMURA, born in 1944 in a Japanese-American internment camp in Arizona, is the son of Jane and the late Rev. Kanmo Imamura. After graduating from Berkeley in mathematics, Imamura entered the Jodo Shin priesthood representing the 18th generation of priests in his family lineage. He served as a priest for fifteen years, and later earned an M.S. and doctorate in counseling and psychology. Since 1988, he has lived with his wife and two sons in Olympia, Washington, where he teaches at The Evergreen State College.

WES JACKSON was born in 1936 on a farm near Topeka, Kansas. He studied biology and botany in Kansas and earned a Ph.D. in genetics from North Carolina State University. After several years in academia, Jackson founded The Land Institute in Salina, Kansas, in 1976, where he continues as president. His books include *New Roots for Agriculture* (1980), *Meeting the Expectations of the Land*, (edited with Wendell Berry and Bruce Colman, 1984), and *Altars of Unhewn Stone* (1987).

FRANK JONES was born in Liverpool, England, in 1915, and earned degrees at Manitoba and Oxford (where he was a Rhodes scholar), and later at Wisconsin (where he earned a doctorate in 1941). Professor Emeritus of English and Comparative Literature at the University of Washington, Jones had earlier taught at Reed College (between 1948 and 1954), where he knew Gary Snyder, Lew Welch, and Philip Whalen. He won a National Book Award in 1970 for his translation of Bertolt Brecht's *St. Joan of the Stockyards*.

HISAO KANASEKI was born in Japan in 1918. He has taught American Literature and English at numerous distinguished universities in Japan, including Doshisha, Kobe, and currently Komazawa University in Tokyo, where he lives with his wife and two daughters. He has been a Fulbright Visiting Fellow and Lecturer at Yale and Columbia, as well as at San Diego State University. His books in Japanese include *Notes Towards Modern American Poetry* (1977), *The Navajo Sand Paintings* (a selection of essays on modern American poetry and art, 1980), and *The Oral Poetry of the American Indians* (1988).

TOM KILLION was born in San Francisco in 1953, and grew up in Marin County. An acclaimed woodcut artist, Killion has traveled widely and worked in the Sudan as an administrator in a camp for Ethiopian refugees. He graduated from the University of California, Santa Cruz, and later earned a Ph.D. in African history from Stanford. A trade edition of his landscape prints, *The Coast of California*, was published by Godine in 1988. Beginning in fall 1990, he will be a professor of African history at Bowdoin College in Maine.

CAROLE KODA was born in Merced County, California, in 1947, to second-generation Japanese-American rice farmers. After graduation from Stanford University in psychology, she moved back to the Central Valley, where she taught elementary school and began rock climbing in the Sierra. In 1974 she began to work for a community clinic in Livingston, California, and graduated from UC Davis with a master's in health services in 1980 and from the Physician Assistant program; this work supported her walnut and almond orchards. Her first daughter, Mika, was born in 1978, and in 1985 her second daughter, Kyung Jin, came from Korea. Since summer, 1988, she has lived at Kitkitdizze with her daughters.

JAMES KOLLER, born in Illinois in 1936, has lived in Washington, California, New Mexico, Illinois, and Maine. He has been the editor of Coyote's Journal and Coyote's Books since 1964, and his books include *California Poems*, *Poems for the Blue Sky*, *Fortune*, and *Roses Love Sunshine*. Novels anticipating publication include *I Went to See My True Love* and *An American I Ching*. His paintings and collages have recently appeared in shows in Portland, Maine, and Santa Fe.

JAMES LAUGHLIN founded New Directions in 1936 and continues as its publisher and editor. A prolific writer and poet, his current new books include *The Bird of Endless Time* (Copper Canyon Press), *Random Essays* (Moyer Bell), and *William Carlos Williams and James Laughlin: Selected Letters* (Norton).

GARY LAWLESS was born in Belfast, Maine, in 1951, and graduated from Colby College in East Asian studies. He lived at Kitkitdizze in the summer of 1973, and is known for his poems and down-east story telling. Co-owner of Gulf of Maine Books in Brunswick and editor/publisher of Blackberry Books, Lawless is active in Earth First! and bioregional organizing in the Gulf of Maine region. With Beth Leonard, he is caretaker of Chimney Farm, in Nobleboro, Maine. His most recent book of poems is *First Sight of Land*.

URSULA K. LE GUIN was born in Berkeley in 1929 and has lived in Oregon for many years. She has published about thirty volumes of prose and poetry, and her latest book is *Way of the Water's Going*, text and photographs about California.

J. MICHAEL MAHAR was born in 1929 and raised in Portland, Oregon. He earned degrees in anthropology from Reed College and Cornell University, and has taught at the University of Arizona, Department of Oriental Studies, since 1958. He has lived for several years in Asia, and his research and interest areas include the Untouchables caste and Gandharan art. He has also served as president of the Arizona ACLU.

MICHAEL McCLURE was born in Kansas in 1932 and has lived in the San Francisco Bay Area since 1954. He first read his poetry at the Six Gallery reading in October 1955. Currently working on his book-length poem *Fleas* and a new manuscript titled *Rebel Lions*, McClure performs at colleges and rock and roll halls with Ray Manzarek, keyboardist of the Doors. "What we are doing looks like 'poetry and jazz on stage' but sounds like blues, jazz, classical, and Balinese—and it has a strong environmental and political stance." He is an advisor for the Dry Lands Institute in the Southwest.

SCOTT McLEAN was the editor of *The Real Work*. He earned a Ph.D. in German literature from the University of California, Santa Barbara, and has also studied at San Diego State College, the Free University of Berlin, and at the Eberhard-Karls University in Tubingen. He teaches in the Comparative Literature program at Davis and lives outside Nevada City with his wife, Patricia, and his son, David. He is a member of the Royal Tibetan Navy Counter-Clockwise Marching Band.

TIM McNULTY is a poet, conservationist, and nature writer living with his family in the foothill country of Washington's Olympic Peninsula. His books of poetry include *Pawtracks* (Copper Canyon Press), *Last Year's Poverty* (Brooding Heron Press), and *As a Heron Settles a Shallow Pool* (Exiled-in-America Press). His nature writings have been translated into German and Japanese, and his most recent book, *Washington's Wild Rivers—The Unfinished Work*, was published in 1990 by The Mountaineers Books in Seattle.

RICHARD NELSON is the author of *Hunters of the Northern Ice, Hunters of the Northern Forest, Shadow of the Hunter*, and *Make Prayers to the Raven*, which was made into an award-winning PBS television series. He has worked extensively as an anthropologist among Inuit and Athabaskan Indians for more than two decades, and currently lives in a small town on the northwest Pacific coast. *The Island Within* (North Point Press) is his most recent book.

MAYUMI ODA was born in Japan in 1941 and is a graduate of Tokyo University of Fine Arts. She lives in a verdant garden setting near the Green Gulch Zen Center in Muir Beach, California. *Goddesses* is her most recent book.

ARTHUR OKAMURA was born in California in 1932 and graduated from The Art Institute of Chicago. He has taught for many years and has exhibited widely. As illustrator, Okamura has co-authored books by Robert Creeley and Robert Bly. *Magic Rabbit* was published in 1989 by Poltroon Press, Berkeley. He lives in Bolinas.

DAVID PADWA was born in New York City in 1932, graduated from the University of Chicago at age 18, did graduate studies in political science, and then completed law school at Columbia University. He founded and was chief executive of several high-technology companies and has been on the faculties of three universities. Presently he is Policy Research Fellow at the National Center for Atmospheric Research. He has traveled widely in Asia, climbed extensively in the Alps, and participated in two Himalayan mountaineering expeditions. The father of three, he lives in Boulder, Colorado.

DALE PENDELL was the editor of *Kuksu: Journal of Backcountry Writing*. He lives with his extended family in Santa Cruz and is writing systems software for laser printers and publishing occasional chapbooks as Exiled-In-America Press. "Next year is still floating."

WILL PETERSEN was born in Chicago in 1928, and lived for many years in Japan where he was a student of Noh, and involved with *origin*, second series, in the early 1960s. A painter, printmaker, translator, and poet, his brush work illustrated the Totem Press—Corinth Books editions of *Myths & Texts*. The editor of the journal *Plucked Chicken* until 1980, Petersen currently lives in Evanston, Illinois, with his wife, the artist Cynthia Archer.

TOM POHRT was born in 1953 and is known for his distinctive illustrations of animals and traditional peoples. He illustrated the Bear Claw Press calendars: *Totem Animal* (1976) and *Bear—Circumpolar Traditions Among Northern Peoples* (1977), and provided illustrations for books by Howard Norman, Jim Heynan, and Gary Snyder. Pohrt's recent books include *Miko—Little Hunter of the North*, with Bruce Donehower (Farrar, Straus & Giroux) and *Crow and*

Weasel, with Barry Lopez (North Point Press). He lives in Ann Arbor, Michigan.

JEROME ROTHENBERG was born in New York City in 1931, and graduated from City College (New York) and the University of Michigan. He is the author of more than forty books of poetry, including *Poland/1931*, *Khurbn*, and *Poems for the Game of Silence*. An innovator in ethnopoetics, total translation, and performance poetry, Rothenberg was the co-founder and editor of the journal *Alcheringa* and also edited the ground-breaking anthologies *Technicians of the Sacred*, *Shaking the Pumpkin*, *America a Prophecy*, and *Symposium of the Whole*. He lives in Encinitas and teaches at the University of California, San Diego.

NANAO SAKAKI is a legendary wandering Japanese poet and teacher. He has spent much time in the mountains and deserts of the American West. His book of poems, *Break the Mirror*, was published by North Point Press in 1987.

STEVE SANFIELD was born in 1937 and raised and educated in New England. After college he worked for a time in Hollywood as a news editor, scriptwriter, and publicist. A poet and storyteller, Sanfield has also been an editor with *Zero—A Journal of Contemporary Buddhist Life and Thought* and *Kuksu*. His books of poetry include *Wandering*, *A New Way*, and *He Smiled to Himself*. His children's books deal with Afro-American and East European Jewish culture and folktales, and include *A Natural Man* and *The Adventures of High John the Conqueror*. He has lived on San Juan Ridge since 1969.

RON SCOLLON was born in Michigan in 1939 and has lived primarily in Alaska since 1968. He graduated from Hawaii with a B.A. in Japanese linguistics in 1971, and earned a Ph.D. in linguistics in 1974. He and his wife, Suzie, have worked as sociolinguists for many years. Their book, *Responsive Communication: Patterns for Making Sense*, was published by The Black Current Press in 1986. Scollon, his wife, and their two children currently live in Seoul, Korea, where he and Suzie teach at the Sogang University English Institute.

SUZIE SCOLLON was born in Honolulu in 1946 and graduated from Reed College in 1969. She has worked variously as a researcher with octopuses, participated in archeological digging, tried her hand at scriptwriting, and performed linguistic research in Fort Chipewyan, Alberta, as part of a Ph.D. in linguistics earned from Hawaii. Primarily based in Alaska since 1969, she and her family are currently living in Seoul, Korea.

GEORGE SESSIONS teaches philosophy at Sierra College in Rocklin, California. He has written extensively in the area of eco-philosophy and deep ecology and is coauthor, with Bill Devall, of *Deep Ecology* (Peregrine Smith Books, 1985).

GEN SNYDER was born in San Francisco in 1969, and grew up on San Juan Ridge. He has worked as a gardener and landscaper, and currently lives in Arcata, California, where he also attends school at the College of the Redwoods.

GARY SNYDER has just finished a prose book, *The Practice of the Wild*. His current involvement in the ecological and social issues around forestry and mining coincides with his plan to resume work on *Mountains and Rivers Without End*, and his ongoing personal practice of the wild.

JIM SNYDER was born and raised in California, and brought early to the Sierra by his parents. He began working as a volunteer in Yosemite in 1958 and then on trail crews in the 1960s to put himself through college. In 1989 Snyder was appointed Park Historian for Yosemite National Park, where he lives.

KAI SNYDER was born in Kyoto, Japan, in 1968, and lived on San Juan Ridge from 1970 to 1985. He attended the University of California, Santa Cruz, for three years, then lived and traveled in Japan for one year on a fellowship. He currently attends the University of California, Berkeley, where he is majoring in conservation and resource studies.

CHARLENE SPRETNAK is the author of *Lost Goddesses of Early Greece*, *The Spiritual Dimension of Green Politics*, *Green Politics: The Global Promise* (with Fritjof Capra), and the forthcoming *States of Grace*. She is also the editor of an anthology, *The Politics of Women's Spirituality*.

WILL STAPLE was born and raised in the San Francisco Bay Area and attended the University of California at Berkeley in the 1960s. He assisted in building the main house at Kitkitdizze and later established himself on adjacent community land, WEPA. He has worked as a carpenter, mental health counselor, and Poet-in-the-Schools in Grass Valley, Nevada City, and North Columbia. An earlier book of his poems, *Passes for Human*, is available, and *Never Give Up This Savage Religion* is forthcoming.

ROBERT SUND was born in 1929 in Olympia, Washington, and grew up on a small farm in the Chehalis River valley. The author of *Bunch Grass* and *Ish River*, he currently lives in the Skagit River delta, the heart of the Ish River country, where he works as a poet, painter, and calligrapher. Now gathering poems for his next book, *The River With One Bank*, he is also preparing two books of translations, *The Fluteplayer's Joy* (from the Swedish of Rabbe Enckell), and *Bringing Friends Over* (poems of Bashō, Buson, Issa, and other poets of 17th- and 18th-century Japan), for which a calligraphic edition is planned.

LEE SWENSON was born in 1939 and has been involved in anarchist and decentralist political and cultural activities for three decades. Formerly director of the Institute for the Study of Nonviolence and the Farallones Institute, Swenson now lives in Berkeley where, with his wife, Vijaya Nagarajan, he raises his two children, and joins with friends under the rubric of the Recovery of the Commons Project.

GIOIA TIMPANELLI was born in 1936 in New York, and has been a central figure in the renewal of storytelling in America for many years. She is the author of *Traveling Images and Observations*, an Italian traveling diary, and *Tales from the Roof of the World: Four Tibetan Stories* (Viking). She has won two Emmy Awards for her work as an educational television producer, writer, and broadcaster, and, in 1987 received the Women's National Book Association Award. She and her husband, the architect Kenneth Hewes Barricklo, live in the Hudson River valley.

ROBERT M. TORRANCE was born in Washington, D.C., in 1939, and received a B.A. and Ph.D. at Harvard and an M.A. from Berkeley. He has taught comparative literature at Harvard and Brooklyn College, and, since 1976, at the University of California, Davis. Torrance has translated plays by Sophocles and has written two books, *The Comic Hero* and *Ideal and Spleen*, on "the crisis of transcendent vision" in major poets since the late 18th century. He is currently working on a manuscript on the spiritual quest as a central dimension of human experience, and on an anthology of writings concerned with the interrelation between humans and the natural world.

ANNE WALDMAN was born in 1945 in New York and graduated from Bennington College. In 1974, she co-founded, with Allen Ginsberg, The Jack Kerouac School of Disembodied Poetics at the Naropa Institute in Boulder, Colorado, where she directs and teaches in the Writing and Poetics and the Summer Writing Programs. Known for her energetic performances, Waldman's books of poems include *Fast Speaking Woman, Skin Meat Bones,* and *Helping the Dreamer (New and Selected Poems, 1966–1988),* and she is also featured in a video entitled *Eyes In All Heads.* She lives in Boulder.

BURTON WATSON was born in 1925 in New Rochelle, New York. He graduated from Columbia College and in 1956 received a Ph.D. in Chinese from Columbia University. From 1951 to 1955 he was a graduate student in Chinese studies at Kyoto University, and later lived in Kyoto and Osaka for a number of years. He has taught at Columbia, Stanford, and Kyoto universities and, since 1973, has devoted full time to translation work. Watson's numerous translations from Chinese and Japanese include *The Complete Works of Chuang Tzu* and *From the Country of Eight Islands: An Anthology of Japanese Poetry* (with Hiroaki Sato). *The Columbia Book of Chinese Poetry* and *The Rainbow World* (essays) are his latest books. He has most recently lived in Japan and Hong Kong but will be returning to New York in fall 1990 to teach at Columbia.

PHILIP WHALEN was born in 1923 in Portland, Oregon. He was in the US Army Air Corps 1943–1946, after which he attended Reed College and received a B.A. in Literature and Languages in 1951. Whalen worked as a lookout in the North Cascades for three seasons—Sauk Mountain in 1953, and Sourdough Mountain in 1954 and 1955. A figure in the San Francisco Poetry Renaissance, he also lived in Japan in 1966–1967 and 1969–1971, and was associated with the San Francisco and Santa Fe Zen Centers for many years. Most recently he has been the resident teacher at the Hartford St. Zen Center in San Francisco. His many books of poems include *On Bear's Head* and *Heavy Breathing*; his novels *You Didn't Even Try* (1967) and *Imaginary Speeches for a Brazen Head* (1972) were reprinted in 1985 as *Two Novels.*

ALAN WILLIAMSON is professor of English at the University of California,

Davis. He has published two books of poems, *Presence* (1983) and *The Muse of Distance* (1988), both from Knopf. An earlier book of criticism, *Introspection and Contemporary Poetry*, is available from Harvard University Press.

PAUL WINTER was born in Altoona, Pennsylvania, in 1939 and attended Northwestern University, where he formed the first of his many jazz groups. The Paul Winter Consort has toured in 35 countries over the years, and their recordings include *Road* (which was carried to the moon in 1971 aboard Apollo 15), *Icarus*, *Common Ground*, *Missa Gaia / Earth Mass*, *Concert for the Earth*, *Canyon*, and, most recently, *Earth: Voices of a Planet*. Winter is known for his pioneering musical interactions with wild animals and the natural environment. In addition, he has performed for years in the Soviet Union to celebrate that country's natural and cultural beauty, and has actively encouraged peace and understanding between the U.S. and the U.S.S.R. He lives on a farm in Connecticut in the foothills of the Berkshires where he directs Living Music Records.

PHILIP YAMPOLSKY is Professor of Japanese at Columbia University. He is the author of *The Platform Sutra of the Sixth Patriarch* and *The Zen Master Hakuin: Selected Writings*. *Selected Writings of Nichiren*, edited by Yampolsky and translated by Burton Watson, was published in 1990 by Columbia University Press.

KATSUNORI YAMAZATO was born in Okinawa (Mototbu Peninsula) in 1949, and graduated from the University of Ryukyus in 1972 with a B.A. in English. He received an M.A. from the University of Hawaii in 1974, and a Ph.D. in English from the University of California, Davis, in 1987. Yamazato teaches American literature at the University of the Ryukyus, and lives in Okinawa with his wife and two children.

INDEX

"A Quiet Day With Friends" (San-
field), 117
Abbey, Edward, 362, 363
Adelaide Crapsey-Oswald Spengler
Memorial Society, 27, 207
Aitken, Robert, 164, 278, 279, 301,
315–316, 367
contributor, 291–298
notes on life, 429
Akiba, Kenji, 98, 101
Alaska Humanities Forum, 419, 424
Aliesan, Jody, 258
Allen, Donald, *See New American
Poetry: 1945–1960, The*
Allen, Robert (Bobo), 12, 27
American Academy of Arts and
Letters, Snyder's induction into,
275
American Anthropological
Association
"Anthropology and Poetry,"
Snyder's participation in, 22,
395
Ananda Meditation Retreat, 124,
146–147
Anderson, Jeremy
contributor, 30–31
notes on life, 429
Arts and Crafts Movement, 353–354
Axe Handles (Snyder), 40, 104,
132, 133, 151, 152

Back Country, The (Snyder), 35, 93,
123, 127, 128, 231, 256, 269, 452
Baker, Carol, 11, 25, 37
and Bobby (Bill), 11, 25
contributor, 24–29
notes on life, 429
Baker, Richard, 275–276, 306, 355, 358
Baker, Will, 276
contributor, 43–49
notes on life, 429

Banyan Ashram (Suwanose Island),
See Tribe, The (*Buzoku*)
Barzaghi, Jacques, 341
Bartlett, Lee, 276, 278
Bashō, 231, 297
Bay Area, *See* San Francisco Bay
Area
Bellon, Jacquie
contributor, 320
notes on life, 429
Bellyfulls (Sakaki), 95, 97, 98, 104
Berg, Peter, 125, 159
contributor, 376–391
notes on life, 429
Berman, Morris, 390
Berry, Den, 169
Berry, Don, 24, 27
Berry, Wendell, 131, 135, 281, 287, 426
contributor, 252
notes on life, 430
Bidney, David, 393
Bioregionalism, 125, 169, 367–369,
384–391
Blue Cloud, Peter, 340
Bly, Robert, 243
Bookchin, Murray, 390
Boyd, Bruce, 136, 137
contributor, 115–116
notes on life, 430
Brand, Stewart, 308
Break the Mirror (Sakaki), 104
Brower, David, 308, 363, 366, 367
Brown, Jerry, 21, 164, 340, 341–342,
387, 388–389
Buckley, Thomas
contributor, 411–415
notes on life, 430
Buddhism, *See* Zen Buddhism
Buddhist Peace Fellowship, 301
Buddhist Temple and Study Center
(Berkeley), 299
Bunnell, Sterling, 381

Burke, Clifford, 258
  contributor, 452 (colophon)
  notes on life, 430
Buzoku, See Tribe, The (*Buzoku*)

Cairnie, Gordon, 255, 412
California State Arts Council, 21,
  164–165, 341, 387–388
Callenbach, Ernest, 388, 390
Callicotte, Harriet, 169–173, 426
Carson, Rachel, 362
Chambers, Paul and Carrol, 11, 24,
  27
Charles, Leonard, 148
Chen, Shih-hsiang, 55, 270
City Lights Bookstore, 14, 354,
  376
Cold Mountain (Han-shan), 56, 57,
  73, 259, 269, 419
Collins, Robin, 10–11, 392
Commoner, Barry, 308
Conner, Bruce, 378
Corman, Cid, 56–57, 58, 82–83,
  235, 236, 303
Corr, Michael
  contributor, 111
  notes on life, 430
Coughlan, Jimmy, 113, 136
Coyote, Peter, 120, 130, 383
  contributor, 157–168
  notes on life, 430
Craig, Al, 65
Crandall, Jerry
  contributor, 3–7
  notes on life, 430
Cranston, Reverend (The Shadow),
  24–25
Crapsey, Adelaide, *See* Adelaide
  Crapsey-Oswald Spengler
  Memorial Society
Crater Mountain Lookout (Washing-
  ton), 30–31, 263, 265
Curry, Robert, 388

Dachtler, Doc, 131, 136, 137, 153
  contributor, 113–114
  notes on life, 430
Dalenberg, Claude, 299
Daley, Michael, 258
Dasmann, Raymond, 366, 384, 386–
  387, 388

Davidson, Robert
  contributor, cover illustration
  notes on life, 430
Davis, R. G., 377
de Angulo, Jaime, 123, 354, 355
"Describing My Feelings" (Wei Yeh),
  260
Dharma Bums, The (Kerouac), 20,
  35, 122, 157
  influence of, 126, 331, 421
  Snyder represented as Japhy Ryder
  in, 20, 122, 143, 157, 203, 365,
  412
Diamond, Stanley, 22, 367, 395
  contributor, 405–410
  notes on life, 431
Diamond Sutra, The, 293, 296, 297
Diggers, the, 158, 159, 162, 163,
  377, 381, 383–384, 387
Digger Papers, The, 378, 380
diPrima, Diane, 123, 377, 412
Dockham, Chuck, 308
Dodge, Jim, 388
  contributor, 143–156
  notes on life, 431
Drugs, 13, 20, 65, 67, 209, 236, 242,
  377, 378
Duncan, Robert, 237, 244
Durham, Eddie, 11, 24, 25

Earth Day (1970), 366, 367, 372
Earth First!, 283, 362
Earth House Hold (Snyder), 31, 100,
  123, 133, 246, 263, 265, 266, 294,
  295, 366, 373, 422
Ehrlich, Paul, 308, 366, 372
Elliot, Harley, 169
Ellsberg, Dan
  contributor, 331–339
  notes on life, 431
Ellsberg, Patricia, 336, 337
Environmental Conservation (Das-
  mann), 366
Environmental Handbook, The
  (Brower), 367
Epsteiner, Fred, 301
Erdrich, Louise, 281
Eshleman, Clayton, 58
  and Barbara, 352
  contributor, 231–242
  notes on life, 431

Essays, Snyder's
  "Anyone with *Yama-bushi* Tenden-
      cies," 102
  "Buddhism and Anarchism," 120,
      293
  "Buddhism and the Coming
      Revolution," 266, 293
  "Four Changes," 367–369, 371–374
  "Good, Wild, Sacred," 369
  "North Sea Road," 125, 387
  "Poetry and the Primitive," 245
  "Poetry, Community, and Climax,"
      133
  "Introduction (Recovery of the
      Commons Bundle #1)," 357–358
  "Re-inhabitation," 388
  "Suwa-no-se Island and the
      Banyan Ashram," 100, 103
  "The Woman Who Married a
      Bear," 221–222, 227, 228
  "Why Tribe," 100, 101, 234–235, 266
Ethnopoetics, 22, 245, 263, 395–397
Everett, Ruth, *See* Sasaki, Ruth
      Fuller Everett
Everson, William, 255, 370
"Excelsissimus" (Jones), 288

Farallones Institute, 357
Federal Bureau of Investigation
      (FBI), Snyder investigated by, 9,
      27
Feminism, 280, 359, 361
Ferlinghetti, Lawrence, 70, 123, 127
First Zen Institute of America (New
      York), *See* Zen, zendos, temples
      and study centers
First Zen Institute of America in
      Japan (Kyoto), *See* Zen, zendos,
      temples and study centers
Folsom, Edwin, 369
Foreman, Dave
  contributor, 362–364
  notes on life, 431–432
Foster, Nelson, 164, 301
French, David H., 422
  and Kay, 13
  contributor, 16–22
  notes on life, 432
Friends of Creation Spirituality,
      359
Friends of the Earth, 367, 389

Frisco Bay Mussel Group, 388–389
Fujimoto, Ryugyu, 299
Fuller, Ruth, *See* Sasaki, Ruth Fuller
      Everett
Fup (Dodge), 151–152

Gard, Richard, 299
"Gary Snyder" (Hadley), 287
Gass, Alison, 11, 28
George, Dewey, 414
Gilbert, Sandra, 276
Ginsberg, Allen, 19, 29, 44–49, 70,
      77, 123, 127, 235, 236, 237, 275–276,
      280, 281, 302, 306, 354, 355, 377,
      379, 402
  contributor, 203
  notes on life, 432
Giorgio, Bob
  contributor, 1
  notes on life, 432
Girl Who Married a Bear, The
      (McClellan), 221
Gold, Jeff, 137
Goldhaft, Judy, 125, 381, 387
Gorsline, Jeremiah (Jerry), 144–147,
      387
Goto, Zuigan (Roshi), *See* Zen,
      Masters
Graham, Bill, 377
Graham, Dom Aelred, 303
Grandpa William, 348, 350
Graves, Morris, 251
Greenpeace, 340
Green, Sam, 258
Greensfelder, Bob, 308, 314
Grogan, Emmett, 379
Grolier Book Shop, 255, 412
Grosjean, Glen, 299
Grumbine, R. Edward,
  contributor, 371–375
  notes on life, 432
Gustaitis, Rasa, 388

Hadley, Drummond
  contributor, 287
  notes on life, 432–433
Halloween, *See* San Juan Ridge,
      Halloween rituals at
Halper, Jon
  contributor, ix–xi (introduction)
  notes on life, 433

Hansen, Paul
  contributor, 259–262
  notes on life, 433
Han-shan, 56–57, 123, 248, 267, 268, 269
  See also Cold Mountain
Hanson, Kenneth, 18
Harper, Ed, 11, 24
Harris, Clarence, 37
Harris, John, 343
Hayward, Claude, 379
Hearn, Lafcadio, 14, 74
Helm, Michael, 151
Hennessy, Lois Snyder, 7, 8–9. 28, 169, 173
He Who Hunted Birds in His Father's Village: The Dimensions of a Haida Myth (Snyder), 17, 227–228
Hewitt, Geof, 154
Hicks, Jack
  contributor, 275–284
  notes on life, 433
Hoang, Jenny, 301
Ho-ching (Lin Pu), 259
Hoffman, Michael, 276, 278–279, 284
Holthaus, Gary, 419
House, Freeman (Linn), 387
Howard, Victoria, 399–402
"Howl" (Ginsberg), 45, 70, 77
Huang, Al, 341
Human Be-In, 378–380
Hybart, Burt, 131
Hunter, Celia, 362, 363
Hunter, Neale, 95, 97–98
Hymes, Dell, 16, 17, 22, 422
  contributor, 392–404
  notes on life, 433

Illich, Ivan, 354–355, 357
Imamura, Kanmo and Jane, 299–301
Imamura, Ryo
  contributor, 299–301
  notes on life, 433
Industrial Workers of the World, The, 13, 25, 203, 244, 379
Inner Heat, *See* People of the Inner Heat
Institute for the Study of Non-violence, The, 357

Iriya, Yoshitaka, 63, 71, 73
Ish River, 251, 258
Ishi, 139

Jackson, Robert, 299
Jackson, Wes, 169
  contributor, 426–427
  notes on life, 433–434
Jacobs, Melville, 399
Jay, Tom, 258
Jeffers, Robinson, 219, 220, 255, 268, 355
Johns, Maria, 221
Johnson, Diane, 276
Jones, Frank, 44–45, 47
  contributor, 288
  notes on life, 434
Jones, Jimmy, 37, 40–42
Jones, LeRoi, 243

Kaizo, 96
Kakuzo, Okakura, 250
Kamaike, Barbara and Susume, 239
Kanaseki, Hisao, 63, 101
  contributor, 70–75
  notes on life, 434
Kato, Mamoru, 94, 98
Kawamura, Leslie, 299
Keeler, Greg, 153, 284
Kehler, Randy, 336, 338
Kelly, Robert, 240, 243
Kenji, Miyazawa, 73–74, 264, 271
Kerouac, Jack, 20, 35, 76, 122, 140, 143, 157, 203, 299, 302, 324, 355, 365
Killion, Tom
  contributor, 33, 51
  notes on life, 434
Kindscher, Kelly, 169–173
Kingston, Maxine Hong, 281
Kitkitdizze, 75, 104, 113–114, 160–161, 203, 249, 366–367
  activities, 124–125, 129, 133–135, 145–147, 216, 297–298, 309, 323–324, 356
  apprenticeships at, 122–126, 145
  construction, 115–116, 130, 148, 160–161, 338–339, 355–356
  friends visiting, 144–145, 159–162, 297, 342, 366–367, 381, 383–389

named for plant, 160, 306
    See also San Juan Ridge;
    Snyder, Gary, at Kitkitdizze;
    Zen, zendos, temples and
    study centers, Ring of Bone
    Zendo
Koch, Kenneth, 209
Koda, Carole, 203
    contributor, 321–325
    notes on life, 434
Koller, James
    contributor, 285–286
    notes on life, 434–435
Krassner, Paul, 380
Kroeber, Alfred, 42, 410
Kunitz, Donald, 276, 278, 284
Kyger, Joanne, 66, 73, 94, 162, 203,
    235, 240

Lambert Street house, 10–12, 24–29
Lampe, Keith (Ponderosa Pine), 144
Land Institute, The, 426
Lang, Julian, 411
Lascaux, 232
"Late Afternoon Cherishing
    Thoughts of Master Jun" (Wei
    Yeh), 261
Laughlin, James
    contributor, 246–247
    notes on life, 435
Lawless, Gary
    contributor, 122–126
    notes on life, 435
Lawrence, D. H., 219, 231, 265
Left Out in the Rain (Snyder), 105,
    137, 265, 266, 268
Le Guin, Ursula K., 281
    contributor, 201–202
    notes on life, 435
Leopold, Aldo, 362, 363
Lin-chi lu (*Rinzai-roku*), 64, 69, 70
Loeffler, Jack, 308
Logsdon, Gene, 169
Lopez, Barry, 281
Lu Ji, 270

Macy, Joanna, 301
Mahar, J. Michael, 11, 13–14
    contributor, 8–13
    notes on life, 435

Marchbanks, Roy, 36–38, 40
Marshall, Bob, 363
Martien, Jerry, 388
Marxism, 21, 280, 294, 360
Matthiessen, Peter, 281
Maybeck, Bernard, 353–354
Mayhew, Leon, 278
Mazama, 6
Mazamas, the, 6
McCarthyism (Senator Joseph
    McCarthy, and Committee), 9,
    17, 20–21, 72
McClellan, Catherine, 221
McClure, Michael, 76, 123, 134, 204,
    402
    contributor, 204–206
    notes on life, 435
McCorkle, Locke, 13
McCormick, Gavin, 98
McLean, Scott, 278, 282, 284, 367
    and Patricia, 131
    contributor, 127–138
    notes on life, 435
McNulty, Tim
    contributor, 254–258
    notes on life, 435–436
Mead, Margaret, 308
Meehan, J. C., 4
Meiji, Etsuko, 65, 82
Mendelsohn, Everett, 334
Milliman, Lynn, 148
Mills, Stephanie, 390
Miura, Isshu (Roshi), *See* Zen,
    Masters
Miyamoto, Shoson, 299
Mocion, Tony, 153
Monkey Wrench Gang, The (Abbey),
    363
Montgomery, John, 140
Moore, Stanley, 9, 392
Morgan, Julia, 353–354
Moth, Luna, 387
Mountaineering and hiking, *See*
    Snyder, Gary, mountaineering
    and hiking
Mountains and Rivers Without End
    (Snyder), 280, 437–438
Muir, John, 36, 219–220, 362, 363, 365
Murie, Martin, 11, 12, 24, 27
Murphy, Forrest (Spud), 37–40

Myths & Texts (Snyder), 209, 243, 257, 264, 265, 267, 285, 395–396, 405, 410, 418, 452

Naess, Arne, 365, 367, 369
Nagasawa, Tetsuo, 94, 98, 101
Nakamura, Hajime, 299
"Naming Gary" (Le Guin), 201–202
Nash, Roderick, 390
Nature and Culture (UC Davis program), 281–282
Nearing, Helen and Scott, 342
Nelson, Richard
  contributor, 344–351
  notes on life, 436
Nemirow, Steve, 315
New American Poetry: 1945–1960, The (Allen), 57, 243, 377
North Columbia Cultural Center, 131, 136–137
Nowick, Walter, 55, 64, 80

O'Connor, Michael, 258
Oda, Mayumi
  contributor, 289
  notes on life, 436
"Ode to Myself at Forty" (Wei Yeh), 262
Oelschlanger, Max, 365
Okamura, Arthur
  contributor, 329
  notes on life, 436
Old Ways, The (Snyder), 42, 224–225, 350, 388
Olson, Charles, 204, 236, 244
Oregonian, (Portland),
  Lois Snyder Hennessy's work at, 8, 28
  Snyder as copyboy, 7
origin, 82–83, 235, 236–237, 242
Origins of the Family, Private Property and the State, The (Engels), 280
Ortiz, Simon, 305–306

Pacific Northwest, 3–7, 30–31, 224–226, 254–258
  See also Lambert Street house; Reed College; Snyder, Gary, childhood and adolescence; Snyder, Gary, mountaineering and hiking; Snyder, Gary, work

Paddock, Joe and Nancy, 169
Padwa, David
  contributor, 302–311
  notes on life, 436
Parker, Catherine, 301
Passage Through India (Snyder), 94–95, 98
Peattie, Noel, 276
Pendell, Dale
  contributor, 312–319
  notes on life, 436
Pentagon Papers, 336–339
People of the Inner Heat, 114
Peripheral Canal, 388–389
Petersen, Will, 56, 65, 66, 243, 299
  contributor, 76–89, 199
  notes on life, 436
Pine, Ponderosa, *See* Lampe, Keith
Piper, Nelson, 276, 278
Places on Earth (UC Davis program), 282
Planet Drum, 125, 386, 387
Planet Drum Foundation, 386, 389, 390
Pleasant, Marty, 38
Poems, Snyder's
  "Above Pate Valley," 256
  "All the Spirit Powers Went to Their Dancing Places," 257
  "As for Poets," 74
  "Avocado," 257
  "Axe Handles," 270
  "The Bath," 249
  "Bedrock," 249
  "A Berry Feast," 393
  "Burning 3," 267
  "Burning 10," 285
  "By the Tama River at the North End of the Plain in April," 101–102
  "A Curse on the Men in Washington, Pentagon," 378
  "Dullness in February: Japan," 105, 266–267
  "For All," 136, 320
  "For the Boy Who Was Dodger Point Lookout Fifteen Years Ago," 127
  "For the Children," 257, 258
  "For Nothing," 257
  "Hay for the Horses," 248, 415

"High Quality Information," 204–206

"Hitch Haiku," 269

"The Humpbacked Flute Player," 244–245

"Hymn to the Goddess San Francisco in Paradise," 128

"I Went Into the Maverick Bar," 126

"Journeys," 254–255

"Kyoto Born in Spring Song," 257

"Look Back," 40

"Logging 8," 256

"March," 93–94

"The Market," 237

"Mid-August at Sourdough Mountain Lookout," 256, 412

"Milton by Firelight," 38

"Mother Earth: Her Whales," 266, 340

"Off the Trail," 326–327

"Original Vow," 414

"The Persimmons," 137–138, 280

"Piute Creek," 81, 83, 256

"Prayer for the Great Family," 250

"Removing the Plate of the Pump," 132

"Riprap," 35, 36, 42, 52–53, 252–253

"The Sappa Creek," 86

"September," 76

"7: VII," 128

"Smokey the Bear Sutra," 345, 367, 414

"Song of the Taste," 128, 257

"The Sweat," 280

"T-2 Tanker Blues," 86, 377

"True Night," 317

"Versions of Anacreon," 265

"A Walk," 216–219

"Walking the New York Bedrock," 166–167, 280

"Wave," 256

"What Happened Here Before," 229

"What You Should Know to Be a Poet," 123–124

"Yase: September," 88

Poetry readings, Snyder's, 18, 19, 45–49, 70, 127, 276, 279, 309, 356
  Alaska, 345, 422
  Arcata, 144, 366
  Conference on the Rights of Nonhuman Nature, 366
  Kansas Prairie Festival, 169
  Los Angeles, 301
  Maine, 123
  New York, 209
  Reed College, 18, 19
  Sacramento, 366
  San Juan Ridge, 115, 136–137
  Sierra College, 312–313
  Six Gallery, 76
  UC-Davis, 275–276
  UC-Santa Barbara, 127
  University of Iowa, 143
  University of Washington, 43–49
  Vermont, 153
  Yasuda Seimei Hall, 101

Pohrt, Tom
  contributor, 91
  notes on life, 436–437

Polyani, Karl, 357

Population Bomb, The (Ehrlich), 366

Portland, Oregon, See Lambert Street house; Reed College; Snyder, Gary

Pound, Ezra, 14, 21, 203, 207, 219, 243, 264, 265, 270, 271, 273, 274

Practice of the Wild, The (Snyder), 321–322, 437

Psyche, 99

Pulitzer Prize, 119

Raise the Stakes, 390

Ramsey, Jarold, 394

Real Work, The (Snyder, ed. McLean), 367

Recovery of the Commons Project, 357–358

Reed College, 9–14, 16–23, 24–28, 203, 207, 280, 392, 421, 422, 424

Regarding Wave (Snyder), 101–102, 256–257

Reinhabiting a Separate Country: A Bioregional Anthology of Northern California (Berg), 388

Reinhabitory Theater, The, 387, 388

Reisner, Marc, 281–282

Reisner, Zac, 147

Rexroth, Kenneth, 70, 71, 74, 76, 120, 123, 127, 231, 251, 255

Reynolds, Lloyd, 16–17, 26–27, 421, 424
Ring of Bone Zendo, *See* Zen, zendos, temples and study centers
Rinzai-roku, *See Lin-chi lu*
Riprap, 36, 252–253
    backcountry lifestyle, 37–42
Riprap (Snyder), 35, 40, 72, 83, 249, 252–253, 255, 259, 412, 415
Robertson, David, 282, 284
Roche, Judith, 258
Roditi, Edouard, 303
Roethke, Theodore, 416
Rothenberg, Jerome, 242
    contributor, 243–245
    notes on life, 437
Ryder, Japhy, 20, 122, 143, 157, 203, 313, 331, 333, 412
    See also The Dharma Bums

Sakaki, Nanao, 75, 94, 95–98, 101, 105, 107–109, 125, 128, 129, 305, 367, 425
    contributor, 107–109
    notes on life, 437
Sakiak, 345, 350
Samperi, Frank, 236
Sanfield, Steve, 114, 131
    contributor, 117–119
    notes on life, 437
San Francisco Bay Area, 13–14, 352–354, 376–381
San Francisco Zen Center, 125, 355
San Juan Ridge, 117–119, 120, 129, 131, 133–135, 136–137, 164, 203, 275–276, 279, 297, 306, 308, 313, 356, 388
    Halloween rituals at, 117, 129, 298
Sappa Creek, The, 65–66, 83–88
Sasaki, Ruth Fuller Everett, 14–15, 55, 56, 62–63, 64, 66–69, 70–74
Savage, Melissa, 308
Schaefer, Edward H., 259
Schloegel, Irmgard, 303
Scollon, Ron
    contributor, 416–420
    notes on life, 437
Scollon, Suzie
    contributor, 421–425
    notes on life, 437

Seeger, Pete, 342
Sessions, George
    contributor, 365–370
    notes on life, 437
Shapiro, Karl, 275, 276
Shepard, Paul, 367
Shippee, Paul, 383–384
Shoemaker, Jack and Vicki, 155
Shrader, Steve, 143
Sierra Club, 366, 367, 388–389
Simpson, David, 387
Smith, Hiram, 397–398, 403
Snyder, Anthea, 8, 9
Snyder, Gary
    as Japhy Ryder, *See* Ryder, Japhy
    at Kitkitdizze, 104, 113–114, 115–116, 124–126, 145–147, 159–162, 297–298, 306, 309, 321–325, 338–339, 341–342, 355–356, 366–367, 388
        See also Kitkitdizze; San Juan Ridge
    books, *See* individual titles
    childhood and adolescence, 3–7, 8–13, 224–226, 275
    college and graduate education, 9–13, 14, 16–23, 24–28, 207, 392–394
        See also Lambert Street house; Reed College
    contributor, 169–173, 326–327
    criticism of, 123, 135, 282, 283–284, 379, 396, 405
    essays, *See* Essays, Snyder's
    family background, 169–173, 224
        See also Snyder, Gary, childhood and adolescence
    in India, 68, 73, 94–98, 203, 235, 264
    in Japan, 54–57, 60, 63–69, 70–75, 77–83, 93–95, 98–105, 107–109, 203, 235–236, 241, 246, 293, 296, 300, 303–304, 332–335
    in Kansas, 169–173
    in San Francisco Bay Area, 13–14, 28–29, 30, 76–77, 157, 158–159, 246, 299–300, 352–354
    investigated by FBI (Federal Bureau of Investigation), 9, 27
    marriages and family, *See* Callicotte,

Harriet; Hennessy, Lois
Snyder; Snyder, Harold; Snyder, Anthea; Gass, Alison;
Kyger, Joanne; Uehara, Masa;
Snyder, Kai; Snyder, Gen;
Koda, Carole
mountaineering and hiking, ix,
3–4, 5–6, 12, 29, 30–31, 35, 53,
78, 81–82, 102, 129, 140, 162,
203, 216, 223–224, 324–325,
326–327, 366, 374, 416–417,
418
notes on life, 437–438
poems, *See* Poems, Snyder's
poetry readings, *See* Poetry
readings, Snyder's
Pulitzer Prize, 119
Sappa Creek, The, 65–66, 83–88
Shugendo, *See* Snyder, Yamabushi
teaching at UC Davis, 275–283
Tribe, The *(Buzoku)*, *See* Tribe,
The; Snyder, Gary, in Japan
work, 5, 7, 10, 14–15, 21, 26, 28, 30–
31, 35–37, 38, 40–42, 56, 63–65,
66, 68, 69, 70–71, 73–74, 77,
83–84, 86, 203, 246, 265, 275–
284, 392–393
Yamabushi, 102
Zen, 10, 14–15, 20, 27–28, 30, 47,
64–67, 68–69, 70–74, 88–89,
94, 103–105, 115–116, 121, 143–
144, 156, 157, 164, 167, 168, 203,
217, 219–220, 235, 246, 250, 263,
264, 293–298, 299–301, 304–
305, 307, 308–309, 312–319, 358
Snyder, Gen, 125, 140, 148, 153, 169,
173, 203, 348, 366
contributor, 142
notes on life, 437
Snyder, Harold, 9
Snyder, Jim
contributor, 35–42
notes on life, 438
Snyder, Kai, 58, 75, 100, 103–104, 125,
203, 366, 382, 421
contributor, 139–141
notes on life, 438
Snyder, Lois, *See* Hennessy, Lois
Snyder
Snyder, Masa Uehara, *See* Uehara,
Masa

"So Caught Up In Ourselves"
(Sanfield), 117
Sommers, Roger, 305
Spengler, Oswald, *See* Adelaide
Crapsey-Oswald Spengler
Memorial Society
Spretnak, Charlene
contributor, 359–361
notes on life, 438
Stafford, William, 394
Staple, Will, 125, 308
contributor, 120–121
notes on life, 438
Starsky, Morrey, 416
Stevens, Joe and Sarah, 345, 348, 349,
350
Stilwell, Roy, 11
St. James, Margot, 305
Strickland, Bob, 303, 332
Sund, Robert, 258
contributor, 248–251
notes on life, 438
Suwanose Island (Japan), 75, 94, 99,
100, 102–103, 107–109
Suzuki, Daisetu, 62
Suzuki, Shunryu, *See* Zen, Masters
Swenson, Lee, 152
contributor, 352–358
notes on life, 438

Tada, Lama Tokan, 299
Takeda, Yuiko, 65, 66, 82
Tao Te Ching (Lao-tzu), 150, 204,
292, 326, 376
Tarn, Nathaniel, 17
Tassajara Hot Springs, *See* Zen,
zendos, temples and study
centers
Thomas, Doug, 38, 40, 41
Thompson, Les, 27
with Rosemary and Gregory, 24
Thompson, William Irwin, 340
Thoreau, Henry David, 250–251, 255,
342, 362, 365
Thorn, Charlie, 388
Timpanelli, Gioia
contributor, 221–230
notes on life, 438–439
Tongass National Forest, 344
Tools for Conviviality (Illich), 354
Torrance, Robert M., 282

contributor, 263–274
notes on life, 439
Tribe, The *(Buzoku)*, 75, 93–105, 107–109
Tripp, Bessie, 388
True Night (Snyder/Giorgio), 432
Tschannerl, Janaki, 336
Trucker's, Ma and Pa, 131
Turtle, Bear and Wolf (Blue Cloud), 340
Turtle Island, 104, 165, 306, 363–364, 369, 371, 383, 418, 423
Turtle Island (Snyder), 103, 125, 135, 257, 284, 294, 367, 423

Uehara, Masa, 75, 101–102, 103–104, 113, 115, 124–125, 139, 148–149, 161, 203, 249, 297, 303, 308, 313, 342, 359, 366–367, 381, 394
United Nations Conference on the Environment (Stockholm), 308, 385
Unno, Taitetsu, 299
Uyeda, Yoshifumi, 299

van de Wetering, Janwillem, 67
Van Newkirk, Allen, 384
Velde Committee (on un-American Activities), 9, 27
"Voyant" (Waldman), 210–215

Wên Fu (Lu Ji), 152, 270
Wagstaff, Chris, 276
Waldman, Anne
contributor, 209–215
notes on life, 439
Wallace, David Rains, 281
Watson, Burton, 63, 71, 73, 269, 303
contributor, 53–59
notes on life, 439
Watts, Alan, 236, 299, 302–303, 305, 338, 354
and Jano, 305
Wavy Gravy, 308
Wayman, Alex, 299, 303
Wei Yeh (Wei the Wild), 259–262
Welch, Lew, 12, 13, 16, 25, 27, 158, 203, 308, 315, 393
Wellings, Julie, 303, 304
Wertheimer, Richard, 381

Whalen, Philip, 11, 12, 13–14, 24, 25, 27, 28, 58, 73, 76, 203, 236, 299, 303, 402, 412
contributor, 207–208
notes on life, 439
Wheeler, Erich, 24, 27
White, Lynn, 366
Wilderness Society, The, 11, 12, 362
Williamson, Alan
contributor, 216–220
notes on life, 439–440
Williams, William Carlos, 154, 203, 207, 219, 248
Wilson, Mark, 144–147
Winter, Paul
contributor, 340–343
notes on life, 440
Wobblies, *See* Industrial Workers of The World
Wooden Fish, The (Snyder), 304–305
Writer's Theater, The (UC Davis), 282
"Written in the Honorable Lin's Room..." (Wei Yeh), 262
"Written On the Wall at the Recluse Yu T'ai-chung's" (Wei Yeh), 261

Yamamoto, Sanehiko, 96
Yamao, Sansei, 98, 100, 101
Yamazato, Katsunori
contributor, 93–105
notes on life, 440
Yampolsky, Philip, 73, 303
contributor, 60–67
notes on life, 440
Yanagida, Seizan, 63, 69, 71
"Yes, It's Really Work!" (Sund), 251
Yevtushenko, Yevgeny, 342
Yosemite National Park, 35–42, 203, 265

Zahnhiser, Howard, 363
Zen Buddhism, 56, 60, 62–64, 67, 104–105, 143–144, 157, 208, 217–218, 220, 244, 296, 299–301, 382–383
American, 164, 246, 298, 299, 301, 383
See also, Zen Buddhism, Zen,

zendos, temples and study
  centers, Ring of Bone Zendo
Buddhist Peace Fellowship, 301
concepts, 156, 167, 208, 217–
  218, 220, 246
Masters (roshis)
  Aitken, Robert, 164, 278, 279,
    293, 301, 315–316, 367, 429
  Chao-chou, 291–292, 297
  Goto, Zuigan, 62, 67–68
  Ikkyu, 79
  Lin-chi, 70
  Miura, Isshu, 71, 77–78
  Oda, Sesso, 294, 295, 296
  Ogata, 303
  Sasaki, Joshu, 315
  Sasaki, Sokei-an, 62, 70
  Suzuki, Shunryu, 218, 220, 355
zendos, temples, and study centers
  Buddhist Study Center (Berke-
    ley), 299
  Daitoku-ji, 56, 62–63, 70, 73, 77,
    94, 235, 246, 293, 303
  Diamond Sangha, 309, 429

First Zen Institute of America
  (New York), 62, 70
First Zen Institute of America in
  Japan (Kyoto), 14–15, 28,
  63, 64, 66–67, 68, 69,
  71, 73–74, 78
Horyuji, 303
Kennin-ji, 61
Koon-ji, 71
Ring of Bone, 131, 155, 164, 203,
  278–279, 298, 308–309,
  315, 367
Ryoanji, 331–332
Ryosen-an, 70, 71, 73, 304
San Francisco, 125, 355
Shokoku-ji, 57, 64, 71, 81, 303
Tassajara Hot Springs, 355
at Kitkitdizze, 115, 124, 164, 246,
  297–298, 313–316
  See also San Juan Ridge
Zen Catholicism (Graham), 303
Zen Dust, 68
Zen Mind, Beginners Mind (Suzuki),
  218, 220

Clifford Burke:
WE'RE STILL MAKING BOOKS

Hard to guess how many of us "first woke up" with the help of Gary Snyder's books: most of those early volumes of poetry still hold special places on our shelves (Who would let go of his or her copy of *Myths & Texts* or *The Back Country*?). With luck, those books, even to the individual copies of them, may last for hundreds of years, to be the vehicle of awakening to generations that will hopefully need less impetus than ours did.

We are still making books because there's this mysterious random quality to them, and a durability and ubiquity and tidiness that we may never find in tapes or video cassettes or floppies. We can hope that future generations will actually pack *The Back Country* into the back country, like we did.

Yet the book is a demanding object that uses resources and technologies pretty intensely, and books often get trashed and fill landfills when the making is done with disrespect and merely for money. But we're creating a responsible post-industrial bookmaking. This book has been printed on recycled paper, for instance. The computer/photographic techniques used in setting the type (Matt Carter's Galliard, chosen for its quirky Reynoldsesque italic) are far less damaging than the old hot lead method, though we are still looking for some alternative to photographic chemistry. Inks made from soy oil rather than petroleum have recently been introduced into book printing, and generally printers have become more mindful of the waste from their work.

All these recall the days of early printing when type was used over and over rather than cooked into the air; when paper was made from fibers other than wood (and could be again—what about sisal, or *hemp*?); when all ink used a linseed oil vehicle; when craft rather than commerce made a thing to last for centuries.

We strive for right livelihood, and we trust in the book to carry the message of our awakening to the future, where they will see at least that we tried, and will know for sure if we succeeded.